THE CONTINENTAL MODEL

THE CONTINENTAL MODEL

Selected French Critical Essays of the Seventeenth Century, in English Translation

EDITED BY

Scott Elledge and Donald Schier

Published by CARLETON COLLEGE *and the*
UNIVERSITY OF MINNESOTA PRESS, *Minneapolis*

Library of Congress Catalog Card Number: 60-10192

PUBLISHED IN GREAT BRITAIN, INDIA, AND PAKISTAN BY THE OXFORD UNIVERSITY PRESS,
LONDON, BOMBAY, AND KARACHI, AND IN CANADA BY THOMAS ALLEN, LTD., TORONTO

Permission to use the notes to Fontenelle's "Digression on the Ancients and the
Moderns" from Robert Shackleton's edition of *Entretiens sur la pluralité des mondes
and digression sur les anciens et les modernes* (Oxford University Press, 1955) has
been granted by Mr. Shackleton and Oxford University Press

Preface

Our aim in collecting and editing these essays was to make available to students of English literary history some of the chief works of those seventeenth-century French critics who most influenced the climate of opinion in which English criticism flowered. Anyone who begins a serious study of any English critic from Dryden, Temple, and Dennis to Warton, Hurd, and Twining soon comes to wish that he knew first-hand the criticism of Boileau, Rapin, Le Bossu, Bouhours, Corneille, and others. Boileau is usually to be found in English and in French in the average college library, but many of the others are not. The present volume is an attempt to put the rarer works within the reach of all students. To be sure, a serious student of literary criticism should read French, and it may be argued that the present collection should consist of the original essays — not of translations. It was not primarily the quiet knowledge that many serious students of English literature do not read French easily that persuaded us to collect translations, but rather the fact that most of the influential French critics were translated into English during the last part of the seventeenth century and that these translations, though they were not always elegant or precise, have for the student of English literary history the virtue that they preserve the English vocabulary and idiom in which many English writers first considered and discussed the French ideas.

Fifty years ago J. E. Spingarn called attention to this "large mass" of French criticism that was translated in England before the end of the seventeenth century, and the *Cambridge Bibliography of English Literature* later illustrated his point in great detail. Useful as we thought a selection from these translations would be, however, we soon decided that to limit the contents of our book to those critics who happened to have been translated long ago would be unnecessarily to limit its usefulness. Chapelain's essays and Bouhours's *Entretiens,* for example, have never been translated, and only two of Corneille's discourses are available in English. Consequently, some of the neat unity of our original plan was sacrificed by the introduction of seven translations which Mr. Schier made for this book.

No anthology can please everybody, of course — or entirely please the anthologists themselves, whose hardest task is simply to choose. And perhaps their wisest procedure is not to raise questions by trying to justify their choices. But since in the notes we have explained why we chose the essays we did, we should perhaps here explain why we omitted certain others.

Our chief criterion was the rarity of the texts. Boileau has not only had the advantage of the Soames-Dryden translation of *L'Art Poétique*; his influence on English criticism has probably already been exaggerated. Of the other major critics, we have tried not to reproduce works available elsewhere, chiefly in two other useful collections: Barrett H. Clark's *European Theories of the Drama* (New York, rev. ed., 1947), and Henry Hitch Adams's and Baxter Hathaway's *Dramatic Essays of the Neoclassic Age* (New York, 1950). Because they limit their subject to dramatic criticism (important as that subject was) and because they are not limited to French or to the seventeenth century, these two books do not serve the same purpose we hope ours will. But, for example, an important demurrer to "the rules" made very early (1628) by François Ogier is adequately represented by a translation of the central part of that essay in Clark's book. We did not, therefore, include Ogier. And since a translation of Corneille's First Discourse is in Clark, and one of the Second in Adams and Hathaway, we have supplied a translation of the Third, though we think other less practical reasons will justify our choice. Among works recently made available by the Augustan Reprint Society and so not included here are Georges de Scudéry's "Preface to *Ibrahim*," André Dacier's *Aristotle's Art of Poetry with Mr. D'Acier's Notes translated from the French*, and Rapin's *A Discourse of Pastorals.*

Malherbe and Vaugelas, since their concern was diction and other matters of style, are not very informative in translation; nor were their works well known in England. This, as well as the relatively small concern in the last half of the century with lyric poetry, accounts for the absence from our collection of essays on the art of the short poem.

Jean-Louis Guez de Balzac, though he may have been the source of many of the ideas of later French critics, was not well known in England, and in any case it was through the essays of Rapin, La Bruyère, and others that the English became aware of his ideas. Concerning the omission of La Mesnardière's *Art Poétique* (1640) and Mambrun's *De Poemata Epico* (1652), we can only say that in our opinion they were not so important or influential as the essays we included.

These latter deal with matters at issue in England: the epic *versus* the romance, the question of the definition of the genres, especially of the romance or novel, the pastoral, the argument that raged about that vexed word "taste," and so forth. We have naturally not attempted to present here in little a panorama of French critical theory of the seventeenth century. Specifically French concerns such as the *Querelle du Cid* are only obliquely represented. Moreover, within the limits of one volume it was not possible to include all the spokesmen on both sides of the controversy between the ancients and the moderns. Most of the authors included here were on the side of the ancients because this was certainly the larger and, we think, the more influential party. However we hope the moderns are not inadequately represented by two of the most eloquent and effective writers of that group, Saint-Evremond and Fontenelle.

We have not tried to make this collection of translations a series of scholarly editions of texts, but we have read the seventeenth- and eighteenth-century translations against the original French text and have made some changes in the interest of accuracy and clarity. Our notes are intended to be helpful but not exhaustive.

We wish to express our gratitude to President Laurence M. Gould and to the Board of Trustees of Carleton College for a grant that made possible this cooperative publishing venture of the College and the University of Minnesota Press. We are indebted to Mr. James Richards, the Librarian of the Carleton Library, who cheerfully helped us obtain books from many collections; to Professor Samuel Monk, who encouraged us to make this book; to Professor Charles Rayment, who gave us the benefit of his advice on certain parts of the text; and to Miss Janet Saltus, who helped prepare our manuscript.

Contents

THE CONTINENTAL MODEL

"But critic-learning flourished most in France." POPE

Jean Chapelain LETTER OR DISCOURSE BY MONSIEUR

CHAPELAIN TO MONSIEUR FAVEREAU, KING'S COUNSELLOR

ON THE BOARD OF EXCISE, CONVEYING HIS OPINION OF THE

POEM "ADONE" BY THE CHEVALIER MARINO

I already knew, both from you and the Chevalier Marino, that you had determined to assemble the learned and detailed observations you have made on his poem *Adone*, and I was overjoyed to think that since this fine work was about to appear, so rare a mind had taken the trouble to reveal subtly its riches and excellence, when I received in your letter the confirmation of what I had believed until then; but your letter is phrased in such a way that you seem to await my answer to learn whether I think such a critical appreciation is likely to redound to your honor, and whether in my opinion the poem is worth the time you would have to give to it. To this I shall reply that I am greatly astonished at two things: the first, that you could now conceive any doubts, however small, about a work which you know to be by that great man, which he communicated to you himself, and whose beauties, as he read it to us, you have often repeatedly admired in my presence; it is as though you had changed and now, alone among critics, refused to recognize that the works of Marino are flawless, and that they bear in his name their inviolable passport. The other thing which astonishes me even more is this: granted that the scorn which the chevalier has several times expressed to us of this poem might have given you serious grounds for doubt; and granted that the modesty you profess so precisely prevents you from depending upon yourself and makes you mistrust that solid judgment upon which others of the most judicious rely so willingly; in short, granted there was real reason to fear and doubt; the astonishing thing is, I say, that among so many skillful people who esteem you and who are at your disposal, you were willing to cast your eyes upon such weakness

3

as mine in the hope and desire of drawing from it some good result. That is indeed a thing of which I do not believe you will be able to clear your conscience. I am a man without a name, without authority, without importance in the world, and if it were not that I fear to contradict a too favorable judgment you once made of me, I should say a man without the learning and the training necessary to speak worthily of so elevated a subject. From this you see what may be expected of me. However, in order not to excuse myself from a thing you order me to do, and from which you leave me no liberty to seek exemption, being unable because of the distance between us to tell you by word of mouth how it appears to me, I shall set my opinion down for you on this paper, protesting beforehand, however, that I disavow my own sentiments from this moment if you judge that they diverge, however slightly, from the goal of truth; nor do I do this without promising myself that you will read the discourse benignly as is your custom, paying attention not to me, who shall write it, but only to the weight and genuineness of the things which are to be said in it.

I say then, in order to answer your question, that I consider the *Adone*, in the form in which we saw it, a good poem, built up and developed in all its novelty according to the general rules of the epic, and the best of its genre which can ever be published.

Now in the reasonable proof of this opinion of mine it might be thought necessary for me to say what *poetry* is, how many kinds of it there are, what the nature is of each, especially of that which the Greeks call *epopoeia* and for which we have not yet found a name, in order to see how, while remaining within these principles — granted that this poem is not typical of the epic — it has been permitted to the poet to introduce a genre different from the traditional one and which may nevertheless be included in the epic as to kind — a point we must demonstrate in order to establish the success of the poem. But since I am speaking to you who are aware of all that, in order not to prolong this essay unnecessarily I shall omit all definitions and divisions as presupposed and sufficiently dealt with by others, and shall concentrate with regard to the first heading, which concerns the basic value of the poem, upon examining three points to be encountered therein which are subject to doubt and to objection, and on the validity of which depends the proof of my position: the *novelty* of the literary genre; the *choice* of the subject; and its *credibility*.

As to *novelty*, I can, in the first place, imagine two kinds: the one blameworthy and unnatural, the other praiseworthy and natural. That novelty

Jean Chapelain

which is unnatural has two subdivisions, of which the first might be called perfect in its imperfection; this occurs when to a body of one nature is conjoined a body of another nature, as was the case with the satyrs in antiquity and in our time with the half-men, half-dogs. Here novelty consists in the excess of monstrosity. The second kind might be called imperfect and occurs when to a body of one nature there is attached another body of the same nature without their being unified and fused, with the result that these two segments do not appear to be and do not produce two distinct beings each independent of the other; we see examples of this in those human monsters having two heads, in hermaphrodites, and in Siamese twins; here the novelty is merely monstrous without excess. Natural novelty is also of two sorts, the first perfect in its perfection, occurring when a non-monstrous thing which has never existed before first comes to light, as when, in a place where water had never appeared, one sees suddenly a clear stream burst forth. The other, less perfect, occurs when, in a thing already known, one discovers some perfection thitherto unrecognized, as if in that same known spring one happened after a while to note some particular virtue which had not been perceived before. Now to reduce these four kinds of novelty to the terms of a fable, that is to say, of the subject of a poem, I include in the first group of the unnatural, daydreams, and the stories nurses tell to children, or, if you prefer, some of the stories of Straparola,[1] the Italian author, in which, without being constrained to do so by the needs of allegory, he makes irrational animals talk and act as men talk and act. In the second I put romances of all kinds if they do not have either unity of action or unity derived from the principal characters. In the first group of natural novelties I include the original discovery of the arts and sciences, as for example, poetry produced by Apollo in his time or by another; that kind of novelty is the most excellent in that it opens the way for those who come afterwards to discover the special virtues of an art. To the second group I assign the invention of genres, as of the heroic by Homer or Orpheus, or of the lyric by Sappho; this kind of invention, although it is really less excellent, has nevertheless much merit in the eyes of those who make the first discovery, and the same is true proportionately of the understrappers. Grant me that word and also those I shall be forced to use in dealing with this subject, because as far as I know our language does not have any words suitable to express these ideas, and I am not bold enough to launch new words for general use. Now, coming back to the subject, I say that the *Adone* is neither of the first nor the second kind of

5

unnatural novelty since, as you know, the fable has unity of action and unity of character and since, for example, there is in it no mixture of sacred history with profane poetry. It does not belong, either, among the first group of natural novelties, because being a poem and an epic poem, as we shall show later, poetry and the epic are presupposed before it. If it has novelty, then, it must be of the second kind, that is to say, of the praise-worthy sort, and that is what I maintain; here are my reasons.

The *significant action*, according to Aristotle, is either represented or narrated. When it is represented tragedy results; when it is narrated epic results. I define a significant action as a notable event, whether of good or of ill fortune, occurring to persons illustrious in themselves or who are made so by the quality of the event. Now of these kinds of actions some can occur in war, as in tragedy the death of Capaneus [2] or the events in the *Antigone*; and in the epic, the death of Hector or that of Turnus; others occur in peace as, in tragedy, *Atreus* [3] or *Medea*. It is true that for the epic there is, as far as I know, no example of this latter kind; but that there may be one is clearly seen in that tragedy and epic do not differ in subject, and that only the way in which the subject is treated, by representation or by narration, sets up a distinction between them. Now it is certainly true that between representation and narration there is difference only in the incidents, for the purpose of both is none other than to set the chosen subject before the eyes, whether by means of scenic display or by words alone (both being instruments of imitation); this being true, nothing can be acceptable in the one which is not acceptable in the other. But there is no doubt that tragic representation accommodates itself to events which have occurred in time of peace, and thus one may soundly conclude that epic narration cannot refuse the same peacetime actions. Otherwise, if the significant action, which occurred in peacetime and was suitable to serve as a subject for the tragic poet, could not so serve for the epic poet, it would follow that they do not both use the same subject, which is against the hypothesis. I do not deny certainly that just as among tragedies those are more frequently seen and are better which are deeply involved in the tumult of war, so among epics those which have war for their subject are the first in dignity, since they have the advantage of events and of the relief given by a stormy background and by violent struggles attendant upon the most important affairs; I mean only that just as the first tragedies do not exclude the others simply because they happen to be favored with a richer subject, so the epic, being of the same eminence and having the same obligations, since a significant action is the subject common to both, cannot reject a second type of itself on the mere statement of the pre-eminence of the first.

Having thus resolved the first problem, and having supposed, as is in fact the case, that the poem *Adone* takes its rise from a deed done in time of peace, accompanied by peaceful circumstances, and which has no complications other than those which peace admits of, nor embellishments other than those which peace allows, it is clear that being new, the poem is of the second class of novelties, the poet having discovered by means of it something new in a kind of writing which was already well known; that is to say he found to be included in the epic besides the heroic, which is a war poem of a kind already familiar, this other which is a poem of peace not previously known, the less so because poets, hitherto enticed by the grandeur of martial subjects as being most susceptible of various encounters and unexpected events having the most remarkable consequences, and ambitious to acquire for themselves a name in the description of something which, like war, is the greatest among human actions, have thrown themselves so avidly and so unanimously upon this kind of poem that they seem to have overlooked the possibility of writing one in the contrary manner. But however overlooked or neglected — I am inclined to think rather the latter — this second has been, insofar as it constitutes another division of the epic, if our friend has considered its basic theory, as I believe, and if he has wanted to put it into practice and to give it vogue, I say not only that his poem is good because it is new and of a praiseworthy kind of novelty, but beyond this that poetry will be infinitely obliged to him as to one who felicitously extends its frontiers and who rightly amplifies and augments its scope and domain.

Since we have proved the reality of this new kind of writing by the example of tragedy, which, merely because it includes deeds of both war and peace, is nevertheless not divided and does not produce two kinds of itself, treating both equally and without difference in style or omission of events, it seems that the epic also, making use of the same deeds, ought to treat them in the same way without any difference in characters or composition; and thus instead of two kinds there would be only one. This, however, was not our conclusion, and I shall say first that although in appearance tragedies of both subjects seem to have only one single mode of composition, they are not so undifferentiated, especially as regards style, that anyone who wished to examine them carefully could not yet find some

7

diversity among them; and secondly I shall say that even if this were not true, the question of treatment is not the same in tragedy and in the epic: for in the first the poet is not concerned with whether the action takes place in war or in peace but only with whether it has particular complications, which results in this, that the subject being one in this respect it can be treated in only one way, whereas in the heroic epic the question of war is important, and so important that without it the heroic would no longer be heroic because the complication, which inseparably constitutes its nature, occurs in it probably only with respect to war, as being the source of its complication and entanglement; and similarly in this new genre the question of peace ought also to enter, in order inseparably to form its essence, which will result in this, that the epic, being divided into two kinds by this means, will require two kinds of treatment. But in a word, when I alleged the tragedy as proof, I ought to have been satisfied that it supported me on the subject of peace as well as that of war; for as far as treating the latter is concerned, the technique is always different depending upon the different considerations which one brings to it, and things are considered either in all their nakedness or with regard to necessary circumstances as we see by the difference between the historian's style and the poet's, even when they are dealing with the same occurrences and the same events. Now since war and peace have notably different tempos and almost opposite circumstances, and since it is necessary to treat things which are different and opposed by differing means, if the difference as such can constitute a separate genre, there is no doubt that since this sort of poem has, in the state of peace which informs it throughout, the difference which can make it a distinct genre, it must then constitute a genre distinct from the heroic and consequently must require different treatment.

And this genre, in view of the opposition between peace and war, will be such, if you please, with respect to the heroic, as comedy, in view of the contrast between an action which is insignificant and one which is significant, is with respect to tragedy, and the same opposition will be found proportionately between the one and the other as exists between comedy and tragedy, provided that the universal rules governing their general constitution and what the poets call consistency are equally observed in them, which will be seen hereafter to be precisely the case with the poem of which we are speaking. And moreover, if we found the conception of this new genre on the basis of a significant action which has occurred in time of peace, I shall say it is necessary that the subject of the poem to which one

8

is willing to grant this designation be significant without an admixture of war; significant, if possible, through its principal characters, and above all significant through the event; that the particular complications be as great as the chosen subject permits while yet not removing it from the relationship which it ought properly to have with the repose of peace and the ordinary events of peacetime; that the composition should thus incline more to simplicity than to complexity as should also the episodes therein principally considered, because of the nature of peace which does not furnish narrative substance, that is to say diversity of action; that all efforts ought to be devoted to descriptions and detail and this more concerning things associated with peace than war, as palaces, gardens, architecture, games, and other similar things, what is not in this category being treated only when necessary and as it were in passing; that love should have the principal place and that everything should issue from it and revolve about it, other subjects being considered only as accessory and ancillary to this one; finally, that comic situations may occur in it, but modest ones, or modestly told: all these conditions are indeed proper to peace, you understand, and yet they do not include the exact contrary of things which are important in war. You know also that the *Adone* everywhere conforms perfectly to this conception, and as the climax of perfection remember that it is a mixed genre yet not debased, as befits its nature which is as it were in suspension between tragedy and comedy, the epic and the romance; it is in some ways grave and lofty, both as regards the characters and the catastrophe, and it is also simple and low both in the actions which precede the conclusion and in the detailed descriptions. I am not speaking here of the style which accompanies it, since it has the same antitheses to the heroic style as its subject has to the heroic subject, but I am certain its novelty will be all the more estimable since the brilliance of antiquity will be found everywhere in it and the graces of the moderns will give it color.

And indeed so many rich and strong conceptions fill the body of the poem that, even if the composition of the poem were irregular, vicious, and haphazard, without any basis in reason (the contrary of which opinion has in part been demonstrated and in part will be demonstrated), nevertheless one would have to admit that the intention of giving the world a poetic genre like this one, where all things may find their place, was never anything but very beautiful and very useful; for how many beautiful inspirations may we believe have been lost or are lost every day for lack of a place where they may be used worthily; and how many profitable things may we think have gone astray and been buried in the ruins of antiquity which, had poets undertaken their expression, regularly or irregularly, would still be alive in the memory of mankind for the public benefit, since everyone knows by experience that there is nothing which is preserved for so long a time, impregnable and invincible to all the shocks of time, as poetic monuments? Oh, how I should extol our friend for having been the inventor and the first advocate of this novelty if I had for his defense only what I have said! But we shall see that the ancients in the two greatest languages practiced what he did before him. I am speaking neither of the *Odyssey* nor of the *Ethiopian History* [4] — both of these compositions have more complications than peace admits of, and it is easy to judge that they were never modeled on the prototype of this poem — but there has come down to us from Musaeus or perhaps from Nonnus [5] a poem very similar to this one, concerning the loves of Hero and Leander; and Claudian elaborated a long poem founded on the rape of Persephone,[6] of which we have a fragment, in the same style and with similar actions although much less unified than those which are here, so that not only on the basis of reason but on that of the most valid authority this novelty will be no more in itself than a renewal and as it were a legitimate correction of a defect which existed in the division of the epic; and thus for being too well founded it will merit less praise. If hereupon it should be claimed that the poems mentioned come to an end in a few lines whereas *Adone* is extremely long, I should reply first that the allegation is not true for Claudian's poem, and that secondly, even if our poet had given himself an unexampled free hand he would have been justified in doing so since the subject-matter of peace allows this, as appears from what has been said above, and since it is only the episodes which he has developed at length, and these episodes, as you know, accommodate themselves to greater or lesser development, there being nothing which controls this in detail except necessity or the poet's preference; this is shown clearly by the episode of Ariadna in the epithalamium of Catullus,[7] which is less necessary and less probable than any one of those which are in the *Adone*, but which all the same has a greater place in this little poem than the principal subject, which concerns the loves of Peleus and Thetis. It can thus be seen that no difficulty arises from this mooted length. Add to this that everything in the poem being excellent, and it being moreover impossible ever to have too many things which are excellent, only the poet loses by that length, and he does not understand, as he has told me a hundred times, why it is taken as binding upon other poems since he wants to be as free in the other major works which he has promised as if he had never thought of this one; in this he shows only too clearly the difference between his mind and that of the ordinary man, for he is unable to do things negligently or pettily, not even those which are petty and negligible.

The question of novelty being thus dealt with, the problem of *choice of subject*, which we have placed second of the three things to be considered, does not consequently need much argument. Choice is said to be good when it is commensurate with the plan one has, and bad in the contrary case; consider the man who, wanting to build a palace, chose a suitable site, the proper materials, and the tools with which to arrange them according to the desired effect: such a man would be said to have chosen well because he kept in view his goal, which is his building, to which goal all those things are related and necessary; but a man who, in order to make a suit or a picture, provided himself with the same equipment and had the same plans would make himself ridiculous and would be said to have chosen ill because he did not consider his goal for which all that equipment is useless. If that is granted, I say the choice of fable for *Adone* is very good and very judicious, and that for this new idea of a poem of peace, which Marino probably stumbled upon, no other subject of greater plausibility or suitability could have been chosen or found, the more so since, as we have said, the action is significant in both ways, occurs in time of peace, is simple rather than complicated, turns entirely on love, and is seasoned with the sweet circumstances of peace and the moderate salt of mirth. But if he had used that fable in an ordinary heroic poem, how reprehensible that would have been! However, that can never have been his intention, and I am convinced that if you forced him to declare what his purpose was, he would tell you that he does not present the poem as heroic or tragic or comic, the term epic alone being suitable to it, although the poem has some admixture of all the other three. And if it is permissible to make a conjecture about these things, one of the principal reasons which probably led him to this choice was to show the existence between two extremes, that of great goodness as seen in the heroic poem, and that of great imperfection as seen in the cluttered romance, of an area to which the poet who could not aspire so high and who would disdain to stoop so low might restrict himself, in order to work with commendation and without fear of losing the title of poet.

After the choice of subject comes the question of *credibility* or the belief

11

which one may have in the subject — a point important above all others since it is said that where belief is lacking attention or feeling also fail; but where feeling does not exist there cannot be any emotion nor consequently any *katharsis*, nor any improvement in the morals of mankind, which is the purpose of poetry. Belief is then absolutely necessary in poetry. But what belief can we have in a fable which is admitted to be a fable? This kind: belief in the meaning which we draw from it; that is to say, the tendency of the imagination to accept that a thing is rather than is not, is acquired in two ways: the one imperfect and incapable of persuading, as being the mere report either of an historian or of another (and I call this incapable of persuading because the sincerity of men is unknown and because most often it is called into question over the slightest difficulty which arises); the other perfect and persuasive because of the probability of the thing reported, whether by the historian or by another; this latter is the natural, efficacious means of acquiring belief to which the first is reduced even when it professes the truth, if it be right that of two stories which are contraries or differently told we always put faith in that which has the greater degree of probability; this happens when the first way is highhanded and subject to rejection, for then the second gains its end gently even while vigorously seizing the imagination of the listener, and by the consistency of the things contained in the report makes him favorable to it. But of these two, since the one is proper to the historian, so one must recognize that the other is proper to the poet, the more so since history treats things as they are and poetry as they ought to be, so that the first cannot accept a false thing however probable it may appear, and the second cannot refuse it provided it has verisimilitude; and the reason for this is the fact that the one considers a detail with the intent only to report it; and that is why in histories cases and events are all different and unregulated as is suitable for what is at the mercy of fortune, for fortune makes the wicked prosper as much as the good, and ruins without distinction of persons the one as well as the other, whereas poetry, one of the sublime sciences which in its classification is not far removed from philosophy, takes first consideration of the universal, treating its subject in detail only with the intention of deducing from it something specific for the instruction of everyone and the common benefit; and that is why in poems the consequences of a good or bad action are always similar, according to the genre; the good man is recognized as such and the wicked man is punished, since their actions result from virtue or vice whose nature it is to reward or to destroy those who follow them; to such an extent is this true that when reading history I learn only what happened to Caesar or Pompey, without any certain profit and without moral instruction, whereas in reading poetry, behind the episodes of Ulysses or Polyphemus I see what one may reasonably suppose will generally happen to any who commit the same acts; just as by that abstraction from the specific which poetry requires of me I no longer consider, in the poems of the ancients, Aeneas as pious and Achilles angry (and the same can be said of all the other actions and passions of mankind) but rather piety with its consequences and anger with its effects so as fully to learn the nature of them. In order to achieve this result the same ancients, urged on by zeal and these considerations, and judging that the truth of events, since they depend on chance, deflected their very laudable intentions through fortuitous and uncertain happenings, with one accord banished the truth from their Parnassus, some composing by caprice without mixing in anything that was truthful while others contented themselves with changing the truth and altering it insofar as it was opposed to their idea; but not one of them made a practice of recalling it except when it accommodated itself to them, that is to say, to justice and reason, and unless it had verisimilitude, which in this instance, rather than truthfulness, serves as the instrument by which the poet puts man on the road to virtue; to which end examples of evil are as useful as those of good, provided they be considered as intended for instruction and be requited as they deserve. For all this either the Achilles of Homer or the Aeneas of Virgil will serve as proof, for if we believe certain writers, neither of these was ever so enraged or so virtuous as he has been pictured to us; nevertheless, since Homer and Virgil intended to suggest by their names the psychological dimensions of the deeds attributed to them, they made them so and were in no way concerned if the details of truth suffered, provided mankind in general profited by the verisimilitude. Now since this verisimilitude is a representation of things as they ought to occur, according as human judgment, born and trained to the idea of good, foresees and determines them; and since the truth is reduced to this and not this to the truth, there is no doubt that because verisimilitude is an attribute of poetry (that is to say, since the poet treats only what ought to be and since what ought to be is always compatible with verisimilitude, for these two things are reciprocal) and since this verisimilitude stimulates the imagination and makes the reader judge that everything came about easily as described, as he does not judge truth to have done except insofar as it has

13

verisimilitude, there is no doubt, I say, that poetry should be believed since it has in its favor that which in itself produces belief, whereas history proceeds more highhandedly and has in its favor only the naked truth which cannot be believed without other aid and comfort. Thus it will suffice for the approval of a poem that it have verisimilitude because of the quick impression which verisimilitude makes upon the imagination, the latter being captivated and controlled by it as the poet intends.

Having thus discussed the subject in general, we may apply what we have said to our friend's poem in this way: it is clear that if one wishes to deny the truth of the plot, and the succession of events seems likely to make us admit its fabulous quality — although this is not certain in view of the fact that there is mention in writing of the tears shed for Adonis, and since according to the ancient rhapsodes and mythologists there is no fable, especially of those concerning the deities, which was not founded upon some real event — the poem will not cease for that reason to follow the laws of art and will not lose credibility, because truth is not of the essence of poetry, and even if truth should be found there, since it is considered not truth but only fable, for the reason that we have discussed, and since verisimilitude alone is sought for, as long as the poem has that quality as you know it does, so long will it have credibility for men; and the more it loses through historical inaccuracies the more it will gain through a sufficiency of probability.

In order to show further the right and necessary falseness of poems I could have instanced the allegory with which they ought to be associated, but since allegory is irrelevant to the discourse on verisimilitude, it being a self-conscious operation of the intellect as it moves from one outward appearance to another and not of the imaginative faculties, I have reserved a discussion of it for this place. *Allegory*, then, according to the general opinion of learned men, is a part of the conception of the poem, and is the second fruit which one can gather from it. Now as it happens that allegory is most often incompatible with the real sequence of events, poets obliged to include it will always prefer rather to falsify the truth, which occurs in their works only incidentally, than to neglect the allegory which must be there by the nature of things; of this we have a notable proof in the fables Aesop gave to his country. Have they any verisimilitude, let alone truth, insofar as concerns the speeches, words, subtleties, foresight, and other things which he attributes to his animals? And yet they have come down to us with the general applause of mankind, who, on reading the fable, go

14

straight to its meaning (that is to say, to the other reality which is meant), by usefully applying what Aesop has said about an impossibility to what is possible, without troubling to examine its degree of possibility; this indicates more than clearly that in the other fables, I mean in ordered poems closer to us than Aesop's, and overlooking the test of truth as an unimportant thing, we need consider only whether the desired profit is in fact found in them.

At this point, if I am not mistaken, the qualities which could keep this poem from being a poem, that is to say good in its poetic genre, have been sufficiently clarified and it has been sufficiently shown that they do not deprive this work of the nature of a poem. There remain now to be considered those which would make it a poem, and it will be proved, if possible, that *Adone* has all the principal qualities of epic poems hitherto accepted; and as for those which it has not, I shall show that it could not have them without impropriety; and consequently that it is good in the highest degree. This is the second premise of the proposition which we must now try to establish with complete proof.

In any narrative poem I consider two things: the *subject* and the *manner* in which it is treated. The first consists in the structure of the fable, which, according to my personal division, properly includes *plot* and *structure* and to a lesser degree *consistency* and *passions*. The second is the *style*, which serves to express all these things and includes *conceits* and *phrasing*. But each of these has its own rules and conditions which as the poem approaches them more closely make it more a poem, that is, bring it closer to perfection. Let us see how *Adone* accommodates itself to them.

First I divide the *plot* of any poem into two aspects, the first *diversity*, the second the *marvelous*. This diversity is acquired in two ways, from the *nature* of the subject and from its *episodes*. That diversity which arises from its nature is like an emanation of things flowing spontaneously from the natural abundance of the subject; thus in the heroic poem the events which constitute the complication, and without which the poem would not be heroic, are said to engender diversity arising from the nature of the subject; and in this new kind of poem about peace, ordinary, uncomplicated events would produce it also if tranquillity could admit of a diversity of incidents and not the contrary. The diversity which results from the episodes is like an assemblage of things which are suitable to the subject but not essential to its nature: for example, (1) in the heroic poem everything which enters into the fable without contributing to the principal event

15

and which nevertheless is suitable to it, which will probably be very little because its complicated nature gives it enough subject-matter in itself without its being forced to seek more elsewhere; and (2) in this new conception all that enters uselessly or unnecessarily into the poem but still without impropriety, which may be a great deal in view of its natural poverty — all these things, I say, are considered to produce the diversity engendered by episodes. The first diversity makes the fable necessary, the second enriches it with ornament. The *marvelous* has the same sources; the nature of the subject produces the marvelous when by a concatenation of causes not forced nor extrinsic to the action one sees events produced which are either unexpected or out of the ordinary; the marvelous takes place in the *episodes* when the fable is sustained by ideas and richness of language only, so that the reader neglects the subject to dwell on the embellishments. But before including these things in our remarks we must assume that the analysis of any poem consists, first of all, in the recognition of its subject so it may be related to the theory of the poetic genre, and then in determining whether the poem observes the rules laid down for the genre.

To come down to cases then, because it has a new subject and because it constitutes a new genre opposed, as we have said, to the heroic, to which belong the first kinds of diversity (those which arise from the nature of the subject), and because of the nature of its new idea, which is to have more episodes than subject-matter, the *Adone* does not accommodate itself to these first kinds of diversity and dwells rather on the latter kinds which result from the episodes in which it is so rich. Now it dwells on these not because there are no diversity and nothing of the marvelous of these first kinds in the body of the fable insofar as it admitted of them, but mostly because the poem must, for the perfection of its type, treat of what the heroic poem has not been able to treat of; and since the one is sustained only by its events which occur in war and troubles, so the other maintains itself only by means of simple, vain events furnished by an action occurring in the tranquillity of peace; despite this, however, the poet has neglected nothing in the *Adone* of what might increase both the diversity and the marvelous in the nature of the subject itself; his interweaving of the plot elements, in the form in which we saw it, if you remember, testifies sufficiently to that; and to prove that he would have done wrong to have gone about it in any other way, I shall argue as follows. If, in order to produce more diversity and more of the marvelous of the first kinds in the *Adone*

16

than there are, Marino had introduced other subjects than those which are there, as he would have had to do to achieve that result, these subjects would have had to be either of the same type or of a different one; if of the same he must have inserted important actions by the gods other than those which belong to the fable, for of unimportant actions there can be no more, I mean of those which merely enhance the subject; but if he had included other important actions, even though they enhanced the subject, the action would have been dislocated and consequently could be criticized according to our second subdivision under *novelty* as being against nature; that is to say that other important actions would have stifled the principal one and the *Adone* would no longer be the handsome Adonis but a many-headed Hydra. If the actions inserted had been of a different kind, i.e., human actions, they must either have served the general plan of the work or not. Those which would so have served could have been either important or unimportant; if important they would have dislocated the unity of the action neither more or less than important actions of the same kind, and moreover would have added to that dislocation a difference in kind, which is no small difference. As for unimportant actions, they are to be found in the poem as are those of the same kind, as many, indeed, as the subject allowed, and handled both in the ancient style, which is the manner I hold in highest esteem for this kind of effect, and in the modern, which I should not approve of in this poem if it appeared in more than one canto (divine certainly in itself and called by the author *Gli Errori*) because of the absurdity which the mixture of genres and the confusion of periods seems to me to bring about; but if he had made the actions of a different kind, not subordinate to the plan, they would all have been important actions with the result that the same difficulties noted above would have been encountered, and hence the composition could have shown only the opposition between the divine and the human, which would have been monstrous and not suitably knit together and so would have fallen into the first classification of unnatural novelties and would have had no unity of action, nor consistency of genre, nor suitable connective cladding. So much for diversity. As for the marvelous, now, it could not be made greater in the poem except by adding new occasions for it; but this could not be, both because of what has been said about diversity and because the poet cannot attribute to a received fable (as he can to history) another event than that known to be part of it; and the reason, I think, is that the relation between history and what is accepted as true is the same as that between poetry and what is accepted as probable; now just as the historian, having once received and recognized the truth as such, cannot alter it in any way at all, that is to say, can neither add to nor take away from it, so the poet, receiving a fable from another writer and recognizing it as probable, that is to say as having previously been reduced to verisimilitude, that immutable object of poetry, confines himself to the fable without being able to innovate in any way whether by suppressing part of it or by adding to it of his own invention; hence just as we say that truth must play the role of verisimilitude in history as far as the historian is concerned so that he can change nothing in it however useful he thinks that might be, so one may say that a fable having veri-similitude must take the place of truth for poetry as far as the poet is concerned, and so for the same reason he must not alter it, however advantageous it might be for him to do so. But to return to the subject, since the poet could add nothing to the subject-matter, so he could not disclose other marvels in the poem than those which are there since the fable is in itself more than fully treated and all possible artifice had been employed in it. Granted even that he was free to make that addition, aside from the fact that the fable would then have been overladen (which would have been against his original conception) he would also have run the risk of creating a diversity of action as has previously been said in the discussion of diversity. Now the unity of action, among the general rules which every epic poem must observe, is in especial the principal one without which the poem is not a poem but a romance. If then to preserve that unity the poet has kept himself within the limits of the chosen fable, although this procedure is in itself sterile as far as the first ways of producing diversity and marvels are concerned, he has done only what he had to do, and the seeking of diversity and the marvelous according to the other ways is suited to the conception of his new poem.

If you should now ask me which of these two manners seems to me the nobler, that which arises from the nature of the subject or that which arises from the episodes only, or, to clarify the matter by an example, whether it is the heroic which has an inherent complication or this new genre which has unalterable tranquillity, I shall admit in all simplicity that it is the first according to my lights, and I consider the other only second to this, even though several reasons might make me think otherwise. For if among these reasons you consider the fable you will remember that the ancients recognized three kinds: the first the Romans called *motoria* since

18

it contained in itself the agitation and entanglement which subsequently appeared in the treatment of the subject, these being artfully arranged to bring about a happy or unhappy ending as required by the subject; the second was called *stataria* since it was less agitated and more tranquil than the other, consisted of ordinary events, and ended without great ceremony so that the spectator came to believe in it; the third was called *mixed* since it partook of the one and the other. Now to say which of these three was the most esteemed among the ancients would be difficult, and it would appear obvious that the calm one enjoyed no less consideration than the others since they often made use of it, and since poetry with its special procedures does more for it than for the two others. Here is why. The purpose of poetry being utility, although this is achieved by means of pleasure, it appears likely that whatever has utility as its object, i.e., whatever tends toward utility, is more estimable for that very reason than whatever has as its object pleasure alone, i.e., whatever halts at pleasure; and thus fables which are in good moral standing since they have utility as their goal are more important to poetry than those whose morality is dubious since they have as their object pleasure alone. That the calmer kind of fables have utility as their object I see no reason to doubt; for if the utility of poetry consists in the purgation of vicious passions, it is clear that this effect is obtained rather from those poems which are not complicated and entangled than from those which are. That this is true everyone will admit: what is to produce a purging must do so by constant application and without slackening, by continuous effort and without interruption; and the fact is that the simplicity of calm fables gives them this quality in the highest degree since they never leave their subject and are bound to give a detailed description only of the passion which is their subject, a state of things which is far from being characteristic of those fables which have complexity inherent in their nature, for that complexity scatters the descriptions about piecemeal and through the jumble of many different events blunts the effect and weakens the vigor which any one of them in its simplicity might have. Therefore the ancients, taking this into consideration, were as careful as possible even in their great poems not to overload them with subjects, recognizing that although in their diversity and capacity to produce the marvelous they might cause pleasure, they also obscured the goal of utility at which all good writers aim their inventions; that is in part why romances are so scorned among the learned, for without any idea of perfection to which they may conform they pile adventure

19

upon adventure, and include fights, love-affairs, disasters, and other things, of which one well treated would make a laudable effect, whereas together they destroy each other, and so romances remain at best the amusement of fools and the horror of the sophisticated who cannot bear even to look at them, knowing that in their confusion they are remote from the purpose of poetry: for to purge it is first necessary to move, and since one cannot move another without first making an impression on him — an impression which is produced by ways both suitable and continuous — and since moreover these tales, by the quality as well as by the quantity of their subject-matter, are utterly incapable of making an impression, one cannot reasonably hope for that purgation through them. As opposed to these and even to heroic poems, since in the conception of the new poem diversity does not consist in events whose number or entanglement may distract from or destroy the impression, but in descriptions which help to create it and consequently to produce the desired utility, it is obvious that we may say the goal of poetry is fully achieved by the new poem and that for this reason the new genre would take first place. All this is part of what he might say on the subject who wished to praise everything in the poem and to show everything in it to be at the highest degree of excellence. But since that is by no means my intention here, and since I am not willingly carried away by appearances when I have some knowledge of the truth, the conclusion I come to in the matter is this: it is certain that the real purpose of poetry is utility which consists in the purgation we have described above but which is obtained from pleasure alone as a gate is taken by storm, so that without pleasure there is no poetry and on the other hand the more pleasure to be found in it the more poetical it is and the better it achieves its purpose which is utility. Now the pleasure of any reading may be divided into three kinds: when it comes from those events which are separate and plain, without arrangement; when it comes from descriptions alone, that is to say, when events are subordinated to descriptions; and when events and descriptions both produce pleasure by a judicious and moderate combination so that the one does not hinder the other and the events nevertheless appear to have the advantage. The first is an abuse in poetry and is not proper to it as much as to history; it occurs without the authority of any good ancient poet. Hence when we consider the nudity of ancient poems of bad form, and the confusion and multiplicity of their principal actions, we may liken them to modern romances whose wild structure the stupid public adores because it has a

20

natural liking for imperfection. The new conception of a poem of peace is related to the second kind of pleasure in reading, and here poetry is found in its absolute purity free from anything foreign to it except such as may serve as a foil. The last kind raises poetry above itself and causes it to be embodied, without in any way altering its nature, in a subject which it wishes to treat for the subject's sake and not its own; to this kind is attributed the conception of the heroic poem. Now that we have excluded the first kind of pleasure from any poetical composition, no one can deny that of the remaining two the first, which arises from descriptions alone, is as far below the other, which includes events clothed in description, as description alone is inferior to the thing described; or one might say that since the description merely makes use of the event as a foil, it is inferior to the event (attribute to necessity the tiresome repetition of this term, but I consistently mean by it the subject) which uses description as a mere accompaniment; thus when description makes use of the event, since the event is not the most important element in the amalgam, it is not found in the description in all its perfection, whereas when the event makes use of description, the event itself is entirely there since it is most important, and the description, although not equally important, is nevertheless as perfect as if it were; this is because description is the essence of poetry and ought never to be lacking in it. And thus on the one hand, if the first kind of these remaining two types of pleasure, which assimilates to itself this new conception, is more purely poetic, that is to say, if it more than the other confers on the writer the name of poet, because the virtue of any artisan, among whom we include the poet, is not judged by the richness of his material but by the rarity of his skill in treating it, on the other hand the second type of pleasure, which is induced by the traditional epic poem, will be more richly poetic, being aided and carried to perfection by the predominance of the event which is perfect in itself; I mean which is considered to be perfect in its form and which is treated primarily because of the goodness inherent in it. These are the reasons which have led me to say, while recognizing the form of the *Adone* as partaking of this new conception, that it yields the first place to the form of the heroic poem and that it must be content with the second place which its nature gives it.

To *plot* may be reduced the parts of the poem generally called *quantitative*, that is to say the complication of the fable and its unraveling (if I may imitate the Italians in the formation of these terms which do not in any way express what is meant by the interweaving of the parts of the fable

21

and its development). Now although these parts are not to be found in the *Adone* insofar as concerns the kind of principal action so much esteemed among the writers of heroic poems, i.e., the marvelous, with or without recognitions, yet they are there just the same; but if they are there in something less than perfection the defectiveness of the subject is the cause of it. Now it was proved above that the choice of this subject was made necessary by the novelty of the above-mentioned conception, and because in that conception the subject-matter, or event, was least considered. Of the subdivisions included under the composition of the fable, the second of those properly so-called is the structure, of which, if it is to be good, two things are usually required: the first, that the poet should not begin his narration *ab ovo*,[8] seeking the first cause of the action and having the story proceed in the same order as it occurred in time, as Statius and Silius Italicus wrongly did, not to mention that Lucan could have done otherwise; the other that the peripeteia, I mean the conversion or the change of fortune,[9] must occur in it, whether the change be from good to bad or from bad to good. If it is argued that the author of *Adone* has transgressed this first law, I say he could not have observed it, or at least that he ought not to have done so. But it seems obvious to me in the first place that he could not have followed it, for if he had given another arrangement to the work than the one it has, if, for instance, he had begun the story at the arrival of Adonis in the forest of Cyprus or in the palace of love or even further back, it is clear he would irremediably have lost the chance to inform the reader of Venus' passion, a thing which cannot be passed over since it is absolutely of the essence of the fable, he would, I say, have lost the chance, for since Amor alone knew of this passion it would have been inconsistent with the proper behavior of a son toward his mother to present him as boasting to anyone of his vengeance; it would also have been unreasonable, for his boasting would have given him cause to fear the anger of Venus and to anticipate some new punishment from her; and as far as Apollo and Neptune are concerned, both of whom knew something of this vengeance because they had helped in it, they could not tell it to others either except at the cost of a serious departure from the subject of the fable, and even then there would have been a great loss both in the general outline of the affair and in the details which enter into it so usefully; all these things Amor alone knew. In the second place it appears that the author ought not to have followed the rule even if he had been able because that reversal of chronology which is sought in poems is in itself more a recourse and an expedient than a beauty, a necessity, even an embarrassment rather than something marvelous; I mean that the judicious ancients made use of it not expressly to produce that highly recommended suspense, which is nevertheless very different from the marvelous as will be clear to anyone who examines the question, but only to recall and as it were to reincorporate in the body of their compositions what could have happened before the previous year, in which their action is described as having occurred; and they proceeded in this way for several reasons: the first, in order to restrict the course of the action to one year, a period whose limits were accepted by all those who wished successfully to treat a significant action in narrative poetry as the limit of one natural day was accepted by all who wrote for the stage; the second, so as not, through continuous narration, to overload their poems with more main actions, even if they were related to a single one, than the subject could profitably admit of; and the third, so as not to corrupt their works by several different actions each independent of the other, which would have made their writings defective in unity. For if the action of their poems had not lasted longer than a year or had not contained more subject-matter than their perfection required, or had not included independent actions, it is obvious that authors would not have forsaken the natural order which is not forced for another where there is constraint and where the imagination is overworked; the example of Claudian is decisive on this point as is that of others like Musaeus and Nonnus who follow the easy order. But in the *Adone* the fable does not stretch beyond a year, nor is the crowd of events very great, nor is what precedes the love of Venus very separate from the main action, and so it was not necessary, in order to avoid these evils, to have recourse to that ὕστερον πρότερον;[10] the poet would then have been mistaken if he had subjected himself to this law and forsaken the natural way which, as long as it is convenient, is always the best. Now the change of fortune in the poem is of the most pathetic kind even though it is lacking in the marvelous for the reasons we have set forth above, and is of the kind most efficacious in purging the passions, especially the tragic passion; but alas! with what circumstances is it accompanied! Considering all these things, I have been a hundred times astonished at what our chevalier has said and repeated to me, that he was not satisfied with the poem, and that if it were to be done over again he would give it a different form; but then I thought that in his case the greatness of his intelligence furnished him ideas which could not be arrived at by reasonable discourse, each idea being unknown to all until he discovered it; and besides, since I could not come to any other conclusion, I thought that what he said was only to test me and to set me thinking, especially since until now I have not been able to conceive of anything which is opposed to this interpretation.

After the proper subdivisions of composition we come now to those aspects of a poem which are less closely related to the composition, of which the first has been designated *consistency*. It could be defined as a natural inclination, confirmed by practice, whether for good or for evil, which is likely to be found in poetic characters endowed with four conditions (as the ancients said, but with only two as I hold): *goodness, propriety, resemblance*, and *equality*; now the first two are reciprocal since what is good is proper and what is proper is good, so that happenings attributed to an evil nature, even though they are evil in themselves, must be called good since they are proper to the person. For example, if cruel men like Diomedes or Mezentius [11] were introduced into a poem, the consistency of their cruelty would be considered good because it would fit them; thus Armida's [12] artifice and magic are good, not morally speaking but from the poetic point of view. Otherwise, in making a poem, the poet would be forced to shape it entirely of virtuous people, which is against usage and against reason. The latter two, on the other hand, which are resemblance and equality, are also the same thing, or almost so, since the one requires that the character presented be made similar to what has been learned about his inclinations through tradition or by the testimony of authors; and the other demands, if the character has not hitherto been known for one habit rather than another, or if he is entirely invented, that he be made to continue throughout the poem in the same posture as was attributed to him at first; one might just as well say that a character presented must be such throughout the poem as he was when either borrowed from another or created by the author at the beginning. But that these conditions of consistency have been precisely observed in the *Adone* is obvious, and first, as far as the good and the proper are concerned, should anyone obstinately try to erect the good into a category different from the proper, I answer that among good things love is considered to be very good and even the severest critic could class it no lower than among the neutral things, which is all one to the poet; aside from the fact that only the outcome of things determines their goodness or badness, if the outcome of the loves of Adonis by their disastrous end, as in tragedies, is to purge away the filth that is found in that passion, it is good, and renders the whole action good with respect to this end; but if one dwells on the proper instead, what is more proper to youth and beauty than the chase and the amorous passions? Secondly, regarding the similar and the equal, no matter how they are considered, what is there in this poem either received from tradition or entirely invented by the poet, which is not consistent to the end? Instead of making a more precise demonstration of this I shall trust to your memory so as not to bore you with details.

The *passions*, following our classification, constitute the second subdivision of these secondary aspects of composition and seem to be of the same type as consistency, being derived from it, for passion is nothing but a perturbation supervening in the animal faculty through a strong operation and, if I dare put it that way, an extraordinary tension of the natural inclination. As for that, the ordinary rules for the expression of the passions are known to you, and I shall say only that all those relating particularly to love are so efficaciously and skillfully handled in the *Adone* that the poet has left far behind him the most famous writers in this genre; and I dare say that those who follow his example most closely in the future still will never come very near to him. You have examples of this very clearly set forth in the beginning of his book and there is no need to examine them more closely here.

The subject having now been justified, the question of style arises, and of this we have made two divisions, the *conceits* and the *phrasing*. Concerning the *conceits*, all of whose differences and effects you are familiar with, I shall say boldly that this noble mind has so excelled in this work that I do not believe, either in the case of the passions or in that of the descriptions, that similar felicities have ever occurred to a human mind. It is really in this aspect of his work that he has achieved diversity and the marvelous, things which other poets seek in the mere invention of episodes; and in this respect where another might have been cloying and disgusting, he has succeeded in being so charming and agreeable that the length of the poem will seem inadequate to anyone who has some little judgment of what good reading is. As for the phrasing, now, if I am allowed without reproof to judge the beauty of a tongue which is not natural to me, the diction is so beautiful in itself, so Tuscan, so carefully chosen, so pregnant, that never has there been a poet in whatever language who had this gift in a higher degree than he; and of conceits and phrasing he has compounded a style which, whether in sweetness or in seriousness, as well as

25

in really poetic inspiration, has no equal unless in certain ancient authors, and which will never be surpassed except by Marino himself.

But because this style is free and diffuse and because some even of the ancients have made judgments against it in their writers, calling it garrulousness, it will be good to see whether Marino's style, which follows that of the ancient writers, is subject to the same objection and whether it deserves blame or praise. It is an accepted maxim that any style must be suitable to the subject, the more so, as they say, because words are the natural expression of the idea, and the idea is nothing but the pure image of the thing itself. Now there are three kinds of subjects to which all others may be reduced: one is called grave or elevated, another humble or low, and the third a mixture of both; this last is called intermediate because it is small with respect to the great or the extraordinary, and great with respect to the ordinary and the petty. The first kind of subject includes all heroic deeds, the cyclical rise and fall of nations, the ruination or establishment of illustrious families, brave enterprises, and similar things; the second includes trickery, examples of gullibility, light loves, the quarrels and reconciliations which occur in civil and peaceful life among people of low estate and which do not produce public disturbance because of the low rank of the people involved; the third includes plots made up of mixtures of those events which are attributed to particular persons, even those who are great and illustrious, but which produce no other consequence than complaints and tears instead of wars and the subversion of the state. But as a thing is said to be average when it appears to partake of the two opposed extremes, so a subject is more properly called intermediate when it includes the serious and low; the seriousness may be found in the people and the lowness in the passions or ordinary events, or else the seriousness may be in the event and the extraordinary passions, and the lowness in ordinary people and circumstances. In ancient times the masters of eloquence sought in these three kinds of subjects the different forms or characteristics of style needed to treat them properly according to their differences; and to the first they assigned, if it was simply tragic, the style they merely called serious; if it was heroic also, that called both grave and magnificent, i.e., figured — you can easily see why; for the second they prescribed a common, trivial, discursive, smooth-flowing style, correct and understandable but knavish and jesting; to the third they assigned a style which was also intermediate, having some admixture of each of the others but sweetened and tempered — something of the serious and the magnificent in those places where the subject resembled the heroic or the tragic whether in dealing with people or events; and something of the popular or the common in those, whether concerning events or people, where it resembled the ordinary and the comic. Once these points are agreed upon, if one considers the nature of the subject of *Adone*, there is no doubt that it will be seen to belong to the genre of the intermediate subject, nor that in consequence the subject had to be treated in the intermediate style. Now the theory of this style requires that things be expressed clearly but not basely, this latter quality being an inconvenience ordinarily associated with its characteristic frankness (which we would interpret as clarity if we should some day begin to want to understand thoroughly what true learning consists of), the more so since to bring things before the eyes one must descend to details and to the statement of relationships and subordinations which, however, it seems impossible to explain without baseness; Homer himself in so doing fell into this pit. But the greater the difficulty in finding this intermediate style which is expressive but not distasteful to the reader, the greater also the praise due to the mind which found it and to the judgment which had the skill to make use of it precisely in a subject which not only permits this but requires it for its own perfection; you may judge particularly whether the fable of *Adone* does this by what we have said about it above. If then our friend used this style on this occasion he must have done so more by judicious choice than by compulsion, and he merits special praise for this as being the first of the moderns who has ventured upon detailed description, in which the essence of poetry consists (I mean by this its energy and imitation) and that, moreover, without having played his subject false and without having stooped to what is base; consider, I beg of you, what subject he chose in order to achieve this success, and how elevated it is in its simplicity. No one denies that of all things the vastest and most susceptible of different facets is human passion, the unique image of raw nature, nor that among all the passions love and jealousy hold first place; now consider whether these are found in the *Adone* and in what way. In truth one could scarcely find a plot or any development of a fable involving the marvelous which is worthy of being compared with that simple way of narrating which Marino has reestablished in his poem, wherein both as regards passions and descriptions that magnificent clarity, that is to say — if I may — that floridity or elegance of style, has been maintained with such complete possession of the ideas, so great care for the language and such precise regard for the scan-

27

sion of the verse and the conformity which ought to exist between the verse and the subject, that no one could ask for more: I find this all the more worthy of admiration since these are the thorniest things in poetry and the last to be mastered. If Scaliger, that great critic of the preceding century, were still alive, I do not doubt that in approving this work he would point out what we have shown here nor that the same thing for which he blamed Lucan, whose subject did not allow him to expatiate, would cause him to praise Marino, whose subject required that he treat it as he did. What leads me to this conjecture is the fact that Scaliger did not criticize copiousness in Claudian, whose intemperance is not slight, nor in Ovid, who expatiated to excess, whatever Quintilian may have said, for Scaliger no doubt realized that the one was fleshing out a simple fable which needed these external aids to give it relief, and that the other was giving life and speech to passions which are inexhaustible springs whose end is never seen. But since I said that the style of the *Adone* is perfect in its genre, I am sure you understand that it has all the qualities and general conditions of a good style, i.e., that the narration is very smooth, that the comparisons are naturally clear, being drawn from things well-known, finally, that as to the transitions nothing is left to be desired; and that thus since the principal virtue of this conception lies in the excellence of the style, and since this latter is the most excellent of all to the despair of carping critics, you see that the poem *Adone*, because of its style, will never have an equal in its genre. That is why, without dwelling at greater length on this final point, and without mentioning either the allegory included in the fable, as being sufficiently elucidated by the poet in the discourses with which he makes a practice of prefacing each canto, or the courageous competition into which he has entered with the ancients on the most important of their subjects, including the phrasing and even the conceits, as well as the detailed inventions hitherto unattempted by any other than himself, I shall, so as not to follow indiscreetly on your traces, conclude this wearisome catalogue by affirming to you as I did at the beginning that I consider *Adone*, in the form in which I remember having seen it, a good poem built up in all its novelty according to the general rules of the epic, and as the best in its genre which will ever be published.

Such then is the opinion you wanted from me concerning our friend's work; to support it more firmly I could have extended to greater length the things I have said in few words, for I should still have much to say if I were speaking to a person less understanding or less predisposed in favor of Marino, that is to say, in favor of the truth. Now should the affection which you have for him lead you to think I have meanly praised him here, remember you did not set me that task, and consider that in taking up my pen in order to satisfy you I have not intended to crown him with laurel but to show you succinctly that I knew why he deserved the crown. It seemed to me, since I was required only to give my opinion about his poem, that I was satisfying my obligation by telling you in plain words what I thought of it and the reasons why I held that opinion; and because of my nature you ought to have expected that I would not force my feelings in return for the friendship which Marino is kind enough to have for me; indeed, if there had been in the poem the slightest thing which I judged severely you would find it noted here in all freedom because, as I say, I do not love my friends more than my frankness and because I do not know what it is to squeeze out praise for them at the expense of the truth, consideration for the truth being so dear to me that what might disturb me about this essay would not at all be to have praised wrongly — that causes me no worry — but not having you before me so that if what I have said is perhaps subject to objection, I might hear your arguments and defend myself by replying to them at once, or else if the objections were unanswerable, so that I might relinquish my error immediately, ask for mercy, and profit from my shame by learning what I did not know. Had you wanted to compel me to panegyrize and praise Marino to the skies as he deserves, either I should have asked you for a longer time in which to prepare or I should have asked you to do it yourself, using that admirable pen which both in prose and verse and in one language or the other recognizes no rival which aims higher than it does. But allow me to tell you what I think: since I have no reason to suppose you wanted that from me, neither can I believe you waited until you had my opinion to make up your mind on this subject; I know too well both your ability and my own lack of knowledge to have any faith in such an idea as that, which without edifying you in the slightest would have entirely destroyed that modesty which alone my friends have until now esteemed in me; and I cannot come to any other conclusion than that you wished to test whether your authority was powerful enough to lead me into vanity and to induce me to think myself capable of making a judgment on the matter, preferring to inflict on yourself an annoying reply rather than not to plumb my weakness to the depths; and if this were true I should have nothing to oppose to that subtle scheme but my affection and the vow of cheerful compliance with which I have bound myself to you, and which, since your first request made me shut my eyes to any other consideration, has led me to reply to you as I have done on the subject of the *Adone*, and obliges me further to tell you that you ought to carry out the fine plan you have of working on the poem; and to show you more clearly that I believe you should do so and that there is in it honor to be won for you, I boldly warn you that if you do not do it I shall try my best to accomplish the task; you will have, then, to address yourself to it, first in your own interest and secondly to deliver Marino from the well-grounded fear he would have, should I undertake it, of coming ill-arrayed from my hands. Farewell.

% 1646

Jean Chapelain ON THE READING OF THE OLD ROMANCES,

DIALOGUE FOR MONSEIGNEUR JEAN-FRANCOIS-PAUL DE

GONDY, ARCHBISHOP OF CORINTH AND COADJUTOR IN THE

ARCHBISHOPRIC OF PARIS, LATER CARDINAL DE RETZ

You complain, my Lord, of not having been present at the conversation which Monsieur Ménage, Monsieur Sarasin, and I [13] had a few days ago on the reading of our old romances, and you show some regret that things were said there in your absence which one would not have expected so miserable a subject to call forth. What can I answer, except that there was never a more legitimate complaint? For indeed that diversion was owing to you for many reasons and among them because it began or at least it was conceived in your presence, during the journey we made last autumn with you. But, my Lord, permit us in our turn to complain that we missed you sorely on that occasion; I especially, who was, I do not know how, led to talk the most, particularly desired that you might have been there to hold me to moderation, to set me right, and to enlighten my darkness. There are so few things you do not know, your learning is so broad, your judgment so clear, you express yourself so lucidly, so forcefully, so eloquently, that if you had been present one might indeed have said that nothing was overlooked in the thorough discussion of the question. If it was through some mistake that you were not present, it must have been fortune's mistake and one for which we are all ready to make amends. We may still help you to enjoy that conversation, for all traces of it are not effaced; and I will wager that my bad memory will recall them easily and also will portray them faithfully for your satisfaction. However, because you are not always at leisure and because this recital could not be delayed without running the risk of being less exact and of losing many of its essential parts, it is best to commit it to paper so that you may pass

31

your time with it free of constraint and it may await your leisure without spoiling. I shall report the exact words as they were uttered by each of us without any embellishment except that which they derive from the subject and which is sometimes found in spontaneous discourse where nothing is premeditated.

If I were speaking to another than you, my Lord, I should have to describe the temper and the qualities of the men who took part in the discussion, and inform you of the goodness, the learning and the wit for which Monsieur Ménage is remarkable and of the fine and varied knowledge which Monsieur Sarasin has acquired and which is added to the quickness of his mind and strengthened by his experience in the affairs of the world. I should have to give you a little sketch of my own inclinations and undertakings, and in showing you my faults I should reveal to you also my boldness in having embarked upon a work so little proportioned to my talents. But since the first has been a friend of yours for so long, since the second holds so high a place in your esteem, and since, for my part I am, to my shame, so well known to you, I shall not take the time to paint our collective portrait, for in any case it could only make us all blush, each in a different manner. I shall only say, my Lord, without other preliminary, that when these two gentlemen came to visit me a few days ago they caught me over a book which you have no doubt heard of but which probably you have never been tempted to read. Monsieur Ménage, who is completely devoted to the ancient Greeks and Romans and whose knowledge of them scarcely allows him to admit that there is good to be found in anything the moderns may do, discovering me with this book [14] which even the moderns mention only with scorn, said to me with his usual gaiety and making sport of me, "What! so this is the Virgil you have taken as a model, and Lancelot is the hero in whose image you are forming the Count de Dunois? I confess I should not have expected that of a man to whom antiquity is not unknown and whom we have heard speak reasonably of its philosophers, its poets and its orators."

I was forestalled in my answer by Monsieur Sarasin who had formerly taken pleasure in that kind of reading and with whom I had discussed it more than once.

"*Lancelot*," said he, "is not his Virgil but his Ennius, in whom, as in manure, he thought he might find a ruby or a diamond with which to deck his Maid. I have read that book and did not find it too disagreeable. Among the things in it which pleased me is this: that I saw in it the source of all the romances which for four or five centuries were the most refined diversion of the courts of Europe and prevented barbarism from mastering the world completely."

"You praise it," said I, "far beyond what it deserves. It is a barbarous thing which barbarians liked, but it is not so throughout. It is better however to let Monsieur Ménage keep whatever opinion of it he likes than to force him to listen to a defense of it. I shall merely defend myself, for I should not want him to leave here convinced that I have lost all taste for good literature because he found me seriously engaged upon a book which he thinks very bad and which in his estimation is no less Gothic in the events than in the characters. He will be very much surprised and will feel very much indebted to me when he learns that it was only out of respect for him that I became attached to it. The fact is that when Monsieur Arnauld came back this winter from Dunkirk laden with so fine a conquest [15] and when that event had reawakened the desire I have always had of casting my eyes on this book so as to observe a little in it the language and the style of our ancestors, I decided to read it principally in the hope of finding there important matter for the *Treatise on the Origins of Our Language* which our scornful friend has started and which is already far along, but he shall know nothing more of it. We have dug up this treasure for him but we shall keep it hidden from him; we shall give it to Monsieur Conrart [16] who wants it for a work of the same plan or even a vaster one, and God knows how well he will make use of it with the solid sense he has and the good taste he shows in these matters."

"If I believed that," replied Monsieur Ménage, "I should be mortified at the hastiness of my judgment and angry at myself for having scorned so useful a book."

"In my opinion you should take him up on that," said Monsieur Sarasin to me, "and while he is in that good humor you can overwhelm him with those riches whose existence he doubts."

"I beg you to do so," went on Monsieur Ménage; "indeed, I defy you, if begging is not enough, so that whether out of kindness or out of spite you will do me a favor I hardly dare hope for."

"You could do that favor for yourself," I replied, "and it cannot be a great one if it is not even worth the seeking. You have only to read and note. However bad you may consider this book to be, it must be for you a classic work; its antiquity gives it that status, and the difference between the language of the book and your own proves its antiquity only too well.

You will have the pleasure of finding in it words so old that they are all worn out; indeed, they are dead in the language, for they are not intelligible or are so only through what goes before or what comes after. You will see others so strange that, since you will not be able to understand them by guesswork or by any other way, you will have to fall back on Monsieur de Salmonet, who will enlighten you through the perfect knowledge he has of his language, provided the words do not have an English root or do not come from Scotland. You will sometimes be in doubt owing to the resemblance to be found there between French sayings and phrases and those in Spanish and Italian which are either their originals or copies of them. You will see a good many which are no longer in use but whose source is not hard to find. On the other hand you will encounter some which have come down to us from remote times not only in their purity but even in their elegance, so that they are among our most agreeable expressions and are heard only among the best speakers. You will find there noun and verb formations, sequences of pronouns, omissions of the articles, constructions, and inversions which seem ridiculous to most of those who read them, but which will serve as torches to light your way more easily to an understanding of the dependence of French on Latin. In a word, you will observe there, through a comparison of the old style and the new, what changes the language has undergone, how it shed bit by bit its original rusticity, and by what roads it passed to arrive at the sweetness, the majesty, and the abundance which we now find in it. And do not think you will have to cover much ground in order to obtain examples of all these things. Each page — why do I say each page? — each sentence, each line will furnish you with such a quantity that if you are embarrassed it will be by their number."

Monsieur Ménage, confused by my remarks and not certain of how to judge them, said that all those statements were fine and that half of them would justify him in having a good opinion of the book if they were as solidly established as they were boldly advanced.

I replied, as I had already said, that proof would be easy and that we should not have to go far; but in order to teach him not to take people at their word I would not give him proof: rather he should find it himself.

"What!" said he, "will you be so cruel, so rigorous? To refuse to convince me and to want me to convince myself! If it is as easy as you say, you cannot decently refuse me, and so I am suspicious of your argument. Well, well, since I must, I shall investigate, and we shall see at leisure if there are grounds for believing in all you say. However, as a single favor, I shall ask you for just one example of that elegance which is both old and new, which has traversed so many ages without being corrupted, and which is not less beautiful now because it was beautiful five hundred years ago. If you can show me that miracle I shall have no more trouble in believing the rest and shall not want a fuller illustration."

"I prefer," said I, "that you should seek the illustration yourself, and if I give you the example you ask for, it is on the condition that you will do so. Could anyone say nowadays in a nobler way that he loves someone extremely than by saying 'He is the man I love best in all the world?' Yet this was said more than four hundred years ago, as can be shown by more than twenty places in this book."

"But if that turn of phrase," he answered, "is as usual as you say it is, it seems to me modern enough so that I should deduce from it the contrary conclusion, and instead of believing it is old because it is in the book, I should say for that very reason that the book is not old."

"There is wit," I replied, "in twisting the argument in that way, but there is no solidity. For since this book is filled with terms either unknown or no longer used, and elegant turns of phrase are only scattered through it, the presumption in favor of its antiquity is much stronger than that of its modernity. But we are not reduced to mere presumption. We have conclusive proofs and unimpeachable witnesses. Three hundred years ago Boccaccio mentioned Lancelot, Tristan, and Gallehaut of the Distant Isles as heroes celebrated by writers of the past. About three hundred and fifty years ago Petrarch spoke of them and of their adventures as dreams and reveries. More than thirty years before him Dante says that Lancelot was the cause of a tragic event which, as he calculated, could not have been very recent. Thus you can see as clear as daylight that this romance was written more than four centuries ago, and I know no older French books except perhaps the chronicles of Joinville and Villehardouin.[17]

"As for its antiquity," said Monsieur Sarasin, "that is indisputable; a cursory reading is convincing on that point; but I should not believe it is more than four centuries old, and I do not see how you will prove convincingly that it is as much as five."

"Nor do I claim to be able to do so," I replied. "But do you have a good reason to show that it is not so old?"

"My position," he said, "is the negative — a choice I am free to make. The burden of proof is on you."

I was about to reply when Monsieur Ménage said: "You are arguing about nothing and it is of no importance to the question which of you says yes or no. As far as antiquity is concerned I do not consider there is much difference between four centuries and five centuries; and if you proved to me that the book is older than four you could easily make me believe it is close to five."

"So," said Monsieur Sarasin, "after the proof we have given you we have at least won this point from you, that the book is good for something and that the French language may receive from its authority a remarkable enrichment. But," he went on, addressing me, "do you limit its merit to the utility which the language may draw from it?"

"Would that not be enough," I replied, "even if there were no other? I have already told you that when first I began to read it that was the only advantage I sought in it. I admit nevertheless that because its words forced me to look at things I have found in it reason to show Monsieur Ménage, if he makes me angry enough, that other than linguistic profit may be drawn from it."

"That's what comes," cried Monsieur Ménage, "of granting something to people like you. Instead of being happy with the favor you have received, you authorize yourselves by our generosity to make new claims. I should really like to know what other profit can be got from that miserable carcass, which is horrible and repulsive even to the crude and the ignorant. Do you expect to show me in that barbarian a Homer or a Livy? What you propose is scarcely anything less."

"Now, now," I said, "we have not taken leave of our senses and we are not making any such odious comparisons. We know the dignity of those great men and the vulgarity of the writer, whoever he was, that composed the romance. But the main difference we see between Homer and him is in the style and in the mere expression of feelings. We see the first always noble and always sublime in this respect, and the second always rustic and prosy; as to the events they are scarcely truer in the one than in the other; and fables for fables, when I examine them closely I don't know which are the more ingeniously invented or even in which of the two verisimilitude is better observed."

"That is no new opinion of yours," interrupted Monsieur Ménage. "What you are saying reminds me of what you once said on this subject: that just as the poems of Homer were the fables of the Greeks and Romans, so our old romances are the fables of the French and the English."

"I still consider the point well taken," I replied, "and if you are reminding me of it in order to reproach me you are no longer the same man who praised my remark as a reflection which, on the basis of what you said, I might even consider excellent."

"I am not holding it against you," said he, "but I am bringing it up in order to show you on what principle your reasoning is based."

"Well," I replied, "Aristotle, who made a mystery of that poet [Homer] and who took him to be the prototype of his art, attributed to him the glory of following the rules — a glory it is very unlikely he ever aspired to. There is but good and bad luck in this world. If Aristotle were to come back and take it into his head to find the subject-matter of a poetics in *Lancelot* I am sure he would succeed just as well as with the *Iliad* and the *Odyssey*, and that his intelligence or his authority would easily overcome the inconveniences which he might encounter. I can assure you of this at least, that the magic which is everywhere in the *Lancelot* would not be more difficult for him to accommodate to the rules than the divinities which Homer used so eccentrically, whatever the allegorical significance given them by his hollow commentators."

"But," said Monsieur Sarasin, "if you consider magic to be as plausible in poetic machinery as Homer's divinities, why did you rather make use in your *Maid* of angels and demons which are related to those divinities instead of magical operations which not only are established in the old romances but which Tasso himself introduced into his poem with so much success? What reason had you in so free a choice to prefer the old style to the new?"

"The argument is *ad hominem*," said Monsieur Ménage, "and presses him hard; I should very much like to hear the answer."

"You may be sure," I replied, "that the answer is ready, but because it would need a long discussion and would take us far from the subject we are dealing with now, we shall put it aside for another occasion. However since, as you know, that is one of the principal difficulties of modern poetry, I considered its nature and basis when I made the plan of my work, and if I decided not to use magic, the reason was not that I thought it bad but merely unnatural to my subject owing to the circumstances of its time, place, and character and its illumination by the excessively bright light of history; besides that, I should require much more discretion in the use of magic in our romances than in the use of Homer's divinities. Moreover, to speak frankly, since my heroic poem came after so many others, if I wished to distinguish myself from the ordinary I had to do it with the quintessence of art and exquisite verismilitude, moving the action by machinery which might appear necessary but which was not, and show that one can write a poem in the Christian style without going along the beaten track of magic, for that would have deprived me of the glory of originality. But to return to the point from which we started, I beg you to consider what a reasonable reader must think of that division and opposition of celestial powers, of the wounding of Mars and Venus by a mortal man, of Vulcan who sets fire to the Scamander, of Neptune and Apollo who work as laborers in the building of the walls of Troy; decide whether the most subtle allegory can satisfy a reason offended by such absurdities, and whether *Lancelot* contains any extravagances to which a speculative mind might not give interpretations as favorable as those given by the commentators of Homer to his. Nevertheless I respect the antiquity of Homer and I freely admit that in the detail of his works there are seeds of astronomy, geography, the art of oratory and even of philosophy which bear witness to the excellence of his doctrine and which put him above comparison."

"Still you gave him a pretty good drubbing," said Monsieur Sarasin, "and that is the least you can say in his favor without declaring yourself his enemy in everything."

"I said enough good of him," I answered, "so that no one can reasonably accuse me of being opposed to him. What if I had treated him as Scaliger [18] did, and if instead of putting him above comparison I should have preferred not to choose between Virgil and him?"

"But," said Monsieur Ménage, "do you not want us to compare *Lancelot* and Livy?"

"The choice," I replied, "that anyone would claim to make between *Lancelot* and Livy would be as mad as that between Virgil and Livy, between the false and true. *Lancelot* is not Livy because the actions which are narrated in it are remote from any truth. If, however, the romance is not comparable to Livy in historical truth, since it is composed only of fabulous events, I daresay it is comparable to him in the description of mores and customs of which both provide perfect images, the one of the times of which he wrote, the other of those in which it was written."

"You are embarking," said Monsieur Ménage, "on a strange affair — that of presenting as truthful a writer who, by your own admission, is completely imaginative."

Monsieur Sarasin interrupted him to say: "He probably didn't do it without thinking. Before condemning him we must hear him out and see how he will escape the paradox. The point is subtle enough in all conscience and deserves a fuller explanation."

"I am convinced," I replied, "of the truth of the statement I made on the subject, and you will be also when I have finished explaining it, or I am very much mistaken. Yet I make it only as a reasonable guess, and I shall be satisfied if you merely consider it probable. For the first basis of my opinion I accept as a fact that the period in which *Lancelot* was written was a time of deep ignorance, when all the scholarly disciplines were dead, and when not only abstruse and difficult sciences were unknown, but when even history, chronology, and cosmography were as confused as it is possible to imagine. All human subtlety was turned either to scholastic theology or to the thorns of jurisprudence, without anybody's having the slightest suspicion that literature existed in the world, for the Greeks and Romans were known only by name. As a second basis I assume that any writer who invents a fable of which human actions are the subject can only present his creatures and make them act in a way conformable to the mores and beliefs of his time, since it is generally admitted that our ideas scarcely go beyond what we see and hear. Since the author's goal is to please the public, he will seek to attain his goal by events which are easily believed; he will use descriptions only of what ordinarily happens or is usually done because pleasure arises only from nature or from habit, and unless one has a depraved taste it is difficult to find pleasure in chimerical imaginings; there must be a relationship between the object and its persuasive power; if the mind is to accept what is presented to it the thing presented must be either natural or well known, for the unknown and the impossible, far from satisfying the mind, will but prove disgusting. On these bases I think I can say that *Lancelot*, which was composed in the darkness of our modern antiquity, and without the benefit of erudition other than experience with the world, is a faithful narration, if not of what happened among the kings and knights of that time, at least of what everybody was convinced might happen, perhaps because of the traces of similar things which had often occurred in the preceding centuries. I think I can assure you even more emphatically that it is a faithful representation and, so to speak, a certain and exact history of the mores which prevailed in the courts of that time. Just as doctors diagnose the peccant humor of their patients from their dreams, so one can judge the mores and the actions of bygone times from the daydreams in these writings. One of the reasons which does most to confirm me in this opinion is the seriousness with which all Europe took this work and the avidity with which all nations sought diversion in it. Novelty, I admit, attracts the curiosity of men, who are rarely excited by what they already know. But we must distinguish among novelties and say that the novelty of events attracts the curious, but not novelty of mores, which astonishes and wounds more than it pleases. Another reason which persuades me to this belief is the great conformity which we find among the customs, and sometimes even among the actions, which we see represented in this fabulous book and those we find in Gothic, Danish, English, and even French stories of that time or of times closer to our own. Read Olaüs Magnus, Saxo Grammaticus, the original of Polydore Virgil and of Buchanan, our *Lives* of Saint Louis, Bertrand du Guesclin, Marshal de Bouciquaut, and the Chevalier Bayard, our Froissarts and our Monstrelets; [19] you will note, if not in all at least in some, shadows and traces of the things which are developed to excess in this romance and similar writings. I need Monsieur Duchesne at this point, for he would fortify my sentiments by his observations, since nothing of these matters has escaped the vast knowledge he has acquired about our antiquity through the unearthing of so many manuscripts and documents. In his stead I might have asked the help of my neighbor, the Baron d'Auteuil, who is scarcely second to Monsieur Duchesne,[20] had I foreseen that you would involve me in this argument. Since they are not here I shall refer you to what Monsieur de la Colombière has just published in his *Théâtre de Chevalerie*, and which might in itself sufficiently guarantee the truth of what I have been saying." [21]

"That aspect of things," said Monsieur Sarasin, "leaves me with no difficulties whatever, and your conception and its proof have satisfied me much more than I had hoped. And to show you that I am not saying this from mere politeness I shall reinforce your proof with a similar one which has just occurred to me." Then turning to Ménage, he said: "Do you not agree that the old tapestries, old paintings, old statues which have come down to us from our ancestors are the true originals of the clothing, the hair-dressings, and the shoes of their times and that, as those relics show us the styles of the times, one may say, as Monsieur Chapelain has done, that the old romances paint for us to the very life the mores and the customs of those same times?"

"It seems likely," said Monsieur Ménage, "and although at first I found the proposition very strange, to show you my open-mindedness I confess it seems to me not unreasonable and that I should consider it true in a pinch."

"Then," said I, "you agree that this book is both fictional and historical, at least that it is often fictional in the events but historical for the rest."

"But you too must agree," replied Monsieur Ménage, "that there is to be found in it no event which deserves the attention of a man of taste, that it is devoid of all art, of all surprise, of all that stimulates the curiosity, and that very often there is found in it a kind of simple-mindedness which comes very close to silliness and foolishness."

"I willingly admit that," said I, "and even more than you require. I have argued nothing else the whole day. The author is a barbarian who wrote in barbarous times for an audience of barbarians; he never imagined a work might be planned so that it would have a reasonable arrangement, a proper proportion among its parts, a subtle plot, or a natural conclusion. He goes as far as is humanly possible; he is always in the same posture and always sings the same note; he is rough, rugged, antipodal to the graces. When in difficulties his only recourse is to magic, which is always at his command and which he has turned into an art as ordinary as the tailor's or the cobbler's. Finally it can be said that he is entirely lacking in wit and that no one can read a single page of his without a yawn and a headache. I am sure you do not think I have such bad taste as to read this book for anything but its language when I take from serious business the time needed to leaf through it. It seems to me I am giving you full measure by saying as many bad things about this book as you could wish. In exchange I ask in my turn that you take my word for this: that it contains all the good things I have mentioned and more besides, if possible."

"What other good things can you say of it," replied Monsieur Ménage, "after having assured us that it is the historian of the mores of its time and that there is to be found in it a supplement to the annals which have come down to us, but which inform us only of the births and deaths of princes with the events which marked their reigns, whereas this book, as you describe it, makes us familiar with those princes and shows us the depths of their souls?"

"Say rather," went on Monsieur Sarasin, seeing that he was stopping there, "that it reveals to us their character and that of their courtiers, that it teaches us how they talked together, that it shows us how deeply they were imbued with the maxims of true honor, how religiously they held to their word, how they managed their love-affairs, how far they were able to carry on a decent friendship, what gratitude they showed for favors, how high an idea they had formed of valor, and finally what feelings they had about Heaven and what respect for holy things."

"If Monsieur Sarasin," said I to Monsieur Ménage, "had added the customs they invariably followed, he would have left me nothing to say on this subject; for excepting that, you and he have mentioned everything; yet this is enough, as anyone will see who thinks about it, so that if you admit it all to be true, you are compelled to say that this bad book is nevertheless a good one, and that there is profit to be had from it which it would be hard to get elsewhere."

I fell silent after these words, and Monsieur Ménage did not intend to pursue the discourse any further, for he showed himself by his silence to be satisfied with it; but then Monsieur Sarasin replied: "If he will not take your word for it I shall vouch for it with mine, and if need be by my oath as an eye-witness; for I have seen in the book all that you saw there, and if I had not read it I could not have made the same reflections about it you have made and which do not admit of contradiction. Therefore I shall say that anything you might add to what you have said, by way of a fuller explanation of this subject, would be superfluous from my point of view; but from that of Monsieur Ménage it might well be different since he has not seen what I have seen and in the end he is not obliged to believe us without proof."

I replied: "If he could not find out for himself, if we forbade him to read the book, if we required him to take us on trust, you would be right to talk that way and to demand proofs of me for him."

"And besides, have we not sufficiently discussed a subject as base as this one? Have we not wallowed long enough in the depths of barbarism and," went on Monsieur Sarasin, turning to Monsieur Ménage, "as your Mamurra would say, in the cloaca of caliginous centuries and in the bilge of apedestic nations?" [22]

"The choice is mine," said Monsieur Ménage to me, "whether I shall take your refusal for a defeat and hence doubt everything you have claimed up to now."

"There is an eye-witness," I answered, "who gives you his word for it, and even if you doubted mine you would be forced to respect his and not to change your opinion so fast."

"He may doubt my sincerity," said Monsieur Sarasin then, "and yours too, but he cannot allow you to stop when you are so well on the road; the important thing is to confirm the new convert in his faith."

"But," said I, "since you think it necessary, do it yourself, for you can do it incomparably better than I and have the necessary graces as I do not."

"I am not to be caught by such flattery," he replied, "and Monsieur Ménage would not follow the new scent even if I were vain enough to imagine he had nothing to lose by doing so."

"Nevertheless," I said, "you must bear your part of the burden; do not imagine that in this you are a mere onlooker."

"In order to satisfy you," said he, "I prefer to promise him an ample discussion whenever he wants it of one of the points which I have only listed, on the condition that you now give him a sample of each, so that before finishing with you he may be assured that we are honorable men and that we affirm only what can be proved. I do not expect you to treat these subjects profoundly. You would need more time and more breath. A summary and a few light touches will be enough to satisfy him until something better is possible."

"I see there is no way to evade this," I replied, "and moreover you are in my house where you are the masters: it would be uncivil of me not to obey. I shall then point out to Monsieur Ménage that one learns from this romance better than from any history of that period how Christian Europe was; I mean how deeply the nations were really attached to the divine cult. Here are a few evidences of that. Make those knights as eager as you want in their perilous quests, whether to preserve their honor or to aid some oppressed person; yet not a day passes that the author does not have them attend mass, and nothing is clearer in the whole book than the care he takes to have them regular in their duty, even to the point of putting these words occasionally into their mouths: 'I have not missed mass one day of my life if it was in my power to attend.' If he involves them in a doubtful enterprise he has them turn towards a monastery and, in order to take it to witness their promises, has them utter aloud before it the terms of their pledge; or else he has them presented with relics on which they swear that they will do what they have undertaken; this is what they call *swearing by the saints*. I shall not mention his famous Holy Grail with its unexpected appearances and difficult adventures, nor the conditions of virginity, purity, and innocence which he requires of the knight destined to end them."

43

"We can easily believe that," said Monsieur Ménage, "after what we have learned of the zeal of those old days from the narration of the Bishop of Tyre [23] and of Joinville, and from the other histories of the Crusades which have caused so much debate in the east and south."

"You believe it," I replied, "on the word of those writers who are no doubt better than the author of *Lancelot*; but you believe it only because they report generalities whereas in the latter you see the individual actions and the very words of the characters as they were done and uttered by the real men of the period. And if we had not decided to glide lightly over each of these subjects I could show you by an infinite number of examples that you are not at liberty to doubt the powerful impression religion had made on their minds nor the sincerity and the reverence with which they submitted to its mysteries."

"You do not say with what knowledge," pointed out Monsieur Ménage.

"I have already mentioned," said I, "their deep ignorance of everything. But why should their understanding and their knowledge matter when only their piety and their faith are concerned?"

"Indeed," said he, "they must have been very ignorant to have been able to combine the goodness and virtue attributed to them with the insults which, it is said, the author has them utter to passers-by and because of which one or the other usually is left dead at the meeting-place. One must live in the deepest darkness to think it possible to adjust the license of utter wantonness to the humblest devotion, and to suppose unscrupulous slaughters and remorseless debaucheries were in no way contrary to the holy laws these knights professed to follow so exactly. There is reason to think the princes of those times were very brutish and that they knew but little of civil government. Ours are much more civilized, when you examine the question, to have suppressed those odd knights and to have replaced them by captains of the watch through whom they have put an end to those disorders which otherwise would have destroyed society."

"Those old princes and their old subjects," I said, "had a plentiful supply of the ignorance they needed for the adjustment you speak of. They held that all of religion consisted in believing firmly in Jesus Christ, and beyond this they made few general reflections about good and evil where natural inclinations were concerned. The priests themselves barely knew how to read, and instructed the people only through the sermon, as was laid down in their ceremonials. If occasionally one of them chanced to take up the study of literature or to raise his mind to the contemplation of heavenly movements, he was at once taken to be a magician or a heretic. Other men, especially the knights, knew nothing but how to fight well, and the women knew nothing beyond how to love well those who fought well. These were the only principles by which they regulated their actions and feelings."

"Are those not animals you are describing," said Monsieur Ménage, "are they not *silvestres homines,* etc.?" [24]

"I am describing them to you as they were," I answered, "and although if you look at them from the point of view you have taken nothing could be more brutish and more savage, yet if one is willing to take another point of view and to seek the root of things, it would not be impossible to find in them something resembling reason, or at least to show that they were not wholly brutes."

"I beg of you to demonstrate that," said Monsieur Sarasin, "for as to this point I admit I am on the side of Monsieur Ménage and I do not see how they can be excused."

"It is well known," I said, "that among northern peoples might has always made right and that the only virtue they recognize is valor. They feel that courage is the instrument by which one attains ease and security in life, and that without it both the preservation and the increase of property are unthinkable. Imbued with that opinion and deprived of any other kind of understanding, they founded, as we see, their whole policy on power alone, and when they formed states these were always military states. Without having heard of Achilles, each of them behaved like him who *Jura negat sibi nata, nil non arrogat armis.* [25] I am aware that little is known of the manner of their ancient government as it existed in the confines of their native lands such as Gothia and Scandia, Sarmatia and Scythia; [26] but it can easily be judged from the swarms of peoples who formerly came out of them and who, under the names of Cimbrians, Teutons, Huns, Goths, Alans, Danes, and Norsemen, overran and subjugated every part of Europe. All their law was only what is called custom, and they gave themselves up to brigandage and violence as a right of conquest, much as Alexander did. Even when in the course of time they grasped the idea that justice was a concept necessary for the maintenance of society and to give a firm basis for their usurpations, when they found it appropriate to make use of it they refused to trust its administration to the laws. The wisest among them held that crimes could rightly be punished if they were only suspected, and that provided they acted in good faith the same

45

men could be both judges and executioners. On this idea were founded the false and the true quests among their adventures for the protection of the weak and the punishment of the wicked, for which they received a mandate when they were raised to the order of chivalry."

"With the result," said Monsieur Ménage, "that the knights were really officers of the law whom the princes sent after robbers and whom they set on the tracks of salt-smugglers and counterfeiters."

"With the result," I said, "that they resembled an army of men like Hercules sent by their Eurystheuses [27] to purge the world of monsters and tyrants. In truth I do not see much difference between Hercules errant and Lancelot errant; and a man wanting to do justice to everybody would decide that Lancelot and his fellows were nothing but Hercules while Hercules and his fellows were much like Lancelots. But, to come back to our argument, from the custom of exercising justice individually there has come down to us the custom of being unwilling to satisfy an offense against honor through a magistrate or a prince, even though God and reason have set them up no less for this than for robberies and murders; and to insist on reparation by our own hands as if the honor of a gentleman could be vindicated only by the sword, not the sword of justice but that of the individual who considers himself offended. And that abuse, gentlemen, is a relic of the former brutality of the French which the light of the Gospel and the authority of the laws have not yet been able to root out from the souls of their descendants. From the same source come those other customs, which are not less barbarous, and which are preserved still in Scotland and in the Isles, as well as those which the inaccessible forests of Ireland have preserved intact and uncorrected for so many centuries whether they concern the tyranny of the lords or the servitude of the vassals, the freedom and purity of marriage, or the security of the weak against the unbridled violence of their powerful neighbors. All this means that the French and the English, being the successors of these brutal tribes, before experience and teaching had uprooted their uncivilized habits, apparently observed the same ways of behaving and put all their trust in valor, using it either to preserve or to increase the extent of their domination. Justice counted for almost nothing among them, and it was a great thing when princes dispensed it once in their lives while making a progress through their provinces as is still done today among the northerners. Ecclesiastics were shut up in hermitages and monasteries; valor reigned alone by its own right, and to it alone pleasures and honors were reserved. The knights were the favored class and the sole arm of the monarch, who for the reasons I have mentioned fed that courage by all the means which those crude times and the sensual bent of youthful minds could suggest to his imagination. For this was invented that Round Table, which was nothing but an Order similar to that of the Garter, to the honors of which were admitted none but those who by acts of superlative valor had deserved to be made companions of the king. So it came about that those who had obtained that highest of favors preferred to die a hundred times rather than to fail their lord once, or to lose the name of brave men by refusing dangers or even by not seeking them out. And because valor was sovereign in the hearts of young men, and because the hearts of persons of that age can be touched only by love of glory and love of women, so as to strengthen the former by the latter, the policy of those olden days was to erect into a kind of law the idea that a lady's heart was the prize of courage, thereby sharpening the fidelity which vassals owed to their lord by the hope, not only of glory, but also of the pleasure which the possession of beauty gives. For this reason princes had established in their courts promiscuous and public love-making as a praiseworthy thing — a situation which has been imitated among modern courts in that of Isabella of Castile and Catherine de Medici; with this single difference that in the earlier ones it was unimportant whether a villainy occurred, for each lady was free to satisfy her lover without being disgraced. This was openly done with the connivance, or rather, at the suggestion of the kings, who were hindered in their own designs by the modesty and virtue of the ladies, since these served only to rebuff knights who were not civilized enough to participate in a long affair and who had no conception of Platonic love. The same princes, for the same ends, had suggested to the ladies that of all the virtues valor alone was to be prized in a knight, and if they wanted something besides it should be faithfulness in love."

"And for them," said Monsieur Sarasin, "the obligation on this last point was reciprocal and the amusing thing is this: the learned lawgivers required that mistresses be faithful to their lovers when they could easily deceive them without being discovered, whereas wives were allowed to be unfaithful to their husbands, provided the scandal was public."

"If we take these things for granted . . ." I went on.

"That is exactly right, 'take for granted,'" interrupted Monsieur Ménage, "for I see no proofs of all this and I should put you in a difficult position if I were to deny the truth of what you say."

"I do not have," said I, "any individual author by whom I can prove this to you, but I do have the author of the *Lancelot* itself, the author of *Tristan*, and the whole swarm of writers of old romances such as *Merlin*, *Arthur*, *Perceforest*, who all agree on the same points and who all wrote in an age when minds were not very inventive or were incapable of reacting against the mores and customs of the times. And the agreement of so many writers about such circumstances as these may pass for partial proof which is enough in this kind of a situation where I promised you only reasonable guesses defensible only before people as pliable as yourself. But since what leads you to be more suspicious of my supposition is what I am telling you about the promiscuity of the ladies of that time — a promiscuity based on the idea that it brought no dishonor — I think I can make their behavior seem more than probable to you by citing a custom maintained in Scotland long after Christianity had been accepted by which the kings had first pleasure after the marriage of their principal ladies, and the great lords a similar tribute from those of their vassals, a custom once observed in Normandy as we see by the dues which certain lords still collect on this precedent at the marriage of their subjects. Now anyone who considers this situation carefully will see that it is of the same nature as that which I accept on the testimony of the romances, except that it is even more reprehensible since it was not excused by love and was but mere brutality. If we take these things for granted, then it does not require great subtlety to conclude that even though the expedient chosen by the princes was violent and indecent, nevertheless it served their ends; and that if they were inexcusable insofar as concerns fairness and modesty they could be justified on grounds of logic and necessity since their limited diligence led them to no other way of maintaining and extending their power."

"If the point is not entirely proved," said Monsieur Sarasin, "it is at least colorable, and I am inclined to believe it."

"If Monsieur Ménage," I replied, "had the same inclination, I should be satisfied and should ask no more."

"I shall not tell you my opinion," responded Monsieur Ménage, "because I am still in doubt, and my decision is not yet made."

"In my opinion," said Monsieur Sarasin, "we should not wait for your decision, and it would be better," he said, turning to me, "for you to continue to show him the other good qualities of this book according to your observations and reflections."

"Let us settle them in a few words," I said, "since we are pledged to discuss them, and let us be careful not to be as lengthy on the remaining points as we have been on this one. First, the style of conversation between these knights and their ladies, which is, as I suppose, that of the time when the book was written, was simple and unadorned, without anything genteel or charming in it, but sensible, clear, and laconic, saying only what was necessary but everything that was essential, *morata* rather than *urbana*, [28] somewhat like the Roman speech of Numa's day; [29] in a word, not very gallant but very solid. From this you will conclude that it is not a clever book or one from which we learn how to behave in good company. On the other hand you see in it the quality of the mind of this past century; you can see how far its barbarism had come on the road to reason; finally you can see what progress the French nation has made in four or five hundred years, not only in language but in the arts of discourse, which is not a disagreeable subject for consideration nor an entirely useless piece of knowledge. Besides this, one may note in these rustic adventures how deep-rooted in the hearts of these knights errant were the love of fairness and the hatred of injustice as these were conceived by them; hence the violent deeds they did in their fights against those whom they met in their quests most often grew out of other violent deeds done to ladies, orphans, and generally to the weak and the deserving.

"From this one may rise to a consideration very different from the last if we are but willing to note how far the centuries which approach our own, as they have come closer to the light of reason, have fallen away from virtue, and if we but consider into what disorders and corruptions souls have fallen from having, as I may say, eaten of the fruit by which they distinguish good from evil. But if there is anything in this kind of reading which pleases me, it is the high point of honor of which each knight makes a precise profession, and the never-ending fear they have lest they do or say something by which their reputation may be in any way smirched or lest they have something with which to reproach themselves even though they alone know of it. If I am touched by anything in the book it is that jealous care for their pledged word, the principle of always doing exactly what they have promised — an ethic worthy of the admiration of more civilized ages, which, because it was constantly practiced, leaves far behind the empty ostentation of the theory that one can teach by precepts. For, although these knights often give a promise very lightly and carry it out at an unsuitable time, what we must complain about is the awkwardness of the writer who plots badly and applies that virtue badly; but what we must esteem is the fixed and resolute intention of the men of those times never to fail in their word, whatever harm may come to them from standing by it.

"What shall I say to you of their undying gratitude for favors done them, their eagerness and the labors they undertook to find an opportunity for repayment, and their conviction that they were always indebted even after they had doubly repaid? I include here their obvious displeasure when they considered they had not shown deep enough appreciation for services received, and the penitences which they imposed upon themselves. These are virtues common to the principal characters of the book and which appear so uniform in it that one cannot doubt they were ordinary in those old days, provided one recalls my supposition that if he wanted to please his contemporaries, the writer could not give his heroes mores other than those of the time. I leave you to judge whether such noble impulses and praiseworthy habits could sow bad seed in the minds of readers; whether the knights who had them were not decent barbarians and admirable boors, and whether there are not grounds for surprise that our sophistication may be enlightened as to its duty by their ignorance; whether blind men like these can serve as guides to those who see as well as we do; and finally whether they did not have great virtues in terms of pure nature while we are covered with vices in the midst of the teachings of art.

"As for valor it is at its apogee among them; I do not say this because of the greatness of their acts, which are almost always exaggerated and impossible, but because of their great contempt for life when their honor was ever so slightly engaged, because of their brave way of fighting, and because of their honest admission of their disadvantage when the worst had happened. I am willing to say that in this our century is their equal and that among the nobility of our times there are but few cowards capable of foul play or the denial of a favor received. I maintain only that those ruffians of the past, who cheated in nothing else, were, in single combat, as shrewd as any of us; and as for frankness, civility, courtesy, modesty in talking of themselves, as well as for vigor and bravado, if they did not surpass us, at least they were not inferior to us, and could boast of having carried that aspect of military virtue to the refinement it has today; that is to say they could boast of having taught it to us, though it be almost the only good lesson we have been willing to take from them. If we wish to talk now of their perfect friendship, based as it was on esteem and virtue, who were ever nobler or more ardent friends than Lancelot and Gallehaut, or to put it better, Gallehaut and Lancelot, as soon as the former had been told of Lancelot's extraordinary merit?

"See the effects of this friendship. Because of it alone he gave back to King Arthur his life and the kingdom which he had almost entirely taken away, and, as a climax of deference, asked pardon of the King for his own victory and offered him in homage his own estates. He allowed Guinevere to have a larger share of Lancelot than himself. For love of Lancelot he took her in when Arthur drove her from Logres. Finally he died of sorrow at the news of Lancelot's death. Achilles did not love Patroclus so much nor Theseus Pirithoüs, and there is nothing approximating this in the *Toxaris* [30] although it was written to celebrate perfect friendship, and after so many years learned men have imagined nothing more perfect. Our own times furnish no comparable examples; what am I saying, furnish no examples? Men of our day do not even conceive such examples, or if they conceived them would laugh at them as empty vaporings and would call mad a man warmed by so fine a passion."

"But even if we granted you all that, said Monsieur Ménage, "and even if we accept all these points as sound, how will you deal with the question of the gallantry of your old knights, since it could not have been very admirable; even you have admitted that they were entirely lacking in wit?"

"I have not promised," I answered, "to justify this romance in all respects, and from the way I have spoken of it you must have seen that I was far from approving everything in it. Speaking frankly, the question of Lancelot's gallantry is one which I should not like to undertake to defend, especially since I am convinced that while love may exist without wit, for that passion has its seat more in the heart than in the head, it is very unlikely that there can be gallantry in which wit has no part and which hence is totally devoid of grace. Even so, if I condemned all the gallantry of Lancelot I should be afraid of the trap into which the author of *Don Quixote* fell when he made game of the knights errant and their strange adventures merely because he failed to consider, as we have done, the times in which they were active and the accepted mores of the period. For if it were allowable to turn to ridicule whatever is not the usage of our century or the place in which we live there is nothing so serious and so true in antiquity or foreign literature in which a clever wit might not find substance for his own amusement and that of others. For myself, I hold that we must be just and that we must look at things with all their attendant circumstances in order to make a sound judgment. Our way of pleasing the ladies and of persuading them of our love is completely contrary to that of ancient times. Shall I for that reason esteem only ours to be good? I am not presumptuous enough to believe that there is nothing good except what I do. I shall not call Lancelot's gallantry bad; I shall merely say it is different from ours, and if it achieved the same effect as ours why should I grudge the admission that it is just as good? I shall not say it, however, because I prefer gallantry to be gallant and I admit that Lancelot's is crude. But to satisfy everybody I think one must say that gallantry is an equivocal term which sometimes designates the art of pleasing the ladies so as to be loved by them, and sometimes the love of them, devoid of method and art. By the first definition we can agree that Lancelot is the least gallant of men, that he has no idea of how to get into his mistress's good graces by studied words and by the art of following her about; that he does not seek to win her by the handsome ordering of his person, and that he does not depend on the elegance of his attire, on melodious serenades, or on striking ballet-like attitudes. By the second definition there was never so perfect a gallant as Lancelot. He does not pretend to be in love, he really is; he loves as much in absence as in presence; the mere sight of Guinevere puts him beside himself, makes him speechless, and incapable of any other thought. He is frenzied at the thought of having displeased her, and this thought sends him out to race through the fields; he invokes her in his greatest perils; he is faithful to her when he has the greatest opportunities to betray her; he belongs to her more than to Galahad, although Galahad bore for him the most ardent friendship that was ever seen.

"You must judge which of these two kinds of gallantry is the more obliging to the ladies and whether the latter is as ridiculous as it appears to the bloods of the present time. For myself I shall not decide so delicate a question in which stylish prejudice does not allow natural freedom of choice. I shall say only that one cannot condemn, except at the risk of being over-bold, the second kind of gallantry, where the lady is sincerely adored and where, instead of words, she is given deeds; in which the eyes and the ears find less satisfaction but where the mind and the heart find it whole and entire. Indeed, I should have great difficulty in replying to anyone who, in its defense, would show me how noble is that gallantry which proves passion by seeking dangers, as also by blood and victories, and how great an advantage it has over that which finds its proofs only in coquetries and assiduities or, at most, in dinners, concerts, and jousting.

"I should have great difficulty in persuading him that a fine dance-step is more valuable than a good sword-thrust, that handsome furniture or elegant races are more important than jousts with whetted blades or than bitter fights to the death or gifts of vanquished prisoners. If he were to add that the state of society at that time gave value only to such actions as these, and hence that ladies could admire no others and thought themselves loved and well served only by them; or finally that tourneys, combats, and quests were the style of those times as courts, the comedy, and balls are in ours; if I did not grant that he was right to prefer that kind of gallantry to ours, nevertheless I should be forced to concede that it can in no way be considered ridiculous."

"If he were to speak to me," said Monsieur Sarasin, "as you pretend he might do, I should reply as you say you should, and only the most unjust man in the world would not hear both sides of the argument and would decide on the testimony of only one litigant."

"It seems to me," said Monsieur Ménage, "that I am of your opinion, and that this point has been as well examined as the others."

"After that," I replied, "I have nothing more to say in order to prove to you that however bad this book may be, there is yet something good in it, and it is not entirely disgraceful for me to have been found with it by a scholar like yourself."

"You have only the customs left to discuss," he said, "and then you will have discharged your duty towards us."

"I have grown hoarse with talking," I answered, "and for the customs I am tempted to refer you to the authority on customs in the kingdom of Logres, [31] I mean the book *Lancelot* itself where you will find them thick-sown; or perhaps you will prefer to await the publication of the *Treatise* which Monsieur Le Fèvre, the great antiquary, is devoting to them,[32] for he supports almost all his observations by passages he takes from *Lancelot*, of which he makes his chief stock as far as customs are concerned. In general I shall say only that they have the character of the mores of that remote time, and whether they be true or false it is obvious that most of them were instituted to give security to the ladies and to feed the valor in the souls of the knights; but the first objective serves the second. I shall cut this discussion short and leave the matter obscure so that you will be curious enough to seek enlightenment."

At this statement I arose as did they, though they were complaining I had skimped on this last part, especially Monsieur Ménage, whose appetite had been whetted by this legal matter and who would have been much interested in seeing then and there what Gothic jurisprudence was like and what affinity it might have with Roman law. He threatened to complain to you, my Lord, and said to me as I walked with them to the door, "Yes, I shall look over the Lancelot code, and I shall even study it with Monsieur Seingeber; it would be amusing if he were to abandon the Code of Justinian for this new one."

"Anything can happen," said I, "if it be only to change your field of study and to avoid ever finishing what you have begun."

Monsieur Sarasin was much amused at this reproach, and both went away laughing, thus showing much satisfaction at the conversation we had had, although it was excessively long for so scanty and meager a subject.

Jean-Francois Sarasin DISCOURSE ON TRAGEDY OR RE-

MARKS ON "TYRANNIC LOVE" BY MONSIEUR DE SCUDERY

The *Amour tyrannique* by Monsieur de Scudéry is so perfect and so finished a poem that if Time had not grudged to the age of Louis the Just the birth of Aristotle, or if Monsieur de Scudéry had written during the Alexandrian Empire, I really think the philosopher would have modeled a part of his *Poetics* on that excellent tragedy and that he would have drawn from it examples as beautiful as those from the *Oedipus*, which he particularly admired.

Since this divine man, having noted all the faults of the Greek poets and reduced to rule what he found excellent in their works, has taught us what opinion we ought to have of the poems of others and the rules we ought to follow for our own, there has not perhaps been a single dramatic writer who has profited so well from his remarks nor so faithfully followed his precepts as Monsieur de Scudéry.

If this were to be a critical discourse instead of an essay dedicated to the merit of my friend and to the defense of his play, I should have to include here a complete examination of the tragic writers, to raise many objections and to produce many quotations and examples; but since I write only to enhance his reputation I shall content myself with pointing out the beauties of his work without paying any attention to the vices of others and without establishing his reputation on the ruin of theirs; and I shall have accomplished my purpose if I confirm the learned in the good opinion they have of this play and leave all my readers persuaded of its excellence.

Should I be obliged later on in my discourse to compare with this work certain passages from the ancients, my purpose will be to reinforce my defense by this means; and if I should happen to challenge them I shall do so without tediousness or affectation and even then only where it appears to me necessary. Indeed, I have no intention of burdening this essay with useless erudition nor of planning out exactly its composition.

Panegyrists need the graces of eloquence and the strength of rhetoric but those who write commentaries do not, and since I am simply making a few remarks about *L'Amour tyrannique* rather than a eulogy of it, I shall put elocution by for another occasion. I shall be satisfied to treat this subject with the order and simplicity which are proper to the argumentative style.

However, since this style is ordinarily thorny and since very plain order is dry and barren I shall temper that harshness and barrenness in certain places so as to provide some source of pleasure for the mind.

Before making a judgment of this tragedy (for that is how we shall describe it and not as a tragicomedy, for reasons which we shall put forward in their proper place), we must see what are the purpose and usefulness which these compositions are assumed to have and what has been taught about them by the philosopher we are following. For since all works approach perfection in proportion as they come nearer to fulfilling their purpose, we shall be easily able to examine later whether the same is true of Monsieur de Scudéry's and whether it has the degree of perfection we hope to find in it.

Since the tragic muse is principally concerned with stirring the passions of the audience through the appalling adventures she represents before them, Aristotle thought the purpose of tragedy was to calm those passions and to restore to the spectators' souls that tranquillity and serenity which she had taken away from them. He thought pity and terror were the passions stirred by tragedy and hence that tragedy ought to repress them and reduce them to a reasonable level of intensity after having excited and stirred them; and he calls that way of calming our souls the expiation or, if you prefer, the purgation of the passions and tensions.

This was his opinion of those passions:

He did not include them among the vices nor did he allow them to be numbered among the virtues, and so without defending them and without banishing them from human life he hoped that wise men might become accustomed to them and come to a reasonable decision concerning how far and when they ought to accept and receive them.

This excellent familiarity with them was to result, in his opinion, from the presentation of tragedies, for just as we acquire perfection in an art through practice so we achieve temperance in the passions when we are used to seeing those things which excite them in our imagination.

Good surgeons calmly dress the most dangerous wounds, while the inexperienced tremble at the task. Habit produces in physicians an insensitivity toward their patients, and veteran regiments who come to grips daily with the enemy attack him without the fear and the indiscipline which are common in raw recruits.

The same thing is true of a man who sees suffering every day: he is touched by it but only to the point proper to a wise man, and the fact that he sees habitually spectacles which produce terror and pity in him results in his being moderate and serene.

Since these things are presented in the theatre and since the stage re-echoes with the cries of Hecuba, Electra, and Antigone; since we see there Oedipus, Atreus, and Aegisthus and since the stage may properly be called the tiltyard of the passions, it is also to the performance of these tragic poems in which these personages appear that one must go in order to mould the passions and to lead them to that perfect philosophical reasonableness to which they never attain without contributing much to the acquisition of virtue and the mastery of learning.

Such was the opinion of Aristotle concerning the purpose of tragedy, which for that reason he called *the government of the passions*. It is clear from this that he was not of the opinion of those who consider the final purpose of these sublime compositions to be the pleasure of the people. We particularly want to make that statement here so as to enlighten those others and so as to judge whether Monsieur de Scudéry's work may excite those violent emotions which prepare the mind for virtue and discipline and whether it has that degree of perfection which we hope to find in excellent tragedies.

For this reason we must examine it according to the rules of the philosopher and judge from the way its separate parts conform to the rules how well the whole conforms to the idea of tragedy. Thus we shall follow the methodical clarity which is always characteristic of the Sage's teachings, and even jealousy will have no grounds for alleging that we are flattering Monsieur de Scudéry, for we shall be examining his composition according to the severe precepts of the greatest critic in the world.

That remarkable man has defined tragedy as follows: "Tragedy is the imitation of a serious action, complete and proper in its magnitude, which through action and not only by speech excites pity and terror, but afterwards leaves a moderate reasonableness in the mind of the spectators."

From the above definition we have eliminated rhythm and music, which are not now in use.

The philosopher, I say, having thus defined tragedy, divides it into six essential parts, of which the final two are related to the others and depend upon them.

The first four are Plot, Character, Thought, and Diction; the last two are Spectacle and Song.

Since of these latter two the first is the concern only of the scenic designer and the second, which made all the charm of the ancient stage, is no longer in use on our own, we need speak only, if we have the leisure, of the remaining four, which concern the poet, in order to see whether our author has a thorough knowledge of them and whether he has made proper use of them in his *L'Amour tyrannique*.

Just as the Plot, which Aristotle takes to be the subject of tragedy, and which includes both the action and the arrangement of the action, which he calls *the structure of the incidents*, is the first in the order of his division so it is first in the order of excellence. The philosopher adduces beautiful arguments in its favor; he calls it *the soul of a tragedy* and claims that without it tragedy cannot be perfect.

Indeed, since the purpose is always the most important thing, the reason for all actions and that upon which everything else depends; since the purpose of tragedy is the representation of human good or ill fortune; and since men are neither fortunate nor unfortunate except insofar as they act; it follows that the plot is the most important part of the tragedy because it includes the action, and the action includes that happy outcome or that catastrophe whose representation is the purpose of tragedy.

And certainly, since without a plot a poet making use of Character, Thought, and Diction, as well as other things, would no more make a real play than a painter would make a good picture by mixing confusedly black lacquer, ultramarine blue, and other colors without representing anything; and since on the contrary with one single action a poet could well make a fine tragedy just as a painter can draw a beautiful figure with red chalk or charcoal, I see no reason to doubt that the plot is the principal part of a thing which cannot exist without it, or that it ought to be considered before the other parts of a composition since they depend upon it so completely.

Moreover, since the last thing men learn in the arts, and that only after much practice and diligence, is what is excellent and perfect in them, the ancient poets who did not yet know how to treat the plot by rule, although they made divine use of the other aspects of tragedy, are adequate witnesses that the plot, which they came to understand only at the end of their period, is beyond all doubt the perfection and crown of a fine tragedy.

If I had to give examples in support of this last argument, our own drama would provide enough of them for me, and I should not be forced to hunt them up among the fragments of Greek drama. Among us tragedy is relatively new and so, although we see it in its full perfection, we also saw its infancy; for this reason the same poets who now give us well-composed works produced very unsatisfactory ones in the past.

Not so very long ago the plot was what they paid least attention to; they worked only on the versification and treated indifferently all sorts of subjects. Provided that in their plays they had mixed up love and jealousy, duels, disguises, prisons, and shipwrecks on a stage divided into several areas, they considered they had written an excellent dramatic poem:

Post hoc
securi cadat an recto stet fabula talo.[1]

In this regard we are under great obligation to Monsieur Mairet, [2] who was the first to take care in plotting the action, who cleared the way for correct works with his *Sylvanire* and who restored the dignity of tragedy with his *Sophonisbe*; one may well say of him that he was born for the glory of our century and for that of our nation's poetry. A little later Monsieur de Scudéry's *La Mort de César* [1636] was successfully presented. This play is certainly incomparable in its kind and no doubt always will be, for the vigor of its ideas and the magnificence of its verse make it worthy of the majesty of ancient Rome, and it follows the rules in its every aspect. Since then some of our authors have learned from a more precise study of dramatic art how important the plot is and how absolutely necessary to the perfection of tragedy; they have since then produced several fine pieces and happily made amends for their first transgressions.

I have dilated somewhat upon the importance of the plot before examining that in my friend's work so as to show how necessary the plot is and how much glory he deserves for having handled it so well.

I claim to have noticed this technical excellence in his work and a part of this essay will be devoted to demonstrating it.

A thing cannot be called beautiful unless it has the order and magnitude which are suitable and proportionate to its nature. The closer a thing comes to this optimum magnitude the more it approaches perfection, and conversely it is defective in proportion as it exceeds or falls short of that optimum size. Tall men are handsome but dwarfs and giants are deformed.

The same thing is true of the plot of a tragedy; for it, too, there is an optimum magnitude; and just as bodies are not beautiful without being of a certain size, so a tragedy cannot be beautiful if it is not of a certain length, and if it does not attain that optimum length which is proper to it and which through its very nature it cannot exceed without becoming defective.

Although Aristotle leaves the exact length to the poet's judgment he nevertheless restrains him with certain rules. He thinks the action may grow and be continued until it is absolutely necessary, because of the nature of the thing represented, to bring about the climax, which is its last development, for it is then that good fortune turns to bad or disaster becomes felicity.

One needs no other example than that of *L'Amour tyrannique* to clarify that doctrine and to show how completely the play conforms to it.

Tiridate, having driven Tigrane and Polyxène to Amasia, takes the town by assault. This victory does not satisfy him; he must have the husband and wife who are the objects of his hatred and his love as well as the causes of the war. At that moment misfortune causes the unhappy lovers to fall into his hands. He will have no happiness unless he possesses Polyxène and puts her husband to death; he therefore decides upon these violent actions and the lovers choose to die. Tigrane begs poison of his wife; she sends it to him. Tiridate intercepts it and owing to an ambiguous letter thinks his own life is at stake. This changes his love to hatred and he debates whether to put both Tigrane and Polyxène to death. He decides to do so. He gives the order. This, it seems to me, is the last development which the action had necessarily to reach and beyond which it could not go without changing course. This is also the point at which the poet brings it to an end and the moment when Polyxène's brother, who seizes the tyrant unawares, changes the misfortune of the lovers into supreme joy and the happiness of Tiridate into unhoped-for disaster, from which, however, he escapes through the recognition of his faults and the goodness of those he had unjustly offended.

I shall not mention here Orosmane or Ormène even though these two characters do much to complete the greatness of the tragedy and play important roles in its denouement and structure; that is a pleasure which I leave to my readers and one which will serve to enlighten them as to the ingeniousness of the poet's plotting.

Indeed, when I consider the smoothness with which the action is led to its climax I must confess that I am entranced; Aristotle did not prescribe anything better, and Monsieur de Scudéry has followed his precepts exactly.

The second rule laid down by the philosopher for the greatness of a tragedy is the one called by our dramatic writers *the unity of time,* for the action occurs in time and, depending upon the time needed for its completion, it may be described as great, small, or excessive. This rule, according to Aristotle, was invented to relieve the memory of the spectators, and since actions embracing several years or several days would be too complicated for the memory to retain them without effort, and since actions completed in a few hours would not occupy it enough, the philosopher has considered it proper to limit the length of the action to the time of one full day and has established the principle that those events which might occur between two suns are the only ones suitable to tragedy.

And certainly, leaving aside the effort and attention needed to follow the representation of actions occurring over several years and which would have burdened the memory of the audience and wearied their patience, the composition of tragedies without the unity of time would not have been an art at all. The episodes which Aristotle urges on the playwright so strongly and which must be treated so delicately would have been banished from it; it would not have been necessary to choose a plot and to plan them carefully; a single tragedy could have been made from the history of a whole century; the masterpieces of the greatest poets would have been exposed to the depredations of the lowliest versifiers.

This defect, for all it is so gross and contrary to common sense, was not avoided by all the Roman poets. Certain of their works are deformed by this irregularity; the time-span of Plautus's *Amphitryon* covers nine full months, involving as it does the love of Jupiter for Alcmena, her pregnancy, and the birth of Hercules as well as his conception. All this is the result of Plautus's eagerness to present the universe with this giant-killer, and his reluctance to end the play before the demi-god is born.

The tragic author who has described the death of Hercules on the stage and whose plays are included among those of Seneca, although in Heinsius's [3] opinion they are not by him — that tragic author fell into the same fault; his stage is divided into several places and his actions last several days. In the beginning he presents Hercules to us in Euboea; later he has him offer sacrifices on the Cenaean Promontory, and it is there that he takes the shirt stained with the blood of Nessus; it is there that the poison begins to take effect; it is in that place that he amazes himself by crying out:

Hic caelum horrido
clamore complet.[4]

It seems to me it would have been proper for the poet to finish his torments in that same place and that he might easily have lighted his funeral pyre from the flames of his sacrifice. The poet should have remembered that it takes four days to go from the Cenaean Promontory to Mount Oeta, where he has Hercules die; he should have considered that it was not proper to burn Hercules slowly nor credible that a poison of which he had said

Quidquid illa tabe contractum est labat [5]

should act with such delay and take its effect only in this long space of time.

Our modern writers, who for the most part have broken the rule we are speaking of, have not been prepared to do it so lightheartedly as the ancients.

They have sometimes included a succession of several years in the same tragedy; nor have they been satisfied to sin only for the learned, for their faults have been made public, and the audience has been amazed to see the same actors grow old in the course of the play so that those who had been lovers in the first act appeared decrepit in the fifth.

No doubt the desire to include a number of effective episodes in their plays and the fear that a period of twenty-four hours would not afford enough of them led these writers into this mistake; the charm of the spectacle brought them to revolt against the severity of the tragic precepts, and the large number of events which a long time-span so easily provided induced in them a scorn for those plots which they considered less attractive because they were more close-knit and Aristotelian.

They will pardon me if I point out that they have not considered carefully what events may happen in one day and that they have boisterously condemned a rule which they did not clearly understand; this would not have happened if they had sought instruction, with reflection, in good poets; they would have found there well-filled days and many events occurring in a few hours; they might even, in the events of one day, have had enough material left over for a second tragedy, or they might have had to be satisfied with the occurrences of a few hours only, or even been forced to cut out superfluous events from that very period of time in which they were afraid of not finding enough action for a single play.

They must agree with me that the day which was the last of the siege of

62

Troy as well as of Priam's empire was one of those busy days filled with a succession of events. Would anyone want more events than are there, and could one not very rightly and properly take those included between this line of the second book of the *Aeneid*

Ergo omnis longo soluit se Teucria luctu [6]

and this one

Hic finis Priami favorum etc.? [7]

It seems to me there is a good deal of subject-matter there, enough to fill a day; and I do not see that our dramatic writers can complain of the shortness of a time in which they find a group of such considerable events and so many important actions.

On the contrary that multitude of events compressed into one day is so important and so beautiful that this very compression is one of the reasons why Aristotle did not hesitate to prefer tragedy to the epic and to find in favor of Sophocles against Homer. Here is what he says in the final chapter of his *Poetics*:

ἔτι τῷ ἐν ἐλάττονι μήκει τὸ τέλος τῆς μιμήσεως εἶναι: τὸ γὰρ ἀθροώτερον ἥδιον ἢ πολλῷ κεκραμένον τῷ χρόνῳ.[8]

Our author, who recognized the importance of that maxim, has observed it religiously; among the many things which take place on the stage he was careful to include skillfully arranged episodes and external embellishments; he has made good use of all the time he was able to devote to the subject, but he was able to stay on this side of the furthest time limit instead of going beyond it; if they examine his play carefully and make allowance for the time needed to carry out the actions it involves, all just critics will conclude that he could have had several hours left over and that he was not in too much of a hurry.

Indeed, if we agree that not much time is needed to take an almost unwalled town, concerning which Tiridate says

The rams have breached the wall that girds the town;
The first assault which I am now to lead
Will end the war and win the kingly crown

and if we consider that the tyrant was hated by his own soldiers, as Pharnabase tells him

It seems your men their arms but sadly bear,
In spilling foeman's blood they shed a tear

and nobly deceived by Phraarte, the Prince of Phrygia was able to reach

63

a point only three leagues from his camp without Tiridate's being informed of this move, the prince having indeed come

> with wagons light,
> Through shadows' favor marching in the night,
> By forests' darkness hidden from all sight.

It is obvious that since these two actions, which must be the two longest in the play, need no more than a few hours for their accomplishment, the rest of the action might easily take place in much less time than that between two suns; thus it is easy to justify what is true in itself and to judge a play justly, provided one be free of boredom and preoccupation.

A writer who neglects the rule which our poet has so happily observed will ordinarily neglect also the one calling for unity of action. This rule is not less important nor less difficult, and it is not easy to arrange things so that in a long period of time only those things occur which are not detached from each other and which can all be related to the same subject.

The term "unity of action" has not been well understood and so has brought about many mistakes; even today it causes writers to make strange errors. Many have understood it to mean the actions of a single hero such as Theseus, Hercules, or Achilles as opposed to the actions of different men which are all related and connected with the same goal; hence on this bad foundation they have constructed works whose parts had no connection or relationship and they made poems about an accumulation of different actions because they had all happened to the same man. Good tragic writers have carefully avoided this mistake and even in the epic Homer and Virgil have escaped it; and although the time-span of their works is much greater than in the tragedy and although there was room for an infinite number of actions, they nevertheless admitted only those which were related to the same purpose and which were necessary for the ornamentation of the poems. Thus Virgil, whose purpose is only to bring Aeneas to the shores of the Tiber, took care not to describe to us all that had ever happened to him; and Homer has not told us everything he knew about Ulysses' adventures, nor did he treat the Trojan war like that poet whom Horace makes game of in the *Ars poetica*:

Nec gemino bellum Troianum orditur ab ovo.[9]

I cannot resist mentioning here an error of Joachim du Bellay's [10] which I regret; he considered it strange that the writers of his time did not work on the adventures of Amadis or Lancelot or Tristram of Lyonesse, for he took those books to be legitimate subjects for an epic poem and imagined that the *Orlando Furioso* of Ariosto followed the rules of the genre.

And in my opinion Ronsard, carried away by that mistaken opinion, would have made his Francus a knight errant if he had gone ahead with his poem and had departed from the *Aeneid*; at least he had already begun to involve him with giants and to have him enter the lists to defend ladies' honor. Thus we see that those great men did not yet have a knowledge of the rules of poetry although they were well read in the poets.

It is then not what happens to a single person that makes unity of action but rather the actions of several men if these actions can all be related to the same subject.

One may use *L'Amour tyrannique* as an illustration of this doctrine, for we see in it how all events are related to the violent love of Tiridate and depend upon it. Polyxène, on the point of falling into the tyrant's hands, begs her husband to kill her and makes him swear to go on living after her so as to avenge her; she obtains both these desires after much difficulty, and Tigrane, thinking he has killed her, enters the camp of Tiridate in disguise intending to stab him. He turns to his sister for help and she, instead of helping him in this bloody design, tries to dissuade him from it by pointing out that Polyxène is not dead but a prisoner. This piece of information produces the effect that is to be expected on a passionate heart, and he is led to scorn all other considerations; as he is about to throw himself into the crowd of Tiridate's guards to assassinate him, Tigrane is recognized and arrested.

If you connect these various ornaments to their goal or purpose, which we have described in dealing with the magnitude of the plot, you will find they observe all the rules necessary to that unity of action we are speaking of.

In the first place, all these actions, which can be reduced to one, are so closely related and connected that one cannot be admitted without the succeeding one which depends upon it either through logical necessity or through verisimilitude.

Moreover, not one of them produces its effect if it is separated from the others, whereas all together they conform to the large action of which they are component parts.

Finally, they are so obviously real parts of this whole that not one of them can be cut out without destroying the plot, or at least without changing the nature of the play.

Since all these things are necessary to the unity of action, and since they can all be found in our poem, we must conclude it is perfect in this regard, and that in this regard as in others we should be unjust in withholding the laurel from our author.

No doubt he deserves much praise for this unity but also no less for the unity of place; never has a stage been better arranged or less cluttered than his; and despite the large number of adventures which take place on it the only scene needed is a bastion in the town of Amasia and Tiridate's tents which are so close to it that Ormène says

> And now the favor of Mars upon him falls;
> Already his tents are pitched beneath the walls.

Hardy, [11] who really gave dignity to tragedy (which had been played on platforms built in the streets and at crossroads), among the many defects which the ignorance of his period makes excusable, was especially prone to this one: he could never keep the scene in one place. He changed countries and crossed the seas without scruple and one was often amazed to see that a character who had just spoken in Naples had moved to Cracow while other actors recited a few lines or the orchestra played a tune.

But although almost all his plays have this defect, in no one of them is it more obvious than in the one entitled *Bigamie*; there has never been such an endless peregrination as that play contains. The author made as bold use of Pegasus in it as does Ariosto of the hippogriff; and Count Gleichen in the French play travels as far as Astolfo in the Italian poem.

This defect of Hardy's did not die with him, any more than did the reputation of his works; the writers who followed him kept that changing scene for a long time; their lyres, like those of Orpheus and Amphion, had the privilege of building cities and of removing cliffs and forests; and their stage was like those geographical maps which on their small scale represent the whole extent of the earth.

Nowadays, although the license is no longer permitted and there are no more supporters of that heresy, a few traces of it still remain, and our poets are not diligent enough to protect themselves completely from it: their scene may indeed be in a single city but not in a single place; the audience cannot tell whether the actors are talking in a house or in the street; the stage is like a common room, private for no one and where anyone may do whatever he wants.

Since not a single beauty is missing from *L'Amour tyrannique*, we must also expect not to find a single defect in it; therefore the poet, as we have already said, does not make the walls fall as they did at the trumpets of Jericho, and all events occur in one place.

It is not enough for a tragedy to follow the rules for length, for the time required for the events, and for unity of place and action; if it is to be perfect it must also arouse pity and terror and it must produce these emotions in the souls of the audience.

What is more, these passions and emotions must be caused not only by the lines recited or the things described but also by the arrangement of the action and the nature of the plot, which therefore is of the essence of tragedy and is its principal ingredient, as we have proved above.

And yet, although all good tragedies must necessarily produce these emotions, nevertheless the kind of tragedy we call *mixed*, which the Romans named better than we do *implexam* and the Greeks excellently, as is their custom, πεπλεγμένην, [12] causes these emotions much more intensively than does simple tragedy which contains nothing unexpected, nothing surprising.

My friend's tragedy is of the first kind, and without flattery one can say that it is an excellent one of the kind.

Indeed the reversal of the situation and the recognition, which are two of the aspects of the plot, have so important and so beautiful a place in *L'Amour tyrannique* that perhaps *Oedipus*, which is the only Latin tragedy of that kind which has been preserved, does not accommodate them in a more beautiful or more finished way.

And the reversal, in fact, which may be defined as "an unexpected change in the action and an event contrary to what was expected or awaited," could not be found without much searching, I assure you, which would be more Aristotelian than the one in our play.

Is it not true that when Tiridate appears in that terrible tribunal where he is to condemn Tigrane, Polyxène, his wife, and his father-in-law, when we see come before him those innocent victims loaded with chains and apparently abandoned of all save virtue and constancy, and when the rage of the tyrant and his injustice have pronounced the cruel verdict "Put them to death," is it not true, I say, that everyone pities those crowned victims and believes that heaven has not strength enough to draw them back from a death which is so close and which seems so assured? And yet, in accordance with the nature of the play and the structure of the plot their help arrives. Troilus changes the nature of things. Tiridate falls from that throne to which violence and betrayal had raised him, and by an unexpected reversal and a course of events entirely contrary to the one awaited, Orosmane finds himself in a position to condemn the tyrant.

The arrival of Polyxène's noble brother shows the poet's skill and by the means he used to rescue the princes one may admire his judgment. Several points in the structure of the play allow the audience to foresee this help; they are prepared for it by the brave deception of Phraarte and by the blindness of the tyrant who puts into his hands the command of the army (in which the learned may note a divine bit of technique), and finally they are fully informed of it through the conference between Phraarte and the Phrygian whom Troilus is supposed to have sent to him.

Seneca in his *Agamemnon* made a serious mistake in the very thing from which Monsieur de Scudéry draws one of his principal beauties: Strophius, whom he introduces to save Orestes and Pylades, appears on the stage like a god from the machine. Nobody expected him. In the whole play there is no preparation for this entrance, and it is so far from every-body's thoughts that he is compelled himself to tell his name to the audience;

> Phocide relicta, Strophius Elea inclytus
> palma revertor.[13]

His reason for coming is only to kiss Agamemnon's hand and to rejoice with him over the fall of Troy:

> Causa veniendi fuit
> gratiari amico etc.[14]

But is it not charming of the poet to have him come with the fastest horses in Greece to carry off Orestes and protect him the more surely from his mother's cruelty:

> Vos Graecia nunc teste, veloces equi,
> infida cursu fugite praecipiti loca.[15]

The best one can say of him is that although he took good care for his children's safety, he was not equally careful to save his reputation.

We learn from this that in ancient times writers made serious mistakes and that our critics ought not to praise antiquity so highly at the expense of our century and the works of our day.

The help of Troilus and the fall of Tiridate produce the *anagnorisis*, which is what the philosopher calls that recognition of people, events, places or other things which produces some effect or which causes some important change in the play.[16] It depends upon the reversal, and cannot exist without it, but the converse is not true since the reversal is found alone in many tragedies.

In this play the *anagnorisis* is very natural and easy, for Tiridate, seeing his ingratitude compensated by the good actions of Ormène and hearing her speak these lines:

> If his reign ends so also must my day;
> If he be punished I must also pay.
> His fate and mine forever interlinked . . .

begins to understand these:

> But to free us all from suffering
> We have no dearth of poison . . .

and to realize his crime and the innocence of those he had condemned. From this result his repentance, his reconciliation and finally the remarkable changes in this marvelous play.

Now I, who always judge as much as possible without prejudice, and who ordinarily am more severe than indulgent towards the works of my friends and who try to resemble that good and wise man of whom Horace says

> Fiet Aristarchus, nec dicet, cur ego amicum
> Offendam in nugis? [17]

I admit that I have never thought of the structure of this fable, even without the aid of the poetry and the spectacle, without shedding in secret those tears which no one has been able to keep from shedding at its presentation and which have sprinkled the galleries and the main floor alike.

Certainly, if I have some understanding of poetics and if my friends have not deceived me on that score, I am prepared to state boldly that it is not possible to find an action better suited to tragedy than that of *L'Amour tyrannique* and that Monsieur de Scudéry created a masterpiece when he found that marvelous subject.

I must also point out, without, however, dwelling on the point, how well Monsieur de Scudéry observes that rule by which the reversal and the recognition must lead toward and concern the same end, for we see that just as the unexpected change in the fortunes of Orosmane, Ormène, Polyxène, and Tigrane has for its purpose a happy ending to the play, Tiridate's recognition of his own faults leads to this same conclusion and makes it possible for him to participate in the general felicity.

It must also be said that of all the kinds of recognition (which may be reduced to six: those brought about through natural or accidental marks, by the intervention of the poet, by the memory, by logical deduction, by deceit or finally, without exterior signs, those that are inherent in the fable and in the structure of the plot) this one, on the word of Aristotle himself, is the first and best

πασῶν δὲ βελτίστη ἀναγνώρισις ἡ ἐξ αὐτῶν τῶν πραγμάτων [18]

It is the one our poet has used and through which Tiridate, with an astonishment and a wonder which must really have surprised even him, recognizes by the very writing-tablets which had persuaded him of his kinsmen's crime the fact of their innocence and his own injustice.

These two beautiful details, which are of such great importance, almost escaped me among the infinite number to be found in this excellent piece of work, in part because of the eagerness I bring to this essay which I am writing in a turmoil of enthusiasm; for *L'Amour tyrannique* is a garden which would be completely denuded if we were to pluck only the most beautiful flowers, and besides, the nature of this preface, which is that of a familiar essay rather than of a studied treatise has forced me to eliminate from consideration many extrinsic ornaments in the poem whose effectiveness depend upon a knowledge of recondite literary doctrines; thus I am far from taking into account the lesser beauties of the play and through haste from making the thorough examination of this fertile poem which a man of greater leisure would devote to so advantageous a subject.

The scene of suffering, which the Greeks call πάθος and the Romans *perturbatio*, follows so logically from the reversal and the recognition and depends upon them so completely, that the philosopher makes it the third division of the mixed plot.

This element is not completely banished from what we have called the simple fable nor can there be any tragedy which fails to produce pity and terror either through the artifice of language and what is recited on the stage or through fate and the way things occur. But the really tragic quality is inherent in the dramatic idea and does not depend upon the spoken word or the stage action, for it is the nature of the plot to imitate events which by their occurrence evoke pity and terror.

Moreover, since what can be educed from the interrelation of events is probably preferable to what can be introduced into the plot from the outside (as we said when we were discussing the different kinds of recognition according to Aristotle's classification), it follows that reversals which the plot contains within itself and which are to be found in the very subject are to be more highly esteemed than those inserted into the plot, especially since the former are more logical and more excellent.

The same thing is true of the arguments with which rhetorical technique reinforces eloquence and which Aristotle for that reason esteems much less than those which do not depend on forensic skill; and just as bad orators fell back on laws, witnesses, and pactions because they did not know the real rules of eloquence and could not make proper use of rhetorical effects, so poets of the past and even some of our own day depend upon the actor's skill to evoke pity and terror, the more so because they have none of their own.

These faults are committed by the writer who bloodies the stage, who shows effects produced by magic and unbelievable metamorphoses, and who presents impossibilities to the public view.

> Nec pueros coram populo Medea trucidet,
> nec humana palam coquat exta nefarius Atreus,
> nec in avem Progne vertatur, Cadmus in anguem.[19]

Because of this mistake, Nero, who was born for the eternal shame of poetry, chose plots full of murders which were dangerous and sometimes fatal to the actors, for he took pleasure in seeing real blood shed on the stage and satisfied his lust for cruelty by the presentation of these appalling spectacles. This is what Suetonius [20] reports of that unhappy actor who, while playing before Nero the role of Icarus, fell near the Emperor's chair as he was attempting his first flight and spattered with his blood that bloodthirsty monster.

We may say then that the plot must be so well constructed that even without stage settings or the aid of actors or horrifying spectacles it cannot be listened to or read without producing its effect and without evoking pity and terror.

This is Aristotle's opinion and what sovereign reason requires, and it is what the learned find worthy of applause in our play. For in truth, who does not experience these two passions which are so violent and so appropriate to tragedy? And who can consider without emotion the strange fall of Tiridate? At the moment when he falls from that felicity which injustice and fate had given him he recognizes in himself the enemy and persecutor of his father-in-law, the ruination of all his kingdom, an unfaithful husband, an infamous lover, an incestuous rival, and almost a parricide and executioner of his own kinsmen.

71

Indeed, without adding to all these disasters the torments of Orosmane, Ormène, Polyxène, and Tigrane, without mentioning the disgraceful chains loaded upon these illustrious persons, a man can but tremble with horror and grow soft with pity at the mere recital of these adventures, and has no need for the effects of the stage setting, the vigorous interpretation of actors, or the power of poetry.

If I am permitted in this essay to unveil the secrets of art and to divulge the most jealously guarded mysteries of poetry, this must be because I am speaking in my friend's favor and addressing myself only to the small group of true connoisseurs.

Let us say then both for them and for him that since the change upon which the emotions and the suffering of a play depend can lead only to felicity or to disaster, and since the characters must all be virtuous or vicious or at a point equidistant from these two extremes, the poet must make use of one of these kinds of people to excite pity and horror and thus to achieve the goal which tragedy proposes for itself.

Now as to witnessing the passage of a good man from felicity to ill-fortune: it seems to me that this change will probably not touch the soul in the way we want because, since pity and terror are induced in men by the things they see happening to others and which they fear may happen to themselves, it is unlikely that if a calamity befalls a good man the soul will be moved by these passions or that the spectators will fear misfortune caused by their probity since this latter ordinarily has as its recompense good fortune in life, and this is Aristotle's argument in the various books of his *Rhetoric*.

However, the ill fortune of a bad man is no more useful and certainly produces no more emotion than that of a good man, for it appears to be the effect of divine justice, and the good fortune of the evil man, which always seems unjust, excludes pity. No one commiserates with a wicked man on his downfall because he is believed to deserve that punishment and because no one fears the same for himself since each man takes a flattering view of his own probity and since, to tell the truth, the great majority of men are passably good.

There remains to be considered only that third type of man who is neither deeply criminal nor deeply virtuous and who alone will actually produce the emotions to which dramatic writers aspire and who is defined by the philosopher in the third book of the *Ethics*. He who sins through imprudence does not deserve to be called a good man because he has not lived up to his duty; but he cannot either be called wicked, for his sin is without premeditation, as they say in the schools.

Thus behave those who have yielded up their judgment to one of the passions and who are no longer their own master, who let themselves be carried away by the torrent; just as diseased eyes are poor judges of colors these minds, clouded and deprived of light, act only from the force of the passion, consider right whatever passion dictates, and no doubt are to be pitied because they imagine they are acting heroically when in fact they are committing appalling crimes.

Monsieur de Scudéry's Tyrant is a perfect example of this kind of character, and the confession he makes in Act III, scene 3, reveals this fact to us while showing that love is the cause of all these tragic events.

To begin with, he discovers that he loves Polyxène, his sister-in-law:

> In truth 'tis Polyxena I adore:
> I will not hide this fateful passion more.

Then his passion leads him to believe that it is right to love her:

> She is too lovely not to be desired;
> I have eyes; by her my soul is fired;
> Her glance is like an arrow in my heart;
> Could living man not feel her beauty's smart?

And then he concludes that he would be mad not to feel this passion:

> In truth 'twould be surprising lov'd I not.

Hence we must not be surprised that he is prepared to use any means to win Polyxène, and he continues as follows:

> What though she flee me to the furthest pole
> I'll seek for her where swiftest torrents roll;
> I'll follow her through desert and through wood,
> Across the sea, etc.

He lifts the mask still further and exposes his complete blindness when he is contradicted by the wise Pharnabase who had been his tutor and who tries to recall to virtue that mind possessed by passion. This is what he says after the fall of Amasia:

> If when the battle's done I find my Queen,
> Let her by throngs of witnesses be seen:
> I'll lead this lovely captive weak and tame
> Triumphant through the streets in public shame.
> I hold my love is just when it gives joy.

When we consider the sentence of death he pronounces against this beautiful woman and examine the sentiments caused by so violent and so disprized a love, we must conclude that throughout the play Tiridate has been dominated by a violent passion, that he has done wrong without premeditation as we have said before, and that his intelligence, killed or stifled by his passion, had no share in his crimes.

I am not surprised this play had so many admirers and that everybody left the theater after its presentation with his soul deeply moved and his eyes wet with tears, for the tyrant who is its protagonist, to whom all the events are related, has all the qualities necessary to cause in others the emotions of fear and pity. He is neither too virtuous nor too wicked, for although he does commit evil acts, he is driven to them by a greater force; his misfortune does not come upon him because of his evil-doing, the more so because he thinks it is right both to love Polyxène and to condemn her to death; and finally, in order greatly to increase the pity and horror of the play and to push these emotions to their uttermost limits, at the moment when he sees two kings and two queens in chains at his feet he is himself overthrown, stripped of the purple, constrained to bear the same chains he had imposed upon others and to pass from the extreme of good fortune to a lamentable calamity.

But since the ambitions of many people must come together to bring about all these complications, and one cannot be enough for this purpose, it follows also that these people must be enemies, or neutral towards each other, or joined by friendship or blood so that they may be driven to act.

But since the desire to avenge ourselves and to injure our enemies is certainly innate in us all and the accomplishment of such acts seems to our minds sweeter than honey, as Homer says, and since the reasons for which men hate each other seem rightfully odious to everybody, how shall the means of the vengeance which we choose to wreak upon our enemies touch the spectators who are likely to consider all such means justified? The spectators must be touched by the fear of misfortunes whose causes they detest and they must be made to look with pity upon the misfortunes which they themselves wish to their enemies.

The same remark may be made concerning those disasters which occur among neutral characters who neither love nor hate, who excite no emotions, who act without passion, and whose misfortunes leave no sadness in the soul except that which we are obliged to feel for suffering humanity.

Hence it is only the Tiridates, the Ormènes, the Tigranes, the Polyxènes, the Orosmanes who can terrify and soften our hearts; in other words, it is only the Husbands, Wives, Fathers-in-law, and Brothers- and Sisters-in-law who can touch us deeply; only the misfortunes of people joined by blood and friendship give us terror and pity.

They do this certainly in Monsieur Scudéry's play. The misfortunes he shows on the stage have touched the greatest hearts in the world as well as the lowest, and not one of these spectators came away without having profited from that calming of the passions which is one of the ends of tragedy.

Finally, of all the means by which Aristotle teaches that pity and horror may be excited, the one he prefers, which is that after having committed a crime one be led to acknowledge it,[21] is not omitted from this excellent tragedy.

From the moment that Tiridate condemns his relatives to death he is a criminal, even though his passion really commits the crime, and, as we have said, partially excuses it. He says this himself after having acknowledged his sin; it is remorse which tortures him so agonizingly and makes him wish for death because he holds himself unworthy to live; and this desire for death shows clearly that there is nothing feigned or superficial in his repentance. Here is how he comes to that acknowledgment:

> Now that the blindfold's gone, I see my error:
> At last my crime is clear; I shake with terror.

This is how he begs Ormène to avenge herself:

> Love me no more; in honor you're constrained
> To grant my heart the death which it awaits.
> Take vengeance, punish me, etc.

It is in these terms that he addresses the princes he had persecuted:

> O princes, outraged by my insolence
> Give all your aid to his just indignation;
> Spare not my blood, avenge your degradation.
> I am your foe who must be greatly feared.

And finally this is how he begs for death:

> My death will save you; that's all my desire.

With these lines the complication of the plot, or what the Romans called *connection*, comes to an end; at this point the denouement or resolution of the plot begins.

These two divisions, which contain all the tragic action, are totally opposed, and must be treated in completely different ways: the first includes not only those things which are properly a part of the plot but also those which can be distinguished from it, such as the episodes, the descriptions and whatever is added to increase either the length or the beauty of the work, and in general whatever the poet brings in for the ornamentation of his poem, whereas the second excludes all extraneous beauties, concerns itself only with the subject, and admits of nothing superfluous.

Despite the great number of ornaments which Monsieur de Scudéry's genius and learning have scattered so prodigally throughout his tragedy the episodes must claim a share of our praise as they have contributed to his reputation; he has worked them out carefully; he has not allowed himself the least poetic license; he has varied them for visual effect; now he charms his audience with wonderful descriptions expertly planned like the one in the fourth act where he describes a city taken and given up to fire and pillage; again he touches the soul of the spectators with the sight of nations enslaved; at still other times he makes use of Pharnabase to teach virtue with greater success and with greater pleasure for the listener than are commonly achieved in the schools or in academic chairs.

These episodes derive both from the subject and from the plot; they are useful; and their primary technical advantage is that they serve to advance the action which nevertheless does not move too fast and comes to its end only after having attained the magnitude required by the structure of the plot. Indeed, the sad state of Amasia's citizens does not touch Tiridate; the lessons of its governor do not restrain him from vice; and Ormène does not allow herself to be so far carried away by the description of her country's ruin that she determines upon and consents to the death of its tyrant; these are the moments when the poet has very skillfully worked out the episodes and the purpose for which they are included.

There is nothing like this in the denouement, which is much more severe since its nature does not allow all these ornaments. It contains only action and only matters related to the plot, nothing that can be or ought to be cut out, and nothing extrinsic or not absolutely necessary.

It remains for us only to consider the conclusion of the plot, which is a happy one. This quiet issue from so many troubled and unhappy events, this peaceful conclusion found in the greater number of our tragic plays and appearing to resemble the tone of comedy, has led our poets to describe these plays as tragicomedies. Some poets are convinced that if the ending is not bloody the play cannot be called a tragedy. Therefore they have brought together two contrary things and have made a monster by combining two natures each good in itself, and they have forgotten the precepts of their master:

> sed non ut placidis coeant immitia, non ut
> serpentes avibus geminentur, tigribus agni.[22]

Aristotle, who includes the happy ending in his enumeration of the purposes of tragedy,[23] gives us no reason to share the opinion of those poets. The examples of Alcestis, the two Iphigenias, of Io and Helen support and confirm the example of the present play; and although most tragedies spill blood on the stage and end with someone's death, we need not conclude from this that the ending of all such plays must necessarily be in disaster. Yet above all we must be careful not to mix into them anything comic.

And indeed how convincing would it be for the actors to have the buskin on one foot and the sock on the other, or for them to wear both the chimer and a simple parti-colored dress? How shall a king's orders, the murders, the despairs, the violent deaths, the banishments, the parricides, the incests, the burnings, the battles, the weeping and wailing and funeral pomps, which are things to be found in tragedy, be made compatible with the games, the feasts, the weddings, the avarice of old men, the tricks and drunkenness of the slaves and parasites, which are things to be found in comedy? And who could reasonably imagine that the author would want at one and the same time to excite in the spectators pity and horror, delight and pleasure, tears and laughter, or that he would seek to calm their souls by stirring them deeply, these being the different purposes which the two kinds of plays seek to achieve?

It is for these sound and convincing reasons that we have called *L'Amour tyrannique* a tragedy throughout this essay. But it could also be so described because it is so perfect and so finished that one can truthfully say it lacks nothing which the philosopher prescribes or which the severest critics seek in such works.

Let no one allege here in opposition the *Amphitryon* of Plautus which we have already censured; that author sins against the rules of comedy in almost every one of his plays. Menaechmus is so deeply in love that he seems maddened, and that is a tragic passion; in another comedy Alesimacchus comes on the stage to kill himself, a thing inexcusable in comedy; in short, the authority of a man of whom Horace says

Quam non adstricto percurrat pulpita socco [24]

77

ought not lead another to break the rules which the wisest of philosophers has established.

As far as the Greeks are concerned, the same thing must be said of Euripides' *Cyclops*, which Julius Caesar Scaliger excludes from the canon of true tragedies because it contains too many comic elements; and indeed who could allow in a serious play what the Cyclops says of Bacchus when, in a casual meeting, he asks how it is possible for a god to live in a bottle?

Monsieur de Scudéry knew very well that his play was a tragedy and yet he gave it the title of tragicomedy so as to show that he was willing to conform to accepted custom and that he preferred to accommodate himself to convention instead of following sovereign reason too scrupulously.

Up to this point we have discussed the plot, which the philosopher considers the most important part of tragedy and, unless I am mistaken, we have shown that he was right to call it the soul of tragedy; we have shown that in this respect Monsieur de Scudéry's work is above all praise, and we would have continued to point out in it the consistency of the characters, of the emotions and of the diction (in which discussion we should no doubt have included matter to satisfy the connoisseurs and instruct the ignorant) if a journey which we are about to make beyond the mountains had not prevented us from ending this essay as we had planned.

But aside from the fact that this would have delayed the publication, which is imminent, and would have increased public impatience for a long time, and aside from the fact that our very good friend Monsieur de la Mesnardière has wonderfully treated these three subjects in the great work on poetic theory which he is about to publish,[25] anyone can see how religiously our author has followed the philosopher's precepts.

Aside from all this, I say, we have considered that the plot was the aspect of a play which is least frequently discussed and yet is the most important, and hence that it was right for us to dwell on it and to demonstrate the incomparable beauty in that of *L'Amour tyrannique* which Monsieur de Scudéry has so marvelously invented; and as for character, emotion and diction one would have to be completely lacking in common sense not to recognize in this play the consistency of the first, the nobility of the second, and the majestic purity of the third.

It is true that if we had followed the beaten track of prefaces to books of our day we should also have avoided speaking of the plot, for following the example of other writers we should only have scattered three or four handfuls of flowers in the path of the work, filled two or three pages with words like *good* and *beautiful,* given praise without explaining the reason for it, wearied the reader by useless flattery, and awarded a crown to the author on our own private authority.

But we should no doubt have had the same experience as others have commonly had: nobody would have believed us and instead everyone would have made fun of our eulogies and refused to judge the reputation of our friend on the basis of conventional praise.

It has then seemed best to adduce at every point the authority of reason and erudition and not to praise Monsieur de Scudéry except after having consulted Aristotle, to award no crowns except at the philosopher's hands, and to establish his glory only on a foundation which would have nothing to fear from either the envious or from calumniators.

And yet we freely admit that even with all these advantages our essay would not have sheltered the play from the incursions of those two enemies of beautiful things, and perhaps we ought to have defended further the truths we have just demonstrated and thus to show the envious that we are

Et cantare pares respondere parati [26]

had that great genius of our century, the shame of past centuries and the marvel of those which are to come, the divine CARDINAL DE RICHELIEU, not spared us this labor.

Having been charmed by the play and convinced that only unjust and impertinent things could be written against so perfect a work, this great man forbade its author to reply if ever human malice should attack him to the prejudice of truth.

Therefore we consider that the tragedy is above attack by the envious both because of its own merit and because of the protection (which it would be more than sacrilegious to violate) granted to it by ARMAND, THE TUTELARY DEITY OF LETTERS.

The voice of that ORACLE pronounced these very words: "L'AMOUR TYRANNIQUE" IS A WORK WHICH HAS NO NEED OF BEING SHELTERED FROM ATTACK, FOR IT PROVIDES ITS OWN DEFENSE.

Georges de Scudery PREFACE TO "ALARIC, OR

ROME DEFEATED"

Since the epic poem is closely related in its construction to those ingenious fables we call novels, it is almost superfluous for me to speak of it here, especially since I have treated them rather fully in the foreword to my *Illustrious Bassa* and since, moreover, the happy success of this Grand Vizir and later that of the *Great Cyrus* have sufficiently demonstrated, it seems to me, that I am not entirely ignorant of that kind of writing which I concern myself with sometimes. Nevertheless, since it might be that some who will read this poem have not seen these other works, I thought I should do well to put here a discourse on the epic, so as to show my readers that I have not undertaken to raise up so large a structure without knowing all the proportions and all the arrangements which art teaches.

I have, then, consulted the masters, that is to say Aristotle and Horace, and after them, Macrobius, Scaliger, Tasso, Castelvetro, Piccolomini, Vida, Vossius, Pacius, Riccoboni, Robortello, Paolo Beni, Mambrun, and several others; and, passing from theory to practice, I have reread very carefully the *Iliad* and the *Odyssey* of Homer, the *Aeneid* of Virgil, the *Civil War* of Lucan, the *Thebaid* of Statius, the *Orlandos amoroso* and *furioso*[1] of Boiardo and Ariosto, the incomparable *Jerusalem Delivered* of the famous Torquato Tasso, and a large number of other epic poems in various languages, such as the first books of the *Franciad* of Ronsard and of the *Saint Louis* of Father Le Moine, and that fine poem, *The Conquest of Granada*, the most beautiful work which Italy has given us since Tasso.[2]

Now here are the rules which I have formed from the reading of all these epic poems and which I have followed in my *Alaric* — rules, as I have said, drawn from those of Aristotle and Tasso and from all those other great men, and consequently infallible, provided they are well put into practice.

I say, then, that the writer of an epic poem must think primarily of three things:

He must choose a subject which is suitable to receive the most excellent form which the skill of the poet can give it;

He must give it that form, as I have just said;

And he must embellish it with the rarest ornaments which it may fittingly bear.

Castelvetro,[3] all of whose opinions are not equally well founded, tries to persuade us that the subject of the epic poem must necessarily be drawn from fable; but if that were true, the *Iliad* would be at fault and the *Aeneid* would be worth nothing, since the siege of Troy is factually true and since Aeneas actually came to Italy according to the belief most common among the authors.

Thus for myself I believe, against the opinion of this commentator of Aristotle, that the subject of the heroic poem ought to be true rather than invented, because since the epic poet must in all things cling to verisimilitude, he would fail in that duty if an illustrious action were not described in any historian. Indeed, great actions cannot be entirely unknown, and those which are believed to be completely false do not touch the emotions and give little satisfaction. Ovid has put very pathetic words into the mouth of the abandoned Ariadne, and yet they are very far from making as strong an impression as those of the Dido of Virgil, of the Olympia of Ariosto, and the Armida of Tasso, so certain is it that actions which have verisimilitude, the more so because they have some shadow of truth mixed with the fiction, are more fitted to produce compassion than those in which the fiction is undisguised. Theseus, who was a hero in fact, son of a real king of Athens, was fitted to give verisimilitude to that fable; but Bacchus, whom the poet introduces, spoils everything and makes one ashamed of having shed real tears over a chimerical misfortune. On the other hand, Dido, who never saw Aeneas, or Olympia and Armida, who were never in the real world, call forth real tears for a false misfortune because some trace of truth makes their misfortune seem likely and because there is nothing in their whole adventure which disturbs the feeling of probability.

It is therefore in part for this reason that I have chosen Alaric for my hero, whose great actions are especially described in Procopius in the first book dealing with the wars of the Vandals, in Orosius, Book Seven, Chapter Thirty-eight, and in Ritius in the first book concerning the kings of Spain.[4]

Nowadays the illustrious subject of the epic poem should not, in my opinion, be taken from the pagan histories because (as I have just said, and as Tasso has said before me) all those imaginary gods absolutely destroy the epic by destroying verisimilitude, which is its whole foundation. The argument of the epic poem must, then, be taken from Christian history but not from sacred history, especially since one cannot alter the truth of the latter without profanation, and because without originality, which is the principal contribution of the poet, it is almost impossible for the epic to achieve its full beauty. One must, however, make an exception for the subject which my illustrious friend Monsieur de Saint-Amant[5] has chosen, for it is certain that the life of Moses has all the quality of the marvelous which originality could invent; and since the poet's art has also included convincing narration, his work ought to be as much esteemed by the learned as I esteem his mind and love his person. And certainly I do not doubt this will happen, for although I have seen almost nothing of this poem, the merit of its author and the testimony about it given to me by the Abbé de Villeloing, a very learned man and one whose inclinations are as noble as his birth, do not leave the matter in doubt. But, as a particular exception ought not to change a general rule, I nevertheless hold to my thesis; and I am strongly persuaded that neither pagan history nor sacred history is fitted to furnish an epic subject now, and that alone in our time profane Christian history can provide the marvelous and the probable which are, so to speak, the soul of such a subject. For, following the example of that history, the imagination of the poet introduces into his story angels, evil spirits, and magicians; and thus without shocking probability, the poet amuses the reader with wonders and complicates or unties the knot of the plot in ways which cannot be guessed in advance. By the use of history a single action can be made both marvelous and probable — the first by the extraordinary things magic can do and the second by the acceptance which history finds in the minds of most people.

If now from the primary nature of the fable we pass to the morality of the story, which is its most important part, Tasso will pardon me if I appeal from him to himself, when he says in his *Poetic Discourses*[6] that morality is not the object of the poet, who should think only of providing amusement. No doubt he conceived such an unfortunate opinion in one of those periods when he was not very lucid and when his reason was not free; and he therefore published an elevated retraction as early as the third stanza of his great poem, where he says, following Lucretius whom he is imitating:

> Sai, che la corre il mundo ove più versi
> Di sue dolcezze'l lusinghier Parnaso;
> E che'l vero condito in molli versi,
> I più schivi allettando ha persuaso.
> Cosi all'egro fanciul porgiamo apersi
> Di soavi licor gli orli del vaso,
> Succhi amari, ingannato in tanto ei beve,
> E dall'inganno suo vita riceve.[7]

Indeed if it is true (as he says in several places in his works) that allegory ought to reign over the whole epic poem even though all eyes may not perceive it, is this not to say clearly that the poet must consider the useful at least as much as the pleasant? And that he has as his principal goal not amusement but instruction? Therefore this great man, having returned to a more wholesome opinion, appended to his *Jerusalem Delivered* a long treatise on allegory in which he shows that there is not in it one single action which is not instructive; and he concludes by saying expressly that instruction must be the purpose of the epic poem.

It is for this reason, therefore, that the allegorical meaning reigns in my whole *Rome Defeated*: one is to understand by Alaric, the soul of man; by the spell to which I make him succumb like Ulysses in Calypso's isle, the weakness of mankind — even of the strongest who without the help of grace fall into weaknesses and into strange misfortunes and who with this powerful help rise up and free themselves, as the prince leaves the enchanted castle through the help which heaven gives him; by the magician who persecutes him, the obstacles which the demons always oppose to good purposes; by the beautiful Amalsonthe, the powerful temptation of the flesh; by the great number of enemies who fight against him, the world, which is one of the three that the Christian soul acknowledges, according to the testimony of the Scriptures and of the Fathers; by the invincible resistance of the hero, the liberty of free will; by the continual malice of the demons, the unending war they wage against the soul; and by the capture of Rome and the triumph of the prince, the victory of reason over the senses, over hell and over the world, and the immortal crowns which in the end God gives to virtue.

But Tasso was not alone in so unreasonable an error; Castelvetro, al-

THE CONTINENTAL MODEL

though a great man, carried the incongruity further than he, and after having worn out half his life on the *Poetics* of Aristotle and having put into that book all his Greek and all his Latin, tells us that poetry was invented only *per dilettare, e per ricreare gli animi della rozza moltitudine e del commune popolo.*[8] Here is an art which would truly merit, if such were its goals, that Aristotle should concern himself with giving us its rules; and Castelvetro himself had well made use of his time were his labors fit only the better to entertain the common herd.

> Just as the spider, spinning forth her slime
> Wears out her life and nothing leaves in Time,

as one of our most famous poets has said.[9] But that is not the only heresy of this author, for a few lines later he says [10] that Empedocles, Nicander, Hesiod, Virgil, and several others whom he names are not poets because learning is treated of in their works. He ought to have degraded Homer like the others and even more than the others, for scarcely is there an art or a skill in all of human knowledge which is not to be found in the *Iliad* or in the *Odyssey*. As for me, I am very far from having such debased opinions about the sublimest kind of writing; I hold on the contrary that to be a real poet one must know everything and that the more of learning one sees in a poem the more praiseworthy is the author.

Quintilian would not have been willing to approve the ignorant poetry of Castelvetro in view of what he says of those who read only the poets. *Nec*, he says, *si siderum rationem ignoret, poetas intelligat qui (ut alia omittam) totiens ortu occasuque signorum in declarandis temporibus utantur; nec ignara philosophiae, cum propter plurimos in omnibus fere carminibus locos ex intima naturalium quaestionum subtilitate repetitos, tum vel propter Empedoclen in Graecis, Varronem ac Lucretium in Latinis, qui praecepta sapientiae versibus tradiderunt.*[11]

It is on the basis of this same opinion that Cicero calls that work of Empedocles *egregium poema*,[12] and I shall not cease to be astonished that a man of as much erudition as Castelvetro should have imagined that learning and poetry were separable and that to appear as a good epic poet it was necessary either to pretend ignorance or to be ignorant. In fact, if the common people were to be readers of the epic poem, Horace would have been very foolish to tell us in his *Ars poetica*

> In verbis etiam tenuis cautusque serendis,
> dixeris egregie, notum si callida verbum
> reddiderit junctura novum etc.[13]

84

Much good would it do, in truth, to utter new words before those gentlemen; and all the politeness which he demands of the poet would have a
great effect indeed if it were seen only by the *rozza moltitudine* of Castelvetro.

I am well aware that learning must not be undigested, so to speak, in
the epic poem as it is in the schools, but, after all, it must be there and all
the more relevant because it is hidden. The same Horace teaches us the
restraint to be observed in this matter when he says

> Omne tulit punctum, qui miscuit utile dulci,
> lectorem delectando, pariterque monendo.[14]

But let us return to our subject after this digression which has not, in my
view, been an idle one.

If the masters of the art tell us next that the period of the epic hero
ought not to be so far from our own that the memory of it is entirely dead,
nor so near that one does not dare to mingle invention with reality, I believe that I have remained within that mean distance which they prescribe
for us; for having chosen the period in which Arcadius and Honorius divided the Empire, I find myself almost at the mid-point between the earliest
times and those in which we live.

Aristotle lays it down as one of the principal rules of the epic that the
action it describes must be illustrious, and I do not think I could have
found one more illustrious than the taking of Rome — Rome, I say, which
was the queen of all nations and the admiration of all the universe. Now
since the epic action must be great, the hero who accomplishes it must be
great; and his virtue would not be heroic if it were only moderate. Thus
one sees perfect piety in the person of Aeneas, great valor in Achilles, and
exquisite prudence in Ulysses; and it is by following these rare originals
that I have tried to show in the person of Alaric, so as to present the model
of an accomplished prince, the piety of the first, the valor of the second,
and the prudence of the third.

Not that I have formed him like the Stoic sage who is more the statue
of a man than a man; on the contrary, as Achilles, Ulysses, and Aeneas
experienced love, I have given him a taste of it, following their example;
for, after all, virtue does not consist in not having passions but in having
them and mastering them.

Such, Reader, ought to be the subject of the epic poem; or, to say it in
a few words, the subject should include the authority of history, the ac-

cepted usages of religion, the freedom of poetic fiction, and the grandeur of real events.

But what is called the subject before it has passed through the creative process is called form after the poet has arranged it and constructed a plot from it; and it is for this reason that Aristotle calls the structure of the plot the soul of the poem. Now Tasso compared the subject to what philosophers call primal substance; and it seems to me that in the case of the latter, although it is devoid of all form, the philosophers nevertheless consider its quantity, which is inseparable from it. In the same way it seems to me that the poet must before all else consider the question of quantity; otherwise his subject may appear to be so full in itself that when he later shapes a plot from it he will not be able to deck out that plot in episodes without making it excessively long. Dwarfs and giants are both monsters, and a fine build is equally removed from these excesses of largeness and smallness. For myself, I have so much facility in writing verse and in constructing a plot that a much longer poem than this would scarcely have cost me more; but I was so impatient to show the great Queen for whom I composed this work [15] the profound reverence I have for so great virtue as hers that I have not been able to restrain my zeal; I flatter myself with the hope that by the claw she will know the lion, to use the old proverb.

But to return promptly from this necessary digression, I say I consider that Lucan and Silius Italicus, because they included too many historical events, were not able to ornament their works with that variety of episodes which gives them all their charm; and thus, no doubt, arose the opinion almost universal among men of letters that both are rather historians than poets, although both have much real and true poetry in them, especially the first. For this reason I wanted the length of my poem to be moderate; but moderate as it is, I think that longer ones have few ornaments which are not to be found in mine, even though it has only eleven thousand lines, which is about the length of the *Aeneid* of Virgil.

Homer, our first master, is the one in whose traces I am here following, for in the *Iliad* his argument is only the anger of Achilles and yet owing to the episodes his work is consistently marvelous. But these episodes ought not to be those of which Aristotle speaks, *Quia sic poetae placuit*,[16] but rather those of which he says elsewhere, *Opportet autem et in moribus quemadmodum in rerum constitutione semper quaerere, vel necessarium, vel verisimile.*[17] In fact they must have verisimilitude and must be connected to the principal plot; such are, it seems to me, in my poem, the description of the burning of Alaric's ships, that of the plague, and all the others. Now while I am on the subject of the episodes, I feel I should tell you, Reader, that I am well aware Homer has none so long as the episodic stories in my *Alaric*; but aside from the fact that the narration of the capture of Troy is much longer in Virgil than any of these stories, there are so many which are longer than mine in Ariosto and Tasso that after these three illustrious examples there can be no misgivings on my part about them.

Besides, it is certain that the poet should treat things not as they really were but as they ought to have been, and to change and change again as he wants, without considering either history or truth which are neither his guide nor his goal. Great Virgil so well knew this maxim and practiced it so well that he did not fear in following it to commit an anachronism of four centuries, nor to depict Dido as other than she was, nor to pretend not to be aware of the tragic death of Aeneas, although the divine poet knew well that he had drowned in the Numicius. Since I have worked on the same subject, I have taken the same liberty, and in the case of Alaric's route, as well as in that of the duration of the siege of Rome (which I have reduced to a year's length as being that which an epic action ought to have), I have consulted my reason more than Procopius, for, after all, the poet is not the slave of the historian, and far from following him always, it is the poet's duty to depart from him often and to invent more than he imitates. But whatever freedom originality gives the poet, he must be careful not to alter the principal incidents of a well-known story because he would thus himself destroy the basis of his work. A writer who made bold to say that Rome was destroyed by Hannibal and that Carthage was not destroyed by Scipio would make himself ridiculous. Therefore I conclude that the argument of the epic must be founded upon some real exploit and not on an entirely invented subject, and that is also the reason why among so many things I have imagined in my poem I always mingle truth with invention and the plot with history, for indeed the historian must narrate things as being true and the poet as being convincing.

The unity of action is another of the principal parts of the epic poem; it is there that the beginning, the middle, and the end of the plot must meet as at their center. Therefore I believe the judicious reader will recognize at once that in my work everything leads to the taking of Rome and that through all the obstacles of hell and all the embellishments of the episodes I have always looked upon that as the unique goal which I was to attain, since Aristotle prescribes that unity as such in his *Poetics*, and since Horace follows the same opinion as do all the Greeks and all the Romans, all the ancients and all the moderns. The sky is spangled with stars, the air and the sea are full of birds and fishes, the earth has wild and tame animals, brooks, springs, and lakes, fields, hills, and woods, fruits, flowers, icicles, and snow, houses, tilled fields, deserts, rocky coasts, and precipices; yet all these make only one world. Similarly in an epic poem one finds armies in fighting array or in camp, battles on land or on the sea, the taking of towns, skirmishes and duels, descriptions of hunger, thirst and storms, burnings, seditions, and magic charms, cruel and magnanimous actions, happy and unhappy love affairs; and yet in the midst of such a great diversity unity does not desert the plot any more than it does the world, if the plot is constructed according to the rules of art.

Such, then, ought to be the subject of the epic poem and such the form one ought to give the subject; it remains to be seen what ornaments the form should receive.

Having here to deal with diction, it follows that I must also speak of style because, according to Aristotle and Tasso, style is only the grouping of words and words are but the images of thoughts; hence in speaking of diction one must necessarily speak of style, for it is but a composite of thoughts and words.[18]

There are three kinds of style: the sublime, the ordinary, and the low; but it is the first which ought most to serve in the epic poem, for since the poem contains noble actions it follows that the style with which they are described must be noble also. One must take care that the Muse does not blunder and that she does not pipe on the flageolet under the impression that she is sounding the trumpet. The magnificent, then, befits the epic; nevertheless the ordinary and even the low style can be used, as they are in Virgil, according to the varying social classes of the characters whom the poet makes speak. But it must never be forgotten that as each virtue has a vice which is related to it and which resembles it, as, for instance, liberality and prodigality, temerity and valor, so every kind of perfect style has for near neighbor the faulty; indeed, it is very easy to pass from one to the other. The magnificent degenerates easily into the inflated and the swollen, the ordinary into the weak and sterile, and the low into the coarse and vulgar. The epic, tragic, and comic styles all have different characteristics, but as the musician uses all kinds of tones without leaving his mode, so the epic poet may use these three kinds of style, provided he does it with judgment and provided the sublime always prevails as being essential to the majesty of the epic poem. Now majesty results from the grandeur of the events described, from the splendor of the words, from the modulation, or, better, the cadence of the verse, and from the rich figures of rhetoric such as hyperbole, prosopopoeia, metaphor, comparison, epithets, and all the others which poets and orators use.

What the learned call maxims are also essential parts of the epic, according to the doctrine of Aristotle; therefore I have not failed to put a considerable number of them into my poem. However I admit that I do not agree with one of the commentators of Aristotle who wants an epic poem to be filled with them. They have an imperious quality which smells too much of the dogmatic style if they are very frequent in poetry; besides, I think great actions teach less obviously but also more usefully than do those decorations and stilted sentiments which, in my opinion, must not be used too often; for although the eyes are the most beautiful parts of the human body, they would make a monster of it if it were entirely covered with them; one must abide by the proverb, nothing in excess.

Such, then, Reader, ought to be the subject, form and ornaments of the epic and what the poem ought to contain in its four principal parts: proposition, invocation, dedication and narration. Finally, I am familiar with art, but to put it into practice well

Hoc opus hic labor est.[19]

I lay my work before you, after having lavished on it all my care, and it is for you to judge in a case where I cannot be both judge and defendant.

But before finishing this discourse I wish to anticipate some objections which might be made to me.

The first is to the name of my poem, *Alaric, or Rome Defeated*, for someone will, perhaps, consider the double title useless and even unreasonable, believing that *Alaric* alone would suffice, or merely *Rome Defeated*, the more so since Homer and Virgil seem to be against me because their poems are named simply the *Iliad*, the *Odyssey*, and the *Aeneid*. But, aside from the fact that Tasso is my surety because he called his poem *Il Gofredo, overo la Hierusalem liberata*, the double title is not only useful but necessary. *Alaric* by itself would not say what I mean, for it would seem that I wished to sing of all the actions of that prince although I mean to celebrate only one; and *Rome Defeated*, without the addition of *Alaric*, would not have expressed my intention either, since Rome was defeated more than once, and no one would know, on seeing that title, which defeat I intended to treat. However, by saying *Alaric, or Rome Defeated*, I leave no doubt in the reader's mind either about the hero whom I wish to praise or about the action which I have undertaken to describe.

The second is that since I said at the beginning of this discourse that epic poems and novels have much in common, someone might remark that Heliodorus, Athenagoras, and all the other Greek authors who composed novels like those dealing with Daphnis and Chloe or Clitiphon and Leucippe [20] go at once to the heart of the matter and begin their story in the middle of the adventure rather than at its beginning as in my poem. I admit that, Reader; but so must you admit at the same time that Homer, in the *Iliad* having chosen to sing of the anger of Achilles and in the *Odyssey*, the labors of Ulysses, causes that anger to be born and those labors to begin at the start of the two poems, and afterwards only continues them as long as the two poems last. Virgil did what Homer had done; Lucan did what Virgil had done; and I did what I saw all three of them had done. It is obvious that this is not a thing I was unaware of, since I bring up the objection myself and since I have shown I understand it in my *Bassa* and in my *Cyrus*; but the fact is that even though Ariosto and Tasso did not take exactly the same route, since I have on my side both my masters and theirs, I have been able at least to consider the thing unimportant and to take what I thought was the most direct road to arrive where I wished to go. For it must not be objected that in various places in these Greek and Latin poems past events are discussed, as all these narrations are only episodic embellishments, which are not what these famous poets promised to sing of. Similarly one can see in my poem these same past events in the description of the profligacy of Rome; but since I undertook to celebrate the taking of that famous city, everything I subsequently say leads toward this goal and I do not stop until I arrive at it.

The third is that Tasso did not deal with love in the person of the hero as I do in that of Alaric. I really do not know why this great man proceeded in that way, but I know that I have on my side and opposed to him Homer, Virgil, Boiardo, Ariosto, and all the others, and that after such great examples I need not fear having erred. Decent love is really the fire of Hercules, which by consuming him made him a god, and as it has so elegantly been said by Guevarra, one of the greatest minds in all Spain, *Arde y no quema, alumbra y no daña, quema y no consume, resplandece y no lástima, purifica y no abrasa, y aun calienta y no congoja;* [21] and I think that noble passion will never prevent anyone from saying of Alaric what Homer said of another prince:

βασιλεὺς τ'ἀγαθὸς χρατερὸς τ'αἰχμητής [22]

The fourth is that there is some slight relationship between my episode of the Lusitanian and the beautiful Laplander with that of Olindo and Sophronia in Tasso, since they wish to die for each other like those lovers of Jerusalem, and some resemblances besides, in two or three places, between my poem and some others. But to that I answer two things: first, that there are certain universal notions that come to everybody; and the other, that if one author were to be condemned for imitation, they must all be condemned. Indeed, the *Aeneid* is almost everywhere a copy of the *Iliad*: for example, the death of Turnus, caused by the belt of Pallas which Aeneas recognizes, is an imitation of the death of Hector, caused by the weapons of Achilles which he had taken from Patroclus. The Camilla of the celebrated Mantuan owes her birth to the Penthesilea of the famous Greek,[23] and the Bradamant and the Marphisa of the Ferraran are but images of the first two. The beginning of the *Metamorphoses* of Ovid is that of Genesis; the Alcina and the Armida of Ariosto and Tasso are portraits of Circe; Olindo and Sophronia, of whom I have just spoken, have their inception in the Nisus and Euryale of the Latin poet [24] and in the Medoro of Ariosto; Olympia and Armida were abandoned by their lovers only after Ariadne had been by hers. This Armida has taken from Dido word for word what she says to Rinaldo when he leaves her, as well as all the curses which she utters when he has left her. The Perseus and Pegasus of the ancient fable have contributed to the Astolpho and the hippogriff of the new; the head of the Medusa made the fatal buckler of Atlantes; and I do not doubt that Homer himself took a great many things from the Egyptians among whom he studied. A thousand other relationships as precise as these are found in all celebrated writers, and it has been many centuries since Solomon said there was nothing new under the sun. But I add to the weight of so many examples this statement, that if the reader examines this episode carefully, as well as the other places and the manner in which I have treated them, he will see they are very different from the others; and he will be forced to admit that if the subject is not all my own (which I do not concede), the form is my own absolutely. Marino said that to take from men of his own nation was robbery, but to take from foreigners was conquest, and I think he was right. We study only to learn, and we learn only to show we have studied. The man who annotated the *Jerusalem* of Tasso considered he was doing him an honor by pointing out in the poem two or three thousand places imitated from various authors, and commentators of Petrarch and Ronsard have done the same thing. Yet since I know that originality is more approved than imitation, I have used the latter only sparingly; and although few people have read more than I and although it would have been easy for me to paraphrase or to translate, since I had in my study everything worthy of paraphrase or translation, I have done it very little, finding it too easy to do. The learned will probably note some places imitated from Homer, Virgil, Ovid, Horace, and Lucan, but I have not abused this technique; and if I have taken something from the Greeks and the Romans, I have taken nothing at all from the Italians, the Spaniards, and the French; for it seemed to me that what is study in the case of the ancients is thievery in the case of the moderns.

The fifth is that since the Greeks and Romans in their pride called all other peoples barbarians, and ourselves amongst them, some pedant who still respects that pride may take exception to my having sought among the ancient Goths the ideal of a perfect prince. However, since a Greek sought one among the Persians, I may well find him among the Vandals; moreover, the last King of Sweden and the great Queen who has succeeded him demonstrate that heroes and heroines may be born anywhere and that they have no special climate. Actually, if my procedure were authorized only by the example of the author of the *Aquilée* who took for his hero Attila, King of the Huns, called the Scourge of God, or rather who took him without intending to, if we may believe the first stanza of his poem, even though he is a man of parts and his work worthy of esteem, I doubt if that would suffice; but since great Virgil took a Phrygian for his hero, I surely may take a Goth for mine, for the Phrygians were not more favorably treated by the vanity of the Romans than all the other peoples of the earth. I know it will be argued that this was because Aeneas, rather than Romulus, was the founder of the grandeur of Rome and because he was the ancestor of Augustus; but, in my opinion, this would not be enough to excuse the Latin poet if he had erred, for the national interest of Rome would not give him the right to violate the epic rules. If a Phrygian was not suitable to be a hero, his choice would never be accepted, even though the Caesars were proud to say they were descended from that race and even though the divine poet traced the descent of Aeneas from Dardanus, a native of Italy; for despite all that, he was an Asiatic. But the truth is that

Virgil did not err, nor have I, more than he, in this respect; for I am sure that heroic virtue may be found as well on the shores of the Baltic as on the shores of the Aegean or the Tiber, a fact which all Europe may see from the two great examples I have adduced.

The sixth is that I have given oars as well as sails to ships and galleys, although modern ships do not have both, but those who know antiquity are aware that formerly ships were provided with the two. Thus I have done only what I had to do, for history provides many examples of what I am saying; and even now, in the waters of the Levant, ships are often so arranged.

The seventh objection may be raised by the most recent commentator of the *Poetics* of Aristotle who, since he has condemned valiant women, may disapprove of the fact that I have introduced two of them into my poem. But although I esteem him highly, I need not fear him on this point, since my warlike women are seconded by the Penthesilea of Homer, the Camilla of Virgil, the Marphisa and the Bradamant of Ariosto, and the Clorinda of Tasso. Moreover, if the heroines of story are not enough to overwhelm him, I shall remind him of those of history: Judith, Zenobia, and all the Amazons who in camps and armies preserved their modesty and their reputation. Let him please remember that I have a special advantage in this respect, for not only were two Gothic queens seen in war during antiquity (I mean Thomyris and Amalsonthe, the daughter of Theodoric) but the Swedes Johannes and Olaüs Magnus [25] name in their histories several other ladies of their nation who bore arms and gave evidence of great bravery and modesty. But I do not wish to dwell any longer on this subject; it concerns the illustrious author of *The Maid* [26] rather than myself, and I shall leave to him the task of defending all valiant ladies by defending his heroic shepherdess, whom the attacker will not prevent from triumphing anew.

The eighth concerns the number of books in my poem, for since Homer made the *Iliad* and the *Odyssey* of twenty-four books each and since he was the first, it seems that he ought to establish the rule for all others. However, no one has followed him in this. The *Aeneid* of Virgil has only twelve, as does the *Thebaid* of Statius; the *Pharsalia* of Lucan has ten; the poem of Silius Italicus, seventeen; the *Orlando* of Boiardo, three, divided into sixty-eight cantos; that of Ariosto has forty-six; the *Jerusalem Delivered* of Tasso has twenty like the *Adonis* of Marino; and so for all the others. Therefore, seeing the matter was uncertain and, consequently, unimportant, I wrote my *Alaric* in ten books because this number suited me better than any other.

The ninth concerns certain terms describing the arts of war, navigation and hunting which I used in this work and which will, perhaps, not be familiar to everybody. I thought about that when I used them, and you cannot doubt this, Reader, since I am raising this objection myself before you have seen them. But, to tell the truth, I thought it was better that those who do not know them should take the trouble to learn them than that I should expose myself to the ridicule of those who know by speaking badly of a subject I ought to be familiar with, since I undertake to discuss it. All those who read the *Bucolics* and the *Georgics* do not understand what they describe about farm management; all those who encounter in the *Aeneid* Eurus, Notus, and Africus do not know from what direction these winds blow; and yet Virgil is not censured for having written as he did. There are many places in that poet and in Homer which are understood only by the learned, and it is for those who read to penetrate the meaning and not for writers to appear ignorant. Of course I should not want to use up half my poem, as did Athenagoras and Polyphilus, in naming the orders and dimensions of architecture from the cellar to the roof of a building, because that would be dull. But by using rare words moderately as I have done, I think I have remained within reasonable limits and have not given criticism cause to censure me on this point. Nevertheless, as a favor to those who do not understand the words of which I am speaking, the reader will find an explanation of them at the end of the preface.

The tenth objection, I admit, is a little more difficult to rebut than the nine others, for indeed Alaric, although a Christian, was of the Arian sect; and it appears, since piety is the first virtue which Virgil attributes to his Aeneas, that there is left something to be desired in my hero, whose belief is not very orthodox. But I have not thought this obstacle insurmountable, for aside from the fact that the care with which Alaric preserved all the churches and sacred vessels at the taking of Rome shows him to have had the good sentiments of our religion, another even stronger consideration frees my mind from any kind of misgiving.

Indeed Cyrus, whose illustrious memory I have tried to revive, far from being a Jew or of our religion (which was not yet established), was a pagan; yet hear how a prophet speaks of him, or rather how God speaks of him through the mouth of this prophet:

Haec dicit Dominus Christo meo Cyro (says God, according to Isaiah) cujus apprehendi dexteram, ut subjiciam ante faciem ejus gentes, et dorsa regem vertam, et aperiam coram eo januas, et portae non claudentur. Ego ante te ibo: et gloriosos terrae humiliabo: portas aereas conteram, et vectes ferreos confringam et dabo tibi thesauros absconditos, et arcana secretorum.[27]

Isaiah, in various places in his prophecies, speaks of this conqueror in the same way, and three other prophets, as I have said elsewhere, sing his praises rather than prophesy about him. But lest it be thought that I am singing my own, in the guise of making my defense, I shall say nothing further, Reader, and I shall leave you the freedom to judge my poem.

First, however, I must beg members of the Swedish nation, for the reputation of which, after that of their incomparable Queen, I have just finished this long task, if they should by chance find some error in the geography of their country or in the description of things, to accuse merely my globes, my charts, and my books, which are the only guides available to follow and in whose good faith I have had to trust, having never been to Sweden although I have been in most of Europe.

Furthermore, considering myself under obligation when speaking of the conquests of the great Gustavus to render justice to the merit and valor of those who helped him to accomplish them, I have not failed to acquit myself of this duty; and of all those whose names history has noted I do not think I have forgotten one. But if, by mischance, there should be a gentleman in Sweden or in the German nations who has been unjustly handled in the narrations which we have of that war through the suppression of his great deeds, I beg him, or those of his house if he is dead, not to impute that fault to me and to believe that since there is no greater joy for me than to praise virtue, I should not have refused so just a tribute to his had it been known to me.

As for the order in which I name these high officers, I do not take it from their birth, their responsibilities or their deeds. I celebrate them in my poem one after the other as history shows them to me and at the same time and in the very places where she puts them.

❧ 1657

Francois Hedelin, abbe d'Aubignac THE WHOLE ART

OF THE STAGE

Book I, Chapter 3

WHAT IS TO BE UNDERSTOOD BY THE ART OF THE STAGE

It may seem very rash, or at least superfluous, to treat of poetry after that so many authors both ancient and modern have given us books upon that subject full of learning, and more particularly have taken pains to make observations upon dramatic poetry as being the most agreeable and yet the hardest to succeed in. But if we may believe with Seneca that all truths have not been yet spoken, we may assure it in the subject which I undertake, for all I have seen yet that concerns the stage contains only the general maxims of dramatic poetry, which is properly the theory of the art, but as for the practice and application of those instructions, I never met with anything of that kind hitherto, all the discourses that are upon that subject being only paraphrases and commentaries upon Aristotle with great obscurity and little novelty.

I do not pretend here to trouble myself about satisfying the criticisms of grammarians or the scruples of logicians, who, it may be, will not freely admit of this distinction in an art whose rules seem all to tend to practice. I am sure all the rational and polite learning will not oppose me in it, since it is natural in all arts to distinguish the knowledge of the maxims and the use of them, besides that in the execution of all general rules there are

NOTE: The complete title of d'Aubignac's book gives a good indication of its contents: *The Whole Art of the Stage, Containing not only the rules of the dramatic art, but many curious observations about it, which may be of great use to the authors, actors and spectators of plays, together with much critical learning about the stage and plays of the ancients.* The translation of 1684 says that the book was "Written in French by the command of Cardinal Richelieu, by Monsieur Hédelin, Abbot of Aubignac, and now made English."

observations to be made of which there is no mention when one teaches only the theory, and which nevertheless are of great importance. Thus architecture teacheth the beauty and symmetry of buildings, their noble proportions, and all the rest of their magnificent appearance, but does not descend to express a thousand necessary contrivances of which the master of the house is to take care when he puts his hand to the work. If the art of playing upon the lute were reduced into rules, it could teach only general things, as the number of the strings and touches, the manner of making the accords, the measures, passages, quavers, etc., but still one would be forced to have recourse to the master himself to learn in the execution of all this the nicest way of touching the strings, the changing of the measures, the most graceful way how to give a good motion to one's playing, and many more particulars which could not well be committed to writing and so must either be neglected or learned of the masters themselves.

The same thing has happened to the stage. There have been ample treatises of dramatic poems, the original of them, their progress, definition, species, the unity of action, measure of time, the beauty of their contrivance, the thoughts, manners, language which is fittest for them, and many other such matters, but only in general, and that I call the theory of the stage; but for the observations to be made upon those general rules, as how to prepare the incidents to unite times and places, the continuity of the theatral action, the connection of the scenes, the intervals of the acts, and a thousand other particulars of which there is nothing left in antiquity, of which all the moderns have said so little that it is next to nothing — all this, I say, is that which I call the art or practice of the stage. As for the ancients, if they have writ nothing about it as to the practical part, it is because that perhaps in their time it was so common that they could not believe anybody capable of not knowing it, and indeed if one look into their works and make but the least reflection upon the art they use, one may perceive it almost everywhere.

But for the moderns, they for the most part have been entirely ignorant of it because they have neglected the reading of the poems of those great masters, or if they have read them, it was without taking notice of the nicest beauties with which they are adorned. Therefore it must be set down for a maxim out of context, that it is impossible to understand dramatic poetry without the help of the ancients and a thorough meditation upon their works.

Book II, Chapter 6
OF THE UNITY OF PLACE

After the poet has ordered his subject according to the rules we have given, or, it may be better, which his own industry and study may furnish him with, he must reflect that the best part of it must be represented by actors, which must be upon a stage fixed and determined, for to make his actors appear in different places would render his play ridiculous by the want of probability, which is to be the foundation of it.

This rule of unity of place begins now to be looked upon as certain, but yet the ignorant and some others of weak judgment do still imagine that it cannot but be repugnant to the beauty of the incidents of a play, because that they, happening often in great distance of place, cannot but lose by this constraint, and therefore whatsoever reason you oppose against their imaginations, they fancy a false impossibility in the execution and reject stubbornly all that's said to convince them. On the other side, those that are but half read in antiquity do well perceive the strength of what it alleged for this rule, but yet they make objections so unbecoming a literate thinking man that they have often moved pity in me, though I had more mind to laugh at them. It is the property of little geniuses not to be able to comprehend many things at the same time so as to reduce them to a point, their judgment not being able to assemble so many images as they must have present all at once, and therefore they make so many difficulties that it is easy to see they would be glad that there were reasons wanting to convince them.

As for the truly learned, they are thoroughly convinced of the necessity of this rule, because they see clearly that probability can no ways be preserved without it. But I may boldly say that hitherto no one of them has explained this rule and made it intelligible, either because we do not take the pains of making all the necessary reflections upon the works of the ancients to discover the art which is most commonly hid in them, and which always ought to be so, [under] an apparent necessity of the subject or the interest of the actors; or else because nobody strives to go beyond the first great masters, and what they have neglected is given over most commonly by their followers.

Aristotle has said nothing of it, and I believe he omitted it because that this rule was in his time too well known, the Choruses which ordinarily remained upon the stage from one end of the play to the other marking the unity of the scene too visibly to need a rule for it. And indeed, would it not have been ridiculous that in the play called the *Seven before Thebes* the young women who make the Chorus should have found themselves sometimes before the palace of the king and sometimes in the camp of the enemies without ever stirring from the same place? And the three famous tragedians of the Greeks whose works we have are so punctual in the observation of this rule and do so often make their actors say where they are and whence they come that Aristotle must have supposed too much ignorance in his age and in those who should read these poets if he had gone about to explain so settled a rule. But since the ignorance and barbarity of some past ages have brought such disorder upon the stage to make people in the play appear in different parts of the world on the same stage, it will not be amiss to give here at length the reason of this rule so well practised by the ancients, and that in honor of some of our modern poets who have very handsomely imitated them.

To understand it, then, we must have recourse to our ordinary principle, which is, that the stage is but a representation of things; and yet we are not to imagine that there is anything of what we really see, but we must think the things themselves are there of which the images are before us. So Floridor [1] is much less Floridor than the Horatius of whom he acts the part, for his dress is Roman, he speaks, acts, thinks as that Roman did at that time; but as that Roman could not but be in some place acting and speaking, the place where Floridor appears does represent that where Horatius was, or else the representation would be imperfect in that circumstance.

This truth well understood makes us to know that the place cannot change in the rest of the play since it cannot change in the representation, for one and the same image remaining in the same state cannot represent two different things. Now it is highly improbable that the same space and the same floor, which receive no change at all, should represent two different places, as, for example, France and Denmark, or, within Paris itself, the Tuileries and the Exchange. At least to do it with some sort of color, one should have of that sort of theatres which turn quite round and entire that so the place might change as well as the persons acting, and to do this, the subject of the play ought to furnish some reason for this change, and as that cannot well happen but by the power of God Almighty, who changes as He pleases the face of nature, I doubt it would be hard to make a reasonable play without a dozen miracles at least.

Let it then be allowed for a certain truth that the place where the first actor who opens the play is supposed to be ought to be the same place to the end of the play, and that, it not being in the ordinary course of nature that the place can receive any change, there can be none likewise in the representation, and, by consequence, that all your other actors cannot rationally appear in any other place.

But we must remember that this place which cannot be supposed to change is the area or floor of the stage, upon which the actors walk, and which the ancients called by the name of *proscenium*; for as that represents that spot of ground upon which the persons represented did actually walk and discourse, which could not turn about or change on a sudden or without a miracle, so, when you have once chosen the place where you intend your action to be begun, you must suppose it immovable in all the rest of the play, as it was in effect and really.

It is not the same with the sides and end of the theatre, for as they do but represent those things which did actually environ the persons acting and which might receive some change, they may likewise receive some in the representation, and it is in that that consists the changing of scenes and other ornaments of decoration which always ravish the people and please the best judges when they are well done. So we have seen upon our stage a temple adorned with a noble front of architecture, which, coming to be set open, showed the inside of it where in perspective were descried pillars and an altar and all the other ornaments of a church extremely well done, so that the place did not change and yet had a fine decoration.

We are not, nevertheless, to imagine that the poet's *capriccio* is to rule these decorations, for he must find some color and appearance for it in his subject.

So, for example, he might feign a palace upon the seaside, forsaken and left to be inhabited by poor fishermen. A prince landing or being cast away there might adorn it with all the rich furniture fit for it, after this by some accident it might be set on fire, and then behind it the sea might appear, upon which one might represent a sea fight; so that in all the five changes of the stage the unity of place would still be ingeniously preserved. Not but that the very floor or *proscenium* may change too, provided it be superficially, as if some river should overflow it, as the Tiber did in the time of Augustus, or if flames came out of the earth and covered the face of it. In all these cases the unity of place would not be broke. But, as I have said already, the subject of the play must furnish probable reasons for these changes, which I repeat the oftener because I am still afraid that it will not make impression enough in the reader.

It is not enough neither to say that the floor or stage should represent a place immovable. It must, besides, be a place supposed open in the reality as it appears in the representation, for since the actors are supposed to go and come from one end of it to the other, there cannot be any solid body between to hinder either their sight or motion. Therefore the ancients did use to choose for the place of their scene in tragedies some public place, as that before the gate of a palace, and in their comedies, some part of a town where different streets met and where the houses of the principal actors were supposed to be, because these places were most fitly represented by the empty stage adorned with the figures of those houses. Not that they always followed this, for in the *Suppliants* and in the *Ion* of Euripides, the scene is before a temple, and in the *Ajax* of Sophocles, the scene is before his tent pitched in the corner of a forest. In the *Rudens* of Plautus, it is before the temple and some scattered houses from whence one sees the sea. And indeed all this depends upon the poet's invention, who according to his subject chooses the place the most convenient for all that he has a mind to represent and adorns it with some agreeable appearance.

One may judge from all this how ridiculous was the wall in the *Thisbe* of [the] poet Théophile, it being placed upon the stage and Pyramus and she whispering through it; and when they went out, the wall sunk that the other actors might see one another. For besides that the two places on each side of the wall represented the two chambers of Pyramus and Thisbe, and that it was contrary to all appearance of reason that in the same place the king should come and talk with his confidents, and, much less, that a lion should come and fright Thisbe there, I would fain know by what supposed means in the action itself this wall could become visible and invisible, and by what enchantment it was sometimes in being and then ceased quite to be again. The fault is not less in those who suppose things done upon the stage which have not been seen by the spectators, it not being probable they could have been done without being seen, or else things must be supposed to have been invisible in the reality of the action, upon which, I think, one of our modern poets fell into a great error of this kind, having placed a bastion upon the stage and having afterwards caused the town to be taken by that bastion, which was never seen to be either attacked or defended.[2]

As for the extent which the poet may allow to the scene he chooses,

101

when it is not in a house, but open, I believe it may be as far as a man can see another walk and yet not know perfectly that it is he. For to take a larger space would be ridiculous, it being improbable that two people, being each of them at one end of the stage without any object between, should look at one another and yet not see one another; whereas this distance, which we allow often, contributes to the working of the play by the mistakes and doubts which a man may make by seeing another at a distance. To which the theatres of the ancients do very well agree; for, being as they were, threescore yards in front among the Romans and little less among the Grecians, it was pretty near the proportion we allow them.

I desire the reader, besides, to consider that if the poet did represent by his stage all the places and rooms of a palace or all the streets of a town, he should make the spectators see not only all that happened in his story but all that was done besides in that palace or in the town. For there is no reason to hinder the spectators from seeing all that, nor why they should see one thing sooner than another, particularly considering that since they can see at the same time into the garden of the palace and into the king's cabinet, according to the subject of the play, they must likewise hear and see all that is done there besides the theatral action, except there were an enchantment to show only that which the poet had a mind to and hide all that was not of his subject. Besides, the stage would never be empty of any of the actors, except they went out of the palace or town, for since the place represents the palace with its garden, court, and other apartments, one cannot forbear seeing anyone who should go from any of those apartments into the court or garden, and, by consequence, as long as any of the actors were in the extent represented by the stage, they cannot avoid being seen. To which it cannot be answered that to mark the different apartments there may be curtains to shut and draw, for these curtains are fit for nothing but to toss their inventors in them like dogs in a blanket.

I have spoken so clearly of this in my *Terence Justified* that I have nothing more to say against this gross piece of ignorance.

If it be said besides that the poet has the liberty of showing and hiding what he pleases, I grant it, provided there be a probability that one thing be seen and another not. But there would need a singular invention to contrive that ever and anon the same persons acting and speaking in a palace should be seen and not be seen, for that would be making of the walls to sink and rise, go backwards and forwards every moment. This may be enough to show the error of those who upon the same scene represent

Spain and France, making their stage not only almost as big as the earth, but likewise causing the same floor to represent at the same time things so far distant from one another and that without any apparent cause of so prodigious a change.

We may likewise observe how they are mistaken that suppose in one side of the stage one part of the town, as, for example, the Louvre, and on the other side, another part, as the Place Royale, thinking by this fine invention to preserve the unity of place. Indeed, if two parts or quarters of a town thus supposed were not far from one another, and the space between were really empty of houses, such a thing were not improper, but if between the two places there are many houses and solid bodies, I would then ask how it comes to pass that those houses do not fill up the empty place of the stage, and how, if they do, an actor can see another place at the other end of the stage beyond all these houses, and, in a word, how this stage, which is but an image, represents a thing of which it has no resemblance.

Let it then be settled for a constant maxim that the *proscenium* or floor of the stage can represent nothing but some open place of an ordinary extent where those that are represented by the actors might naturally be in the truth of the action. And when we see it written, 'The Scene is at Aulis, Eleusis, or Argos,' it is not that the place where the actors appear is all that town or province, but only that all the intrigues of the play, as well what passes out of the sight of the spectators as what they see, are treated in that town of which the stage takes up but the least part.

Thus in the prologue of the last comedy of Plautus, the poet, explaining the place of the scene, says that he begs of the Romans a little space in the middle of their noble buildings to transport thither the town of Athens without the help of architects.[3] Upon which Samuel Petit[4] observes that we ought not to imagine that Plautus pretends to place all the city of Athens in that of Rome, but only a small part of it where the things represented in the play did come to pass, to wit, the quarter of the Plotaeans, and of all that quarter only the place where Phronesion lived. And he confirms this by the mending of two Greek words, of which he pretends one Latin one was made by a mistake, and by a verse which he mends by some manuscripts which he had seen, making the Prologue then speak thus: "I abridge here the town of Athens upon this stage during this play, and in this house lives Phronesion."

These are the only authorities of any either ancient or modern authors that I have found concerning the place of the scene. Castelvetro indeed says that tragedy requires but a small space, but since he has not explained himself better, we are not bound to guess in his favor.

These things, then, once settled for the doctrine or theory, I have thought of what follows for the practical part. The poet does not desire to represent to his spectators all the particulars of his story, [but only the principal and most beautiful circumstances. On the one hand he cannot do so since he would have to include too many incidents and transactions; thus he is obliged to suppose some of them to be beyond the view of the spectators. On the other hand he should not do so, since there are a hundred horrible, indecent, low, and almost useless things which he must hide, informing the spectators of them either by a mere narration which corrects them, or by an easy act of the imagination.] He must then first of all consider exactly what persons he most wants and cannot well be without, then let him choose a place where they may probably meet; for as there are places which certain persons cannot leave without extraordinary motives, so there are others where they cannot be without great reason. A nun cannot leave the place of her retreat but upon some pressing motive, and a woman of honor cannot accompany Messalina to the place of her infamous debauches.

Besides, he must observe whether or not in his subject there be not some circumstances or notable incident which it will be necessary to preserve for the beauty of his play and which cannot happen but in a certain place, for then he must accommodate to that the rest of his parts. So he that would show Celadon half dead upon the shore and found there by Galatea must, of necessity, place his scene upon the bank of a river and accommodate to it the rest of the theatral action. Plautus followed this method in his *Rudens*, where he desired to show the relics of a shipwreck and therefore was forced to place his scene on the seaside, where all the rest of his adventures are very dexterously brought to pass.

The poet, having chosen the place, must examine next what things are fittest to be showed with delight to the spectators and be sure to represent them. As for the others not so fit to be seen, they must be told some way that they may be supposed done, and that in places so near the stage that the actor who tells them may be supposed to have been there and back again from the time he has been absent from the stage, or else he must be supposed gone before the play began, for then he may come as far off as you will. All which Terence hath observed in his third comedy, where the

104

two slaves, Syrus and Dromo, had been sent a great while before for Clitophon's mistress, and, by consequence, all that Syrus tells of their negotiation is very credible — what time soever there needed for the dressing of the lady and the doing of all the rest.

And if the things or places to be spoke of in the play have been done too far from the scene or are in themselves too remote, one must bring them nearer in the representation, which may be done two ways: either by supposing that they happened in other places nearer when it is all one to the story (as Donatus [5] observes that in plays country houses are always supposed to be in the suburbs), or else by supposing the places nearer than they really are when it is impossible to change them; but in this last, one must observe not to bring known places so near that the spectator cannot follow the poet in his belief. As, for example, if a man should bring the Alps or Pyrenaean mountains in the place of Mount Valerian that so he might bring an incident to play which else he could not, the scene being at Paris, truly the rigor of the rule would be followed as to the unity of the scene and its decencies, but beauty of the art, which is to please and persuade, would be lost. It is therefore that I cannot approve of this force upon nature as to the distance of places which we see done in the *Suppliants* and the *Andromache* of Euripides, in the *Captives* of Plautus and some other pieces of antiquity. I speak not here of our modern poets, for all the world knows there never was anything so monstrous in this point as the plays we have seen in Italy, Spain, and France, and indeed, except the *Horatius* of Corneille, I doubt whether we have one play where the unity of the scene is rigorously observed — at least I am sure I have not seen any.

It is necessary to give one advertisement more to the poet in this place, which is that none of his actors ought to come upon the scene without some apparent reason, since else it is not probable they should be there, and he must avoid to follow the example of a poet who made a princess come a purpose out of her tent upon the stage which was before it to say some passionate complaints of a secret misfortune of hers, for it was much more probable that she should make them in her tent.[6] Therefore he ought to have feigned either that the company of some people in the tent was importunate and troublesome to her and that to avoid them she came out, or else he ought to have given her some sudden impatience to look out, and then, as naturally upon reflections of our misfortunes we are carried to expressions of them, he might have put in her mouth what words he had thought necessary for his subject. Thus when the passion of some person upon the scene is to be showed by some narration which the spectator has had already and which cannot be repeated without disgust, one must suppose the thing to have been told that person in some place near the scene and make him come in near towards the end of it with words in his mouth expressing the knowledge of the thing and causing the passion he is to show afterwards upon the stage. The examples of this are frequent among the ancients, and the imitation of them cannot but succeed well.

Book II, Chapter 7

THE EXTENT OF THE THEATRAL ACTION, OR OF THE TIME FIT TO BE ALLOWED A DRAMATIC POEM

There is no question more debated than this which I am now treating. The poets make it their discourse, and the players scarce talk of anything else, as well as those who frequent the theatres; nay, the ladies in their *ruelles* undertake to decide it, and all this while the thing is so little understood that I have a great deal of reason to endeavor to explain it carefully. To talk with some knowledge, then, of this matter one must consider that a dramatic poem has two sorts of time, each of which has a different and proper lasting.

The first is the true time of the representation; for though this sort of poem be but an image, and so ought to be considered as having a representative being, nevertheless one ought to consider that there is a reality in the very representation. For really the actors are seen and heard, the verses are really pronounced, and one suffers really either pleasure or pain in assisting at these representations, and there is a real time spent in amusing the audience, that is from the opening of the stage to the end of the play. This time is called the lasting of the representation.

Of this time the measure can be no other but so much time as will reasonably spend the patience of the audience, for this sort of poem being made for pleasure, it ought not to weary and fatigate the mind; and it must not likewise be so short as that the spectators go away with an opinion of not having been well nor enough diverted. In all this, experience is the faithfullest guide and tells us most commonly that a play cannot last above three hours without wearying of us, nor less without coming short of pleasing us. I have seen a very learned gentleman who was present at the representation of the *Pastor Fido* in Italy who told me that never was anything so tedious, it having lasted too long, and that this play, which ravishes the reader because he can lay it by when he will, had most horridly disgusted the spectators.

There is another observation to be made here, which is that the time which we allow the representation may be spent many other ways.

The ancients had in their tragedies many different mixtures, as *mimes, pantomimes,* and other buffoons. These diversions pleased the people, and yet I do not believe they made the representations longer than those of our time, for besides that these interludes were short, their tragedies themselves were not of above a thousand verses and those verses much shorter than our heroic ones. Therefore the poet must take great care that if his play be of the ordinary length, his interludes be not too long, for let them be never so pleasing, they will disquiet the spectator in the impatience which he will naturally have to know the event and success of the story.

The other time of the dramatic poem is that of the action represented so far as it is considered as a true action and containing all that space which is necessary to the performing of those things which are to be exposed to the knowledge of the spectators from the first to the last act of the play.

Now this time is the chief time, not only because it is natural to the poem, but because also it all depends on the poet's invention and is made known by the mouth of his actors according as his ingenuity can suggest him the means of doing it, and this is the time so much talked of in our days. The three Greek tragics, Aeschylus, Euripides, and Sophocles, allow but a few hours to the lasting of the theatral action in their poems, but their example was not followed by the poets who succeed them; for Aristotle blames those of his time for giving too long an extent to the lasting of their plays, which makes him set down the rule, or rather renew it from the model of the ancients, saying that tragedy ought to be comprehended in the revolution of one sun. I do not know whether this rule was observed by those that came after him as by the authors of those tragedies which carry the name of Seneca, which are regular enough in this circumstance. But for all those that I have seen which were made at the reestablishment of learning in Spain and France, they are not only irregular in this point but in all the other most sensible rules, insomuch that one would admire that men of learning should be the authors of them. When I first had the honor to be near Cardinal Richelieu, I found the stage in great esteem but loaded with all these errors and particularly with that of exceeding the

107

time fit to be allowed in tragedy. I spoke of it in those plays which were acted at court, but I was generally opposed and, most commonly, turned into ridicule both by the poets, the actors, and the spectators. And when I, to defend myself, began to allege the ancients, I was paid with this answer, that what they had done was well for their time, but nowadays they would be laughed at if they were here, as if the general reason of mankind could grow old with time. And accordingly we see that at last it has prevailed over prejudice and ignorance to make all the world confess that the time of a tragedy ought to be short and limited. But because even in this there are different interpretations given to Aristotle, and that some poets do believe to circumscribe too narrowly the lasting of the theatral action would be to spoil most of the incidents, I will here give the true explanation of the rule and ways of practising it with success. Aristotle has said that one of the principal differences which is between an epic poem and a tragedy is that the first is not limited in any time and that the second is comprehended in the revolution of one sun. Now though Aristotle does express himself in few words, yet I cannot understand how there was ground for so much dispute. For since he says the revolution of one sun, it cannot be meant the annual revolution, for that is the time generally allowed to an epic poem, and there is none of the most indulgent that have offered to extend the rule to that excess in tragedy. It remains then to say he means the diurnal revolution but as the day is considered two ways — the one with regard to the *primum mobile*, which is called the natural day and is of twenty-four hours, and the other by the sun's presence upon the horizon between his rising and setting, which is called the artificial day. It is necessary to observe that Aristotle means only the artificial day, in the extent of which he makes the theatral action to be comprehended. Castelvetro and Piccolomini upon Aristotle's poetic are of this opinion against Segni, who extends the rule to the natural day of twenty-four hours.[7]

The reason of this is certain and founded upon the nature of dramatic poems, for this sort of poem ought to carry a sensible image of the actions of human life. Now we do not see that regularly men are busy before day nor much after night, and accordingly in all well governed places there are magistrates to watch those who employ the night, naturally designed for rest, in the actions of the day.

Besides, we have said, and it cannot be called in question, that the theatral action ought to be one, and not comprehend any other actions which are not necessary to the intrigue of the stage. Now how can that be

108

observed in a play of twenty-four hours? Would it not be a necessity that the persons acting should sleep and eat and busy themselves in many things which would not be of the subject of the play, and though the poet should say nothing of it, yet the spectators must needs conceive it so.

But, besides, the action of the stage is to be continued and not interrupted or broken. Now that could not be in a play of twenty-four hours; nature could not without some rest endure so long an action, since all that men can commonly do is to be in action for the daytime.

Moreover we cannot omit a reason of the ancients which originally is essential to tragedy, which is that the choruses which they used did not regularly use to stir off the stage for the whole play or at least from the time they first came on, and I do not know with what appearance of probability the spectators could have been persuaded that people who were never out of their sight should have stayed twenty-four hours in that place, nor how, in the truth of the action, they could imagine that those whom they represented had passed all that time without satisfying some necessities of nature.

After all, we can never better understand Aristotle than by those three excellent tragic poets whom he always proposes for examples who have regularly observed not to give above twelve hours to their plays. And I do not think that there are any of their works which do comprehend the whole space between the rising and setting of the sun.

It being most certain that their stage generally opens after sunrise and is shut up before sunset, as one may observe in the comedies of Plautus and Terence, it is therefore that Rossi,[8] an Italian, allows but eight or ten hours. And Scaliger, more rigorously but more reasonably, would have the whole action performed in six hours. It were even to be wished that the action of the poem did not take up more time than that of the representation; but that being hard and almost impossible, in certain occasions the poet has the liberty to suppose a longer time by some hours, in which the music that marks the intervals of the acts, and the relations of the actors upon the stage while others are busy off of it ([together] with the natural desire of the spectators to see the event), do all contribute very much and help to deceive the audience so as to make them think there has passed time enough for the performance of the things represented.

What we have said hitherto of Aristotle's rule might suffer some difficulty in those plays which represent actions that happened in the night, if we did not own that he has forseen the objection when he says that

109

"tragedy endeavors to comprehend its action in the revolution of one sun, or in changing that time a little," for by that means he lets us know that the poet is not always bound to place his action between sunrising and sunsetting, but may take a like time out of twenty-four hours and place his action in the night, as in the *Rhesus* of Euripides and some other plays of the ancients of which we have nothing but fragments in Athenaeus. Nay, he may take some of his time in the day and the rest in the night, as Euripides has done in his *Electra* and Plautus in his *Amphitryon*. They that upon this of Aristotle have said that he gave leave to exceed the revolution of a sun and go some hours beyond did not well understand him, having taken the word "changing" for "exceeding."

But without standing upon this scrupulous niceness, I must tell the poet that he need not fear to spoil his play by straitening his incidents in so small a compass of time; for quite contrary, it is that which shall make his play agreeable and wonderful, it is that which will afford him the means of introducing extraordinary surprises and passions which he may carry as far as he will. Let him consider well *Horatius, Cinna, Polyeucte,* and *Nicomedes,* the latter works of Monsieur Corneille, and I believe he cannot but agree to it.

Now, to contribute for my share to the necessary means of practising this rule, I here deliver my thoughts.

First, let the poet be very careful in choosing the day in which he will comprehend all the intrigues of his play, and that choice ought generally to be made from the most noble incident of the whole story, that is, from that incident which is to make the catastrophe and to which all others do tend, like lines to their center; and if he be free to take what day he will, his best will be to pitch upon that which will most easily bear the assemblage and concurrence of all the incidents of the stage. So Corneille, being to represent the death of Pompey, took the last day of his life because he could not do otherwise, but when he was to make his *Cinna,* he chose what day he pleased for to facilitate the bringing in of the conspiration of Cinna with the deliberation of Augustus whether he should forsake the Empire or no. The choice being thus made, the next sleight is to open your stage as near as it is possible to the catastrophe, that you may employ less time in the negotiation part and have more liberty in extending the passions and discourses which may please; but to execute this luckily the incidents must be prepared by ingenious contrivances, and that must appear upon occasion in the whole conduct of the action.

110

This we may observe in the *Ion* of Euripides, the *Amphitryon* of Plautus, and the *Andria* of Terence. Corneille practises it likewise well in *Horatius* and *Cinna*. The stage in *Horatius* is opened but a moment before the combat of the three Horatiuses against the three Curiatiuses who are told of their being chosen to fight against each other as soon as they come upon the stage. And Cinna had already made his conspiracy before the opening of the stage, which opens just before the sacrifice which was to be the pretext of the execution of it.

Things being thus disposed, the poet must next study to bring together the incidents all in one day so artfully that there appear no force nor constraint in the effecting of it. And to succeed in this he must rectify the time of those things that happened before the opening of the stage, and suppose some of them to come to pass that day, though they really happened before, but he must join them with so much art as they may seem to be naturally connected and not put together by the poet's invention.

Thus Sophocles makes that Creon, who was sent to Delphos to consult the Oracle, comes back just at the same time that the news comes to Thebes of the death of Polybius, king of Corinth, though these two things did not happen on the same day. So Plautus makes Amphitryon return victorious that very night that Alcmena is brought to bed of Hercules. But that which one must particularly have a care of is not to conjoin the time of the incidents with so much precipitation that probability be destroyed by it, as in the *Suppliants* of Euripides, the *Captives* of Plautus, and some other pieces of the ancients which I cannot approve of, though for some other considerations they are not unexcusable. They are indeed according to the rule of time, but without any of the graces of the art. In a word, we must still remember that Aristotle, in giving his rule of the confining tragedy to the revolution of one sun, means that the poet ought so to press his imagination as to order all the events of his theatre in that time, but so as not to offend probability, which is always the principal rule and without which all the others become no rules at all.

Book IV. Chapter 5

OF DIDACTIC DISCOURSES OR INSTRUCTIONS

This is new subject in our dramatic art, I not having found anything in those authors who have composed great volumes about it, and I am the first that have made observations upon it such as I may boldly say ought not to be despised by our poets.

I understand then by didactic discourses those maxims and general propositions which contain known truths and are only applied in the play according as the subject will allow, tending more to instruct the audience in the rules of morality than to explain any part of the intrigue afoot. An example may illustrate the thing better. Suppose then the poet had a mind to treat this proposition: "The gods are just, and were they not so, they would cease to be gods." Or this: "A general instinct cannot be suspected of error." Or this: "A subject that rebels against his prince is criminal." I say that a poet often endeavors to set out some of these maxims by a great number of verses upon which he demurs a great while, leaving all that time his subject and the intrigue of the stage and keeping himself still upon general notions.

Now as to these didactic discourses, I distinguish them into two sorts; some I call physical and the others moral ones.

I call those physical or natural which make a deduction or description of the nature, qualities, or effects of anything, without distinction whether it be in the rank of natural or supernatural things or of the number of artificial compounds.

Under the notion of moral discourses I comprehend all those instructions which contain any maxim of religion, or politics, or economics, or that anyways regard human life.

To come after this to my observations, we must lay it down as a maxim that all these didactic discourses are of their own nature unfit for the stage because they are cold and without motion, being general things which only tend to instruct the mind but not to move the heart, so that the action of the stage, which ought to warm our affections, becomes by them dull and indifferent. Young people who come to read Euripides and Sophocles admire the first much more than the latter, and yet Sophocles almost always carried the prize from Euripides upon the stage and that by the judgment of all the Athenians. This mistake of the young reader proceeds from this, that they being themselves not thoroughly instructed in those maxims and finding a great many of them in Euripides, as well about religion as politics and moral ones, they are charmed to see such truths so nobly expressed, and the things themselves, being new to them, please them beyond measure. It is for this that Quintilian, in his precepts of rhetoric, advises young people to the lecture of Euripides before Sophocles. In all which they do not observe that Sophocles makes the groundwork of his plays of those very truths as well as Euripides, but he does it with so much art that

112

he utters them in a pathetic manner as well as in a didactic one; whereby the people of Athens departed almost always pleased and charmed by the high passions which Sophocles fills his stages with, but were more used to Euripides's maxims which he so often beats over to them and by that means did not consider them as anything rare and extraordinary. And from thence it proceeds that in our modern plays those very places in which the poets have labored by noble verses and high words to express some great maxim have least succeeded, because that falling into the didactic way they forsake the business of the stage and let the action cool. From thence it comes likewise that all actors that appear with the pedantic character of teaching, such as are the governor of a young prince, a doctor, a governess, or the like, are still ill received by the audience; the very presence of them displeases and imprints the character of ridicule upon the most serious piece. I am confident that if the Linco in *Pastor fido* appeared upon our stage, he would be hissed off of it, notwithstanding all the good counsel he gives Sylvio; and that which makes me believe it the sooner is that one of our best modern plays lost half its due applause by there being a governor to a young prince who was giving him advice in the midst of most violent passions with which he was tormented, that being neither the time, nor the stage the place, for such instructions.

We do not see neither that either astrologers, conjurers, high priests, or any of that character do much take, for the very reason that they can hardly speak without pretending to teach or else talk in generals of the power of the gods, the wonderful effects of nature, and such things which cannot fail of being tedious when they are prolixly expressed. Scaliger will not allow them in the very epic poems; much less can they be received in the dramatic but ought to be quite banished the stage.

We must observe, besides, that physical instructions about nature and its effects are yet less welcome than moral ones, because that it is hard an actor should speak so long as to explain the nature of a thing without disgusting the audience, which soon grows weary of being ill taught the thing the poet would have him learn; which together with the little concern the no passion of the stage raises in him makes the whole very disagreeable. We have a notable example of this in *Mariamne*,[9] where a long discourse is made of the nature of dreams. The thing is very fine, and the nature of them well explained, but it interrupts an agitation of the stage begun by Herod's trouble at his waking. The audience would fain know the cause of his disturbance and the particulars of his dream, but instead of that,

113

there is a long discourse of the nature of dreams in general, to which the spectator gives but little attention as being thereby disappointed of his chief expectation.

To all this it may be objected that the stage is a place of public instruction, and that the dramatic poet is to instruct as well as please, and therefore that didactic discourses may be proper enough or at least ought not to be condemned.

I confess that the stage is a place of instruction, but we must well understand how that is meant. The poet ought to bring his whole action before the spectator, which ought to be so represented with all its circumstances that the audience be fully instructed; for as dramatic poetry does but imitate human actions, it does it only to instruct us by them, and that it does directly and properly. But for moral maxims which may incite us either to the love of virtue or stir us up to hate vice, it does it indirectly and by the *entremise* of the actions themselves; of which sentiment Scaliger is so much as I dare quote him for my warrantee in this opinion. Now this may be done two ways: the first, when the action of the stage is so judiciously managed that it shows the force of virtue triumphing in the midst of persecutions, after which it is often happily rewarded, but if it is totally overwhelmed by them it remains glorious even in its death. By this all the deformities of vice are discovered; it is often punished, but when even it triumphs and overcomes, it is in abomination with the audience who thereupon are apt to conclude with themselves that it is better to embrace virtue through the hazard of persecution than to follow vice even with hopes of impunity.

It is thus principally that the stage ought to be instructive to the public — by the knowledge of things represented; and I have always observed that it is not agreeable to the audience that a man who swerves from the way of virtue should be set right and repent by the strength of precepts and sentences. We rather desire it should be by some adventure that presses him and forces him to take up reasonable and virtuous sentiments. We should hardly endure that Herod should recall his sentence against Mariamne upon a remonstrance of one of the seven wise men of Greece; but we are pleased to see that after the death of the queen, his love becomes his tormentor, and, having opened his eyes, drives him into so sincere a repentance that he is ready to sacrifice his life to the regret he has for his crime.

As for the other way of teaching morality, it depends much on the in-

François Hédelin

geniousness of the poet when he strengthens his theatral action with divers pithy and bold truths, which being imperceptibly worked into his play are, as it were, the nerves and strength of it. For, in a word, that which I condemn in common didactics is their style and manner of expression, not the things themselves, since those great truths which are, as it were, the foundation of the conduct of human actions, I am so far from banishing them off the stage that quite contrary I think them very necessary and ornamental — which to attain I give these following observations.

First, these general maxims must be so fastened to the subject and linked by many circumstances with the persons acting that the actor may seem to think more of that concern of his he is about than of saying fine things; that is, to speak in terms of rhetoric, he must reduce the thesis to the hypothesis and of universal propositions make particular applications, for by this means the poet avoids the suspicion of aiming to instruct pedantically, since his actors do not leave their business which they are about. For example, I would not have an actor spend many words to prove that "Virtue is always persecuted," but he may say to the party concerned, "Do you think to have better measure than virtue has always had, and can you expect to be privileged from persecution more than Socrates or Cato?" And so continue a little, speaking still to the party present and upon the subject in hand, by which means these discourses seem a little to keep off from being too general precepts and so, disgust the less.

Secondly, in all these occasions the poet must use figurative speech, either by interrogation, irony, or others that his fancy shall suggest; for these figures, by not circumstancing minutely the general propositions, make them more florid, and so, by ornaments, free them from the didactic character. As, for example, if there be a design of advising a young woman to obey her parents, instead of preaching downright obedience to her, I think an irony would do better. As thus: "That's a fine way indeed for a virtuous young lady to attain the reputation of a good daughter, to be carried away by her own passions and neglect not only the censure of the best sort of people but break through all the fences of duty and honor."

My third observation is that when any of these great maxims are to be proposed bluntly and in plain words, it be done in as few as may be; by that means they do not cool the stage but add something to the variety of it. But there must be care taken that this do not happen in the midst of a violent passion, for besides that in those cases men do not naturally speak sentences, the actor cannot then appear with that moderation which those

115

reflections require. Seneca is very guilty of this fault in all his tragedies, where most commonly in the heat of passion all his fine commonplaces are bestowed upon the audience.

We have, nevertheless, some examples of didactic propositions made in direct terms and at length, not without some success, in Corneille, which to attain as well as he requires the same ingenuity and art. The expressions must be strong and seem to have been said only for that particular subject to which they are applied, and that requires a particular genius and much study to accomplish.

I have observed, besides, that common truths, though in a didactic style, yet do very well upon the stage in the mouth of a rogue or a cheat when his character is known; for the spectator is delighted to see him cunningly use all the maxims and discourses of a good man to intents and purposes quite contrary, so that by that means it is all figurative and moves the attention of the audience.

One may likewise successfully enough burlesque all these common truths, but that can be performed nowhere but in comedy, where, by that means, they forsake their natural state and are disguised under a new appearance which causes both variety and ornament. But tragedy in its own nature is too grave to admit of anything so low and buffoon as this would be; neither do I remember to have met with anything of that kind in any serious tragedy — I say serious tragedy because that in satirical tragedy there was admitted a mixture of heroic actions and low buffooneries, and therefore this disguising of serious precepts might have room among the rest in them.

❧ 1660

Pierre Corneille OF THE THREE UNITIES OF ACTION,

TIME, AND PLACE

The two preceding discourses and the critical examination of the plays which my first two volumes contain have furnished me so many opportunities to explain my thoughts on these matters that there would be little left for me to say if I absolutely forbade myself to repeat.

I hold then, as I have already said, that in comedy, unity of action consists in the unity of plot or the obstacle to the plans of the principal actors, and in tragedy in the unity of peril, whether the hero falls victim to it or escapes. It is not that I claim that several perils cannot be allowed in the latter or several plots or obstacles in the former, provided that one passes necessarily from one to the other; for then escape from the first peril does not make the action complete since the escape leads to another danger; and the resolution of one plot does not put the actors at rest since they are confounded afresh in another. My memory does not furnish me any ancient examples of this multiplicity of perils linked each to each without the destruction of the unity of action; but I have noted independent double action as a defect in *Horace* and in *Théodore*, for it is not necessary that the first kill his sister upon gaining his victory nor that the other give herself up to martyrdom after having escaped prostitution; and if the death of Polyxène and that of Astyanax in Seneca's *Trojan Women* do not produce the same irregularity I am very much mistaken.

In the second place, the term unity of action does not mean that tragedy should show only one action on the stage. The one which the poet chooses for his subject must have a beginning, a middle, and an end; and not only are these three parts separate actions which find their conclusion in the principal one, but, moreover, each of them may contain several others with the same subordination. There must be only one complete action, which leaves the mind of the spectator serene; but that action can become complete only through several others which are less perfect and which, by serv-

117

ing as preparation, keep the spectator in a pleasant suspense. This is what must be contrived at the end of each act in order to give continuity to the action. It is not necessary that we know exactly what the actors are doing in the intervals which separate the acts, nor even that they contribute to the action when they do not appear on the stage; but it is necessary that each act leave us in the expectation of something which is to take place in the following one.

If you asked me what Cléopâtre is doing in *Rodogune* between the time when she leaves her two sons in the second act until she rejoins Antiochus in the fourth, I should be unable to tell you, and I do not feel obliged to account for her; but the end of this second act prepares us to see an amicable effort by the two brothers to rule and to hide Rodogune from the venomous hatred of their mother. The effect of this is seen in the third act, whose ending prepares us again to see another effort by Antiochus to win back these two enemies one after the other and for what Séleucus does in the fourth, which compels that unnatural mother [Cleopatra] to resolve upon what she tries to accomplish in the fifth, whose outcome we await with suspense.

In *Le Menteur* the actors presumably make use of the whole interval between the third and fourth acts to sleep; their rest, however, does not impede the continuity of the action between those two acts because the third does not contain a complete event. Dorante ends it with his plan to seek ways to win back the trust of Lucrèce, and at the very beginning of the next he appears so as to be able to talk to one of her servants and to her, should she show herself.

When I say that it is not necessary to account for what the actors do when they are not on stage, I do not mean that it is not sometimes very useful to give such an accounting, but only that one is not forced to do it, and that one ought to take the trouble to do so only when what happens behind the scenes is necessary for the understanding of what is to take place before the spectators. Thus I say nothing of what Cléopâtre did between the second and the fourth acts, because during all that time she can have done nothing important as regards the principal action which I am preparing for; but I point out in the very first lines of the fifth act that she has used the interval between these latter two for the killing of Séleucus, because that death is part of the action. This is what leads me to state that the poet is not required to show all the particular actions which bring about the principal one; he must choose to show those which are the most ad-

118

vantageous, whether by the beauty of the spectacle or by the brilliance or violence of the passions they produce, or by some other attraction which is connected with them, and to hide the others behind the scenes while informing the spectator of them by a narration or by some other artistic device; above all, he must remember that they must all be so closely connected that the last are produced by the preceding and that all have their source in the protasis which ought to conclude the first act. This rule, which I have established in my first *Discourse*, although it is new and contrary to the usage of the ancients, is founded on two passages of Aristotle. Here is the first of them: "There is a great difference," he says, "between events which succeed each other and those which occur because of others." [1] The Moors come into the *Cid* after the death of the Count and not because of the death of the Count; and the fisherman comes into *Don Sanche* after Charles is suspected of being the Prince of Aragon and not because he is suspected of it; thus both are to be criticized. The second passage is even more specific and says precisely "that everything that happens in tragedy must arise necessarily or probably from what has gone before." [2]

The linking of the scenes which unites all the individual actions of each act and of which I have spoken in criticizing *La Suivante* is a great beauty in a poem and one which serves to shape continuity of action through continuity of presentation; but, in the end, it is only a beauty and not a rule. The ancients did not always abide by it although most of their acts have but two or three scenes. This made things much simpler for them than for us, who often put as many as nine or ten scenes into each act. I shall cite only two examples of the scorn with which they treated this principle: one is from Sophocles, in *Ajax*, whose monologue before he kills himself has no connection with the preceding scene; the other is from the third act of Terence's *The Eunuch*, where Antipho's soliloquy has no connection with Chremes and Pythias who leave the stage when he enters. The scholars of our century, who have taken the ancients for models in the tragedies they have left us, have even more neglected that linking than did the ancients, and one need only glance at the plays of Buchanan, Grotius, and Heinsius, of which I spoke in the discussion of *Polyeucte*, to agree on that point. We have so far accustomed our audiences to this careful linking of scenes that they cannot now witness a detached scene without considering it a defect; the eye and even the ear are outraged by it even before the mind has been able to reflect upon it. The fourth act of *Cinna* falls below the others through this flaw; and what formerly was not a rule has become one now through the assiduousness of our practice.

I have spoken of three sorts of linkings in the discussion of *La Suivante*: I have shown myself averse to those of sound, indulgent to those of sight, favorable to those of presence and speech; but in these latter I have confused two things which ought to be separated. Links of presence and speech both have, no doubt, all the excellence imaginable; but there are links of speech without presence and of presence without speech which do not reach the same level of excellence. An actor who speaks to another from a hiding-place without showing himself forms a link of speech without presence which is always effective; but that rarely happens. A man who remains on stage merely to hear what will be said by those whom he sees making their entrance forms a link of presence without speech; this is often clumsy and falls into mere pretense, being contrived more to accede to this new convention which is becoming a precept than for any need dictated by the plot of the play. Thus, in the third act of *Pompée*, Achorée, after having informed Charmion of the reception Caesar gave to the king when he presented to him the head of that hero, remains on the stage where he sees the two of them come together merely to hear what they will say and report it to Cléopâtre. Ammon does the same thing in the fourth act of *Andromède* for the benefit of Phinée, who retires when he sees the king and all his court arriving. Characters who become mute connect rather badly scenes in which they play little part and in which they count for nothing. It is another matter when they hide in order to find out some important secret from those who are speaking and who think they are not overheard, for then the interest which they have in what is being said, added to a reasonable curiosity to find out what they cannot learn in any other way, gives them an important part in the action despite their silence; but in these two examples Ammon and Achorée lend so cold a presence to the scenes they overhear that, to be perfectly frank, whatever feigned reason I give them to serve as pretext for their action, they remain there only to connect the scenes with those that precede, so easily can both plays dispense with what they do.

Although the action of the dramatic poem must have its unity, one must consider both its parts: the complication and the resolution. "The complication is composed," according to Aristotle, "in part of what has happened off stage before the beginning of the action which is there described, and in part from what happens on stage; the rest belongs to the resolution.

Pierre Corneille

The change of fortune forms the separation of these two parts. Everything which precedes it is in the first part, and this change, with what follows it, concerns the other." [3] The complication depends entirely upon the choice and industrious imagination of the poet and no rule can be given for it, except that in it he ought to order all things according to probability or necessity, a point which I have discussed in the second *Discourse*; to this I add one piece of advice, which is that he involve himself as little as possible with things which have happened before the action he is presenting. Such narrations are annoying, usually because they are not expected, and they disturb the mind of the spectator, who is obliged to burden his memory with what has happened ten or twelve years before in order to understand what he is about to see; but narrations which describe things which happen and take place behind the scenes once the action has started always produce a better effect because they are awaited with some curiosity and are a part of the action which is being shown. One of the reasons why so many illustrious critics favor *Cinna* above anything else I have done is that it contains no narration of the past, the one Cinna makes in describing his plot to Emilie being rather an ornament which tickles the mind of the spectators than a necessary marshaling of the details they must know and impress upon their memories for the understanding of what is to come. Emilie informs them adequately in the first two scenes that he is conspiring against Augustus in her favor, and if Cinna merely told her that the plotters are ready for the following day he would advance the action just as much as by the hundred lines he uses to tell both what he said to them and the way in which they received his words. There are plots which begin at the very birth of the hero like that of *Héraclius*, but these great efforts of the imagination demand an extraordinary attention of the spectator and often keep him from taking a real pleasure in the first performances, so much do they weary him.

In the resolution I find two things to avoid: the mere change of intention and the machine. Not much skill is required to finish a poem when he who has served as the obstacle to the plans of the principal actors for four acts desists in the fifth without being constrained to do so by any remarkable event; I have spoken of this in the first *Discourse* and I shall add nothing to that here. The machine requires no more skill when it is used only to bring down a god who straightens everything out when the actors are unable to do so. It is thus that Apollo functions in the *Orestes*: this prince and his friend Pylades, accused by Tyndarus and Menelaus of the

121

death of Clytemnestra and condemned after prosecution by them, seize Helen and Hermione; they kill, or think they kill the first, and threaten to do so the same with the other if the sentence pronounced against them is not revoked. To smooth out these difficulties Euripides seeks nothing subtler than to bring Apollo down from heaven, and he, by absolute authority, orders that Orestes marry Hermione and Pylades Electra; and lest the death of Helen prove an obstacle to this, it being improbable that Hermione would marry Orestes since he had just killed her mother, Apollo informs them that she is not dead, that he has protected her from their blows and carried her off to heaven at the moment when they thought they were killing her. This use of the machine is entirely irrelevant, being founded in no way on the rest of the play, and makes a faulty resolution. But I find a little too harsh the opinion of Aristotle, who puts on the same level the chariot Medea uses to flee from Corinth after the vengeance she has taken on Creon. It seems to me there is a sufficient basis for this in the fact that she has been made a magician and that actions of hers as far surpassing natural forces as that one have been mentioned in the play. After what she did for Jason at Colchis and after she had made his father Aeson young again following his return, and after she had attached invisible fire to the gift she gave to Creusa, the flying chariot is not improbable and the poem has no need of other preparation for that extraordinary effect. Seneca gives it preparation by this line which Medea speaks to her nurse:

Tuum quoque ipsa corpus hinc mecum aveham; [4]

and I by this one which she speaks to Aegeus

I shall follow you tomorrow by a new road.

Thus the condemnation of Euripides, who took no precautions, may be just and yet not fall on Seneca or on me; and I have no need to contradict Aristotle in order to justify myself on this point.

From the action I turn to the acts, each of which ought to contain a portion of it, but not so equal a portion that more is not reserved for the last than for the others and less given to the first than to the others. Indeed, in the first act one may do no more than depict the moral nature of the characters and mark off how far they have got in the story which is to be presented. Aristotle does not prescribe the number of the acts; Horace limits it to five; [5] and although he prohibits having fewer, the Spaniards are obstinate enough to stop at three and the Italians often do the same thing. The Greeks used to separate the acts by the chanting of the chorus, and since I think it reasonable to believe that in some of their poems they made it chant more than four times, I should not want to say they never exceeded five. This way of distinguishing the acts was less handy than ours, for either they paid attention to what the chorus was chanting or they did not; if they did, the mind of the spectators was too tense and had no time in which to rest; if they did not, attention was too much dissipated by the length of the chant, and when a new act began, an effort of memory was needed to recall to the imagination what had been witnessed and at what point the action had been interrupted. Our orchestra presents neither of these two inconveniences; the mind of the spectator relaxes while the music is playing and even reflects on what he has seen, to praise it or to find fault with it depending on whether he has been pleased or displeased; and the short time the orchestra is allowed to play leaves his impressions so fresh that when the actors return he does not need to make an effort to recall and resume his attention.

The number of scenes in each act has never been prescribed by rule, but since the whole act must have a certain number of lines which make its length proportionate to that of the others, one may include in it more or fewer scenes depending on whether they are long or short to fill up the time which the whole act is to consume. One ought, if possible, to account for the entrance and exit of each actor; I consider this rule indispensable, especially for the exit, and think there is nothing so clumsy as an actor who leaves the stage merely because he has no more lines to speak.

I should not be so rigorous for the entrances. The audience expects the actor, and although the setting represents the room or the study of whoever is speaking, yet he cannot make his appearance there unless he comes out from behind the tapestry, and it is not always easy to give a reason for what he has just done in town before returning home, since sometimes it is even probable that he has not gone out at all. I have never seen anybody take offense at seeing Emilie begin *Cinna* without saying why she has come to her room; she is presumed to be there before the play begins, and it is only stage necessity which makes her appear from behind the scenes to come there. Thus I should willingly dispense from the rigors of the rule the first scene of each act but not the others, because once an actor is on the stage anyone who enters must have a reason to speak to him or, at least, must profit from the opportunity to do so when it offers. Above all, when an actor enters twice in one act, in comedy or in tragedy, he must either lead one to expect that he will soon return when he leaves the first time, like Horace in the second act and Julie in the third act of *Horace*, or explain on returning why he has come back so soon.

Aristotle wishes the well-made tragedy to be beautiful and capable of pleasing without the aid of actors and quite aside from performance.[6] So that the reader may more easily experience that pleasure, his mind, like that of the spectator, must not be hindered, because the effort he is obliged to make to conceive and to imagine the play for himself lessens the satisfaction which he will get from it. Therefore, I should be of the opinion that the poet ought to take great care to indicate in the margin the less important actions which do not merit being included in the lines, and which might even mar the dignity of the verse if the author lowered himself to express them. The actor easily fills this need on the stage, but in a book one would often be reduced to guessing and sometimes one might even guess wrong, unless one were informed in this way of these little things. I admit that this is not the practice of the ancients; but you must also allow me that because they did not do it they have left us many obscurities in their poems which only masters of dramatic art can explain; even so, I am not sure they succeed as often as they think they do. If we forced ourselves to follow the method of the ancients completely, we should make no distinction between acts and scenes because the Greeks did not. This failure on their part is often the reason that I do not know how many acts there are in their plays, nor whether at the end of an act the player withdraws so as to allow the chorus to chant, or whether he remains on stage without any action while the chorus is chanting, because neither they nor their interpreters have deigned to give us a word of indication in the margin.

We have another special reason for not neglecting that helpful little device as they did: this is that printing puts our plays in the hands of actors who tour the provinces and whom we can thus inform of what they ought to do, for they would do some very odd things if we did not help them by these notes. They would find themselves in great difficulty at the fifth act of plays that end happily, where we bring together all the actors on the stage (a thing which the ancients did not do); they would often say to one what is meant for another, especially when the same actor must speak to three or four people one after the other. When there is a whispered command to make, like Cléopâtre's to Laonice which sends her to seek poison,[7] an aside would be necessary to express this in verse if we were to do without the marginal indications, and that seems to me much more intolerable

124

than the notes, which give us the real and only way, following the opinion of Aristotle, of making the tragedy as beautiful in the reading as in performance, by making it easy for the reader to imagine what the stage presents to the view of the spectators.

The rule of the unity of time is founded on this statement of Aristotle "that the tragedy ought to enclose the duration of its action in one journey of the sun or try not to go much beyond it." [8] These words gave rise to a famous dispute as to whether they ought to be understood as meaning a natural day of twenty-four hours or an artificial day of twelve; each of the two opinions has important partisans, and, for myself, I find that there are subjects so difficult to limit to such a short time that not only should I grant the twenty-four full hours but I should make use of the license which the philosopher gives to exceed them a little and should push the total without scruple as far as thirty. There is a legal maxim which says that we should broaden the mercies and narrow the rigors of the law, *odia restringenda, favores ampliandi*; and I find that an author is hampered enough by this constraint which forced some of the ancients to the very edge of the impossible. Euripides in *The Suppliants*, makes Theseus leave Athens with an army, fight a battle beneath the walls of Thebes, which was ten or twelve leagues away, and return victorious in the following act; and between his departure and the arrival of the messenger who comes to tell the story of his victory, the chorus has only thirty-six lines to speak.[9] That makes good use of such a short time. Aeschylus makes Agamemnon come back from Troy with even greater speed. He had agreed with Clytemnestra, his wife, that as soon as the city was taken he would inform her by signal fires built on the intervening mountains, of which the second would be lighted as soon as the first was seen, the third at the sight of the second, and so on; by this means she was to learn the great news the same night. However, scarcely had she learned it from the signal fires when Agamemnon arrives, whose ship, although battered by a storm, if memory serves, must have traveled as fast as the eye could see the lights.[10] *The Cid* and *Pompée*, where the action is a little precipitate, are far from taking so much license; and if they force ordinary probability in some way, at least they do not go as far as such impossibilities.

Many argue against this rule, which they call tyrannical, and they would be right if it were founded only on the authority of Aristotle; but what should make it acceptable is the fact that common sense supports it. The dramatic poem is an imitation, or rather a portrait of human actions, and

125

it is beyond doubt that portraits gain in excellence in proportion as they resemble the original more closely. A performance lasts two hours and would resemble reality perfectly if the action it presented required no more for its actual occurrence. Let us then not settle on twelve or twenty-four hours, but let us compress the action of the poem into the shortest possible period, so that the performance may more closely resemble reality and thus be more nearly perfect. Let us give, if that is possible, to the one no more than the two hours which the other fills. I do not think that *Rodogune* requires much more, and perhaps two hours would be enough for *Cinna*. It we cannot confine the action within the two hours, let us take four, six, or ten, but let us not go much beyond twenty-four for fear of falling into lawlessness and of so far reducing the scale of the portrait that it no longer has its proportionate dimensions and is nothing but imperfection.

Most of all, I should like to leave the matter of duration to the imagination of the spectators and never make definite the time the action requires unless the subject needs this precision, but especially not when probability is a little forced, as in the *Cid*, because precision serves only to make the crowded action obvious to the spectator. Even when no violence is done to a poem by the necessity of obeying this rule, why must one state at the beginning that the sun is rising, that it is noon at the third act, and that the sun is setting at the end of the last act? This is only an obtrusive affectation; it is enough to establish the possibility of the thing in the time one gives to it and that one be able to determine the time easily if one wishes to pay attention to it, but without being compelled to concern oneself with the matter. Even in those actions which take no longer than the performance it would be clumsy to point out that a half hour has elapsed between the beginning of one act and the beginning of the next.

I repeat what I have said elsewhere,[11] that when we take a longer time, as, for instance, ten hours, I should prefer that the eight extra be used up in the time between the acts and that each act should have as its share only as much time as performance requires especially when all scenes are closely linked together. I think, however, that the fifth act, by special privilege, has the right to accelerate time so that the part of the action which it presents may use up more time than is necessary for performance. The reason for this is that the spectator is by then impatient to see the end, and when the outcome depends on actors who are off stage, all the dialogue given to those who are on stage awaiting news of the others drags and action seems to halt. There is no doubt that from the point where Phocas exits in the fifth act of *Héraclius* until Amyntas enters to relate the manner of his death, more time is needed for what happens off stage than for the speaking of the lines in which Héraclius, Martian, and Pulchérie complain of their misfortune. Prusias and Flaminius, in the fifth act of *Nicomède*, do not have the time they would need to meet at sea, take counsel with each other, and return to the defense of the queen; and the Cid has not enough time to fight a duel with Don Sanche during the conversations of the Infanta with Léonor and of Chimène with Elvire. I was aware of this and yet have had no scruples about this acceleration of which, perhaps, one might find several examples among the ancients, but the laziness of which I have spoken will force me to rest content with this one, which is from the *Andria* of Terence. Simo slips his son Pamphilus into the house of Glycerium in order to get the old man, Crito, to come out and to clear up with him the question of the birth of his mistress, who happens to be the daughter of Chremes. Pamphilus enters the house, speaks to Crito, asks him for the favor and returns with him; and during this exit, this request, and this re-entry, Simo and Chremes, who remain on stage, speak only one line each, which could not possibly give Pamphilus more than time enough to ask where Crito is, certainly not enough to talk with him and to explain to him the reasons for which he should reveal what he knows about the birth of the unknown girl.

When the conclusion of the action depends on actors who have not left the stage and about whom no one is awaiting news, as in *Cinna* and *Rodogune*, the fifth act has no need of this privilege because then all the action takes place in plain sight, as does not happen when part of it occurs off stage after the beginning of the act. The other acts do not merit the same freedom. If there is not time enough to bring back an actor who has made his exit, or to indicate what he has done since that exit, the accounting can be postponed to the following act; and the music, which separates the two acts, may use up as much time as is necessary; but in the fifth act no postponement is possible: attention is exhausted and the end must come quickly.

I cannot forget that although we must reduce the whole tragic action to one day, we can nevertheless make known by a narration or in some other more artful way what the hero of the tragedy has been doing for several years, because there are plays in which the crux of the plot lies in an obscurity of birth which must be brought to light, as in *Oedipus*. I shall not say again that the less one burdens oneself with past actions, the more favorable the spectator will be, because of the lesser degree of trouble he is given when everything takes place in the present and no demands are made on his memory except for what he has seen; but I cannot forget that the choice of a day both illustrious and long-awaited is a great ornament to a poem. The opportunity for this does not always present itself, and in all that I have written until now you will find only four of that kind: the day in *Horace* when two nations are to decide the question of supremacy of empire by a battle; and the ones in *Rodogune, Andromède,* and *Don Sanche.* In *Rodogune* it is a day chosen by two sovereigns for the signature of a treaty of peace between the hostile crowns, for a complete reconciliation of the two rival governments through a marriage, and for the elucidation of a more than twenty-year-old secret concerning the right of succession of one of the twin princes on which the fate of the kingdom depends, as does the outcome of both their loves. The days in *Andromède* and *Don Sanche* are not of lesser importance, but, as I have just said, such opportunities do not often present themselves, and in the rest of my works I have been able to choose days remarkable only for what chance makes happen on them and not by the use to which public arrangements destined them long ago.

As for the unity of place, I find no rule concerning it in either Aristotle or Horace. This is what leads many people to believe that this rule was established only as a consequence of the unity of one day, and leads them to imagine that one can stretch the unity of place to cover the points to which a man may go and return in twenty-four hours. This opinion is a little too free, and if one made an actor travel post-haste, the two sides of the theater might represent Paris and Rouen. I could wish, so that the spectator is not at all disturbed, that what is performed before him in two hours might actually be able to take place in two hours, and that what he is shown in a stage setting which does not change might be limited to a room or a hall depending on a choice made beforehand; but often that is so awkward, if not impossible, that one must necessarily find some way to enlarge the place as also the time of the action. I have shown exact unity of place in *Horace, Polyeucte,* and *Pompée,* but for that it was necessary to present either only one woman, as in *Polyeucte*; or to arrange that the two who are presented are such close friends and have such closely related interests that they can be always together, as in *Horace*; or that they may react as in *Pompée* where the stress of natural curiosity drives Cléopâtre from her apartments in the second act and Cornélie in the fifth; and both

128

enter the great hall of the king's palace in anticipation of the news they are expecting. The same thing is not true of *Rodogune*: Cléopâtre and she have interests which are too divergent to permit them to express their most secret thoughts in the same place. I might say of that play what I have said of *Cinna*, where, in general, everything happens in Rome and, in particular, half of the action takes place in the quarters of Auguste and half of it in Emilie's apartments. Following that arrangement, the first act of this tragedy would be laid in Rodogune's antechamber, the second, in Cléopâtre's apartments, the third, in Rodogune's; but if the fourth act can begin in Rodogune's apartments it cannot finish there, and what Cléopâtre says to her two sons one after the other would be badly out of place there. The fifth act needs a throne room where a great crowd can be gathered. The same problem is found in *Héraclius*. The first act could very well take place in Phocas's quarters, the second, in Léontine's apartments; but if the third begins in Pulchérie's rooms, it cannot end there, and it is outside the bounds of probability that Phocas should discuss the death of her brother in Pulchérie's apartments.

The ancients, who made their kings speak in a public square, easily kept a rigorous unity of place in their tragedies. Sophocles, however, did not observe it in his *Ajax*, when the hero leaves the stage to find a lonely place in which to kill himself and does so in full view of the people; this easily leads to the conclusion that the place where he kills himself is not the one he has been seen to leave, since he left it only to choose another.

We do not take the same liberty of drawing kings and princesses from their apartments, and since often the difference and the opposition on the part of those who are lodged in the same palace do not allow them to take others into their confidence or to disclose their secrets in the same room, we must seek some other compromise about unity of place if we want to keep it intact in our poems; otherwise we should have to decide against many plays which we see succeeding brilliantly.

I hold, then, that we ought to seek exact unity as much as possible, but as this unity does not suit every kind of subject, I should be very willing to concede that a whole city has unity of place. Not that I should want the stage to represent the whole city, that would be somewhat too large, but only two or three particular places enclosed within its walls. Thus the scene of *Cinna* does not leave Rome, passing from the apartments of Auguste to the house of Emilie. *Le Menteur* takes place in the Tuileries and in the Place Royale at Paris, and *La Suite* shows us the prison and

129

Mélisse's house at Lyons. *The Cid* increases even more the number of particular places without leaving Seville; and since the close linking of scenes is not observed in that play, the stage in the first act is supposed to represent Chimène's house, the Infante's apartments in the king's palace, and the public square; the second adds to these the king's chamber. No doubt there is some excess in this freedom. In order to rectify in some way this multiplication of places when it is inevitable, I should wish two things done: first, that the scene should never change in a given act but only between the acts, as is done in the first three acts of *Cinna*; the other, that these two places should not need different stage settings and that neither of the two should ever be named, but only the general place which includes them both, as Paris, Rome, Lyons, Constantinople, and so forth. This would help to deceive the spectator, who, seeing nothing that would indicate the difference in the places, would not notice the change, unless it was maliciously and critically pointed out, a thing which few are capable of doing, most spectators being warmly intent upon the action which they see on the stage. The pleasure they take in it is the reason why they do not seek out its imperfections lest they lose their taste for it; and they admit such an imperfection only when forced, when it is too obvious, as in *Le Menteur* and *La Suite*, where the different settings force them to recognize the multiplicity of places in spite of themselves.

But since people of opposing interests cannot with verisimilitude unfold their secrets in the same place, and since they are sometimes introduced into the same act through the linking of scenes which the unity of place necessarily produces, one must find some means to make it compatible with the contradiction which rigorous probability finds in it, and consider how to preserve the fourth act of *Rodogune* and the third of *Héraclius*, in both of which I have already pointed out the contradiction which lies in having enemies speak in the same place. Jurists allow legal fictions, and I should like, following their example, to introduce theatrical fictions by which one could establish a theatrical place which would not be Cléopâtre's chamber nor Rodogune's, in the play of that name, nor that of Phocas, of Léontine or of Pulchérie in *Héraclius*, but a room contiguous to all these other apartments, to which I should attribute these two privileges: first, that each of those who speaks in it is presumed to enjoy the same secrecy there as if he were in his own room; and second, that whereas in the usual arrangement it is sometimes proper for those who are on stage to go off, in order to speak privately with others in their rooms, these latter might meet the former on stage without shocking convention, so as to preserve both the unity of place and the linking of scenes. Thus Rodogune, in the first act, encounters Laonice, whom she must send for so as to speak with her; and, in the fourth act, Cléopâtre encounters Antiochus on the very spot where he has just moved Rodogune to pity, even though in utter verisimilitude the prince ought to seek out his mother in her own room since she hates the princess too much to come to speak to him in Rodogune's, which, following the first scene, would be the locus of the whole act, if one did not introduce that compromise which I have mentioned into the rigorous unity of place.

Many of my plays will be at fault in the unity of place if this compromise is not accepted, for I shall abide by it always in the future when I am not able to satisfy the ultimate rigor of the rule. I have been able to reduce only three plays, *Horace*, *Polyeucte*, and *Pompée,* to the requirements of the rule. If I am too indulgent with myself as far as the others are concerned, I shall be even more so for those which may succeed on the stage through some appearance of regularity. It is easy for critics to be severe; but if they were to give ten or a dozen plays to the public, they might perhaps slacken the rules more than I do, as soon as they have recognized through experience what constraint their precision brings about and how many beautiful things it banishes from our stage. However that may be, these are my opinions, or if you prefer, my heresies concerning the principal points of the dramatic art, and I do not know how better to make the ancient rules agree with modern pleasures. I do not doubt that one might easily find better ways of doing that, and I shall be ready to accept them when they have been put into practice as successfully as, by common consent, mine have been.

Charles de Saint-Evremond SELECTIONS FROM

"THE WORKS OF M. DE SAINT-EVREMOND"

1668

A DISSERTATION ON RACINE'S TRAGEDY CALLED
"THE GRAND ALEXANDER"

Since I have read *The Grand Alexander*, the old age of Corneille does not so much alarm me, and I am not so apprehensive that the writing of tragedies will end with him.[1] However, I could wish that before his death he would adopt the author of this piece, and like a tender father give a right cast to the judgment of one who alone deserves to be his successor. I wish that he would give him a good taste of antiquity, which he enjoys to so much advantage; that he would make him enter into the genius of those dead nations, and know judiciously the character of heroes that are now no more. This is, in my opinion, the only thing which is wanting in so great a genius. Some of his thoughts are strong and bold; his expressions equal the force of his thoughts. But then you must give me leave to say he is not acquainted with Alexander or Porus. By his performance one would think that he had a mind to give the world a greater idea of Porus than of Alexander, in which it was not possible for him to succeed; for the history of Alexander, as true as it is, has much of the air of a romance in it, and for an author to make a greater hero than him is to affect to deal in fiction, and rob his work not only of the credit of truth but the agreeableness of probability. Let us not therefore imagine anything greater than this conqueror of the world, otherwise our imaginations will range too far and soar too high. If we would give other heroes an advantage over him, let us take from them the vices which he had and give them the virtues which he had not. Let us not make Scipio greater, although there never was amongst the Romans a soul so aspiring as his; he should be made more just, more disposed to do good, more moderate, more temperate, and more virtuous.

132

Charles de Saint-Evremond

Let not those that are most partial to Caesar against Alexander allege in his favor either passion of glory, greatness of soul, or firmness of resolution. These qualities are so conspicuously shining in the Grecian that to have had them in a higher degree would have been to have had them to excess; but let them make the Roman more wise in his undertakings, more dexterous in his affairs, one that better understood his own interests and was more master of himself in his passions.

A very nice judge of the merits of men is contented to compare to Alexander the man whom he thought worthy of the highest character. He durst not attribute to him greater qualities, but took away from him the bad: *Magno illi Alexandro, sed sobrio nec iracundo simillimus.*[2]

Perhaps these considerations influenced our author in some measure; perhaps, to make Porus the greater man without diving into fables, he thought it convenient to lessen his Alexander. If that was his design, it is impossible for him to have executed it better, for he has made him so moderate a prince that a hundred others may be preferred to him as well as Porus. Not but that Hephestion gives us a fine idea of him, that Taxila and Porus himself speak advantageously enough of his greatness; but when he appears himself he has not force enough to sustain it, unless out of modesty he has a mind to appear an ordinary man amongst the Indians in a just repentance for having been ambitious to pass for a god amongst the Persians. To speak seriously, I can here discern nothing of Alexander but his bare name; his genius, his humor, his qualities appear to me nowhere. I expect to find in an impetuous hero such extraordinary motions as should excite my passion, but I find a prince of so little spirit that he makes no manner of impression upon me. I imagined to find in Porus a greatness of soul which would be somewhat more surprising to us; an Indian hero should have a different character from one of ours. Another heaven, if I may so speak, another sun and another earth produce other animals and other fruits. The men seem to be of another make, by the difference of their faces, and still more, if I dare say so, by a distinction of reason. Both their morals and a wisdom peculiar to their climate seem there to overrule and guide another sort of men in another world. Porus, however, whom Quintus Curtius[3] describes an utter stranger to the Greeks and Persians, is here purely French. Instead of transporting us to the Indies, he is carried into France, where he is so well acquainted with our humor that he seems to have been born or at least to have passed the greatest part of his life among us.

133

They that undertake to represent some hero of ancient times should enter into the genius of the nation to which he belonged, of the time in which he lived, and particularly into his own. A writer ought to describe a king of Asia otherwise than a Roman consul: one should speak like an absolute monarch, who disposes of his subjects as his slaves; the other, like a magistrate, who only puts the laws in execution, and makes their authority respected by a free people. An old Roman should be described furious for the public good, and moved by a fierce sense of liberty, different from a flatterer of Tiberius's time, who knew nothing but interest, and abandoned himself to the slavery of the age. We should not make the same description of persons of the same condition and the same time when history gives us different characters of them. It would be ridiculous to make the same description of Cato and Caesar, Catiline and Cicero, Brutus and Mark Antony, under pretence that they lived at the same time in the same republic. The spectator, who sees these ancients represented upon our theatres, follows the same rules to judge exactly of them as the poet doth to describe them well, and the better to succeed in this he removes his mind from all that he sees in fashion; he endeavors to disengage himself from the humor of his own time, he renounces the inclination of his own nature if it is opposite to that of the persons represented: for the dead cannot know our manners, but reason, which is of all times, may make us entertain theirs.

One of the greatest faults of our nation is to make all center in it, even to that degree as to call those very persons strangers in their own country who have not exactly either our air or manners. Upon this score we are justly reproached for not knowing how to esteem things but by the relation they have to us, of which Corneille made a sad but undeserved experiment in his *Sophonisbe*. Mairet, who described his [Sophonisbe as] unfaithful to old Syphax, in love with the young and victorious Massinisse, pleased the whole world, in a manner, by hitting upon the inclination of the ladies and the true humor of the courtiers. But Corneille, who makes the Greeks speak better than the Greeks, the Romans than the Romans, the Carthaginians than the citizens of Carthage speak themselves — Corneille, who is almost the only person that has a true taste of antiquity, has had the misfortune not to please our age for representing [the genius of these nations, and preserving] the true character of Hasdrubal's daughter. Thus to the disgrace of our judgments, he that has surpassed all our authors, and has, in this respect, perhaps, even surpassed himself by al-

134

lowing to those great names all that was their due, could not oblige us to do him the same piece of justice, being enslaved by custom to set a value on those things the present mode recommends, and little disposed by reason to esteem those qualities and sentiments which are not agreeable to our own.

Let us then conclude, after so long a reflection, that Alexander and Porus ought to have preserved their characters entire; that it was our business to view them upon the banks of Hydaspes such as they were, not theirs to come to the banks of the Seine to study our nature and speak our thoughts. The speech of Porus should have had something more unusual and extraordinary in it. If Quintus Curtius has made himself admired for his oration of the Scythians, where he gives them thoughts and expressions natural to their nation, this author might have rendered himself as much admired by representing to us the rarity of a genius of another world.

The different conditions of these two kings, in which both of them behaved themselves so gallantly, their virtue differently exercised in the variety of their fortune, bespeak the attention of historians, and oblige them to describe them to us. The poet, who is at liberty to add to the truth of things, or at least to set them off with all the ornaments of his art, instead of using colors and figures to embellish them has taken away much of their beauty; and whether the scruple of saying too much of them did not suffer him to say enough, or whether it is owing to the barrenness of his invention, he falls vastly short of the truth. He might have entered into their most private thoughts, and have drawn from the bottom of those great souls, as Corneille has done, their most secret motions; whereas he scarce goes so far as their bare outside, little curious to remark well what appeared, and little prying to discover what lay concealed.

I could have wished that our author had laid the stress of his skill in giving us a just representation of those great men, and that in a scene worthy of the magnificence of the subject he had carried the greatness of their souls as high as it was possible. If the conversation of Sertorius and Pompey had such an influence upon our minds, what should not we expect from that of Porus and Alexander upon a subject so uncommon? I could likewise have wished that the author had given us a greater idea of this war. And, indeed, the passage of the Hydaspes is so strange that it is hardly to be conceived: a prodigious army on the other side the river, with terrible chariots and elephants, at that time formidable; the lightning, thunder, and tempests, which occasion a general confusion, and above all,

135

when so large a river must be passed over in skins; in short, a hundred dreadful things which astonished the Macedonians, and which made Alexander say that at last he had found a danger worthy of himself; all this, I say, ought to have raised the imagination of the poet, both in the description of the preparations and the recital of the battle.

However, he scarce mentions the camps of these two kings, whom he robs of their true character to enslave them to imaginary princesses. All that is either great or valuable amongst men, the defense of a country, the preservation of a kingdom, does not excite Porus to the battle; he is encouraged to it by the beautiful eyes of Axiana alone, and the design of his valor is only to recommend himself by it to her. Thus knights-errant are described when they undertake an adventure, and the finest genius, in my opinion, that Spain has produced never makes Don Quixote enter the lists before he has recommended himself to Dulcinea.

A maker of romances may model his heroes according to his fancy. Neither is it of great importance to confine oneself religiously to the true character of an obscure prince, to whose reputation we are perfect strangers. But those great persons of antiquity, so famous in their age, and better known amongst us than the living themselves, the Alexanders, the Scipios, and the Caesars, ought never to lose their characters in our hands. For the most injudicious spectator perceives that he is offended when an author ascribes faults to them which they had not, or when he takes from them virtues which had made upon his mind an agreeable impression. Their virtues, once established, interest our self-love near as much as our own real merit, and it is impossible to make the least alteration in them without making us feel this change with violence. Above all things, we ought not to injure the reputation of their genius in the war to render them more illustrious in their amours; we may give them mistresses of our own inventing, we may mix passion with their glory, but let us take care of making an Antony of an Alexander, and not ruin a hero confirmed for so many ages merely to favor a lover of our own creating.

To banish love out of our tragedies as unworthy of heroes is to take away that secret charm which unites our souls to theirs by a certain tie that continues between them. But then to bring them down to us by this common sentiment, don't let us make them descend beneath themselves, nor destroy what they possess above men. Provided this discretion be observed, I dare affirm that there are no subjects where so universal a passion as love is may not be introduced naturally and without violence. Besides, since women are as necessary in the representation as men, we should give them frequent occasions to speak of that which is most agreeable to their nature, and [of] which they talk better than anything else. Take away from some of the fair sex the expression of amorous thoughts and from others those private familiarities into which the mutual confidence they have in each other leads them, and you reduce them for the most part to very tedious conversations. Most of their motions as well as their discourses should be the effects of their passion; their joy, their sorrow, their fears, and their desires ought to have a little tincture of love in order to be taking.

If you introduce a mother rejoicing for the happiness of her dear son, or afflicting herself for the misfortune of her poor daughter, her satisfaction or her grief will make but a weak impression upon the spectators. To affect us with the tears and complaints of this sex, show us a mistress that bewails the death of a lover, and not a wife that laments the loss of a husband. The grief of mistresses, which is tender and endearing, has a far greater influence upon us than the affliction of an inveigling, self-interested widow, who, as sincere as she happens to be sometimes, always gives us a melancholy idea of funerals and their dismal ceremonies. Of all the widows that ever appeared upon the theatre, I can endure none but Cornelia, [4] because instead of making me think of fatherless children and a wife without a spouse, her affections, truly Roman, recall to my mind the idea of ancient Rome and of the great Pompey.

This is all that may reasonably be allowed to love upon our theatres: let our writers be contented with this, so far even as the severest rules of the drama will allow of it, and let not its greatest favorers believe that the chief design of tragedy is to excite a tenderness in our hearts. In subjects truly heroic, a true greatness of soul ought to be maintained above all things. That which would be pleasing and tender in the mistress of an ordinary man is often weak and scandalous in the mistress of a hero. She may entertain herself, when alone, with those inward conflicts she feels in herself; she may sigh in secret for her uneasiness, and trust a beloved and virtuous confidante with her fears and griefs. But supported by her glory and fortified by her reason, she ought always to remain mistress of her passions, and to animate her lover to great actions by her resolution instead of disheartening him by her weakness.

It is, indeed, an indecent sight to see the courage of a hero softened by tears and sighs; but then, if he haughtily contemns the grief of a beautiful

137

person that loves him, he rather discovers the hardness of his soul than the resolution of his heart.

To avoid this inconvenience, Corneille has no less regard to the character of his illustrious ladies than to that of his heroes. Emilie encourages Cinna to execute their design, [5] and answers all the scruples that oppose the assassinating of Augustus. Cleopatra has a passion for Caesar, and leaves nothing undone to preserve Pompey.[6] She had been unworthy of Caesar if she had not declared against the base treachery of her brother, and Caesar undeserving of her if he had been capable of approving so infamous an action. Dircé, [7] in *Oedipus*, vies greatness of courage with Theseus, turning upon herself the fatal explanation of the oracle which he would apply to himself out of love to her.

But above all we ought to consider Sophonisbe, [8] whose character might be envied by the Romans themselves. We ought to behold her sacrifice the young Massinisse to old Syphax for the good of her country; we ought to see her hearken as little to the scruples of duty in quitting Syphax as she had done to the sentiments of love in losing Massinisse. We ought to see her subject the strongest inclinations, all that binds, all that unites us, the most powerful ties, the most tender passions, to her love for Carthage and her hatred for Rome. In a word, we ought to see her, when being utterly abandoned, not wanting to herself, and when those hearts which she had gained to save her country failed her expectations, to owe to herself the last support, to preserve her glory and her liberty.

Corneille makes his heroes speak with so exact a decorum that he had never given us the conversation of Caesar with Cleopatra if Caesar had believed that he had any work upon his hands at Alexandria, as beautiful as it is, even to that degree as to make an amorous discourse agreeable even to indifferent persons that should hear it. He had certainly let it alone but that the Battle of Pharsalia was fully won, Pompey dead, and all his party dissipated. As Caesar then believed himself to be the master of all, an author might justly enough make him offer a glory of which he was in full possession and a power in all probability well settled. But when he discovered Ptolemy's conspiracy, when he beheld his affairs in an ill condition and his own life in danger, he is no more a lover that entertains his mistress with his passion, but a Roman general that acquaints the queen with the danger that threatens them, and leaves her in haste to provide for their common security.

It was therefore very ridiculous to busy Porus wholly with his love just

before a great battle which was to decide his destiny, nor is it less preposterous to make Alexander quit the field when the enemy begin to rally.
One should have introduced him impatient to find out Porus, and not
make him leave the fight with precipitation only to pay a visit to Cleophile
— he that was never troubled with any such amorous disorders, and who
never thought a victory complete till he had either destroyed or pardoned.
That which is harder upon him still is that he is made to lose much on one
side without gaining anything on the other. He is as indifferent a hero in
love as in war, and thus the history is disfigured without any ornament to
the romance. We find him a warrior whose glory cannot inflame our courage and a lover whose passion cannot affect our tenderness.

This is what I had to say of Alexander and Porus. If I have not regularly
tied myself to an exact criticism, it is because instead of entering into particular criticism I rather chose to enlarge myself upon the decorum that
ought to be observed in the discourses of heroes and the difference of their
characters; upon the good and ill usage of the tenderness of love in tragedies, which is rejected too severely by those that ascribe everything to the
motions of pity and fear, and is too nicely pursued by those that have no
relish but for these sorts of sentiments.

1671

OF READING AND THE CHOICE OF BOOKS

I am as fond of reading as ever because it depends more particularly on
the mind, which decays not like the senses; but in truth, I seek in books my
pleasure rather than my instruction. As I have less time for practice I have
less curiosity to learn. I have more need of a stock of life than of methods
of living, and the little that remains is better entertained and cherished by
things agreeable than instructive. The Latin authors afford me the most,
and I read whatever I think fine a thousand times over without being
cloyed.

A nice choice has confined me to a few books, in which I seek rather
sound than fine wit, and the true taste (to use a Spanish expression) is
generally found in the writings of considerable men. I am pleased to discover in Tully's *Epistoles* both his own character and that of those persons
of quality that wrote to him. As for Tully himself, he never divests himself
of his rhetoric, and the least recommendation to his most intimate friend
is as artificially insinuated as if he were to prepossess a stranger in an affair

139

of the greatest consequence in the world. The letters of the rest have not those turns, but in my mind they have more good sense than his, and this makes me judge very advantageously of the great and general abilities of the Romans at that time.

Our authors perpetually cry up the age of Augustus upon the account of Virgil and Horace, and perhaps more yet upon the score of Maecenas, who encouraged men of learning, than for those men of learning themselves. It is certain, nevertheless, that their parts as well as courages began at that time to decay. Greatness of soul was converted to circumspect conduct, and sound discourse to polite conversation; and if we consider what remains of Maecenas, I know not whether he had not something effeminate which was made to pass for delicate. Maecenas was Augustus's great favorite, the man that pleased and whom all the polite and sprightly wits endeavored to please; now is it not likely that his judgment overruled the rest, that they affected his manner and aped, as much as they could, his character?

Augustus himself leaves us no great idea of his Latinity. What we see of Terence; what was reported at Rome of the politeness of Scipio and Lelius; the remains of Caesar; and what we have of Cicero, with the complaint of this last for the loss of what he calls *sales, lepores, venustates, urbanitas, amoenitas, festivitas, jucunditas*; [9] all these together, I say, make me believe, upon better consideration, that we must pitch on some other time than that of Augustus to find the sound and agreeable wit of the Romans, as well as the pure and natural graces of their tongue.

It may be said that Horace had a very nice palate in all these matters, which persuades me that the rest of his contemporaries had not. For the nicety of his relish consisted chiefly in finding the ridicule of others. Were it not for the impertinencies, false manners and affectations which he laughed at, his sense would not at this very day appear so very just.

1671

OF POETRY

I own the Augustan age to have been that of excellent poets, but it follows not that it was that of sound judgment. Poetry requires a peculiar genius that agrees not overmuch with good sense. It is sometimes the language of gods, sometimes of buffoons; rarely that of a gentleman. It delights in figures and fictions, always beside the reality of things, though it be that only that can satisfy a sound understanding.

Not but that there is something noble in making agreeable verses; but we must have a great command of our genius: otherwise the mind is possessed with something foreign which hinders it from the free management of itself. "He's a blockhead," says the Spaniard, "that can't make two verses, and a fool that makes four." I own if this maxim prevailed over all the world we should want a thousand fine works, the reading of which gives us a very delicate pleasure; but this saying respects men of business rather than professed poets. Besides, those that are capacitated for such great performances will not resist the force of their genius for what I can say, and it is certain that amongst authors those only will write few verses who find themselves more cramped by their own barrenness than by my reasons.

Excellent poets are as requisite for our entertainment as great mathematicians for our use; but it is sufficient for us to be acquainted with their works, and not to engage ourselves in the solitary enthusiasm of the one, or to exhaust our spirits in meditation like the other.

Comic poets are of all most proper for the converse of the world, for they make it their business to draw to the life what passes in it and to express the sentiments and passions of men. How new a turn soever may be given to old thoughts, that sort of poetry is very tedious which is filled with similes of the morning, sun, moon, and stars. Our descriptions of a calm and a tempestuous sea represent nothing which the ancients have not expressed much better. Nowadays we have not only the same ideas, but the very same expressions and rhymes. I never hear of the harmony of birds but I prepare myself for purling streams; the shepherdesses are always lolling upon fern, and you may sooner find a grove without a shade in its proper seat than in our verses. This must necessarily at length be very tedious, which cannot happen in comedy, where with pleasure we see those things represented which we may perform, and where we feel motions like those we see expressed.

A tale of woods, rivers, meadows, fields, and gardens makes but a very languishing impression upon us unless their beauties be wholly new; but what concerns humanity, its inclinations, tendernesses, and affections, finds something in the inmost recesses of our souls prepared to receive it; the same nature produces and receives them, and they are easily transfused from the actors to the spectators.

OF ANCIENT AND MODERN TRAGEDY

There were never so many rules to write a good tragedy by, and yet so few good ones are now made that the players are obliged to revive and act all the old ones. I remember that the Abbé d'Aubignac wrote one according to the laws he had imperiously prescribed for the stage. This piece had no success, notwithstanding which he boasted in all companies that he was the only French writer who had exactly followed the precepts of Aristotle; whereupon the Prince of Condé said wittily: "I am obliged to Monsieur d'Aubignac for having so exactly followed Aristotle's rules, but I will never forgive the rules of Aristotle for having put Monsieur d'Aubignac upon writing so bad a tragedy."

It must be acknowledged that Aristotle's *Art of Poetry* is an excellent work; but, however, there is nothing so perfect in it as to be the standing rules of all nations and all ages. Descartes and Gassendi have found out truths that were unknown to Aristotle. Corneille has discovered beauties for the stage of which Aristotle was ignorant; and as our philosophers have observed errors in his *Physics*, our poets have spied out faults in his *Poetics*, at least with respect to us, considering what great change all things have undergone since his time. The gods and goddesses amongst the ancients brought everything that was great and extraordinary upon the theatre, either by their hatred or their friendship, by their revenge or their protection; and among so many supernatural things, nothing appeared fabulous to the people, who believed there passed a familiar correspondence between gods and men. Their gods, generally speaking, acted by human passions; their men undertook nothing without the counsel of the gods, and executed nothing without their assistance. Thus in this mixture of the divinity and humanity there was nothing which was not credible.

But all these wonders are downright romance to us at this time of day. The gods are wanting to us, and we are wanting to the gods; and if, in imitation of the ancients, an author would introduce angels and saints upon our stage, the devouter sort of people would be offended at it and look on him as a profane person, and the libertines would certainly think him weak. Our preachers would by no means suffer a confusion of the pulpit and theatre, or that the people should go and learn those matters from the mouth of comedians which themselves deliver in their churches with authority to the whole people.

Charles de Saint-Evremond

Besides this, it would give too great an advantage to the libertines, who might ridicule in a comedy those very things which they receive at church with a seeming submission, either out of respect to the place where they are delivered or to the character of the person that utters them.

But let us put the case that our doctors should freely leave all holy matters to the liberty of the stage; let us likewise take it for granted that men of the least devotion would hear them with as great an inclination to be edified as persons of the profoundest resignation; yet certain it is that the soundest doctrines, the most Christian actions, and the most useful truths would produce a kind of tragedy that would please us the least of anything in the world.

The spirit of our religion is directly opposite to that of tragedy. The humility and patience of our saints carry too direct an opposition to those heroical virtues that are so necessary for the theatre. What zeal, what force is there which Heaven does not bestow upon Néarque and Polyeucte? And what is there wanting on the part of these new Christians to answer fully the end of these happy gifts? The passion and charms of a young, lovely bride make not the least impression upon the mind of Polyeucte. The politic considerations of Félix, as they less affect us, so they make a less impression. Insensible both of prayers and menaces, Polyeucte has a greater desire to die for God than other men have to live for themselves. Nevertheless this very subject, which would make one of the finest sermons in the world, would have made a wretched tragedy if the conversation of Pauline and Sévère, heightened with other sentiments and other passions, had not preserved that reputation to the author which the Christian virtues of our martyrs had made him lose.

The theatre loses all its agreeableness when it pretends to represent sacred things, and sacred things lost a great deal of the religious opinion that is due to them by being represented upon the theatre.

To say the truth, the histories of the Old Testament are infinitely better suited to our stage. Moses, Samson, and Joshua would meet with much better success than Polyeucte and Nearchus, for the wonders they would work there would be a fitter subject for the theatre. But I am apt to believe that the priests would not fail to exclaim against the profanation of these sacred histories, with which they fill their ordinary conversations, their books, and their sermons; and to speak soberly upon the point, the miraculous passage through the Red Sea, the sun stopped in his career by the prayer of Joshua, and whole armies defeated by Samson with the jawbone

143

of an ass — all these miracles, I say, would not be credited in a play because we believe them in the Bible; but we should be rather apt to question them in the Bible because we should believe nothing of them in the play.

If what I have delivered is founded on good and solid reasons, we ought to content ourselves with things purely natural, but at the same time, such as are extraordinary; and in our heroes to choose the principal actions which we may believe possible as human, and which may cause admiration in us as being rare and of an elevated character. In a word, we should have nothing but what is great, yet still let it be human. In the human, we must carefully avoid mediocrity, and fable in that which is great.

I am by no means willing to compare the *Pharsalia* to the *Aeneid*; I know the just difference of their value; but as for what purely regards elevation, Pompey, Caesar, Cato, Curio, and Labienus have done more for Lucan than Jupiter, Mercury, Juno, Venus, and all the train of the other gods and goddesses have done for Virgil.

The ideas which Lucan gives us of these great men are truly greater, and affect us more sensibly, than those which Virgil gives us of his deities. The latter has clothed his gods with human infirmities to adapt them to the capacity of men; the other has raised his heroes so as to bring them into competition with the gods themselves. *Victrix causa deis placuit, sed victa Catoni.*[10] In Virgil, the gods are not so valuable as the heroes; in Lucan, the heroes equal the gods.

To give you my opinion freely, I believe that the tragedy of the ancients might have suffered a happy loss in the banishment of their gods, their oracles, and their soothsayers.

For it proceeded from these gods, these oracles, and these diviners, that the stage was swayed by a spirit of superstition and terror, capable of infecting mankind with a thousand errors, and overwhelming them with more numerous mischiefs. And if we consider the usual impressions which tragedy made at Athens in the minds of the spectators, we may safely affirm that Plato was more in the right, who prohibited the use of them, than Aristotle, who recommended them; for as their tragedies wholly consisted in excessive motions of fear and pity, was not this the direct way to make the theatre a school of terror and of pity, where people only learnt to be affrighted at all dangers, and to abandon themselves to despair and every misfortune?

It will be a hard matter to persuade me that a soul accustomed to be terrified for what regards another has strength enough to support misfortunes that concern itself. This perhaps was the reason why the Athenians became so susceptible of the impressions of fear, and that this spirit of terror which the theatre inspired into them with so much art became at last but too natural to their armies.

At Sparta and Rome, where only examples of valor and constancy were publicly shown, the people were no less brave and resolute in battle than they were unshaken and constant in the calamities of the Republic. Ever since this art of fearing and lamenting was set up at Athens, all those disorderly passions which they had, as it were, imbibed at their public representations, got footing in their camps and attended them in their wars.

Thus a spirit of superstition occasioned the defeat of their armies, as a spirit of lamentation made them sit down contented with bewailing their great misfortunes when they ought to have found out proper remedies for them. For how was it possible for them not to learn despair in this pitiful school of commiseration? The persons they usually represented upon it were examples of the greatest misery and subjects but of ordinary virtues.

So great was their desire to lament that they represented fewer virtues than misfortunes, lest a soul raised to the admiration of heroes should be less inclined to pity the distressed; and in order to imprint these sentiments of affliction the deeper in their spectators, they had always upon their theatre a chorus of virgins or of old men, who furnished them upon every event either with their terrors or their tears.

Aristotle was sensible enough what prejudice this might do the Athenians, but he thought he sufficiently prevented it by establishing a certain *purgation*, which no one hitherto has understood, and which in my opinion he himself never fully comprehended. For can anything be so ridiculous as to form a science which will infallibly discompose our minds, only to set up another, which does not certainly pretend to cure us? Or to raise a perturbation in our souls for no other end than to endeavor afterwards to calm it by obliging it to reflect upon the dejected condition it has been in?

Among a thousand persons that are present at the theatre, perhaps there may be six philosophers who are capable of recovering their former tranquility by the assistance of these prudent and useful meditations; but the multitude will scarce make any such judicious reflections, and we may be almost assured that what we see constantly represented on the theatre will not fail, at long run, to produce in us a habit of these unhappy motions. Our theatrical representations are not subject to the same inconveniencies

145

as those of the ancients were, since our fear never goes so far as to raise this superstitious terror, which produced such ill effects upon valor. Our fear, generally speaking, is nothing else but an agreeable uneasiness, which consists in the suspension of our minds; it is a dear concern which our soul has for those subjects that draw its affection to them.

We may almost say the same of pity as it is used on our stage. We divest it of all its weakness, and leave it all that we call charitable and human. I love to see the misfortune of some great unhappy person lamented; I am content with all my heart that he should attract our compassion; nay, sometimes, command our tears; but then I would have these tender and generous tears paid to his misfortunes and virtues together, and that this melancholy sentiment of pity be accompanied with vigorous admiration, which shall stir up in our souls a sort of an amorous desire to imitate him.

We were obliged to mingle somewhat of love in the new tragedy, the better to remove those black ideas which the ancient tragedy caused in us by superstition and terror. And in truth there is no passion that more excites us to everything that is noble and generous than a virtuous love. A man who may cowardly suffer himself to be insulted by a contemptible enemy will yet defend what he loves, though to the apparent hazard of his life, against the attacks of the most valiant. The weakest and most fearful creatures — those creatures that are naturally inclined to fear and to run away — will fiercely encounter what they dread most to preserve the object of their love. Love has a certain heat which supplies the defect of courage in those that want it most. But to confess the truth, our authors have made as ill an use of this noble passion as the ancients did of their fear and pity; for if we except eight or ten plays where its impulses have been managed to great advantage, we have no tragedies in which both lovers and love are not equally injured.

We have an affected tenderness where we ought to place the noblest sentiments. We bestow a softness on what ought to be most moving; and sometimes when we mean plainly to express the graces of nature, we fall into a vicious and mean simplicity.

We imagine we make kings and emperors perfect lovers, but in truth we make ridiculous princes of them; and by the complaints and sighs which we bestow upon them where they ought neither to complain nor sigh, we represent them weak, both as lovers and as princes. Our great heroes upon the theatre do often make love like shepherds; and thus the innocence of a sort of rural passion supplies with them the place of glory and valor.

If an actress has the art to weep and bemoan herself after a moving, lively manner, we give her our tears at certain places which demand gravity; and because she pleases best when she seems to be affected, she shall put on grief all along, indifferently.

Sometimes we must have a plain, unartificial, sometimes a tender and sometimes a melancholy whining love, without regarding where that simplicity, tenderness, or grief is requisite; and the reason of it is plain: for as we must needs [have] love everywhere, we look for diversity in the manners, and seldom or never place it in the passions.

I am in good hopes we shall one day find out the true use of this passion, which is now become too common. That which ought to sweeten cruel or calamitous accidents, that which ought to affect our very souls, to animate our courage and raise our spirits, will not certainly be always made the subject of a little affected tenderness or of a weak simplicity. Whenever this happens, we need not envy the ancients; and without paying too great a respect to antiquity, or being too much prejudiced against the present age, we shall not set up the tragedies of Sophocles and Euripides as the only models for the dramatic compositions of our times.

However, I do not say that these tragedies wanted anything that was necessary to recommend them to the palate of the Athenians; but should a man translate the *Oedipus*, the best performance of all antiquity, into French, with the same spirit and force as we see it in the original, I dare be bold to affirm that nothing in the world would appear to us more cruel, more opposite to the true sentiments which mankind ought to have.

Our age has at least this advantage over theirs, that we are allowed the liberty to hate vice and love virtue. As the gods occasioned the greatest crimes on the theatre of the ancients, these crimes captivated the respect of the spectators, and the people durst not find fault with those things which were really abominable. When they saw Agamemnon sacrifice his own daughter, and a daughter too that was so tenderly beloved by him, to appease the indignation of the gods, they only considered this barbarous sacrifice as a pious obedience, and the highest proof of a religious submission.

Now, in that superstitious age, if a man still preserved the common sentiments of humanity, he could not avoid murmuring at the cruelty of the gods like an impious person, and if he would show his devotion to the

147

gods, he must needs be cruel and barbarous to his own fellow-creatures; he must, like Agamemnon, offer the greatest violence both to nature and to his own affection. *Tantum religio potuit suadere malorum,* says Lucretius,[11] upon the account of this barbarous sacrifice.

Nowadays we see men represented upon the theatre without the interposition of the gods; and this conduct is infinitely more useful both to the public and to private persons, for in our tragedies we neither introduce any villain who is not detested, nor any hero who does not cause himself to be admired. With us, few crimes escape unpunished and few virtues go off unrewarded. In short, by the good examples we publicly represent on the theatre, by the agreeable sentiments of love and admiration which are discreetly interwoven with a rectified fear and pity, we are in a capacity of arriving to that perfection which Horace desires: *Omne tulit punctum, qui miscuit utile dulci,*[12] which can never be effected by the rules of the ancient tragedy.

I shall conclude with a new and daring thought of my own, and that is this: we ought, in tragedy, before all things whatever, to look after a greatness of soul well expressed, which excites in us a tender admiration. By this sort of admiration our minds are sensibly ravished, our courages elevated, and our souls deeply affected.

1672

ON THE CHARACTERS OF TRAGEDIES

I formerly designed to write a tragedy; but what I found the hardest matter of all was to defend myself from a secret suggestion of self-love, which will not easily suffer a man to lay aside his own temper to take up that of another. I remember that I drew my own character without ever designing it, and that the hero dwindled insensibly into the little merit of St. Evremond, whereas St. Evremond ought to have raised himself to the great virtues of his hero. It fell out with my passions as it did with my character, for I expressed my own motions while I endeavored to express his. If I was amorously inclined, I turned everything upon love; if I found myself inclined to pity, I was not wanting to provide misfortunes for it. I made the actor speak whatever I found within my own breast at home, and, in short, represented myself under the name of another. Let us not quarrel with the heroes of our tragedies for being too liberal of their tears, which they should only shed upon proper occasions; they are the poet's own tears, whose natural temper being too compassionate, he is not able to resist their tenderness, which he has formed within himself. If he could content himself only with entering into the sentiments of his heroes, we might expect that his soul, which he only lends to grief for a few moments, might observe some moderation; but when authors take it to themselves, they express in reality what they ought only to represent as probable. It is a secret to know how to express ourselves justly in what relates to the thoughts, but infinitely more in what concerns the passions, for it is more difficult for the soul to disengage itself from passions than for the mind to divert its thoughts. The passions, it is true, ought to be lively, but never strained; for if it were left to the spectators to choose one of two extremes they would much sooner pitch on the defect than the excess. He that does not carry on the passions far enough does not content his audience, and merits no applause; but he that pushes them on too far wounds the imagination, and must expect to be exploded for his pains. The former gives us the pleasure to supply his defects by our own invention; the latter gives us the trouble to retrench his superfluities, which is always painful and tiresome. When the heart, for instance, finds itself touched so much as it ought to be, it endeavors to comfort itself; and as of our own natures we return from our passions to our judgment, we judge not very favorably of tenderness and tears. Those of the most unfortunate ought to be managed with great discretion, for the tenderest spectator soon dries up his: *cito arescit lacrima in aliena miseria.*[13]

In truth, if we see a person too long afflicted upon the theatre we either laugh at his weakness, or the long pitying of a tedious torment, which renders the misfortunes of another our own, offends nature, which ought only to be touched. Every time that I go to hear our most moving tragedies, the tears of the actors draw forth mine with a secret pleasure which I find in being moved; but if the affliction continues I am uneasy, and impatiently expect some turn of the scene to deliver me from these melancholy impressions. I have frequently seen it happen in those long discourses of tenderness that towards the end the author gives us another idea than that of a lover, whom he designs to represent. This lover sometimes commences a philosopher and reasons gravely in his passion, or by way of lecture explains to us after what manner it is formed. Sometimes the spectator, who at first suffered his imagination to range with the person represented, comes home to himself and finds that it is not the hero but the poet that speaks, who in doleful strain of elegy would needs have us weep at some feigned misfortune.

An author mistakes when he thinks to get my good opinion at this rate; he provokes my laughter when he pretends to possess me with pity. But what is more ridiculous even than this is to hear a man declaim eloquently on his misfortunes. He that takes a great deal of pains in describing them saves me the trouble of condoling with him; it is nature that suffers, and it is she that ought to complain. She sometimes loves to speak her private thoughts in order to gain relief by it, but not to expatiate eloquently to show her fine parts.

Neither have I any mighty opinion of the violence of that passion which is ingenious to express itself with great pomp and magnificence. The soul when it is sensibly touched does not afford the mind an opportunity to think intensely, much less to ramble and divert itself in the variety of its conceptions. It is upon this account that I can hardly bear with Ovid's luxuriant fancy. He is witty in his grief, and gives himself a world of trouble to show his wit when we expect nothing but natural thoughts from him. Virgil deservedly makes a just impression upon us in which we find nothing either languishing or strained. As he leaves us nothing more to desire in him, so on the other hand he has nothing that offends us, and for this reason our souls behold with pleasure that amiable proportion which shines in all parts of his work.

For my part, I am astonished that in our age, when all dramatic pieces turn upon love, we should be grossly ignorant of its nature and motions; although love acts differently according to the diversity of temper, yet we may reduce all the effects of so general a passion to three principal heads, which are to love, to burn, and to languish.

To love, simply considered, is the first condition of our soul when she moves by the impression of some agreeable object, whereupon is formed a secret complacency in the person that loves; and this complacency becomes at last a devoting oneself to the person that is loved. To burn is a violent condition, subject to inquietudes, to pains, to torments, sometimes to troubles, to transports, to despair; in a word, to everything that agitates us and disturbs our repose. To languish is the finest movement of love; it is the delicate effect of a pure flame which gently consumes us; it is a dear and tender malady which makes us hate all thoughts of a cure. We entertain it secretly in the bottom of our hearts, and if it comes to discover itself, our eyes, our silence, a sigh that escapes us, a tear that drops in spite of us express it infinitely better than all the eloquence of the most elaborate discourse. As for those long conversations of tenderness, those sighs we hear incessantly, and those tears that are shed every moment, they may be ascribed to some other cause, for in my opinion they are not so much the effects of love as the folly of the lover. I have a greater respect for that passion than to load it with any scandal which does not belong to it. A few tears are sufficient for a lover to express his love by; when they are immoderate or unseasonable, they rather show his infirmity than his passion. I dare venture to say that a lady who might have some compassion for her lover when she sees him discreetly and respectfully expressing the inquietudes she gives him would laugh at him for a chicken-hearted milksop if he whined and sobbed eternally before her.

I have observed that Cervantes always esteems in his cavaliers a probable merit, but he never fails to lash in good earnest their fabulous combats and their ridiculous penances. Upon this last consideration he prefers Don Galaor to the honest Amadis de Gaule, *Porque tenía muy accommodada condición para todo; que no era cavallero melindroso, ni tan llorón como su hermano.*[14]

One great fault of authors in their tragedies is that they employ one passion for another, as for instance they make it to be grief where it ought only to be tenderness, and on the contrary they introduce despair when it should be grief. Quinault in his tragedies is frequently tender where he ought to grieve in good earnest. In the *Titus*[15] of Racine you find despair where there is scarce occasion for bare grief. History informs us that Titus, who was a cautious, prudent prince, sent back Berenice to Judea that he might not give the least offence to the people of Rome; but the poet makes a desperate lover of him, who is resolved to kill himself rather than consent to this separation.

Corneille is equally faulty in his Titus.[16] He represents him as ready to leave Rome and throw up the empire to go and make love in Judea. In this he trespasses directly against truth and probability, destroying the character both of the private man and the emperor only to ascribe everything to a passion that was extinguished. In short, he makes this prince perfectly besotted on Berenice, whereas he parted from her either as a wise man or a disgusted lover. I own, indeed, that there are certain occasions wherein good sense and even reason itself allows us passion, and in those cases passion ought to carry it above the character. Horace would have us represent Achilles active, choleric, inexorable, one that looked upon himself subject to no laws and owning in his undertakings no other right but what his sword gave him;[17] but then we are to consider that he is only to be painted so in his ordinary temper. This is the character which Homer gives him when he contends for his fair captive with Agamemnon; nevertheless, neither Homer nor Horace would have us extinguish all humanity in Achilles, and Euripides was certainly in the wrong to give him so little love for Iphigenia just upon the point when she was going to be sacrificed. The priest seemed to be touched with compassion, and the lover appeared as it were insensible. If he shows anger it results from his temper, not from his affection for Iphigenia. It will be granted me on all hands that humanity demanded pity; that nature and even good manners required tenderness; and all persons of a true taste will blame this poet for laying too great a stress upon the character of his hero when he ought to have made some allowances to passion. But when a passion is generally known, we ought to ascribe as little as we can to the character of the person.

For instance, if you were to describe Mark Antony after he had abandoned himself to his love, you ought not to paint him with those shining qualities which nature bestowed upon him. Antony besotted with Cleopatra is not Antony the friend of Caesar. Of a brave, bold, active man he is become a weak, effeminate, lazy, whining wretch. Of a man who had in no respect been wanting either to his interest or to his party, we find him wanting to himself and utterly undone by himself.

Horace, whom I mentioned a little above, has laid down the character of old age, which he advises us carefully to observe. If we have an old man to represent, he would have us draw him heaping up riches yet denying himself the use of them, cold, timorous, peevish, melancholy, dissatisfied with the present times, and a zealous admirer of what he saw when he was a young fellow.[18] However, if we are to introduce an old man who is passionately in love we must not give him either coldness or fear or laziness or melancholy; we must make him liberal instead of covetous, and complaisant instead of morose or surly. He must find fault with all the beauties he has seen, and only admire that which enslaves him at present; he must do everything for his mistress, and govern himself by no other will but hers, as thinking to obtain by his submission whatever he loses by the disadvantage of his age:

> He thinks the low submission by him shown
> Will for his age and impotence atone.[19]

152

Such an one was in effect, and as such has been painted by Corneille, the old and unfortunate Syphax. Before he was charmed by Sophonisbe he held the balance between the Carthaginians and the Romans; no sooner did he become a lover in his old days but he lost his dominions and himself together for resigning himself to a woman's will.

When I use the word passion, it is love I mean, for all the other passions serve to form the character instead of destroying it. To be naturally gay, melancholy, choleric and fearful is to have humors, qualities and affections that compose a character; to be very much in love is to take up a passion which not only destroys the qualities of a character but likewise commands the motions of other qualities. It is certain that they who truly love are never hurried to any other passions but according as they humor and strike in with their love. If they have any indignation against a lover, love both provokes and pacifies them: they intend hatred, and cannot cease loving; love excuses ingratitude and justifies infidelity. The very torments of a true passion are pleasures; we feel the pains of it only when it is past, just as after the delirium of a fever we feel the pain occasioned by it. In loving well we are never miserable, but we think ourselves to be so when we cease to love.

> A beauteous She, with all her pow'r,
> Can't make us wretched for an hour.
> Though we must never hope for the possessing,
> Her charms are favors, and her sight's a blessing.

1672?

TO AN AUTHOR WHO ASKED MY OPINION OF A PLAY
WHERE THE HEROINE DOES NOTHING
BUT LAMENT HERSELF

The princess you make the heroine of your play would have pleased me well enough had you managed her tears with more frugality. But you make her shed them so prodigally that when the audience come to themselves this profusion of tears cannot but make the person whom you represent less affecting, and those that behold the representation less sensible. Corneille has had the misfortune to disgust the generality of his spectators in his latter days, because he must needs discover that which is most hidden in our hearts, that which is most exquisite in the passions

153

and most delicate in the thoughts. After he had, as it were, worn out the ordinary passions with which we are agitated, he was in hopes of gaining a new reputation if he touched our most concealed tendernesses, our nicest jealousies, and our most secret griefs. But this studied penetration being too delicate for great assemblies, so precious and painful a discovery has made him lose some esteem in the world, whereas it ought to have procured him new applauses.

It is certain that no man understood nature better than Corneille, but he has described it differently according to the different periods of his life. When he was young, he contented himself with describing its motions; when he was old, he was for discovering its most secret springs. Formerly he ascribed everything to the sentiment; at present, penetration does everything with him; now he opens the heart and its most concealed recesses, whereas he formerly represented it with all its anxieties and agitations. Other authors have succeeded better in complying with the present humor of the age, which loves nothing but grief and tenderness upon the theatre. But I am afraid your tragedy will contribute to rectify the depraved palate of the town, and that the audience will nauseate the insupportable excess of a passion which has the good fortune at present to please.

I own that nothing is so moving as the lively representation of a beautiful person in distress; it is a new sort of a charm, that unites everything that is tender within us by impressions of love and pity mingled together. But if the fair lady continues to bewail her misfortunes too long, that which at first affected us makes us sad, and as we are soon weary of comforting one who takes a pleasure in whining and complaining, we leave her as a troublesome creature in the hands of old women and relations, who know how to manage one in this sad condition by the received rules of condoling.

A writer who thoroughly understands the passions will never exhaust his stock of grief, because this profusion must naturally create an indolence in the spectators which will infallibly end in a general dislike. The first tears are natural to the passion which we express: they have their source in the heart and convey grief from an afflicted to a tender heart. The latter are purely owing to the poet's wit: art has produced them, and therefore nature will not own them. Affliction ought to have something that is moving, and the end of affliction something that is animated, in order to make a new impression upon us. It is likewise requisite that it terminate by good fortune, which finishes misfortunes by joy or by a great

154

virtue which draws our admiration. Sometimes it ends in death, and from thence arises in our souls a commiseration, proper and natural to tragedy. But this never ought to be after long lamentations, which gives us more disgust for the weakness of the person represented than compassion for his misfortunes.

I cannot endure to see a dying person upon the stage who is more lamented by him that dies than by the spectators that see him die. I love great griefs attended with few complaints but deep concern; I love a despair which does not waste itself in words, but where nature is overcome and sinks under the violence of the passion. Long, tedious discourses rather show our desire of life than our resolutions to die; to speak much upon these occasions is to languish in despair, and to lose all the merit of one's grief. *O Silvia, tu se' morta*, and to swoon away like Amintas; "I do not weep, Madam, but I die," and to expire like Eurydice.[20]

Our misfortunes are certainly alleviated by tears and lamenting, and the greatest pain in the world, when it begins to abate, increases our desires of living in proportion as it lessens. It falls out with our reasoning as it does with our tears; if we reason never so little in our afflictions, reason will rather advise us to bear them than to die. Let us relieve, on the theatre, those persons whom we represent lamenting and grieving so excessively. Let us bestow more calamities than tears and long discourses on those who we design should die there.

1676

UPON TRAGEDIES

I confess we excel in dramatical compositions, and without flattering Corneille, I think I may prefer many of his tragedies before those of antiquity. I know the ancient tragedians have had admirers in all times, but am not so sure that the sublime which is ascribed to them is built upon a good foundation. To believe that Sophocles and Euripides are so admirable as we are told they are, one must fancy greater matters of their works than can be conceived from their translations; and in my opinion, language and expression must have a considerable share in the beauty of their tragedies.

Through all the praises which their most zealous and celebrated advocates give them, methinks one may perceive that greatness, magnificence, and above all dignity were things they little understood. Wits they were

155

indeed, but cramped by the frugality of a small republic, where a necessitous liberty was all they had to boast of. When they were obliged to represent the majesty of a great king, they made horrid work with a grandeur that was unknown to them because they saw nothing but low and mean objects, to which their senses were in a manner enslaved.

It is true that their poets, being disgusted with these objects, did sometimes raise themselves to what was sublime and wonderful; but then they brought so many gods and goddesses into their tragedies that hardly anything human was to be found in them. What was great was fabulous; what was natural, mean and contemptible. In Corneille, grandeur seems to have attained the last perfection. The figures he employs when he would embellish it with any ornament are proper and suitable; but for the most part he neglects the pomp of metaphors, and does not plunder the heavens to enrich with its spoils what is considerable enough upon earth. His principal aim is to penetrate into the nature of things, and the full image he gives of them makes that impression which pleases men of sense.

Indeed, nature is to be admired wherever we find it, and when we have recourse to figurative ornaments with which we think to embellish our subject, it is many times a tacit confession that we know not what is proper for it. To this are owing most of our figures and similes, which I cannot approve unless they are rare, altogether noble, and just; otherwise it is nothing else but a trick in the author to drop a subject which he does not understand. How beautiful soever comparisons may be, yet they suit much better with epic poetry than tragedy. In an epic poem the mind seeks to please itself out of its subject; in tragedy the soul, full of sentiments and possessed with passions, does not care to be interrupted by vain, flashy similes.

But let us return to the ancients from whom we have insensibly digressed; and to do them justice, let us acknowledge that they have much better succeeded in expressing the qualities of their heroes than in describing the magnificence of great kings. A confused notion of the grandeur of Babylon spoiled rather than raised their imagination; but they could not be imposed upon as to fortitude, constancy, justice, and wisdom, of which they had daily instances before their eyes. Their senses, being weaned from pomp in a mean republic, gave their reason a greater latitude to consider men in themselves.

Thus nothing took them off from the study of human nature, and from applying themselves to the knowledge of vice and virtue, inclinations and tempers. Hence it is that they learnt to paint their characters so well that juster cannot be desired, considering the time they lived in, if we will be contented to know persons by their actions.

Corneille thought it not enough to make them act: he has dived to the bottom of their soul to find out the principle of their actions; he has descended into their heart, to see how their passions are formed there, and discover the most hidden springs of their motions. As for the ancient tragedians, either they neglect the passions by applying themselves to an exact representation of the incidents, or else they make speeches amidst the greatest perturbations, and amuse you with moral sentences when you expect nothing but confusion and despair from them.

Corneille takes notice of the principal events and exposes as much of the action as decency can allow, but this is not all. He gives the passions all the extent they require, and leads nature without constraining or abandoning her too much to herself. He has banished from the theatre of the ancients all that was barbarous; he has sweetened the horror of their drama by some tender passions of love judiciously interwoven. But then he takes care all along to preserve our fear and pity for tragical subjects that deserve them, without diverting us from real passions to whining, tiresome scenes of love, which though varied an hundred several times are for all that still the same.

As ready as I am to acknowledge the merit of this excellent author, yet I will not pretend that none but his pieces deserve applause in our theatre. We have been pleased and affected with *Mariamne, Sophonisbe, Alcionée, Venceslas, Stilicon, Andromaque, Britannicus*,[21] and many others from whose beauty I would not be thought in the least to derogate because I do not name them.

I avoid being tedious as much as possibly I can, and will only add that no nation can dispute with us the superiority in tragedy. As for those of the Italians, it is not worth the while to speak of them; to name them only is to create a distaste. Their *Peter's Feast*[22] would make a Stoic lose all his patience, and I never saw it acted but I wished the author of the piece had been destroyed with his atheist.

There are some old English tragedies which if some things were retrenched in them might be made admirable plays. In all the rest written in those days you see nothing but a shapeless, indigested mass, a crowd of confused adventures, without any regard to time, place, or decency, where eyes that delight in cruel sights are fed with murders and bodies weltering in blood. Should the poets palliate the horror of them by relations, as it is the custom in France, they would deprive the spectators of that sight which pleases them most.

The men of better breeding among them condemn this custom, which perhaps owes its establishment to something inhuman and savage; but an ancient habit, or the humor of the nation in general, prevails over the delicacy of a few private persons. To die is so small a matter to the English that they want images more ghastly than death itself to affect them. Hence it is that upon very good ground we object to them that they allow too much to their senses upon the stage. We must also bear with the reproach they return upon us of passing to the other extreme, when amongst us we admire tragedies for the little tendernesses of passion which make not an impression strong enough upon the mind. For this reason being sometimes dissatisfied with a passion ill-managed, we expect a fuller emotion from the action of our players. And sometimes we would have the actor, more transported than the poet, lend fury and despair to an ordinary agitation and a common grief. The truth is, what ought to be tender is with us generally but soft; what ought to form pity scarce amounts to tenderness; emotion serves us instead of rapture, astonishment instead of horror. Our thoughts have not depth enough, and passions when they are not thoroughly worked up only excite imperfect motions in our souls, that neither leave them wholly to, nor transport them out of, themselves.

1677

OF THE ITALIAN COMEDY

So much for the French and Spanish comedies; I'll now give my opinion of the Italian. I will not speak of *Aminta, Pastor fido, Filli di Sciro,*[23] and other plays of that nature. I ought to be better acquainted than I am with the graces of the Italian language, and therefore I design to speak only of comedies that are acted upon the stage. What we see in France upon the Italian theatre is not properly comedy, since there is no true plot in it, no coherence in the subject, no character strictly observed, nor regularity in the composition, at least according to the rules of art. In short, it is nothing but a kind of ill-formed consort amongst several actors, each of whom furnishes out of his own head what he judges proper for the part he acts. To take it rightly, it is no more than a medley of impertinent *concetti* in the mouth of lovers, and silly buffoonries in that of their *zanis*. There is no such thing as good sense anywhere in it; but a kind of false wit predominates, either in the thoughts, which are borrowed from the heavens, sun, stars, and elements, or in an affectation of simplicity, which has nothing of true nature in it.

The buffoons, I grant, are inimitable, and of an hundred that I have seen ape and mimic them, not one could ever come near them; and for grimaces, postures, motions, agility, suppleness, and distorting of their faces, which they can vary and alter as they please, it is certain that if one must be a great lover of idle jesting and drollery to be taken with what he hears, he must be also very grave and composed not to laugh at what he sees. A man would affect too great a nicety not to be pleased with their acting because a critic will not be satisfied with their discourse.

All representations wherein the mind has no share in the entertainment are tedious at long run; nevertheless they surprise and are agreeable for some time before they tire us. As buffoonry diverts not a man of breeding but by intervals, it ought to be soon over, and the hearers should not have time enough allowed them to reflect upon the exactness of the discourse and consider what is truly natural. It were well if they observed this conduct in the Italian comedy, where a greater mortification comes upon the neck of another, and the variety, instead of relieving us, brings us only something new to tire us.

The truth is, when you are weary of the buffoons that have too long kept the stage, the lovers step in next to complete your persecution. This, in my opinion, is the worst of punishments to a delicate and nice man, who would with more reason prefer a speedy death before the patience of hearing them than the Lacedemonian in Boccalini had when he chose the gallows before the reading of the tedious history of the war of Pisa written by Guicciardini. If any man, overfond of living, is able to endure so killing a fatigue, instead of some agreeable diversity to refresh his mind, all the change he finds is the impertinence of a doctor that plagues him infinitely more. I know that to represent the follies of a pedant aright he must be made to turn all his discourse upon that sort of learning he is master of; but that without ever answering one single question he should cite a thousand authors with a volubility that puts him out of breath, this is to bring a madman upon the stage, who ought to be sent to Bedlam, and not justly to represent the impertinence of a pedantic scholar.

Petronius goes a different way to work when he ridicules Eumolpus;

the pedantry of Sidias is otherwise managed by Théophile; [24] the character of Caritides in *Le Fâcheux* or *Morose* of Molière is altogether exact, and nothing can be cut off from it without disfiguring the whole piece. These are the ridiculous scholars who may be pleasantly enough represented upon the stage; but is it not a most wretched diversion for a gentleman to be plagued with a pitiful pedant, whom books have besotted and who, as I said, ought carefully to be shut up to conceal from us the frailty of our human condition and the misery of our nature?

But I must not launch out too far in my observations upon the Italian comedy. To sum up then in a few words what I have sufficiently enlarged upon, I say that instead of agreeable lovers you have nothing but affected talkers of love; instead of natural comedians, incomparable buffoons — but still they are buffoons; instead of ridiculous pedants, wretched, mad scholars. There is hardly any part but what is forced, unless it be that of Pantaloon, which is the least esteemed and yet is the only one that does not exceed the bounds of probability.

Tragedy was the chief delight of the ancient commonwealth, and the old Romans, endowed only with a rough virtue, introduced no other examples in their theatres but such as might fortify their natural disposition and entertain their habitual fierceness and austerity. When politeness of conversation was joined to their greatness of soul, then they began to take delight in comedy, and sometimes they were pleased with noble ideas and sometimes diverted with agreeable ones.

As soon as Rome grew corrupted, the Romans forsook tragedy and could not endure to see upon the stage any severe representation of the ancient virtue. From that time, to the ruin of the Republic, comedy was the recreation of the great men, the diversion of the polite, and the amusement of a people either grown loose or civilized.

A little before the civil wars, the Romans were again animated with the spirit of tragedy, their genius secretly disposing and preparing them for the fatal revolutions that happened afterward. Caesar wrote one, and many persons of quality did the like. The troubles ceasing under Augustus and peace being restored and settled, all sorts of pleasures were cultivated. Comedies came again into vogue, the *pantomimi* were in credit, and tragedy still preserved a great reputation. Under the reign of Nero, Seneca was taken up with dire speculations which set him upon writing those tragedies that are still extant. When corruption was at the height and vice universal, the *pantomimi* wholly ruined both tragedy and com-

160

edy. Wit had no more share in plays, and all they aimed at was to divert the spectators with such postures and motions as would give them voluptuous ideas.

The modern Italians think it enough for them to be warmed by the same sun, to breathe the same air, and to inhabit the same country with the ancient Romans; but they leave to their historians to talk of that severe virtue which the Romans practiced, and therefore think they have no need of tragedy to animate them to hard and difficult things which they have no mind to undertake. As they affect the softness of an ordinary, and the delights of a voluptuous life, so they love plays that have relation to both. This has introduced that mixture of comedy and diversion of mimics which we see upon all the stages of Italy. And this is almost all that can be said of the Italians who as yet have appeared in France.

All the present actors of their company are generally good comedians, even those that act lovers; and to do them neither injustice nor favor I must own that they are excellent players who have very bad plays. Perhaps they can make no good ones; perhaps they have reason not to have any. For as the Earl of Bristol was, one day, objecting to Cinthio that there was not probability enough in their pieces, he answered that "If there was more, good comedians with good comedies might go starve."

1677

OF THE ENGLISH COMEDY

There is no comedy more conformable to that of the ancients than the English, as for what relates to the manners; it is not a mere piece of gallantry full of adventures and amorous discourses, as in Spain and France, but a representation of the ordinary way of living, according to the various humors and different characters of men. It is an alchemist, who by the illusions of this art feeds the deceitful hopes of a vain *curioso*. It is a silly credulous coxcomb, whose foolish facility is continually abused; it is sometimes a ridiculous politician, grave and composed, starched in everything, mysteriously suspicious, that thinks to find out hidden designs in the most common intentions, and to discover artifice in the most innocent actions of life. It is a whimsical lover, a swaggering bully, a pedantic scholar, the one with natural extravagancies, the other with ridiculous affectations. The truth is, these cheats and cullies, these politicians and

161

other characters so ingeniously devised, are carried on too far in our opinion, as those which are to be seen upon our stage are a little too faint to the relish of the English; and the reason of that, perhaps, is because the English think too much, and we commonly not enough.

And indeed, we are satisfied with the first images of things, and by sticking to the bare outside we generally take appearance for reality, and the easy and free for what is natural. Upon this head I shall observe by the bye that these two last qualities are sometimes most improperly confounded; the easy and the natural agree well enough in their opposition to what is stiff and forced, but when we are to dive into the nature of things or the natural humor of persons, it will be granted me that the easy will scarce carry us far enough. There is something within us, something hidden, that would discover itself if we sounded the subject a little more. It is as difficult for us to enter in as for the English to get out. They become masters of the thing they think on, though they are not so of their own thoughts; their mind is not at rest even when they possess their subject; they still dig when there is no more ore to be got, and go beyond the just and natural idea, which ought always to be maintained, by carrying their inquiries too far. The truth is, I never saw men of better understanding than the French who apply themselves to consider things with due attention and the English that can shake off their too deep meditations to return to that faculty of discourse and freedom of wit which, if possible, ought always to be had. The finest gentlemen in the world are the French that think and the English that speak.

I shall insensibly run into too general considerations, and therefore must reassume my subject of comedy and observe a considerable difference which is to be found betwixt theirs and ours. It consists in this: that being zealous to copy the regularity of the ancients, we still drive to the principal action without any other variety than that of the means that bring us to it. It is not to be denied but that the representation of one principal event ought to be the sole scope and end proposed in tragedy, for we cannot without some violence and pain find ourselves taken off from what employed our first thoughts. The misfortune of an unhappy king, the sad and tragical death of a great hero, wholly confine the mind to these objects, and all the variety it cares for is to know the different means that contributed to bring about this principal action. But comedy being contrived to divert and not to busy us, variety, in the opinion of the English,

162

is an agreeable surprise and change that pleases, provided probability be observed and extravagance avoided; whereas the continual expectation of one and the same thing, wherein there seems to be no great matter of importance, must of necessity make our attention flag.

Thus instead of representing a signal cheat carried on by means all relating to the same end, they represent several cheats, each of which produces its proper effect. As they scarce ever stick to the unity of action that they may represent a principal person who diverts them by different actions, so they often quit that principal person to show various things that happen to several persons in public places; Ben Jonson takes this course in his *Bartholomew Fair*. We find the same thing in *Epsom Wells*, and in both these comedies the ridiculous adventures of those public places are comically represented.

There are some other plays which have in a manner two plots that are interwoven so ingeniously the one into the other that the mind of the spectators (which might be offended by too sensible a change) finds nothing but satisfaction in the agreeable variety they produce. It is to be confessed that regularity is wanting here, but the English are of opinion that the liberties which are taken in order to please the better ought to be preferred before exact rules, which dull authors improve to an art of tiring their audience.

Rules are to be observed for avoiding confusion; good sense is to be followed for moderating the flight of a luxuriant fancy; but rules must not so constrain the mind as to fetter it, and a scrupulous reason ought to be banished which, adhering too strictly to exactness, leaves nothing free and natural. They who cannot attain a genius which nature hath denied them ascribe all to art which they may acquire, and to set a value upon the only merit they have, which is that of being regular, they employ all their interest to damn any piece that is not altogether so. As for those that love the ridicule, that are pleased to see the follies of mankind, that are affected with true characters, they will find some of the English comedies as much or perhaps more to their relish than any they have ever seen.

Our Molière, whom the ancients have inspired with the true spirit of comedy, equals their Ben Jonson in representing truly the various humours and different ways of men, both observing in their characters a just regard to the peculiar taste and genius of their own nation. I believe they have both carried that point as far as the ancients ever did. But it is

163

not to be denied but that they had a greater regard to their characters than to the plot, which might have better laid together and more naturally unraveled.

1678

UPON OPERAS (TO THE DUKE OF BUCKINGHAM)

I have long had a desire to tell your Grace my thoughts of operas, and to acquaint you with the difference I have observed betwixt the Italian and French way of singing. The occasion that I had of speaking of it at the Duchess of Mazarin's has rather increased than satisfied that desire; therefore I will gratify it in the discourse I now send to your Grace.

I shall begin with great freedom, and tell your Grace that I am no great admirer of comedies in music, such as nowadays are in request. I confess I am not displeased with their magnificence; the machines have something that is surprising, the music in some places is charming, the whole together seems wonderful; but it must be granted me also that this wonderful is very tedious, for where the mind has so little to do, there the senses must of necessity languish. After the first pleasure that the surprise gave them is over, the eyes are taken up, and at length grow weary of being continually fixed upon the same object. In the beginning of the concerts we observe the justness of the concords, and amidst all the varieties that unite to make the sweetness of the harmony nothing escapes us. But it is not long before the instruments stun us, and the music is nothing else to our ears but a confused sound that suffers nothing to be distinguished. Now how is it possible to avoid being tired with a *recitativo*, which has neither the charm of singing nor the agreeable energy of speech? The soul fatigued by a long attention, wherein it finds nothing to affect it, seeks some relief within itself, and the mind, which in vain expected to be entertained with the show, either gives way to idle musing or is dissatisfied that it has nothing to employ it. In a word, the fatigue is so universal that everyone wishes himself out of the house, and the only comfort that is left to the poor spectators is the hopes that the show will soon be over.

The reason why commonly I soon grow weary at operas is that I never yet saw any which appeared not to me despicable, both as to the contrivance of the subject and the poetry. Now it is in vain to charm the ears or gratify the eyes if the mind be not satisfied, for my soul, being in better intelligence with my mind than with my senses, struggles against the im-

164

pressions which it may receive, or at least does not give an agreeable consent to them, without which even the most delightful objects can never afford me any great pleasure; an extravagance set off with music, dances, machines, and fine scenes is a pompous piece of folly, but it is still a folly. Though the embroidery is rich, yet the ground it is wrought upon is such wretched stuff that it offends the sight.

There is another thing in operas so contrary to nature that I cannot be reconciled to it, and that is the singing of the whole piece from beginning to end, as if the persons represented were ridiculously matched, and had agreed to treat in music both the most common and most important affairs of life. Is it to be imagined that a master calls his servant, or sends him on an errand, singing; that one friend imparts a secret to another singing; that men deliberate in council singing; that orders in time of battle are given singing; and that men are melodiously killed with swords and darts? This is the downright way to lose the life of representation, which without doubt is preferable to that of harmony; for harmony ought to be no more than a bare attendant, and the great masters of the stage have introduced it as pleasing, not as necessary, after they have performed all that relates to the subject and discourse. Nevertheless, our thoughts run more upon the musician than the hero in the opera; Luigi, Cavallo, and Cesti are more present to our imagination.[25] The mind, not being able to conceive a hero that sings, thinks of the composer that set the song, and I do not question but that in the operas at the Palais Royal Lulli is an hundred times more thought of than Theseus or Cadmus.[26]

I pretend not, however, to banish all manner of singing from the stage; there are some things which ought to be sung, and others that may be sung without trespassing against reason or decency. Vows, prayers, praises, sacrifices, and generally all that relates to the service of the gods, have been sung in all nations and in all times; tender and mournful passions express themselves naturally in a sort of a querulous tone; the expressions of love in its birth, the irresolution of a soul tossed by different motions, are proper matters for stanzas, as stanzas are for music. Everyone knows that the chorus was introduced upon the Grecian theatre, and it is not to be denied but that with equal reason it might be brought upon ours. So far, in my opinion, music may be allowed. All that belongs to conversation, all that relates to intrigues and affairs, all that belongs to council and action, is proper for actors to rehearse, but ridiculous in the mouth of musicians to sing. The Grecians made admirable tragedies, where they had some singing; the Italians and the French make bad ones, where they sing all.

Would you know what an opera is, I will tell you that it is an odd medley of poetry and music wherein the poet and musician, equally confined one by the other, take a world of pains to compose a wretched performance. Not but that you may find agreeable words and very fine airs in our operas; but you will more certainly find at length a dislike of the verses, where the genius of the poet is so cramped, and be cloyed with the singing, where the musician is spent by too long a service.

If I thought myself capable of giving counsel to persons of quality who delight in the theatre, I would advise them to take up their old relish for good comedies, where dances and music might be introduced. That would not in the least hurt the representation. The prologue might be sung with an agreeable accompaniment. In the *intermedes*[27] singing might animate words that should be as the life of what had been represented; after the end of the play the epilogue might be sung, or some reflection upon the finest things in the play, which would fortify the idea, and rivet the impressions they had made upon the spectators. Thus you might find enough to satisfy both the senses and the mind, wanting neither the charms of singing in a bare representation nor the beauty of acting in a long, continued course of music.

It remains that I give you my advice in general for all comedies where any singing is used, and that is to leave to the poet's discretion the whole management of the piece. The music must be made for the words, rather than the words for the music. The musician is to follow the poet's directions; only in my opinion Lulli is to be exempted, who knows the passions better and enters farther into the heart of man than the authors themselves. Cambert,[28] without doubt, has an excellent genius, proper for an hundred different sorts of music, and all well managed with a just symphony of voices and instruments. No *recitativo* is better understood nor better diversified than his. But as to the nature of passions and the quality of the sentiments that are to be expressed, he ought to receive from the authors those lights which Lulli can give them, and submit to be directed when Lulli, through the strength of his genius, may justly be allowed to be director.

Before I put an end to my discourse, I will tell your Grace what a small esteem the Italians have for our operas, and how great a dislike those of Italy give us. The Italians, who apply themselves wholly to the representa-

166

tion and take a particular care in expressing things, cannot endure that we should give the name of opera to a mixture of dances and music which have not a natural relation or exact connection with the subject. The French, on the other hand, accustomed to the beauty of their entries, the delightfulness of their airs, and charms of their symphony, cannot endure the ignorance or ill use of the instruments in the operas of Venice, and are weary of a long *recitativo*, which becomes tedious for want of variety. I cannot properly tell you what this *recitativo* of theirs is, but I know very well that it is neither singing nor reciting; it is somewhat unknown to the ancients, which may be defined [as] an awkward use of music and speech. I confess I have found things inimitable in the opera of Luigi, both for the expression of the thoughts and the charms of the music; but the common *recitativo* was very tiresome, insomuch that the Italians themselves impatiently expected those fine places which in their opinion came too seldom. I shall in a few words sum up the greatest defects of our operas: one thinks he is going to a representation, where nothing will be represented, and expects to see a comedy, but finds nothing of the spirit of comedy.

So much I thought I might say concerning the different constitution of operas. As for the manner of singing which we in France call *execution*, I think without partiality that no nation can justly vie with us. The Spaniards have admirable pipes, but with their warblings and shakings they seem to mind nothing in their singing but to outrival the nightingales. The Italian singing is either feigned or at least forced; for want of knowing exactly the nature or degree of the passions, they burst out into laughter rather than sing when they would express any joy; if they sigh, you shall hear violent sobs formed in the throat, and not sighs which unawares escape from the passion of an amorous heart; instead of a doleful tone they fall into the strongest exclamations; the tears of absence are with them the downright weeping at a funeral; sadness becomes so sorrowful in their mouths that they roar rather than complain; and sometimes they express a languishing passion as a natural fainting. Perhaps there may be at present some alteration in their way of singing, and by conversing with us they may be improved as to the justness of a neat execution, as we are improved by them as to the beauties of a stronger and bolder composition.

I have seen plays in England wherein there is a great deal of music, but to speak my thoughts with discretion, I could not accustom myself to the English singing. I came too late to find a relish in that which is so different

167

from all others. There is no nation that affords greater courage in the men, more beauty in the women, nor more wit in both sexes. It is impossible to have everything, and where so many good qualities are so common, it is no great misfortune that a good taste is a rarity there. It is certain that it is very rarely to be found, but those persons that have it possess it in as eminent a degree of niceness and perfection as any in the world, being distinguished from the rest of their nation either by an exquisite art or by a most happy genius.

Solus Gallus cantat, none but the Frenchmen sings; I will not be so injurious to all other nations as to maintain what an author has published, *Hispanus flet, dolet Italus, Germanus boat, Flander ululat, et solus Gallus cantat.*[29] I shall leave these pretty distinctions with the author, and only beg leave to back my opinion by the authority of Luigi, who would not endure that the Italians should pretend to sing his airs after he had heard them sung by Nyert, Hilaire, and the little Varenne. On his return to Italy he made all the musicians of that nation his enemies by saying openly at Rome, as he had said at Paris, that to make fine music Italian airs must come out of a French mouth. He made as little account of our songs except those of Boisset, which he admired, as well as the concert of our violins, our lutes, harpsichords, and organs; [he was ravished when he first heard the great bells of Saint-Germain-des-Prés;] and how would he have been charmed with our flutes, if they had been then in use? It is most certain that he was much disgusted with the harshness of the greatest masters of Italy when he had once heard the sweet touch and agreeable manner of the French.

I should be too partial if I insisted only upon our advantages. Therefore I must own that no people have a slower apprehension both for the true sense of words and for humoring the thought of the composer than the French. There are but few who less understand the quantity, and who with greater difficulty find out the pronunciation; but when by long study they have surmounted all these difficulties and are masters of what they sing, nothing comes near them. The same thing happens to us in our instrumental music and particularly in concerts, where we can pretend to nothing very sure or just till after an infinite number of rehearsals; but when once we are perfect in them, nothing can be so just and fine. The Italians, for all their profound skill in music, bring their art to our ears without any sweetness. The French, not satisfied to take away from the skill the first harshness that shows the labor of the composition, find in the beauty of their performance, as it were, a charm for our souls and I know not what that touches, which they carry home to the very heart.

I forgot to speak to your Grace about machines, so easy it is for a man to forget that which he would have laid aside. Machines may satisfy the curiosity of ingenious men who love mathematical inventions, but they will hardly please persons of good judgment in the theatre; the more they surprise, the more they divert the mind from attending to the discourse, and the more admirable they are, the less tenderness and exquisite sense they leave in us to be touched and charmed with the music. The ancients made no use of machines but when there was a necessity of bringing in some god; nay, the poets themselves were generally laughed at for suffering themselves to be reduced to that necessity. If men love to be at expenses, let them lay out their money upon fine scenes, the use whereof is more natural and more agreeable than that of machines. Antiquity, which exposed their gods even at the gates and chimney-corners — antiquity, I say, as vain and credulous as it was, exposed them nevertheless but very rarely upon the stage. Now the belief of them is gone, the Italians in their operas have brought the pagan gods again into the world, and have not scrupled to amuse men with these ridiculous vanities, only to make their pieces look great by the introduction of that dazzling and surprising wonderful. These stage deities have long enough abused Italy, but the people there, being happily undeceived at last, are disgusted with those very gods they were so fond of before, and have returned to plays, which in truth cannot pretend to the same exactness, but are not so fabulous, and which with a little indulgence may pass well enough with men of sense.

It has happened with us as to our gods and machines what happens with the Germans as to our modes and fashions; we now take up what the Italians have laid aside, and as if we would atone for the fault of being prevented in the invention, we run extravagantly into a custom which they brought up preposterously. In truth, we cover the earth with deities, and make them dance in troops, whereas they made them descend with discretion and on the most important occasions. As Ariosto carried too far the wonderful of poetry by a vain profusion of fables, so we strain even fable itself by a confused assembly of gods, shepherds, heroes, enchanters, apparitions, furies, and devils. I admire Lulli as well for the diversion of dances as for what concerns the voices and instruments, but

169

the constitution of our operas must appear very extravagant to those who are true judges of the probable and the wonderful.

Nevertheless, one runs a risk of having his judgment called in question if he dares declare his good taste, and I advise others, when they hear any discourse of operas, to keep their knowledge a secret to themselves. For my own part, who am past the age and time of signalizing myself in the world by the invention of modes and the merit of new fancies, I am resolved to strike in with good sense, and to follow reason though in disgrace with as much zeal as if it were still in as great vogue as formerly. That which vexes me most at this our fondness for operas is that they tend directly to ruin the finest thing we have, I mean tragedy, than which nothing is more proper to elevate the soul or more capable to form the mind.

After this long discourse, let us conclude that the constitution of our operas cannot be more faulty than it is. But it is to be acknowledged at the same time that no man can perform better than Lulli upon an ill-conceived subject, and that it is not easy to outdo Quinault in what belongs to his part.[30]

1678

A DISSERTATION UPON THE WORD "VAST" (TO THE GENTLEMEN OF THE FRENCH ACADEMY)

After I had condemned myself as to the word *vast*, I was in hopes the world would have been satisfied with my recantation. But since the gentlemen of the Academy have thought fit to add their censure to mine, I declare my retractation was not sincere, but the mere effect of complaisance, and a voluntary submission of my thoughts to those of Madame Mazarin. Therefore I resume against them that reason which I quitted for her sake, and which every well-bred man would take a pride to lose to her.[31]

We may dispute with the gentlemen of the Academy the privilege of regulating our language as they please. It doth not depend upon authors to abolish old terms because they dislike them and to introduce new ones according to their own fancy. All the favor we can do them is to make them masters of use, when use does not contradict true reason. Some authors have refined languages; on the other hand, others have corrupted them; so that a man must have recourse to good sense to decide the matter. Never had Rome such a set of noble geniuses as at the latter end of the Republic. The reason is because there was then liberty enough remaining amongst the Romans to give a due force to their minds, and luxury enough to give them politeness and agreeableness. At this time, when the beauty of their language was arrived to its highest pitch, when there was at Rome such admirable men as Caesar, Sallust, Cicero, Hortensius, Brutus, Asinius Pollio, Curio, Catullus, Atticus, and many others whom I need not here cite, it was just to submit to their opinions, and to receive their decisions with docility. But when the language came to be corrupted under the emperors, when Lucan came to be preferred to Virgil, and Seneca to Cicero, was anyone obliged to submit implicitly to the authority of these gentlemen, who then set up for wits? Is not Petronius highly commended by all judicious persons for ridiculing the eloquence of his time, for knowing the false judgment of his age, and giving to Cicero, Virgil, and Horace the praises which they deserved? *Homerus testis et lyrici, Romanusque Virgilius, et Horatii curiosa felicitas.*[32]

Let us proceed from Latin authors to the French. When Nervèze's false eloquence was admired, would not the court have been obliged to any man of good sense who would have undeceived them? When Coëffeteau charmed all the world with his metaphors, and "main-mast sails of eloquence" were thought miraculous; when the florid language of Cohon, which had neither force nor solidity, pleased all the pretended wits and the would-be critics; when the affectation of Balzac, that destroyed the natural beauty of thoughts, passed for a majestic, noble style,[33] would it not have been an important service to the public to withstand the authority which these gentlemen usurped, and prevent the ill taste that each of them differently set up in his own time?

I confess that we have not the same right against the gentlemen of the Academy. Vaugelas, d'Ablancourt, Patru have brought our language to its perfection,[34] and I make no question but that our present authors will keep it up in the same condition wherein the former left it. But if one day a false notion of politeness should make our discourse feeble and languishing; if out of too great a fondness for writing puny tales and novels we should study an affected easiness, which is nothing else but nature ill-copied; if too great an application to purity should at length end in dryness; if, in pursuing always the same method of thought, we should rob our language of its fine turns, and, depriving it of all ornament, should make it barbarous when we intend to render it natural: would it not be reasonable then to oppose these corrupters who would subvert the good and true style to give us another instead of it, as little proper to express noble sentiments as delicate thoughts?

But what have I to do to recall what is past, or to foresee what is to come? I acknowledge the jurisdiction of the Academy; let them therefore decide whether *vast* be a word in use or no. So far as this comes to, I will submit to their judgment. But to know the force and propriety of the word, to be satisfied whether it is an imputation or an honor, they must give me leave to consult reason. This small discourse will show whether I have a true notion of it or no.

I maintained that this term *vast genius* was taken in a good or bad sense according to the things which were joined to it; that a genius vast, admirable, piercing, signified a wonderful capacity, and that on the other side a genius vast and immoderate was a genius that lost itself in rambling thoughts, in bright but airy ideas, in designs too great and not at all proportioned to the means that may render them successful. This opinion, methinks, was moderate enough. I have now a mind to deny that *vast* can ever be a commendation, and that nothing is capable of rectifying that quality. *Great* is a perfection in minds; *vast* always a defect. A just and regulated extent makes the *great*; an immoderate greatness the *vast*. *Vastitas* signifies an excessive greatness. The vast and the dreadful have a great affinity one with another. Vast things differ mightily from those which make an agreeable impression upon us. *Vasta solitudo* is not one of those solitudes that afford a delicious repose, that charm the misfortunes of the miserable; it is a wild solitude, where we are frighted with being alone, where we regret the loss of company, where the remembrance of lost pleasures afflicts us and the sense of present misfortunes torments us. A vast house offers something ghastly to the sight. Vast apartments never made any person desirous of living in them. Vast gardens cannot have either the agreeableness which is owing to art or those graces which nature produces. Vast forests put us into a fright. The sight loses itself in looking over vast plains. Rivers of a reasonable greatness give us the prospect of fine banks, and insensibly charm us with the pleasantness of their gentle streams. Rivers too large, overflowings, and inundations displease by the noise and violence of their billows, and our eyes cannot with any pleasure behold their vast extent. Savage countries that are uncultivated, countries ruined by the desolation of war, lands forsaken and aban-

172

doned, have something of vastness, which produces, as it were, a secret horror within us. *Vastus, quasi vastatus*: vast, signifies almost the same with *laid waste, spoiled*, and *ruined*. Let us pass from solitudes, forests, plains, and rivers to living creatures and men.

Whales and elephants are called *vastae et immanes belluae*. That which the poets have feigned most monstrous, as the Cyclops and the giants, are named vast:

Vastosque ab rupe Cyclopas
prospicio . . .
Vasta se mole moventem
pastorem Polyphemum . . .[35]

Amongst men, those who exceeded the ordinary stature, those whom bigness or height distinguished from the rest, were called by the Latins *vasta corpora*.

Vastus has obtained so far as to be applied to customs and manners. Cato, who had otherwise so many good qualities, was a person *vastis moribus*, according to the Romans. He had nothing of elegance in his discourse, nothing of grace either in his person or his actions; a rough, savage air attended all he did. The Germans, who at present are civilized and polished in many places, loved formerly that everything about them should have something of vastness. Their habitation, their attendance, their equipage, their assemblies, their festivals, *vastum aliquid redolebant*; that is to say, they were pleased with an immoderate greatness wherein there was neither politeness nor ornament. I have observed that the word *vastus* hath four or five different significations in Cicero, but all in an evil sense: *vasta solitudo, vastus et agrestis, vasta et immanis bellua, vastam et hiantem orationem*.[36] The most usual signification of *vastus* is "too spacious," "too extended," "too great," "immoderate."

It may be replied that *vaste* in French does not signify what *vastus* may signify in Latin, in the full extent of its meaning. I confess it. But why should it not keep the most natural, as well as *liberty, favor, honor, affliction, consolation*, and a thousand words of the like nature keep theirs? Besides, there is a reason for *vast* which cannot be pretended for the rest: it is this, that we have never a French term that expresses fully and truly what the *vastus* of the Latins can express; and surely we did not make it French to increase the number of words which signify the same thing, but to give our language a word which it really wanted. We think with more force than we express ourselves. Some part of our thought

173

always stays behind; we very seldom communicate it entirely, and it is by a spirit of penetration more than by the intelligence of words that we enter absolutely into the conceptions of authors. Nevertheless, as if we were afraid to understand aright the thoughts of others, or to have our own comprehended, we weaken those very terms that would otherwise have force to express them. But in spite of ourselves, *vast* will preserve in French the true signification it has in Latin. We commonly say *too vast* as we say *too insolent, too extravagant, too covetous,* and it is the excess of a vicious quality. We do not say *vast enough* because *enough* supposes something just and reasonable, whereas as soon as a thing is *vast* there is an excess, there is too much; *enough* can never agree with it. Let us now examine particularly the vast genius, since that is the subject of the question.

That which we call genius, mind, or soul is divided into three faculties: the judgment, the memory, and the imagination or fancy. The judgment may be commended for being solid, profound, nice in discerning, just in defining; but in my opinion no man of good sense will ever give it the quality of *vast*. It is a common expression that such a one has a memory happy, faithful, fit to receive and preserve images; but I never heard anyone call it *vast* except once, and that too preposterously, in my opinion. *Vast* may be applied to an imagination that rambles, that loses itself, that creates visions and chimeras.

I am not ignorant that some have pretended to praise Aristotle by attributing to him a vast genius. They believed too that this very epithet of *vast* was a great commendation to Homer. We hear it often said that Alexander, Pyrrhus, Catiline, Caesar, Charles V, and Cardinal Richelieu had a vast genius, a vast soul. But if we take the pains to examine them well, we shall find that their great works and their great actions ought to be ascribed to the other qualities of their minds, and their errors and faults imputed to the predominance of *vast*. They had something of vastness, I own it; but still it was a vice in them, and a vice not to be pardoned but in consideration of their virtues. It is an error of our judgment to value them for what cannot be excused but by indulgence. If they had not been almost always great, we should not forgive them for being sometimes vast. Let us come to an examination of their works and actions; let us assign to each quality the effects that really belong to it, and begin with the works of Aristotle.

His treatise of poetry is one of the most finished; but to what are owing so many judicious precepts and so many just observations, but to the clearness of his judgment? Nobody will say that it was to his vast genius. In his *Politics*, which may still serve to guide legislators, he shows himself wise, prudent, and skillful in regulating the different constitutions of states; he was by no means *vast*. No writer ever pierced so far as he into the heart of man, as one may see in his *Morals* and in his *Rhetoric* in the chapter about the passions. But this he performed as a philosopher that knew how to make profound reflections, that had exactly studied his own motions and nicely observed those of other men. Do not found the merit of *vast* upon that, for it had no share therein. Aristotle showed properly a vast genius in his *Physics*, and to that we may truly ascribe all his errors; by that he lost himself in his principles, in his own *materia prima*, in the heavens, in the stars, and in the rest of his false opinions.

As for Homer, he is admirable so long as he is purely human: just in his characters, natural in his passions, wonderful in knowing and expressing well what depends upon our nature. When his vast genius leads him to talk of the gods, he speaks of them so extravagantly that Plato banished him out of his Republic as a madman.

Seneca was in the wrong to represent Alexander as a rash adventurer who owed his grandeur to his fortune. Plutarch seems, in my opinion, to have reason on his side when he attributes the conquests of Alexander to his valor more than to his good fortune. In effect, consider Alexander at his first accession to the throne, and you will find that he showed no less conduct than courage in settling himself in the dominions of his father. A contempt of this prince's youth encouraged his subjects to rebel, and his neighbors to take up arms against him; he punished the seditious and vanquished the restless. When this storm was over, his next step was to get himself chosen general of the Greeks against the Persians, and these measures were so well concerted that one could not have expected more just from the most consummate politician. Thus being chosen, he undertook the war and made the lieutenants of Darius, and even Darius himself, commit a thousand faults without making one himself. If the greatness of his courage had not made him pass for a rash man by the dangers to which he exposed himself, his conduct would have left us the idea of a wise and prudent prince. I describe him to you great and politic in all the fine actions he performed. But you must needs have him *vast*, and it is that single quality that set him upon all his extravagant, preposterous undertakings. An unbounded desire of glory engaged him in a very foolish

175

war against the Scythians; an immoderate vanity persuaded him that he was the son of Jupiter. *Vast* extended as far as his affliction when it carried him to sacrifice entire nations to the manes of Hephaestion. After he had conquered the great empire of Darius he might have been contented with the known world, but his vast mind formed the design of conquering another. As *vast*, he undertook his expedition into India, where his army threatened to abandon him, and where his fleet was near being lost; from whence he returned to Babylon, melancholy, disturbed, uncertain, distrusting both gods and men. Are not these noble effects of the vast soul of Alexander? [37] . . .

1685

OF THE POEMS OF THE ANCIENTS

No man pays a greater veneration to the works of the ancients than myself. I admire the design, the economy, the elevation of spirit, the extent of knowledge which are so visible in their compositions; but the difference of religion, government, customs, and manners have introduced so great a change in the world that we must go, as it were, upon a new system to suit with the inclination and genius of the present age.

And certainly my opinion must be accounted reasonable by all those who will examine it. For if we give quite opposite characters when we speak of the God of the Israelites and of the God of the Christians, though it be the same deity; if we speak otherwise of the Lord of Hosts, of that terrible God who commanded to destroy the enemy to the very last man, than we do of that God patient, meek, merciful, who enjoins to love them; if the creation of the world is described with one genius and the redemption of men with another; if we want one kind of eloquence to set forth the greatness of the Father, who hath made all things, and another kind to express the love of the Son, who was pleased to suffer all: why should there not be a new art, a new genius to pass from the false gods to the true one; from Jupiter, Cybele, Mercury, Mars, Apollo, to Jesus Christ, the Virgin Mary, our angels, and our saints?

Take away the gods from the ancients, and you take from them all their poems. The constitution of the fable is in disorder, and the design of it turned upside down. Without the prayer of Thetis to Jupiter, and the dream which Jupiter sends to Agamemnon, there will be no *Iliad*; without Minerva, no *Odyssey*; without the protection of Jupiter and the assistance of Venus, no *Aeneid*. The gods assembled in heaven, and there debated what was to be done upon earth; they formed resolutions, and were no less necessary to execute than to take them. These immortal leaders of parties among men contrived all, gave life to all, inspired force and courage, engaged themselves in fight; and if we except Ajax, who asked nothing of them but light, there was no considerable warrior that had not his god upon his chariot as well as his squire, the god to conduct his spear, the squire to direct his horses. Men were pure machines whom secret springs put in motion, and those springs were nothing else but the inspiration of their gods and goddesses.

The divinity we serve is more favorable to the liberty of men. We are in his hands, like the rest of the universe, by way of dependence, but in our own to deliberate and to act. I confess we ought always to beg his protection. Lucretius himself asks it, and in that very book where he attacks providence with all the force of his wit he falls a-praying, and implores that power which governs us to be so gracious as to avert all misfortunes from him.

> Quod procul a nobis flectat natura gubernans.[38]

However, we should not introduce this formidable majesty upon every trifling occasion, whose very name ought never to be used in vain. If the false divinities are mixed in fictions, it is no great matter; those are downright fables and vain effects of the poet's imagination. As for Christians, they should give nothing but truth to Him who is truth itself, and they should adapt all their discourses to His wisdom and to His goodness.

This great change is followed by that of manners, which by reason of their being civilized and softened at present cannot suffer that wild and unbecoming freedom that was assumed in former times. It is this change that makes us nauseate the vile and brutal scolding between Achilles and Agamemnon. Upon this score Agamemnon appears odious to us, when we see him take away that Trojan's life whom Menelaus, upon whose account the war was made, had generously pardoned. Agamemnon, the king of kings, who ought to have shown an example of virtue to all the princes and the people, the base Agamemnon kills this miserable wretch with his own hand. It is on the same account that Achilles fills us with horror when he butchers young Lycaon, who entreated him so tenderly

177

for his life. It is then we hate him even to his virtues, when he ties the body of Hector to his chariot and drags him inhumanely to the camp of the Greeks. I loved him as a valiant man, and as the friend of Patroclus; the cruelty of this action makes me abhor his valor and his friendship. It is quite otherwise with Hector: his good qualities return into our minds; we pity and lament him the more for his sufferings; his idea on the sudden becomes very dear and raises all our thoughts in his favor.

Let it not be said in the behalf of Achilles that Hector had killed his dear Patroclus. The resentment of this death doth not excuse him to us. An affliction that could permit him to suspend his revenge, and to tarry till his arms were made before he went to the combat — an affliction so patient ought not to have carried him to this unusual barbarity after the fight was over. But let us acquit friendship of an imputation so odious; the sweetest, the tenderest of all virtues does not use to produce effects so contrary to its nature. Achilles had really this cruelty in the bottom of his nature. It is not to the friend of Patroclus, but to the inhumane and inexorable Achilles, that it belongs.

This all the world will easily agree to. However, the vices of the hero are no faults in the poet. Homer's design was to paint nature such as he saw it, and not to improve it in his heroes. He has described them with more passions than virtues; now passion has its foundation in nature, and virtue is a thing acquired by the improvement of our reason.

Politics had not yet united men by the bonds of a rational society, nor polished them enough for others; morality had not yet accomplished them for themselves. Good qualities were not sufficiently distinguished from the bad. Ulysses was prudent and fearful, provident against dangers, industrious to get out of them, valiant sometimes, when there was less danger to be so than otherwise. Achilles was valiant and fierce, and, what Horace would not set down in his character for him, condescending sometimes to puerile follies. As his nature was uncertain and irregular, hence it came to pass that his behavior was sometimes fierce and sometimes childish. One while he drags the body of Hector in a barbarous manner, now he whines to the goddess his mother, like a child, to drive away the flies from that of Patroclus, his dear friend.

Their customs differ no less from ours than their morals. Two heroes ready for the combat would not amuse themselves nowadays in setting forth their genealogy; but it is easy to observe in the *Iliad*, nay in the *Odyssey* and the *Aeneid* too, that such a method was then practised. Men harangued before they fought, just as they make speeches in England before they are hanged.

As for comparisons, discretion will teach us to use them more sparingly than the ancients. Good sense will render them just, invention new. The sun, the moon, the elements, will lend us no more of worn-out magnificence. Wolves, shepherds, and flocks will not afford us a simplicity too much known and threadbare.

I am of opinion there is an infinite number of comparisons that are more like one another than the things they are compared to. A goshawk that strikes a pigeon, a sparrow hawk that dares the little birds, a falcon that makes a stoop, are liker one another in the swiftness of their flight than the men to whom they are compared for their impetuosity. Take away the distinction of the names of goshawk, sparrow hawk, and falcon, you will find the very same thing. The violence of a whirlwind that roots up trees more resembles that of a storm which raises disorders of another kind than the objects to which it is compared. A lion whom hunger drives from his den, a lion pursued by hunters, a lioness furious and jealous of her whelps, a lion against whom a whole village assembles, and who for all that retires with pride and indignation—all this is a lion differently represented, but still a lion, which doth not afford us ideas different enough.

Sometimes comparisons take us from objects that employ us most by showing us another object that makes an unseasonable diversion. I am ready to consider two armies that are drawn out to engage, and I employ all my thoughts to observe the behavior, order, and disposition of the troops. On a sudden, I am transported to the shores of a sea, which is swelled by the fury of the winds, and I am in more danger to behold ship-wrecked vessels than broken battalions. These vast thoughts which the sea affords me efface the former. Another represents to me a mountain or a forest all on fire. Whither doth not the idea of such a burning carry one? If I were not a perfect master of my own thoughts, I might insensibly be led to the last universal conflagration. From this terrible burning I am hurried to an image of lightning, and these diversions so much take me off from the first image that employed me that I lose entirely that of the battle.

We think to embellish objects by comparing them to eternal, immense, infinite beings; but in truth we lessen instead of advancing them. To say that a woman is as handsome as Madame Mazarin is to praise her more than if you compared her to the sun: for the sublime and wonderful create esteem; the impossible and the fabulous destroy that very commendation which they pretend to bestow. Truth was not the inclination of the first ages; a useful lie and a lucky falsehood gave reputation to imposters and pleasure to the credulous. It was the secret of the great and the wise to govern the simple, ignorant herd. The vulgar, who paid a profound respect to mysterious errors, would have despised naked truth, and it was thought a piece of prudence to cheat them. All their discourses were fitted to [this] advantageous design, in which there was nothing to be seen but fictions, allegories, and similitudes— nothing appeared as it was in itself. Specious and rhetorical outsides hid the truth of things, and comparisons too frequently used hindered the reader from minding the true objects by amusing him with resemblances.

The genius of our age is quite opposite to this spirit of fables and false mysteries. We love plain truth; good sense has gained ground upon the illusions of fancy, and nothing satisfies us nowadays but solid reason. To this alteration of humor we may add that of knowledge; we have other notions of nature than the ancients had. The heavens, that eternal mansion of so many divinities, are nothing else with us but an immense and fluid space. The same sun shines still upon us, but we assign it another course, and instead of hastening to set in the sea it goes to enlighten another world. The earth, which was immovable in the opinion of the ancients, now turns round in ours, and is not to be equalled for the swiftness of its motion. In short, everything is changed, gods, nature, politics, manners, humors, and customs. Now is it to be supposed that so many alterations should not produce a mighty change in our writings?

If Homer were now alive, he would undoubtedly write admirable poems; but then he would fit them to the present age. Our poets make bad ones, because they model them by those of the ancients, and order them according to rules which are changed with things which time has altered.

I know there are certain eternal rules, grounded upon good sense, built upon firm and solid reason, that will always last. Yet there are but few that bear this character. Those that relate to the manners, affairs and customs of the ancient Greeks make but a weak impression upon us at present. We may say of them as Horace has said of words: they have their certain period and duration. Some die with old age.

Verborum interit aetas.[39]

Others perish with their nation, as well as their maxims of government, which subsist not after the empire is dissolved. So it is plain, there are but very few that have a right to prevail at all times, and it would be ridiculous to regulate matters wholly new by laws that are extinct. Poetry would do ill to exact from us what religion and justice do not obtain.

To this servile and too much affected imitation is owing the ill success of all our poems. Our poets have not genius enough to please without employing the gods, nor address to make a good use of what materials our religion could afford them. Tied to the humor of antiquity but confined to the doctrines of this age, they give the air of Mercury to our angels, and that of the fabulous wonders of paganism to our miracles. This mixture of ancient and modern has made them succeed very ill. And we may say that they neither know how to draw any advantage from their fictions nor make a right use of our truths.

To conclude, the poems of Homer will always be a masterpiece, but they are not a model always to be followed. They will form our judgment and our judgment will regulate the present disposition of things.

1685

OF THE WONDERFUL THAT IS FOUND IN
THE POEMS OF THE ANCIENTS

If we consider the wonderful in the poems of antiquity, divested of the fine thoughts, the strong passions, and the noble expressions with which the works of the poets are adorned; if we consider it, I say, destitute of all ornament and come to examine it purely by itself, I am persuaded that to a man of good sense it will appear no less ridiculous than that of knight-errantry. Nay, the latter is in this regard the discreeter of the two because it supposes all pernicious, dishonest, and base things done by the ministry of devils and magicians, whereas the poets have left the most infamous exploits to the management of their gods and goddesses. Yet this hinders not but that poems have been always admired and books of chivalry ridiculed. The first are admired for the wit and knowledge we find in them, and the other despised for the absurdities they are filled with. The wonderful in the poems supports its fabulous extravagance by the beauty of the discourse and by an infinite number of useful discoveries that accompany it. That of chivalry discredits even the foolish invention of its fable by the ridiculousness of the style in which it is written.

Be it how it will, the wonderful in the poems has begotten that of knight-errantry, and certain it is that the devils and conjurers cause much less harm in this way of writing than the gods and their ministers did in the former. The goddess of arts, of knowledge, and wisdom inspires the bravest of all the Greeks with an ungovernable fury, and suffers him not to recover his senses she had taken from him, but only to make him capable of perceiving his folly and by this means to kill himself out of mere shame and despair. The greatest and most prudent of the goddesses favors scandalous passions, and lends her assistance to carry on a criminal amour. The same goddess employs all sorts of artifices to destroy a handful of innocent people who by no means deserved her indignation. She thought it not enough to exhaust her own power and that of the other gods, whom she solicited to ruin Aeneas, but even corrupts the god of sleep to cast Palinurus into a slumber and so to order matters that he might drop into the sea; this piece of treachery succeeded, and the poor pilot perished in the waves.

There is not one of the gods in these poems that does not bring the greatest misfortunes upon men or hurry them on to the blackest actions. Nothing is so villainous here below which is not executed by their order or authorized by their example, and this it was that principally contributed to give birth to the sect of the Epicureans, and afterwards to support it. Epicurus, Lucretius and Petronius would rather make their gods idle and enjoy their immortal nature in an uninterrupted tranquillity than see them active and cruelly employed in ruining ours. Nay, Epicurus by doing so pretended he showed his great respect to the gods, and from hence proceeded that saying which my Lord Bacon so much admires: *Non deos vulgi negare profanum, sed vulgi opiniones diis applicare profanum.*[40]

Now I do not mean by this that we are obliged to discard the gods out of our works, and much less from those of poetry, where they seem to enter more naturally than anywhere else:

Ab Jove principium Musae.

I am for introducing them as much as any man; but then I would have them bring their wisdom, justice, and clemency along with them, and not appear, as we generally make them, like a pack of impostors and assassins.

182

I would have them come with a conduct to regulate, and not with a disorder to confound everything.

Perhaps it may be replied that these extravagancies ought only to pass for fables and fictions, which belong to the jurisdiction of poetry. But I would fain know what art and science in the world has the power to exclude good sense? If we need only write in verse to be privileged in all extravagancies, for my part, I would never advise any man to meddle with prose, where he must immediately be pointed at for a coxcomb if he leaves good sense and reason never so little behind him.

I wonder extremely that the ancient poets were so scrupulous to preserve probability in the actions of men, and violated it after so abominable a manner when they come to recount the actions of the gods. Even those who have spoken of their nature more soberly than the rest could not forbear to speak extravagantly of their conduct. When they establish their being and their attributes they make them immortal, infinite, almighty, perfectly wise, and perfectly good. But at the very moment they set them a-working there is no weakness to which they do not make them stoop; there is no folly or wickedness which they do not make them commit.

We have two common sayings which appear to be directly opposite to one another, and yet I look upon both to be very probable. The one is that poetry is the language of the gods; the other, that there is not such a fool in nature as a poet.[41] Poetry that expresses with force and vigor those impetuous passions that disturb mankind, that paints the wonders of the universe in lively expressions, does elevate things purely natural, as it were above nature, by the sublimity of its thoughts and the magnificence of its discourse, which may justly enough be called the language of the gods. But when poets come once to quit this noble field of passions and wonders to speak of the gods, they abandon themselves to the caprice of their own imagination in matters which they do not understand; and their heat having no just ideas to govern it, instead of making themselves, as they vainly believe, wholly divine, they are in truth the most extravagant fools in the world. It will be no difficult matter to be convinced of this truth if we consider that this absurd and fabulous theology is equally contrary to all notions of religion and all principles of good sense. There have been some philosophers that have founded religion upon that knowledge which men may have of the deity by their natural reason. There have been law-givers too that have styled themselves the interpreters of the will of heaven to establish a religious worship which has not had reason to support it. But to make, as the poets have done, a perpetual commerce, a familiar society, and if I may use the expression, a mixture of men and gods, against religion and reason, is certainly the boldest and perhaps the most senseless thing that ever was.

It remains now to consider whether the character of a poem has virtue to rectify that of impiety and folly. Now, as I take it, we do not ascribe so much power to the secret force of any charm. That which is bad is bad for good and all; that which is extravagant can be made good sense in no respect. As for the reputation of the poet, it rectifies nothing any more than the character of the poem does. Discernment is a slave to nobody. That which is effectually bad is not at all the better for being found in the most celebrated author, and that which is just and solid is never the worse for coming from an indifferent hand. Amongst a hundred fine and lofty thoughts, a good judge will soon discover an extravagant one which one's genius threw out when it was warm and which too strong an imagination was able to maintain against unfixed reflections. On the other hand, in the course of an infinite number of extravagant things, this same judge will admire certain beauties where the mind, in spite of its impetuosity, was just and regular.

The elevation of Homer and his other noble qualities do not hinder me from taking notice of the false character of his gods, and that agreeable and judicious equality of Virgil that pleases all true judges does not conceal from me the little merit of his Aeneas. If among so many noble things which affect me in Homer and Virgil I cannot forbear to remark what is defective in them, so amongst those passages that displease me in Lucan, either for being too flat, or weary me for being too far carried on, I cannot forbear to please myself in considering the just and true grandeur of his heroes. I endeavor to relish every word in him when he expresses the secret movements of Caesar at the sight of Pompey's head; and nothing escapes me in that inimitable discourse of Labienus and Cato, where they debate whether they shall consult the oracle of Jupiter Ammon to know the destiny of the Commonwealth.

If all the ancient poets had spoken as worthily of the oracles of their gods, I should make no scruple to prefer them to the divines and philosophers of our time, and it is a passage that may serve for an example in this matter to all succeeding poets. One may see in the concourse of so many people that came to consult the oracle of Ammon what effects a public opinion can produce where zeal and superstition mingle together.

Charles de Saint-Evremond

One may see in Labienus a pious sensible man who to his respect for the gods joins that consideration and esteem we ought to preserve for true virtue in good men. Cato is a religious severe philosopher, weaned from all vulgar opinions, who entertains those lofty thoughts of the gods which pure undebauched reason and a truly elevated wisdom can give us of them. Everything here is poetical, everything here is consonant to sense and truth; it is not poetical upon the score of any ridiculous fiction, or for some extravagant hyperbole, but for the daring greatness and majesty of the language and for the noble elevation of the discourse. It is thus that poetry is the language of the gods and that poets are wise, and it is so much the greater wonder to find it in Lucan because it is neither to be met with in Homer or Virgil!

Pierre-Daniel Huet, Bishop of Avranches THE ORIGINAL OF ROMANCES

Though I think your curiosity very just, and that it is natural for a person who so perfectly understands the art of writing romances to be inquisitive into their original, yet I know not whether I may with equal justice undertake to satisfy that curiosity. I am without books, I have my head at present full of other matters, and I am not ignorant of the many difficulties wherewith such an inquiry must necessarily be attended. It is neither in Provence or Spain, as some have imagined, we are to trace out the beginnings of this agreeable amusement of a harmless idleness. We must search after them in countries farther off, and in the more remote recesses of antiquity. I will, notwithstanding, endeavor to comply with your desires, for that strict friendship which has been established so long between us gives you a right to demand everything of me, and takes from me the choice of refusing anything to you.

Heretofore by the word *romance* was understood not only such works as were written in prose, but more frequently those that were formed in verse. Giraldi and Pigna, his scholar, in their treatises of romances do scarce allow that name to any else, and propose Boiardo and Ariosto for models.[1] But at present the contrary acceptation prevails, and romances properly so called are fictions of love-adventures, artfully formed and delivered in prose, for the delight and instruction of the readers. I call romance a *fiction* to distinguish it from history, and a fiction of *love-adventures* because love ought to be the principal subject of a romance. It must be written in prose, to conform itself to the custom of the age; it must be contrived with art, under some certain rules, otherwise it will be a confused mass without order or beauty. The chief design of a romance, and which the writer ought in the first place to have in view, is the instruction of his reader, before whom he is to represent the reward of virtue and chastisement of vice. But forasmuch as the mind of man is naturally an enemy to instruction, against which self-love is ever ready to revolt, he must be soothed and deluded by the baits of pleasure, and the author must temper the severity of precept by the agreeableness of example till he has brought the reader insensibly to correct those faults in himself which he cannot but condemn in others. So that delight, which the ingenious romancer seems to make his chief design, is in effect no other than a medium subordinate to the principal end, the instruction of the mind and reformation of the manners; and romances are more or less regular as they come up more or less to this definition. It is only upon such that I intend my present discourse, and I am of opinion that your curiosity is with regard to such only.

I shall not therefore say anything of romances written in verse, much less of epic poems, which besides their being written in verse have several essential differences that distinguish them from romances, though in some other respects there is a great resemblance between them; and since, according to Aristotle's maxim, a poet is more to be distinguished as such by his invention than his verses, the authors of romances may be ranked among the poets. Petronius saith that poems ought to distinguish themselves [by great indirection, by the ministry of the gods] by their surprising turns and their free and hardy expressions, insomuch that they are to be considered rather as oracles proceeding from a divine impulse and spirit full of fury than as an exact regular narration.[2] Romances, on the other hand, are more simple, less elevated and metaphorical, both in the invention and expression. Poems have more of the surprising, but are always [bounded by the] probable: romances have more of the probable, and sometimes [have] something of the surprising. Poems are more regular and exact in the contrivance, but have less of matter, fewer events and episodes. On the other hand, romances have more of these because, having less of the sublime and metaphorical, they do not put the mind so much upon the stretch, but leave it in a condition to fill itself with more variety of different ideas. [Finally], poems have for their subject some action military or politic, and touch only upon love occasionally; on the other hand, love is the principal subject of romances, where war and politics are no other than incidents. I mean this of regular romances, for the greatest part of our old French, Italian, and Spanish romances have less of love and more of fighting, which inclined Giraldi to believe that the word romance is taken from a word signifying in Greek force and courage, because those books were made on purpose to magnify the strength and courage of their

187

paladins. But Giraldi was mistaken, as I shall make appear to you in the sequel of this discourse. Neither do I comprehend under my definition of romances those histories which are notorious for their many falsities, such as that for instance of Herodotus (which however has not so many as it is generally charged withal), Hanno's voyages, the life of Apollonius written by Philostratus, and the like.[3] These writings are true in the main, and false only in some particular points, whereas romances are true in particular facts only, and false in the main. The one consists of truths mingled with some falsehoods, and the other of falsehoods mingled with some truths. I mean that truth has the ascendant in these histories, and falsehood is so prevailing a quality in romances that it will be contrary to no rule if there should not be one word of truth in the whole or in part. Aristotle saith that [that] tragedy is the most perfect whose plot is founded upon some known fact in history, because it carries a greater probability with it than that which is entirely of a new invention; and yet he does not condemn the latter, his reason for which is that though the argument be taken from history, it may nevertheless be unknown to the greatest part of the audience and consequently new to them, notwithstanding which it may prove a general entertainment. The same is to be said of romances, but with this distinction, that an entire fiction of the fable will pass easier in such pieces where the actors are of mean circumstances, as in our comical romances, than in those more lofty ones, where great princes and conquerors are the actors, and whose adventures are illustrious and remarkable, because it is not likely that such great events should have lain so long concealed and neglected by the historians; and probability, which is [not always] allowed in history, is essential in a romance.

I exclude also from the number of romances those pretended histories which are entirely false, both in the whole and in part, invented purely to supply the want of truth. Such are the imaginary originals of most nations, and even of the most barbarous. Such moreover are those gross fictions of Annius the monk of Viterbo, worthy the indignation or contempt of the learned.[4] I make the same difference between romances and those writings as there is between such who with an innocent artifice mask and disguise themselves to divert themselves whilst they are diverting others, and those abandoned wretches who assume to themselves the name and dress of some persons deceased or absent on purpose from the resemblance there is between them to lay claim to and get possession of their estates. In a word, I must likewise deny to fables a place in my definition, for a romance is the fiction of things that might have happened, but never did happen, whereas fables are of things that never were and never can be.

Having thus settled what writings they are that deserve the name of romances, I must affirm that the invention of them is owing to the Orientals, I mean to the Egyptians, Arabians, Persians, and Syrians. I do not question but you will yield me up this point when I have proved to you that most of the famous romancers of antiquity were of those countries. . . .

The Egyptian hieroglyphics serve to instance to what an excess that nation was mysterious. Everything among them was expressed by representatives, everything wore a disguise; all their religion was under a veil, nor were the vulgar suffered to receive any other knowledge of it than what was conveyed to them under the mask of fables; neither was the mask to be taken off but to those they deemed worthy to be initiated into their mysteries. Herodotus saith the Greeks borrowed from them their mythologic divinity, and recounts some stories he had been taught by the priests in Egypt, which, as credulous and as much given to fables as he was, he relates as old wives' tales, which however had something agreeable in them and tickled the curiosity of the Greeks, a people desirous to learn and great admirers of novelties. It was doubtless from these priests that Pythagoras and Plato, in their voyages to Egypt, learned to disguise their philosophy, and hide it under the shadow of mysteries.

As for the Arabians, if you read their works, you will find nothing in them but metaphors, drawn in by head and shoulders, similitudes and fictions; of this sort is their Alcoran. Mahomet saith he composed it in that manner to the end it might be more easily learnt and not easily forgotten. They have translated Aesop's fables into their language, and some of them have composed fables like them. . . . It is my opinion that we had the art of rhyming from the Arabs, and I think there is ground to believe that the Leonine verses are copied from them. For it does not appear that rhymes had met with any reputation in Europe before Tarick and Musa [5] had penetrated into Spain, but we meet with great plenty of them in the ages following, though it may be easy for me to convince you that rhyme was not utterly unknown to the ancient Romans.

The Persians have not come behind the Arabians in the art of lying agreeably. For though in the common usages of life it was reckoned most abominable among them to lie, and there was no fault they punished in their children with so much severity, yet nothing pleased them more in their books and writings, if indeed fictions can deserve the name of lies.

189

To prove this we need only read the fabulous adventures of their great law-giver Zoroaster. Strabo saith that the Persian schoolmasters gave their pupils precepts of morality clothed in fictions. He tells us in another place that no great credit is to be given to the ancient histories of the Persians, Medes, and Syrians, because of the inclination in their writers to fables. For observing that they among them who made it their profession to write fables were in great esteem, they thought the people would be highly delighted in reading relations false and counterfeit, provided they were written with an historical air.[6] Aesop's fables were in such high esteem among them that they claimed the author for their countryman. . . .

There are no poets that come up to the Persians in the liberty they take of lying in the lives of their saints, the origin of their religion, and in their histories. They have so disguised their histories, the true knowledge of which hath been derived to us from the Greeks and Romans, that they are not to be known; and degenerating from that laudable aversion they had heretofore to such as had recourse to lies to serve their interests, they now value themselves upon it. They are in love with poetry to excess; it is the delight of the noble and plebeian. All entertainments are imperfect where poetry is wanting, so that poets abound among them and are known by their splendid garments. Their works of gallantry and amorous stories have been highly celebrated, and discover a national genius to romances. . . .

Those fictions and parables, which remained unconsecrated in the nations before mentioned, became sanctified in Syria. The sacred penmen, accommodating themselves to the humor of the Jews, clothed the inspirations they had received from heaven in parable and allusion. The Holy Scripture is all mystical, allegorical, enigmatical. The Talmudists believe the Book of Job is nothing but a parable invented by the Hebrews. This book, that of David, the Proverbs, Ecclesiastes, the Song of Songs, and all the other sacred canticles, are so many pieces of poetry full of figures that would appear bold and extravagant in our writings, but are familiar in those of that nation. The Book of Proverbs is otherwise called the Parables, because proverbs of that kind, according to Quintilian's definition, are no other than fictions or strings of parables.[7] The Song of Songs is a dramatic piece where the passionate sentiments of the bridegroom and the bride are expressed in a manner so touching and tender that we should be charmed with them if those expressions and figures were [a little more in rapport with] our genius, or if we could divest ourselves of that unreasonable prejudice that gives us a distaste of everything that differs never so little from our own customs. Wherein we insensibly condemn ourselves, since our inconstancy will not permit us to continue long in the observance of the same customs. Our Blessed Saviour himself rarely gives any precept to the Jews but under the veil of a parable. The Talmud is stuffed with a million of fables, every one more impertinent than another. Several of the rabbins have from time to time given explanations of them, or labored to reconcile them to each other, or digested them in particular pieces, and moreover composed many poems, proverbs, and apologues. The Cypriots and Cilicians adjoining to Syria have been the authors of certain fables that have been distinguished by the names of those people respectively, and the aptness the Cilicians in particular had for lying has been exposed in one of the most ancient proverbs among the Greeks. In short, fables were in such great vogue in all those parts that according to the testimony of Lucian there were among the Arabians and Assyrians certain persons whose sole business was to explain those fables, and who from their temperate and regular manner of living enjoyed a much longer life than any others.[8]

But it is not enough to have traced out and discovered the original source of romances; it is now time to consider by what means they found a passage into Greece and Italy. . . .

The Ionians, who were originally of Attica and Peloponnesus, could not forget from whence they sprung; they maintained an uninterrupted commerce with the Grecians; they each of them sent their children from the one to the other to be educated after the custom and manners of the country, whither they were sent respectively. During this free and open communication, Greece, which of itself was naturally inclined to fables, easily learnt from the Ionians how to write romances, and soon became great proficients in the science. But for the clearer understanding of this matter, I will endeavor to recount, in due order of time, such of the Greek writers as excelled in this art.

I can meet with none of them before Alexander the Great, which makes me believe that this art had made but a small progress among them, till by the conquest of Persia they were in a condition to learn it, as it were, at the fountainhead. Clearchus of Solium, a city in Cilicia, who lived in the days of Alexander and was in like manner one of Aristotle's disciples, is the first I can find to have written books of love.[9] Nor do I know whether what he wrote was not a collection of several amorous events drawn out

191

of the vulgar fable, like that compiled afterwards by Parthenius, under the reign of Augustus, and which is preserved down to our times.[10] . . .

I have much the same opinion of the pastorals of the sophist Longus as of the two preceding.[11] For though some learned men in these latter ages have commended them for their elegance and agreeableness, as likewise for their simplicity so proper to the subject, yet there is nothing else commendable in them besides that simplicity which however sometimes descends even to puerility and nonsense. He opens very grossly with the birth of his shepherds, and concludes his work with their nuptials. He never unravels his intrigues but by injudicious machines. Moreover he is so obscene that one must [be a little cynical] to read him without blushing. His style, for which he has been so much commended, is that for which perhaps he is the least praiseworthy; it is a style like that of a sophist, as he was, of the same stamp with that of Eustathius and Theodorus Prodromus,[12] betwixt the orator and historian, and so proper neither to the one or the other; full of metaphors and antitheses, and of those glaring figures that surprise the simple and tickle the ear without benefiting the understanding. Instead of engaging his reader by the novelty of events, the method and variety of matter, and a neat close narration which has however its proper turn and cadence, still advancing in its subject, he endeavors, as most sophists do, to delay him by descriptions foreign to the purpose. He leads him out of the high road, and whilst he exposes him to so many places where he had no business, he wearies his attention and blunts the impatience he had of arriving at the end he desired and which at first was proposed to him. I must confess I translated this romance with some pleasure in my youth, and that indeed is the only age wherein it ought to please. I will not pretend to ascertain the time wherein he lived; none of the ancients have made any mention of him, nor is there anything in him that may give ground for a conjecture, unless it be the purity of his elocution, which inclines me to think him more ancient than the two others. . . .

In the fore-mentioned catalogue I have distinguished those romances that are regular from those that are not so. I call those regular which are framed upon the rules of heroic poetry. The Grecians, by whom most arts and sciences have been brought to so great a perfection that they have been esteemed the first inventors of them, have likewise cultivated the art of romancing, and rough and unshapen as it was among the Orientals, they have worked it into a better form by confining it to the rules of the epopea and uniting in a complete body the several parts that lay without order or relation to each other in the romances that had been composed before them. Of all the Greek writers of romances beforementioned, Antonius Diogenes, Lucian, Athenagóras, Jamblicus, Heliodorus, Achilles Tatius, Eustathius, and Theodorus Prodromus are the only authors that have subjected themselves to those rules. I say nothing in this place of Lucius of Patras, nor of Damascius, whom I have not numbered in the list of romance writers. As for St. John of Damascus and Longus, they might easily have formed their works according to those rules, but they either did not know them or despised them. I know not what the three Xenophons [13] did in that respect, since we have nothing left of theirs to make any judgment upon, nor of Aristides or the rest, who with him were authors of the Milesian fables. However I believe these last observed some rules, as seems to appear from those works that have been written in imitation of them, and have been preserved down to our days, such for instance as Apuleius's *Metamorphosis*, which is regular enough.

These Milesian fables, long before they made that progress in Greece, already mentioned, conveyed themselves into Italy, where they were first entertained by the Sybarites, a people voluptuous beyond imagination; that conformity of humor which happened between them and the Milesians established between them a reciprocal communication of luxury and pleasure, and so firmly united them that Herodotus saith he never knew a better established alliance between any people whatever. From the Milesians therefore the Sybarites learnt the art of fabling, so that the Sybarite tales became as common in Italy as the Milesian were in Asia. It is hard to determine of what construction they were. Hesychius gives us to understand, in a passage that has been much corrupted, that Aesop having been in Italy, his fables grew into great reputation in that country; that improvements were made upon them; that having suffered some alterations, they were called Sybarites, and that they passed into proverbs; but he does not tell us wherein those alterations consisted.[14] Suidas thinks they were like those of Aesop, but in this he is deceived as in many other instances.[15] The old commentator upon Aristophanes saith the Sybarites introduced brutes in their fables, and that Aesop made use of men in his.[16]

This passage is certainly corrupted, for as it is plain that men were actors in Aesop's fables, it follows from thence that the Sybarites made use of brutes in theirs; and this is what the commentator saith in express terms in another place. Those of the Sybarites were diverting, and intended to

193

raise laughter in the readers. I have met with a sketch of one of them in Elian; [17] it is a story he tells us he had taken out of the histories of the Sybarites, that is to say, according to my opinion, out of their fables. You shall be a judge of it from the story itself. A Sybarite boy walking with his schoolmaster in the street met a fellow that sold dry figs, and stole one of them out of his basket; his master severely reproved him for it, but snatched the fig from him and ate it himself. These fables were not only facetious, but extremely smutty. Ovid places the *Sybaritis*, that had been composed a little before his time, in the number of the most debauched pieces. Several learned men have imagined that he thereby meant the work of Hemitheon the Sybarite, of whom Lucian speaks,[18] as of a lump of lewdness. But to me there seems no ground for this imagination, for it does not appear that there was any agreement between that book of Hemitheon and the *Sybaritis*, only that both the one and the other were very lascivious, and this was common to all the fables of the Sybarites. Besides the *Sybaritis*, as has been said before, was written not long before Ovid, and it is notorious that the city of Sybaris was razed by the Crotoniats five hundred years before the birth of that poet. It is therefore most likely that the *Sybaritis* had been composed by some Roman, and so called because written in imitation of the old Sybarite fables. A certain ancient author, whose name I take to be of no moment for you to know, gives us to understand that their style was short and laconic, but that does not prove that their fables had nothing in them of the romance. . . .

If the Romans could without a blush read those fables under the Republic at a time when an austere discipline and rigidness of manners was maintained among them, it is not to be wondered at if, when the commonwealth was subjected to the will of the emperors, and everyone after their examples abandoned themselves to luxury and pleasure, their minds bcame sensible of such as the reading of romances inspired into them. . . .

Hitherto the art of romancing continued in some reputation and figure, but declined at the same time with literature and the empire, when the rugged nations of the North overwhelmed Europe with their ignorance and barbarity. Till then romances had been composed for pleasure and delight, but now fabulous histories began to prevail for want of proper materials for true ones. Thelesin, who is said to have lived about the middle of the sixth century under the reign of King Arthur, so famous in the books of chivalry, and Melkin, who was something younger, wrote the history of their country England and of King Arthur and his Round

Table.[19] Balaeus, who has given them a place in his catalogue, makes mention of them as of very fabulous authors.[20] The same thing may be said of Hunibaldus Francus, who is said to have been contemporary with Clovis, and whose history, as he calls it, is no better than a collection of lies and absurdities.[21]

And now, sir, we are got down to the celebrated piece containing the actions of Charlemagne, which has been very injudiciously ascribed to Archbishop Turpin, though he was not born till two hundred years after.[22] Pigna and some others have been so weak as to believe that romances was so called from Rheims, of which Turpin was Archbishop, because his book, as Pigna will have it, was the fountain from whence most of the romancers of Provence supplied themselves, and was, according to others, the masterpiece of romances. . . . These histories, told in a plausible manner, did not fail to please the ignorant readers, more ignorant, if possible, than their authors. So that no one was at the pains to examine into authentic records, or to be duly informed of the truth before they took upon them to write; they had their materials nearer hand, in their own head and in their own invention, and by this means history began to degenerate into romance. The Latin tongue grew as much neglected and despised in that age of ignorance as truth itself. Your poetasters, balladmongers, storytellers, and *jongleurs* of Provence, in short all those of that country who practised what they called the *gay science*, began in the days of Hugh Capet to romance in good earnest and to roam up and down France vending their romantic wares wherever they came, composed all in the Roman language. For at that time the Provencials were better skilled in literature and poetry than all the rest of France. This language was what the Romans had introduced with their conquests, and which, in time, was corrupted with a mixture of the old Gaulish, which had preceded, and of the Frank, or Teutonic, that succeeded it; insomuch that it was neither Latin nor Gaulish nor Frank, but a medley of them all, wherein however the Roman had the predominance, for which reason it still preserved that name to distinguish it from the particular or mother tongue of each country, whether [the French, or] the Gaulish (or Celtic) or the Aquitanic, or the Belgic; for Caesar tells us these three languages differed from each other, though Strabo saith the difference was nothing else but three different dialects upon the same common language.[23] The Spaniards put the same signification upon the word *Roman* that we do, and call their vulgar tongue *Romancé*. The Roman therefore being what was most universally understood, the Provencials wrote their stories in that language, and they were for that reason called *romances*. These authors passing thus up and down were generously paid for their pains, and well received by the great men of the country where they travelled, some of whom were so taken with them that they often stripped themselves to clothe them. However, the Provencials were not the only people who addicted themselves to that agreeable occupation, for almost all the provinces in France had their romancers too, even as far as Picardy, where they had their *sirvantois*, a sort of amorous pieces, and sometimes satirical. And from hence sprung up such an incredible number of old romances, many of which are extant in print, others are mouldering away in libraries, and the rest have been consumed by time. Even Spain itself, which by degrees grew so fertile in romances, and Italy too, borrowed the art from us. . . . "I may venture to affirm," saith [Giraldi], "that this sort of poetry had its original and beginning in France, and from thence likewise it has probably received its name. The Spaniards learnt this way of poetising from the French, and now at last it has been received by the Italians."

The late Monsieur Saumaise,[24] for whose memory I have a singular veneration, both on the account of his great learning and the friendship there was between us, imagined that Spain, having learnt of the Arabs the art of romancing, taught it the rest of Europe. To support which opinion, it must be allowed that Thelesin, Melkin, both English, and Hunibaldus Francus, who are all three said to have composed their romantic histories about the middle of the sixth century, are at least two hundred years younger than has been hitherto believed; for Count Julian's revolt and the settlement of the Arabs in Spain did not happen till the ninety-first year of the Hegira, in 712 of our Lord, and it would require some time after that for the Arabian romances to take footing in Spain and for those which it is pretended were composed by the Spaniards in imitation of them to be communicated to the rest of Europe. I am far from insisting upon the antiquity of those authors, though I have some right so to do, since the common opinion is on my side. It is very true, as I have already observed, that the Arabians were much addicted to the *gay science*, that is, to poetry, fictions, and fables. This science, which remained in its primitive roughness among them, though reformed and polished by the Greeks, was carried together with their arms into Africa when they made a conquest of that country, though it was no stranger there before; for Aristotle, and Priscian from him, make mention of the Libyan fables,[25] and the romances

196

written by Apuleius and Martianus Capella, before-mentioned, who were both Africans, are instances of the genius of that people. . . . The Spaniards having, in course of time, received the Arabian yoke, received likewise from them their customs, and learnt, in imitation of them, to sing love verses and to celebrate the actions of great men after the manner of the bards in Gaul; but these songs, which they called *romances*, were very different from our modern romances; they were composed on purpose to be sung, and were consequently very short. There has been a collection made of several of them, some of which are so very ancient that they are hardly intelligible. Some of them have served to clear up the Spanish history and reduce events to a chronological series. Their romances, properly so called, are of a much later date; the eldest of them are posterior to our Tristans and Lancelots by several hundred years. Miguel de Cervantes, one of the finest wits that that nation ever produced, has made an excellent judicious [critique] upon them in his *Don Quixote*, wherein the curate and Master Nicholas the barber have much ado to find six among them all that deserve to be saved; the rest are delivered over to the secular arm of the chambermaid to be committed to the flames. Those which were thought worthy to be preserved are the four books of *Amadis de Gaule*, which they pronounce to be the first romance of chivalry that was ever printed in Spain, the model of the rest and the best of them all; *Palmerin of England*, supposed to have been written by a king of Portugal, and thought worthy of a box, like that of Darius, wherein Alexander kept the works of Homer; *Don Belianis, the Mirror of Chivalry*; *Tirante the White*, and *Kyrie Eleison of Montauban* (for there were such learned times wherein *Kyrie Eleison* and *Paralipomenon* were taken for some saints' names), wherein the subtleties of Madam Pleasure-of-my-Life, and the Cheats of the Widow Reposada are highly commended. But these are all of yesterday, when compared with our old romances from which they were in all likelihood modeled, as may be presumed from the conformity of the works and the neighborhood of the nations. He likewise censures romances written in verse, and some other pieces of poetry found in Don Quixote's study; but that is nothing to the present purpose.

If it be objected to me that as we have learnt from the Arabs the art of rhyming it is more than probable that we have in like manner received from the same hands the science of romance, forasmuch as most of our old romances were in rhyme, and that the custom among the French lords to give their clothes to the best versifiers, and which Marmol saith was practised by the Kings of Fez, seems to justify that assertion, I must confess that it is not impossible but that when the French borrowed their rhyme from the Arabs they at the same time learnt from them the custom of using it in romance. I will allow farther that the taste we had before for fable might be augmented and our science in romance improved, from the intercourse our vicinity to Spain and the wars with that nation have introduced between us and the Spaniards; but I do not agree that we owe to them originally this inclination, since we were possessed with it long before it was observed in Spain. . . .

It is very likely that the Italians were first induced to write romances from the example of the Provencials whilst the popes resided at Avignon; as likewise from the example of other Frenchmen, first, when the Normans, and afterwards when Charles, Earl of Anjou, brother of St. Louis, a virtuous prince, a lover of poetry, and himself a poet, carried on the war in Italy. For the Normans, as well as the rest, were dabblers in the *gay science*, and we learn from history that they sung the exploits of Roland just before they began that memorable battle wherein William the Bastard got the crown of England. All Europe was, at that time, involved in a cloud of impenetrable ignorance, though that ignorance prevailed less in France, England and Germany than in Italy, which, in those days, produced a very small number of authors, and hardly one writer of romance. Those of that country who were desirous to distinguish themselves with some tincture of knowledge came for that purpose to study in the University of Paris, the mother of sciences and nurse of the learned. St. Thomas Aquinas, St. Bonaventure, the poets Dante and Boccaccio were students there, and the President Fauchet has proved that Boccaccio has taken most of his novels out of our French romances, and that Petrarch and the other Italian poets have stolen their most beautiful passages [from] the songs of Thibaud, King of Navarre, from Gace's Brussez, from the Chatelain de Coucy, and [from] the old French romancers.[26] It was therefore, according to my opinion, during this intercourse between the two nations that the Italians learnt from us the science of romance, which they owe to us, as well as that of rhyming.

In this manner did Spain and Italy receive from us an art which was the effect of our ignorance and unpoliteness, but the fruit of politeness in the Persians, Greeks, and Ionians. In a word, as necessity compels us for the preservation of our lives to feed upon herbs and roots for want of bread, in like manner, when the knowledge of truth, which is the proper and natural food of the mind, is wanting, we support it with fiction, which is in imitation of truth. And as in the midst of plenty, to regale our taste, we sometimes quit our bread and usual food for the sake of ragouts, so when the mind is possessed of the truth it often quits the study and speculation of it to divert itself in the image of truth, which is falsehood. For the image and imitation are, according to Aristotle, sometimes more agreeable than truth itself, insomuch that two roads directly contrary, that is, ignorance and erudition, politeness and barbarity, often conduct men to one and the same end, the study of fictions, fables, and romances. From hence it is that the nations that are the most barbarous delight in romantic inventions, as those that are opposite love such as are most polite. The accounts of the originals of all the savage nations in America, and particularly those of Peru, are stuffed with fables, as are those of the Goths, which they inscribed heretofore in their ancient Runic characters upon large stones, of which I have seen some fragments in Denmark; and if we had anything remaining of the writings composed by the bards in Gaul to eternise the memory of their nation, I do not question but we should find them embellished with a multitude of fictions.

This inclination to fables, which is common to all men, is not the effect of reasoning, nor does it arise from imitation or custom; it is natural to them, and is riveted in the very frame and disposition of the soul. For the desire to learn and to know is peculiar to man, by which he is as much distinguished from other creatures as by his reason. Nay, the sparks of an imperfect rough-hewn reason are observable in some animals, but the desire of knowledge is found nowhere but in man. And this is, according to my opinion, because the faculties of our mind are of too great an extent, and of a capacity too large to be filled and satisfied with present objects, for which reason she searcheth into what is past and to come, into truth and falsehood, into imaginary spaces and even impossibilities, to find out wherewithal to exercise and satisfy those faculties. Brutes find in the objects presented to their senses sufficient to answer the powers of their mind, and go no farther; insomuch that we never observe in them that impatient thirst which incessantly incites the mind of man to search after new discoveries and [to] proportion, if it be possible, the object to the faculty, and taste therein a pleasure equal to that one finds in appeasing a violent hunger or in drinking after having been long under an impatient thirst. This is what Plato would represent to us in the fable of the marriage of Porus and Penia, that is, of riches and poverty, whose offspring, he saith, is pleasure.[27] The object is denoted by riches, which are not riches but when they are used, without which they remain unfruitful, and will never occasion the birth of pleasure. The faculty is expressed by poverty, and which is barren, and constantly attended with inquietude whilst debarred from riches; but upon their being joined, pleasure becomes the fruit of that union. This exactly squares with the disposition of our mind. Poverty, that is ignorance, is natural to it, and is continually breathing after knowledge, which is riches, and when possessed of it, that possession is attended with pleasure. But this pleasure is not always alike; it sometimes costs us a great deal of labor and pains, as when the mind applies itself to difficult speculations and abstruse sciences, whereof the subject matter is not present or obvious to our senses, and where the imagination, which works with ease, is less concerned and engaged than the understanding, whose operations are very laborious. And forasmuch as we are naturally shocked at the prospect of labor, the mind never engages in those knotty disquisitions but from the prospect of reward, or in the hope of some remote pleasure, or out of necessity. But those discoveries which engage and possess it the most effectually are such as are obtained with the least labor, wherein the imagination has the greatest share, and where the subject is such as is obvious to our senses; but more especially if those discoveries excite our passions, which give the main bias and motion to all the actions of our life. And of this sort are romances, which are to be comprehended without any great labor of the mind or the exercise of our rational faculty, and where a strong fancy will serve the turn with little or no burden to the memory. They do not raise our passions but to allay them, nor do they excite in us either fear or pity but that we may have the pleasure at [last] of seeing those escape out of the imaginary danger or distress wherein they at first had represented them. Love is not raised in us but to the end we may see those happy who are the objects of it, nor is our hatred moved but to give us the satisfaction of seeing those miserable against whom it was excited. In short, all our passions are there agreeably raised and laid. Hence it is that they who are governed more by passion than reason and act more with their imagination than understanding have a more sensible pleasure in romances; not but that the other find a pleasure in them too, but not after the same manner. These are taken with the beauties of the art and with those parts wherein the understanding was most concerned; but those, that is children and ignorants, are only touched with what strikes the imagination, and works upon

200

their passions. They are in love with the fictions purely as such, and carry their thoughts no farther. Now fictions being narrations, that are true in appearance but false in effect, the simple, who look no farther than the outside and content themselves with the appearance of truth, rest themselves there; but they who have a deeper penetration and look into the bottom are apt to disrelish that which has only the appearance of truth. So that, in short, the first love the fiction for the sake of the appearance of truth under which it is disguised; but the later are disgusted at this imaginary truth by reason of the real falsity that is concealed under it, if that falsity is not at the same time ingenious, allegorical, and instructive, and supported by the excellency of art and invention. St. Austin saith somewhere that "those falsities which are significative and contain in them a hidden sense are not properly lies, but figurative truths, made use of by men renowned for their wisdom and sanctity, and even by our Saviour himself upon occasion."

Since therefore it is most certain that ignorance is the inexhaustible fund of falsehoods, and that the inundation of the barbarians who, issuing from the North, overran all Europe and sunk it into such an abyss of ignorance as that it was not able to recover itself out of it till about two hundred years since, is it not highly probable that the same cause produced the same effect here that it has at all times done in other places? And is it not therefore in vain to endeavor to prove that to be accidental which is manifestly natural? So that we are not to doubt but that the French, German, and English romances, with all the fables of the North, are of the country's growth, born upon the place and not transplanted thither, having no other beginning but in histories stuffed with falsehoods and written in those times of ignorance and obscurity, when men had neither industry nor curiosity enough to discover the truth, nor judgment to write it when discovered; that those histories patched up with truth and falsehoods, having been well received by the rude unpolished people, the writers were encouraged from thence to publish some that were all fiction, and those are romances. It is even the common opinion that history heretofore went by the name of romance, which word was afterwards applied to fictions; which is an invincible argument that the one arose out of the other. "Romances," [saith Pigna,] "according to the common opinion in France, were their annals, and for that reason the histories of their respective wars were published under that title likewise; whereupon others, in time, gave their writings the same name, how fabulous soever they were and foreign to truth."

Strabo, in a passage I have already cited, saith the histories of the Persians, Medes, and Syrians are not to be relied upon because the compilers of them, observing what high reputation the fabulists were in, endeavored to advance themselves likewise in the esteem of the people by giving fables the air of histories, that is, by writing romances. From whence we may conclude that the word *romance*, according to all appearance, had the same origin with us as it had heretofore among those nations.

But to return to the [trouvères] of Provence, who in France were the princes of romance: towards the end of the tenth century, their profession became so much in vogue that all the provinces in France, as has been already said, had in time their [trouvères] too. This produced in the eleventh century, and in those that succeeded, an infinite number of romances, both in prose and verse, many of which have, in spite of time, been continued down to us. Of this number were Garin le Loheran, Tristan, Lancelot du Lac, de Bertain, St. Greal, Merlin, Arthur, Perceval, Perceforet, and most of the hundred twenty-seven poets who lived before the year 1300, and upon whom the President Fauchet has written an examen. . . .

It will be sufficient to tell you that all these writings, being the fruits of ignorance, carried in them the marks of their original, and were no other than a heap of fictions bunglingly stitched one to another, and infinitely beneath that sovereign degree of art and elegance to which our nation has since raised the romance. We must confess it is a matter of wonder that at the same time that we have yielded to our neighbors the prize of epic poetry and history we should attain to such a perfection in this, as that their most finished romances come far short of the worst of ours. I am of opinion that this is owing to the politeness of our gallantry and the great liberty in which the men live with the women in France. [The women] are perfect recluses in Spain and Italy, and debarred from the men under so many obstacles that one rarely sees and seldom or never speaks to them. So that [the men] never study the art of agreeable courtship because the opportunities of putting it in practice are so rare. All their study lies in surmounting the difficulties that lie in their way to come at them; when that is done they make the best of their time without standing upon ceremony. But in France, where the ladies are left more at liberty and have no other guards upon them but their own honor, they are more impregnably secured within the bounds of that than they can be under all the locks, within all the grates, and under the care of the most vigilant duennas in Spain. This obliges the men with us to besiege in form that formidable entrenchment, and to employ so much pains and address to reduce it, that courtship is become an art in France almost unknown in other nations. It is this art which distinguishes the French romances from others, and has rendered the reading of them so bewitching that it has introduced among us a neglect of more useful studies. The ladies were the first that were taken with these allurements; they have made romances their entire study, and have so far despised that of the ancient fable and of history that they have quite laid aside those works which heretofore furnished them with their greatest ornaments. And to prevent blushing at that ignorance which they have such frequent occasions of discovering in themselves, they have found it more to their purpose to seem to despise what they do not know than to be at the pains to learn it. The men out of complaisance have followed their example. What the ladies condemn they condemn likewise, and call that pedantry which even in Malherbe's time was thought essential to politeness.[28] The succeeding poets and other [of] our French writers have been obliged to submit to this [verdict], and many of them, observing that the knowledge of antiquity was of no benefit to them, forbore studying that which they durst not put in practice. Thus a good cause has produced a very mischievous effect, and the beauty of our romances has occasioned a contempt of learning of which ignorance has been the unavoidable consequence.

I do not for this reason condemn the reading of them. The best things in the world are never without some inconveniencies, and romances [might have] worse consequences than ignorance. I know what is commonly objected to them: they deaden our devotion, they inspire us with irregular passions, and corrupt our manners. This may happen, and without doubt does happen sometimes. But what may not be perverted by a vicious inclination? Weak minds are contagious to themselves, and turn everything into poison. Upon that account, the reading of history ought to be forbidden because it affords so many pernicious examples, and mythology laid aside where transgressions are warranted from the practice of the gods themselves. A marble statue which was the object of public devotion among the heathens incited a certain young man to brutality and despair. Cherea in Terence [fortifies] himself in the prosecution of a criminal design from a painting of Jupiter, which perhaps was revered by all other spectators.[29] Small regard was had to the sobriety of manners in the generality of the Greek and old French romances, and that through the corruption of the times wherein they were written. Even *Astrea*,[30] and some

203

other romances that succeeded, are in a degree licentious; but the romances of this age, I speak of the good ones, are so free from that imputation that there is not in them a single word or expression offensive to a chaste ear, or an action distasteful to a modest mind. If it is objected that love is therein treated after a manner so refined and insinuating that the bait of that dangerous passion is too easily swallowed by unguarded minds, I answer that it is so far from being dangerous that it is in some sort necessary for young persons to be acquainted with that passion that they may be able to shut their ears against it when it is criminal and know how to conduct themselves in it when it is innocent and honorable. This is evident from experience, which shows us that they who are the least read in love are most open to it, and that the most ignorant are the greatest cullies. Let us add to this that nothing quickens the mind so much or conduces more to the forming and finishing of it than good romances. They are silent instructors that take us up where the college left us, teaching us to speak and live after a method more edifying and persuasive than what is practised there, to whom Horace's compliment upon the *Iliad* may justly be applied, that morality is more effectually taught by them than by the precepts of the most able philosophers.[31]

Monsieur d'Urfé was the first who retrieved them from barbarity, and brought them under a regulation in his incomparable *Astrea*, a piece the most ingenious and polite of any of that kind that had appeared, and which eclipsed the glory Greece, Italy and Spain had acquired before. However, this did not discourage others who followed from entering into the same lists, or so far engrossed the esteem of the public as to leave none for so many beautiful romances as have appeared in France since his time. We cannot behold without admiration those a lady as illustrious for her modesty as her merit has published under a borrowed name, thereby generously depriving herself of a reputation so justly her due, and seeking no other recompense but what flowed from her own virtue, as if whilst she was laboring so industriously for the glory of our nation she was willing to spare our sex the shame of it. But time has done her that justice which she denied herself, and it is [now no] longer a secret that the *Illustrious Bassa*, the *Grand Cyrus*, and *Clelia* are the performances of Mademoiselle de Scudéry, so that the art of writing romances, which can justify itself against censure not only from the commendations given it by the patriarch Photinus but from the examples of those who have dealt in it may at last receive a sanction from her; and after having been cultivated by philosophers, as Apuleius and Athenagoras, by a Roman praetor, as Sisenna, by a consul, as Petronius, by a pretender to the empire, as Clodius Albinus, by a priest, as Theodorus Prodromus, by bishops, as Heliodorus and Achilles Tatius, by a Pope, as Pius II, who wrote the amours of Euryalus and Lucrece, and by a saint, as St. John of Damascus, it is at length arrived to the highest pitch of glory, by being professed by a grave and virtuous virgin.[32] As for you sir, since it is true, as I have made appear, and as Plutarch assures us, that there is no charm can captivate the soul of man so effectually as the contexture of a fable well invented and related, what success may you not promise to yourself from *Zayde*, wherein the adventures are so new and moving, and the narration so just and polite? I could wish, from the concern I have for the glory of that great monarch heaven has placed over us, that we had a history of his illustrious reign, written in a style as noble and with the same accuracy and judgment. The virtues which conduct his great actions are so heroic and that fortune which accompanies them is so surprising that posterity may doubt whether it be a history or romance.

✣ 1671

Dominique Bouhours THE BEL ESPRIT FROM "THE CONVERSATIONS OF ARISTO AND EUGENE"

Eugene and Aristo began their walk with the reading of a work containing both prose and verse which one of their friends had recently composed. They read it attentively, as new things are always read; and after examining it at leisure they were both of the opinion that for a long time nothing had appeared which was wittier or more reasonable.

A man must be very intelligent, said Eugene, to write the kinds of works in which witticisms glitter everywhere and in which there are no paste jewels.

Intelligence alone is not enough, replied Aristo; a special kind is needed. Only the keenest wit produces masterpieces, for it is the quality which gives to excellent pieces of writing the special shape which distinguishes them from ordinary ones, and that characteristic of perfection by which new charms are always to be found in them. But everybody does not have this keen wit I am speaking of, he added, and he who counterfeits the clever man has it perhaps less than another. For there is much difference between being professionally clever and having a keen wit of a certain beauty which I can imagine.

If that beauty of wit which you imagine is a very rare thing, said Eugene, the reputation for cleverness is fairly common; it is the compliment most frequently paid in society. It even seems to me there is no quality more easily acquired. One need only be able to tell a story agreeably or turn a line of verse: a trifle gracefully said, a madrigal, a couplet for a song can often be the basis for a reputation as a wit; and you must agree that it is of these clever talkers and makers of pretty things that we are accustomed to say, He is a bel esprit.

I admit, answered Aristo, that this title has been as freely and unjustly usurped in our time as that of gentleman or marquis; and if the usurpers

206

in the realm of letters were punished as severely as these other usurpers have been in France many people would be degraded from that rank as many have been from the nobility. Those clever gentlemen would have a hard time commanding respect for their madrigals, their jingles, and their impromptus and thus maintaining themselves in their present status; I am sure they would not find in their papers grounds for clinging to the eminence they claim. Their titles are no better than those of false nobles; the name they bear is a name floating in the air unsupported by anything substantial; they have a reputation for wit but without deserving it and without exemplifying it.

The witty man is a foolish type, said Eugene, and I don't know whether I wouldn't rather be a little stupid than to pass as what is ordinarily called clever.

All reasonable men are of your opinion, answered Aristo. Wit has been so much disparaged since its profanation through being made too common that the wittiest men object to the name and avoid being accused of it as though it were a crime. Those who are still proud of the name are not the decent people in society; indeed, they are far from being what they think they are; they are nothing less than beaux esprits, for true beauty of wit consists in a just and delicate discernment which those gentlemen do not have. That discernment shows things to be what they are in themselves, not stopping too soon, as do the common people who do not go below the surface, and not going too far like those refined intelligences which, through an excess of subtlety, evaporate in vain and chimerical imaginings.

It seems to me, interrupted Eugene, that this exquisite discernment is more closely related to common sense than to bel esprit.

True wit, answered Aristo, is inseparable from common sense, and it is a mistake to confuse it with that sort of vivacity which has nothing solid in it. One might say that judgment is the foundation for beauty of wit; or rather bel esprit is of the nature of those precious stones which are not less solid than brilliant. There is nothing more beautiful than a well-cut and well-polished diamond; it shines on every side and on every facet. *Quanta sodezza, tanto ha splendore.*[1] It is solid but brilliant matter, it dazzles but has consistency and body. The union, the mixture, the proportion of the brilliant with the solid give it all its charm and all its value. There is a symbol for bel esprit as I conceive it. It is equally brilliant and solid: it might well be defined as common sense which sparkles. For there is a kind of gloomy, bleak common sense which is hardly less the contrary of wit than is a false brilliance. The common sense I am speaking of is entirely different; it is gay, lively, full of fire, like that which is seen in the *Essays* of Montaigne and in the *Testament* of la Hoguette;[2] it proceeds from a straight and luminous intelligence and from a clear and pleasant imagination.

The just apportionment of vivacity to common sense renders the mind subtle but not vapid, brilliant but not too brilliant, quick to conceive an idea, and sound in all its judgments. With that kind of wit one thinks of things properly and expresses them as well as they have been thought. Much meaning is gathered into few words, everything is said that need be said and only that is said which must be said. The bel esprit is concerned more with things than with words; yet he does not scorn the ornaments of language, neither does he seek them out; the polish of his style does not lessen its strength, and he might be compared to those soldiers under Caesar who, for all they were clean and perfumed, were nonetheless valiant men who fought well.[3]

On the basis of what you are saying, remarked Eugene, there is not much difference between a bel esprit and a rationalist (*esprit fort*).

There is none at all, replied Aristo, if we take the latter expression in its literal meaning, a strong mind. The beauty of wit is a masculine and gallant beauty which has in it nothing soft or effeminate.

But that strength does not consist in doubting everything, in believing nothing, and in being stiff-necked before established truths. According to the remark of a Father of the Church, that kind of strength is the strength of a madman.[4] True strength consists, then, in reasoning well, in getting down to fundamental principles of knowledge and in discovering the most hidden truths. It is right for a thinker to go deeply into the subjects he treats and not to let himself be led astray by appearances. Reasons which satisfy lesser minds are not reasons for him; he always goes straight to his goal by whatever way may best lead there, without being diverted and without dawdling. His principal characteristic is to sweep other minds along in the direction he wishes them to take and to make himself master of them when he chooses. This was one of the qualities of the last Marshal Schomberg;[5] it was said of him as well of Caesar that he talked as courageously as he fought, and that his weapons were not more invincible than his arguments.

But do not imagine that the bel esprit, because he is very strong, is for that reason lacking in delicacy: he resembles Achilles in Homer and Rinaldo in Tasso whose nerves and muscles were extremely strong under a white and tender skin. His solidity and profundity do not keep him from conceiving things with finesse, nor from giving refined expression to all that he thinks. The images by which he expresses his thoughts are like those paintings which have all the technique of art and in addition what must be called a tender and graceful air which charms the connoisseur.

There are excellent minds which have no delicacy and who are proud of having none, as if delicacy were incompatible with strength. Their way of thinking and saying things has no sweetness and no attractiveness. With all their learning and all their subtlety their imaginations are in some way sombre and crude, like that Spanish painter who could make only coarse strokes and who proudly replied one day to those who criticized him for this that he preferred to be *primero en aquella grossería que secundo en delicadeza.*[6]

But men of this turn of mind, however good they may be, are not so felicitous in their works as that painter was in his. The most learned writings and even the most ingenious are judged unfavorably in our day if they are not delicately handled. Besides their solidity and their strength they must have what I shall call an agreeable and flowery quality in order to please people of good taste, and that is what gives individuality to beautiful things. To understand what I mean, remember what Plato says, that beauty is like the flower of goodness. According to that philosopher good things which do not have that flower are only good, and those which have it are really beautiful.

That is to say, added Eugene, that the bel esprit, if we define him Platonically, is a good mind in flower, like those trees which bear fruit and flowers at the same time and in which we see the maturity of autumn allied to the beauty of spring.

Col fior, maturo ha, sempre il frutto.[7]

Those fruits and flowers, Aristo went on, indicate also that happy fecundity which is so fitting in a gifted man. For myself I consider there is not less difference between sterile minds and those which are not than there is between handsome orange trees and mean growths which produce no fruit.

I doubt, interrupted Eugene, whether fertility is a sound indication of beauty of mind. It seems to me that the most fecund minds are not al-

209

ways the most reasonable or the most acute. Great fecundity most often degenerates into an undesirable abundance, into a profusion of false and useless thoughts; and if you examine the question carefully you will see that what you are calling a property of the bel esprit is usually no more than the effect of an unbridled imagination.

I am well aware, replied Aristo, that there is a fertility of mind similar to that of trees which, because they are too heavy-laden with fruit, bear little that is good. The fecundity I am speaking of is not of that kind. It is what I have called a happy fecundity, not only a stock of good things but one which is controlled by common sense. A real bel esprit is like those rich and wise people who live magnificently in every way, yet who nevertheless are not extravagant.

By that criterion, said Eugene, Marino would not be a bel esprit. For never has a more fertile imagination been seen, nor one less controlled, than his. You know this better than I. If he speaks of a nightingale or a rose, he says of it everything imaginable; far from rejecting what presents itself to him, he goes out of his way to seek what does not occur to him; he always exhausts his subject.

I agree, replied Aristo, and I shall also confess to you, he added laughing, that if letters patent for the bel esprit were issued as they are for the nobility I should never approve their being given to those kinds of authors who do not control their ideas or their words, and who leave nothing to be thought or said on the subjects they treat. But not all poets are as mad or as undisciplined as Marino. Some of them are wise and moderate, even among the Italians, though the only example I can give is that of Tasso.

I assure you, said Eugene, that Tasso is not always the most reasonable man in the world. Truly, it is not possible to have more genius than he has. His conceptions are noble and agreeable; his feelings are strong or delicate depending upon what the subject requires; his passions are well handled and well developed, all his comparisons are exact, all his descriptions are marvelous; but his genius sometimes carries him away; in some places he is too flowery; he trifles at rather serious junctures; he is not so respectful as Virgil of all the moral proprieties.

Yet there are in his works such great beauties, replied Aristo, that he may be pardoned these little faults. If he is a little lacking in that good sense which distinguishes Virgil from the other poets still he has an abundance of that sacred fire which makes poets. After all, whatever liberties he takes, he does not lose himself as Marino does and Ariosto.

210

But to go on with our discourse, he continued, a bel esprit is rich in his own resources; he finds in his own understanding what ordinary people find only in books. He studies himself and educates himself, as a learned man said of one of the greatest geniuses France has ever produced.[8] Above all he does not take over the thoughts of others; he does not steal from the ancients or from foreigners the works he gives to the public.

Yet, said Eugene, that is what most of our clever men do. They continually pillage the Greeks and the Romans, the Italians and the Spaniards; and if anyone were willing to examine their works carefully he would discover that the land of Belles Lettres is full of robbers and that Mercury, who presides over the arts and sciences, is also, and not without cause, the god of thieves, as Bartoli cleverly remarks in his *L'Uomo di lettere*.[9] For while criticizing those who steal the thoughts of others I have no desire to steal this one from its author.

While forbidding larceny to the bel esprit, Aristo went on, I do not intend to forbid him to read good books; I do not even claim that his reading ought to be useless to him. I am willing for him to imitate the great models of antiquity if only he tries to surpass them in his imitation; but I cannot allow him to do like those minor painters who limit themselves to copying the originals and who would produce nothing beautiful if the masters of the art had not done so before them.

I am also perfectly willing for him to use at certain junctures thoughts from good authors provided that he adds new beauties to them, and following the example of bees who change into honey what they take from flowers, not only that he chooses what is good in books but that besides he makes his own what he chooses, and that he turns it into something better through the usage he makes of it. This is one of the great talents of Voiture;[10] he has made himself inimitable through imitating others; he knows admirably the art of drawing the best from, and of showing off the thought of, his authors; the lines he sometimes borrows from Terence and Horace seem made for his subject and are even more beautiful in the places where he puts them than in those whence he took them, just as precious stones are more beautiful when mounted in rings than in the rocks whence they are extracted.

But do not suppose that all of the beauty of wit can be reduced to this. Besides what I have just mentioned, it demands a nature able to acquire all the artistic skills, a lofty and broad intelligence, unlimited and unsurpassed. For beauty of wit is like that of the body: little men, however well formed, are not handsome, in Aristotle's opinion; at best they are only agreeable, because to have the advantage of stature is an essential part of beauty. Thus the little genius who is limited to a single thing, the maker of pretty verses who can do only that with whatever charm and decorum, is not a bel esprit, say what you will; he is really only a wit and it would be enough for him to be accepted on that footing in society.

Moreover, to be a bel esprit it is not enough to have a solid, profound, delicate, fertile, just, and universal intelligence; the mind must have besides a certain clarity which all great geniuses do not have. For some of them are naturally obscure and even affect obscurity; a large proportion of their ideas are so many enigmas and mysteries; their language is a kind of cipher which can be understood only through divination. Among modern Spaniards Gracián is one of these incomprehensible geniuses; he can rise very high, he has subtlety, strength, and common sense; but most of the time the reader doesn't know what he means as perhaps he doesn't know himself; some of his works seem made to defy understanding.

However, there ought to be neither obscurity nor confusion in what comes from a bel esprit; his thoughts and expressions must be so noble and so clear that the most intelligent of his readers admire him and the least intelligent understand him. Malherbe, who was no doubt a great genius, tried above all to give this quality of clarity to all that he wrote; and you know that when he had composed a work he read it to his servant before showing it at court in order to find out whether he had completely succeeded, believing that works of the intelligence do not achieve entire perfection if they are not filled with a certain beauty which is accessible even to the crudest of men.[11] It is plain to you, of course, that this beauty must be simple and unstudied, free of pretense and artifice, if it is to make its effect; and on that basis you can judge those writers who are not natural, who are always stilted in expression, and who try never to say anything except what surprises and dazzles.

Heavens! how you please me, said Eugene, in excluding from the company of the beaux esprits those eternal sayers of witticisms and maxims; those copiers and apes of Seneca; those Mancini, Malvezzi, and Loredans [12] who are always trying to shine through clever remarks or *vivezze d'ingegno*, as they say in their language. For to tell the truth, I cannot bear them, and I have trouble putting up with Seneca himself because of his perpetual witticisms and antitheses.

Nothing outrages common sense more than that, said Aristo, and in

212

my opinion it is a greater defect to shine excessively than not to shine enough.

There is nothing finer than the conception you have of the bel esprit, answered Eugene. I very nearly said there is nothing finer than this picture of you, for you have, as it were, painted yourself in the picture you have just made, so much does it resemble you.

If I painted myself, said Aristo, smiling, it was so flatteringly that I do not recognize myself. But to answer you seriously, he added, I have too low an opinion of myself to believe that I am a good model of the bel esprit; I do not aspire so high and I should be ridiculous to do so.

But one must not aspire to it, said Eugene. One must not even be grateful that one is a bel esprit in order really to be one; and if I dared touch the picture you have drawn, I should add to it modesty as a last trait. It is a quality which gives relief to all the others and which is not less becoming to a bel esprit than to a pretty woman.

I am entirely of your opinion, answered Aristo, and I admit that I detest nothing so much as certain mediocrities who try very hard to be imposing. They have in their behavior, their movements, and even in the tone of their voice a quality of pride and self-sufficiency which leads one to judge that they are well satisfied with themselves. They profess never to be favorably impressed by anything and to find something to criticize in everything. Every work of literature seems to them pitiable, but on the other hand they admire all that they do themselves. In company they often take an oracular tone and decide every question highhandedly. They make a great mystery of their works perhaps from affectation, or in order to excite further the curiosity of those who want to see them, or because they judge few people capable of admiring them at their full value. Those works are hidden treasures which they show only to three or four of their admirers.

There is another class of minds, continued Eugene, who are less mysterious but who are not less convinced of their own merit. No sooner have they tossed off some trifle than they present it to everybody. They are always ready to recite their madrigals and odes in order to attract a little praise; they shamelessly praise themselves and are the first to burn incense in their own honor. However, the real bel esprit has the qualities of a real hero who never talks of what he has done. He avoids general applause, and far from pushing himself in where he is not wanted, he hides as much as he can.

213

I don't know, said Aristo, whether there might not be more modesty in less affectation. You have heard of that woman whom Nero loved so much, and you know that she was not very respectable. Yet, if we are to believe Tacitus, she rarely showed herself and never went out unveiled.[13]

A bel esprit ought, in my opinion, keep the temperament of Tasso's Sofronia, who was as modest as she was beautiful.

Non coprì sue bellezze, e non l'espose.[14]

He need not always keep his works a mystery, but neither must he show them everywhere; he must neither hide himself through affectation nor show himself through vanity.

Now I see, said Eugene, why the real bel esprit is so rare. Qualities as contrary as vivacity and common sense, delicacy and strength, not to mention the others, are not often found together. But I should like very much to know, he added, whence come all the qualities which make a man a bel esprit.

They come, replied Aristo, from a fortunate temperament and a certain arrangement of the organs: they are the result of a well-made and a well-proportioned head, of a well-tempered brain filled with a delicate substance, of an ardent and luminous bile made firm by melancholy and softened by the blood. The bile gives brilliance and profundity, melancholy gives good sense and solidity, the blood, charm and finesse.

I do not understand all this, said Eugene, about bile, blood and melancholy, for indeed I cannot believe that spiritual qualities more angelic than human owe what they are to what we have in common with the animals; and I do not see how the humors which stagnate in the body can be the principle of the noblest operations of the soul.

I have read in some Platonic philosopher or other, replied Aristo, that however material these humors may be they create great minds more or less as the vapors of the earth make thunder and lightning. This philosopher's idea is subtle and ingenious. I think he means that the spirits of the blood and the bile glow in the brain as a warm exhalation catches fire in a cold and damp cloud; that these glowing spirits spread through the head that *dry splendor* which according to Heraclitus makes the soul wise and intelligent; that as in corporeal things there is nothing which has less matter and more virtue, which is purer and more alive than these spirits, therefore that the flame which comes from them is the subtlest, livest and most ardent that exists in nature; that it is this flame which illumines the reason and at the same time warms the imagination; that this flame renders visible to the soul the physical shape of things and shows all things to the soul in their true light; in a word, that it is by the light of this good fire that the understanding discovers and contemplates the most hidden truths; and that it is perhaps this fire which shines in the eyes of intelligent people and distinguishes them from the stupid, whose gloomy, somber eyes sufficiently indicate that they have in their heads only a black and dark fire better suited to befog the soul than to illumine it.

Those are truly beautiful visions, said Eugene, and perhaps the daydreams of poets as much deserve belief as the ideas of those philosophers.

Even though you were to call Abelard himself a dreamer and a visionary, replied Aristo, I must tell you his idea about the differences among minds. His dear Heloïse one day put to him the question you have asked me. He answered that all men have a looking-glass in their head, and this answer was based on the words of Saint Paul [15] to the effect that we see as in a glass darkly during this life; but he added that crude minds had a dull glass and subtle minds a shining, clear one which represented objects distinctly to them. He meant that bile mixed with blood formed in the brain a kind of polished, shining surface to which melancholy served as the silver.

Whatever you may say, continued Eugene, and whatever your amorous doctor may say, I cannot make myself believe that souls borrow their light from bodies, and that beauty of mind is a perfection foreign to the spirit itself. I should rather believe that the perfection of the body depends on that of the spirit, or at least that the excellence of the spirit comes from the nobility of the soul.

I am aware that all souls are of the same kind, but that is no hindrance, if we are to believe the most reasonable philosophers, to their having special perfections which distinguish them adequately from each other, as the stars have differing degrees of clarity or differences in other qualities although they are all composed of the same matter. In truth, all reasonable souls are images of God; all are marked by the light of His countenance as the prophet says; but there exist some in which that light is better seen and in which the characteristics of its divine beauty are more deeply graven; these are the noblest and the most perfect, the most intelligent and the most ingenious. For as some figures made in wax with the same seal are clearer and better shaped than others owing to nothing but the hand that pressed down the seal, so the perfection found in some souls results from the fact that the image of God is better imprinted upon them; the greater strength of this impression makes them in some way more spiritual and more divine.

But if that is true, said Aristo, how does it come about that although the soul is incorruptible and unalterable by its nature, the mind is altered by a vapor which rises to the brain and sometimes takes away the reason?

The reason is that the noblest souls, answered Eugene, are like painters who, however skillful they may be, can do nothing without the instruments of their art. The good disposition of the organs and the special tempering of the humors do not alone make souls intelligent and ingenious, any more than delicate brushes and fine paints make excellent painters; but the organs and the humors are instruments needed by the soul if it is to act while it is in the body; once these instruments are spoiled the soul no longer acts or acts only imperfectly however perfect it may be in itself. The soul is then comparable to a good painter who has poor brushes and poor paints.

What you say is clever, interrupted Aristo, but after all, the philosophers you believe the wisest are not better founded on reason than the others; and I am very much afraid, he added laughingly, that if that nobility of soul, to which they attribute excellence of intelligence, were to be examined, the criteria by which they judge it would be found to be false. The best decision, in my opinion, is not to take sides in disputes where the truth cannot be recognized; and the most reasonable men perhaps are those who reason least about matters like that.

However that may be, Eugene continued, it is certain that nature alone does not make the bel esprit. The most fortunate native endowment must be completed by a good education and by that experience with the world which refines the intelligence and makes common sense more subtle. Thus it comes about that professional scholars are usually not beaux esprits; as they are always buried in study and have little intercourse with respectable people, their minds do not have that special politeness and that indefinable charm which they must have. Not that learning is in itself opposed to beauty of mind, but rather that the great doctors and those who know the most Greek and Latin ordinarily do not know how to use their knowledge.

It is also certain, he added, that no matter what principle such beauty comes from, there is more than one kind of bel esprit. For besides those we have mentioned up to now who excel in letters and who have acquired all the knowledge study can give, there are others who, although they have studied almost nothing except society, have all they need in order to succeed in conversation.

The characteristic of men like that is to speak well and easily and to give an entertaining twist to whatever they say; in company they always return very clever answers; they always have some subtle question to propose and some amusing story to tell with which they urge on the conversation or stimulate it when it begins to languish; once they are fairly started they say a thousand amazing things; they are skilled in witty badinage and clever chaff when the conversation is gay, but they also manage very well in serious ones; they think soundly on all subjects which are brought up and they always speak solid sense.

There is also another kind of bel esprit who can be called the diplomat or the statesman. Such a man has a clear, judicious, active intelligence suited to affairs; with one glance he looks into the heart of the matter and analyzes all its attendant circumstances and all its consequences; he finds at once all the expedients and the means by which the most difficult affairs can be handled and made to succeed. But he sees only what must be seen and only as much as he need see in order to come to a sound decision and make a reasonable choice, for it is sometimes a weakness in practical life to be too profound and too intelligent; many different points of view and different approaches dissipate the mind and often hinder execution; the time for action is spent in deliberating.

Such men are born for the government of States, for they conceive only great plans, useful to the country and glorious to the Prince; this happens especially when the Prince, convinced of their ability, their faithfulness, and their zeal, turns over to them the direction of affairs. Since they have both great intelligence and much experience they take no false measures and make no false advances. Then if fortune, which is not always in agreement with prudence, does not favor all their enterprises, they profit from their bad luck, imitating those wise steersmen who make use of contrary winds as well as of favorable ones. In negotiations they conduct themselves with great skill and in a very delicate way; first they lay bare the thoughts of him with whom they are dealing while hiding their own; they insinuate their point of view into his mind; they urge him to it on the ground of his own interest; they handle and steer him so well that he imagines he will get what he wants by agreeing with them and ends by giving what they want without even knowing he is giving. Such were Cardinal

217

Richelieu and Count Olivares, the two most famous ministers that France and Spain have ever had.

Those are the different characteristics of the bel esprit. These three kinds of beauty, although they are different, are occasionally found in one person. For not to mention the ancients and foreigners, Cardinal Duperron and the late Monsieur d'Avaux [16] were equally well suited to letters, to conversation, and to business; there are others among us who scarcely yield to these great men and who are equally capable of writing a work of literature, of telling a pleasant story, and of negotiating a peace treaty.

However, generally speaking, these three talents are only rarely found together. Men skilled in affairs do not ordinarily succeed in literature; but also the most polished and precise authors do not always shine in conversation. The first group have more solidity than finesse; the study of statecraft completely occupies them; they count other kinds of knowledge as nothing. The second group are too delicate and too touchy; they are almost never satisfied with what occurs to them; they almost never say anything when they are in company through thinking about what they mean to say. Since they are accustomed to sink into a brown study in order to phrase their thought well, they are most often absent-minded; they are often gloomily silent in a gay conversation, but also, since they have their heads full of their own compositions, they sometimes talk too much; they draw all the conversation to themselves and leave no chance for others to talk.

Conversational wit is a natural wit, opposed to labor and constraint; it is the opposite of learning and skill in affairs; thus we see that those who have this talent are ordinarily idlers whose principal occupation is the paying and receiving of visits. Hence, if one looks deeply into these things, it seems that these different kinds of wit are incompatible, and even that they require completely contrary natural predispositions.

Although it may seem, said Aristo then, that the bel esprit must belong to one of the various classes you have just marked out, yet he belongs to every one of those classes, for he is born ready for anything and has in himself talents such that he will succeed in whatever he wishes to undertake. The apparent diversity comes less from the nature of wit than from the subjects on which it is exercised. Great men who excel in certain things because they applied themselves to these in their youth would perhaps have succeeded equally well in others if they had brought to them as much care and application.

Chance, which takes a hand in the way men live and which often is the determining factor in the profession they embrace, ordinarily makes the difference we see among intelligences. Some find themselves led, I do not know how, to establish their reputation and fortune through poetry; for this they need only to have succeeded with a sonnet inspired by passion or perhaps by mere caprice; the praise which results from this is tempting bait which leads them to try a second; the high opinion one comes easily to have of oneself urges the writer on to something greater; he reads the poets, he studies the fables, he consults the masters of the art; in a word he specializes in poetry and bit by bit becomes a professional poet almost without being able to be anything else. Now if these excellent poets do not always have a talent for business or for conversation the reason is that they have taken another road from the beginning, and instead of studying politics and seeing the best people they have devoted themselves to books and writing.

The diplomatic bent is generally given pre-eminence and usually called the great talent and the great capacity, yet it does not differ from these others except by the exalted quality of its subject matter, for one cannot suggest anything more noble than to protect the interests of Princes, to enter into their most secret designs, to reconcile their differences, and to govern their lands. This is the sublimest and most glorious occupation of the mind; nothing so flatters the self-esteem, nothing better satisfies ambition than the dazzling titles of Ambassador, of Plenipotentiary, and Minister of State. Those who have been raised to these high dignities have a quality of grandeur and authority which distinguishes them from the rest of men; they are on earth what in heaven are the angels of the first order, those who approach closest to God's throne, who are illumined directly by Him and who are destined for the most important things.

However, when one examines the situation, it becomes apparent that it is chance which makes these great men by leading them sometimes into countries and into houses where by accidental and unforeseen encounters they accept employment from ambassadors and ministers. This decision requires them to concern themselves with affairs; application causes them to succeed in them and in time makes them eligible for the first offices of the State. Thus it is really chance which leads a bel esprit to play a leading part in the theatre of this world while chance, too, leaves others in dust and darkness. For assuredly there are men of parts who are unknown and unused because they have no employment to show them off and to compel them to work.

I admit, said Eugene, that chance contributes much to the formation of a statesman, but it can do nothing without nature; for however favorable opportunities may be, and however industrious a man may be, few reach the dignity of Prime Minister without a talent for great affairs. For despite what you say, genius is a particular skill and a certain talent which nature gives to certain men for certain tasks. Some have it for painting and others for verse; it is not enough to have intelligence and imagination to succeed in poetry: one must be born a poet and to have that natural bent which depends neither on art nor on study and which derives in some way from inspiration.

I am of the same opinion about diplomacy and statecraft. It is not enough to be well educated and even very wise in order to succeed in it; one must have a special gift for governing other men's minds under the Prince's authority, so as to command while obeying. This has led a Spanish political writer to declare that aptitude and intelligence are the two principal causes for the advancement and the glory of a great man. *Genio y ingenio los dos ejes del lucimiento de prendas: el uno sin el otro felicidad a medias, no basta lo entendido, desease lo genial.*[17]

It is true that this natural bent, however powerful it may be, languishes as you might say, and is stifled outside the uses to which it is fitted because its development and activity require a certain subject-matter. But if we consider talent in itself, we see that it is independent of luck and fortune; it is a gift of heaven in which the earth has no part; it is this divine something which makes a bel esprit whom the providence of God has destined to the government of an Empire, which makes him, I say, naturally good and just, zealous for the glory of his prince and for the good of his country, equal to the most difficult enterprises, firm and constant in the most trying situations, impenetrable to the most piercing gaze, insensible to pleasure, indefatigable in work, free and tranquil in reverses, and always master of himself as of his affairs which, great as they are, are always subordinate to his talent.

Not that such a minister as I am imagining is limited only to affairs. Since his mind is almost infinitely broad, he has a tincture of every science; when he wishes he can even make eloquent speeches and hold his ground in an academy of beaux esprits as he does in the council of a powerful

220

monarch; but after all, political genius is his dominant quality and his true characteristic.

I am very much pleased with that portrait of the perfect minister, said Aristo, and what pleases me most is that apparently you have not made an imaginary portrait. If I am not mistaken, your statesman is more real than Aristotle's Philosopher or Seneca's Sage; I am happy about this for the honor of our nation, for, to tell you the truth, I should be very much chagrined if France were no more important than Greece or Italy.

The Greeks and Romans, replied Eugene, are so jealous of the glory of their nation that one cannot argue about any aspect of it without quarreling with them and without having to answer for this to the bravest and cleverest men alive. For myself, he continued, laughing, since I do not like to make enemies, I prefer to yield to the Greeks and Romans and to confess in good faith that all countries are sterile in heroes when compared with ancient Greece and ancient Italy.

At least you must admit, said Aristo, that the bel esprit is found in all countries and all nations; thus, as there once were Greek and Roman beaux esprits, so there are now French, Italian, Spanish, English, even German and Russian ones.

A German or Russian bel esprit is an oddity, answered Eugene, and if there are some in the world, they must be like those spirits which never appear without causing astonishment. Cardinal Duperron once said of the Jesuit Gretser, *He is very intelligent — for a German*, as if a very intelligent German were a miracle.[18]

I allow, interrupted Aristo, that the bel esprit is rarer in cold countries because nature in those parts is drearier and more languishing so to speak.

Say rather, remarked Eugene, that the bel esprit as you have defined him is not at all compatible with the coarse temperament and the massive bodies of northern peoples.

I do not mean, he added, that all northerners are stupid; there is wit and learning in Germany and Poland as elsewhere; but all things considered, our bel esprit is unknown there, as is that art which is not learned in school and whose first rule is politeness; or if they are both known there it is only as foreigners whose language is not understood and to whom one cannot become accustomed.

I am not even sure that the Italian and Spanish beaux esprits are of the same kind as ours; of course they have some of the same qualities and characteristics, but I rather doubt whether the resemblance goes any further

221

and whether they have precisely the character you have described. For after all this character is so suited to our nation that it cannot be found outside of France, whether because it results from some quality of the climate, or because our national spirit contributes something to it, or finally because it is the fate of the French nation to have this fine quality of mind today when other peoples do not have it.

I am astonished, answered Aristo, that a man who fears to be at odds with the Greeks and Romans should be willing so lightheartedly to have on his hands the Spaniards, the Italians, the Germans, the Poles, the Russians, and all the other nations of the earth. But joking aside, he went on, I think you are very bold to criticize all foreigners in that way. For myself, since I dislike equally the arbitrariness of settling a question and the unpleasantness of ruffling another's temper, I prefer to believe the bel esprit at home everywhere, and I have no desire to be more difficult than the satiric poet who was prepared to say that great geniuses are born everywhere.

I know that some countries are more hospitable to the things of the mind than others, that Attica was of all the nations of Greece the most fertile in beaux esprits, nor do I deny that France is at least the equal of Attica in this. But it does not follow that the other countries are as sterile as you say; after all, minds are not like gold or precious stones which nature forms only in certain places on earth; minds are to be found in cold and hot climates as well as in temperate ones and among barbarous nations as well as among civilized ones.

But if the bel esprit is to be found in all countries, said Eugene, it is certainly not found in all centuries, for some are crude and stupid, dominated by barbarism and ignorance, as was the tenth century when people were so simple-minded and so stupid that as soon as a man knew a little Greek he passed for a necromancer.

There are also centuries of the intelligence, said Aristo, and one need not be deeply versed in history and chronology to be aware that Alexander's time was fecund in beaux esprits. By Alexander's time I mean not only the period during which that famous conqueror lived but the years just before his birth and after his death. It was then that Anacreon, Socrates, Pindar, Euripides, Sophocles, Aristophanes, Isocrates, Plato, Aristotle, and Demosthenes flourished. Everybody knows that the age of Augustus was among the Romans the century of the bel esprit and of rational thought, of good authors and of good literature.

222

The fourth Christian century was one of the most fertile in great geniuses. For aside from Arius, who is so famous for the harm he did to Christendom, Valens, Ursacius, and Eusebius, all defenders of that heresiarch's doctrine, Julian the Apostate, and another Julian, the disciple of Pelagius, all these were bad men and good thinkers; and we might mention Themistius the Philosopher and Libanius the Sophist; there was in that century a large number of holy fathers as remarkable for the grandeur of their intelligence as for the sanctity of their lives. It is the century of Chrysostom, Jerome, Epiphanius, Ambrose, and Augustine.

How does it come about, interrupted Eugene, that one century is more or less intellectually inclined than another?

If you put that question to an astrologer, replied Aristo, he would not fail to give the responsibility to the stars, and he would probably say that the revolution and the conjunction of certain stars whose influences act to a greater or lesser degree upon the human mind are the only cause of that difference. But since I am not an astrologer, I prefer to believe it results in part from a good or a bad education, and that intelligences are subtler or coarser depending upon the degree to which they were cultivated in youth.

But would you believe that sometimes only one bel esprit is needed to civilize a whole nation? Malherbe [19] reformed the idea of poetry in France and gave us a taste for good verse. It can be said that Voiture taught us the easy and delicate way of writing which is now in fashion. Before him the would-be wit spoke only pure Balzac, and great thoughts were expressed in long words.

The rivalry which develops among certain persons and even among certain nations does much to civilize a century; ambition often has the same effect as rivalry. A thousand intelligent men spring up in a nation where intelligence is a means to success; thus in the ancient republics where a man achieved high office through his eloquence and his knowledge there were many great orators and excellent philosophers. There have always been learned men in times when princes loved knowledge.

How does it happen, do you think, that in the last century literature flourished so much in Italy if not because Lorenzo de' Medici and Leo X were so fond of it? And was it not that same fondness in Francis I which caused France in his reign to become refined and learned after having been crude and ignorant in the preceding reigns? The bent which a Prime Minister may have for a particular branch of study induces others to apply themselves to it, and so with time they will excel in it. The passion of Cardinal Richelieu for the theatre carried the Comédie Française to its highest perfection and has brought about the birth in our century of dramatic poets who almost surpass the ancients.

It seems to me, said Eugene, that times of peace also contribute a great deal to the refining of mankind, for as you know the Muses naturally love repose and silence; they cannot live in the midst of violence and noise. Beaux esprits are rare in wartime whether because war, which has in it something wild and savage, prevents minds from taking a polish or because those who have ambition turn their thoughts to weapons and choose valor as did Caesar, who, in Quintilian's opinion, might have disputed with Cicero pre-eminence in eloquence.

Periods of war, said Aristo, are not always incompatible with learning; they are sometimes very favorable not only to the grandeur of nations but also to the perfection of the mind, and without seeking foreign examples we may say that we were never more polished than while war was raging between France and Spain.

I think, he went on, that new heresies do no little to banish barbarism and ignorance; the passion on the one side to establish and defend a new doctrine, the zeal on the other to combat and destroy it urge on the two parties to study and ordinarily produce very remarkable works. For leaving old heresies aside, we perhaps owe, if it is permitted to speak in this way, we owe, I say, to recent ones some of the embellishment of our language and the polish of our century.

Could one not add, said Eugene, that nature makes an effort from time to time to produce extraordinary geniuses and then afterwards remains sterile for several centuries as if her most recent productions had exhausted her and as though she needed rest after so much labor?

One could also add, rejoined Aristo, that there is in all this a kind of doom, or to speak in a more Christian way, some disposition of Providence which is impenetrable. For this barbarism or refinement of minds passes from country to country and from century to century by ways often unknown to us. At one time a nation is crude, at another, refined. In the time of Alexander the Greeks were more productive than the Romans; in Caesar's time the Romans were more productive than the Greeks.

The last century was for Italy a century of learning and refinement; it produced more beaux esprits than the country had seen since the days of Augustus. The present century is for France what the last was for Italy;

one might say that all the intelligence and all the learning of the world are now among us and that all other nations are barbarous when compared with the French. It is not an advantage or an excellence in France to be intelligent, because everybody is. Almost everyone has had a little education, almost everyone speaks well and writes genteelly. The number of good authors and of makers of beautiful things is infinite; the number of learned academies increases every day; in short, I know of nothing more ordinary in the Kingdom than the refined good sense which used to be so rare here.

Moreover, the bel esprit is not limited to men of letters; it is found among men of the sword and persons of the highest quality who in previous reigns were generally ignorant. We have princes who can compete in wit as well as in valor with Scipio and Caesar, and I personally have the honor of knowing one [20] who in the flower of his age has all the critical discernment and the maturity it is possible to have. This young prince has many charms in his person which make him, proud as he is, the most likable man in the world. Long ago I compared him to Tasso's Rinaldo and applied to him these four lines as through the spirit of prophecy:

> L'età precorse, e la speranza; e presti
> Pareano i fior, quando n'usciro i frutti.
> S'el miri fulminar fra l'arme avvolto
> Marte lo stimi; Amor, se scopre il volto. [21]

But I shall leave aside his courage and handsomeness and speak only of his mind. However cold his face may appear he has much vivacity and fire, but this fire is not outwardly visible at all times and the vivacity is all in a subtle and penetrating intelligence which nothing escapes. He understands the shadings in everything; he judges works of literature with an admirable finesse; everything he says is just and full of good sense even when he utters trifles, for despite his wise and serious air he often takes part in witty and graceful badinage when the occasion presents itself.

He knows all the literary languages, and he has taken from learning all that a person of his quality ought to know, so that he speaks very well and in a princely way on every subject without aping the scholar and without being pretentious. You must add to this a clear and well-instructed mind which always leads him to choose the right side, a noble and lofty soul which makes him capable of anything, and finally a certain individual quality of mind which the finest bel esprit does not have.

We have besides, dukes, marquesses, and counts who are very witty and very learned, who handle the pen and the sword equally well and who know as much about planning a ballet or writing a history as about establishing a camp or lining up an army for battle. We have also duchesses, marquises, and countesses who may be the equal of the dukes, marquesses, and counts and who are real beaux esprits.

I did not suppose, interrupted Eugene, that a woman could be a bel esprit, and whatever you may say I am inclined to doubt that she can have all the qualities which are necessary really to be one. That bright flame and that good sense you spoke so well of do not result from a cold and moist complexion; the cold and moisture which make women "weak, timid, indiscreet, light, impatient and talkative" as one of our good authors has clearly shown in his *Art of Knowing Men,*[22] prevent them from having the judgment, the solidity, the strength, and the precision which bel esprit demands. That phlegm with which they are filled and which gives them their delicate coloring does not agree well with delicacy and vivacity of mind; it blunts the cutting edge of the intellect and dims its light. If you reflect on this question you will see that what is brilliant in women partakes of the nature of lightning which dazzles for a moment and which has no solidity; women shine a bit in conversation, and provided the talk be of trifles they do well; but beyond this they are not very reasonable. In a word, nothing is thinner or more limited than the female mind.

What you say is true in a general way, answered Aristo, and I admit there is a kind of contradiction between beauty of the mind and that of the body, this latter being woman's share; but that does not keep certain ones from being exceptions to the general rule. They are the ones who, as far as their minds are concerned, have none of the imperfections of their sex and to whom nature has given, it seems, a special temperament.

One may count among those privileged women the famous Grecian who invented a new kind of verse and who was called the tenth Muse;[23] the virtuous Cornelia, the mother of the Gracchi; the wise and learned Athenaïs whose merit brought her to the throne of Constantinople;[24] the illustrious Mary Stuart whose beauty, learning and virtue all Europe admired; Vittoria Colonna, Marchesa de Pesquere,[25] Isotta Nogarola,[26] Serafina Contarini,[27] Oliva Margareta Sarrochi,[28] all four Italian women; Margaret Moore[29] and Elizabeth Tanfield,[30] English; Isabel de Roseres, Spanish;[31] Catherine of Portugal, Duchess of Bragança;[32] Marguerite de Valois, sister of Francis I, who was called by the beaux esprits of her time the Tenth Muse and the Fourth Grace; Queen Margaret;[33] the Princess de Conti, daughter of Henri, Duke of Guise; [34] Mademoiselle de Gournay, whom Montaigne called his daughter and Justus Lipsius his sister; and many others who were the ornament of their country and of their time, not to mention those who are still alive.

Besides a talent for literature, an aptitude for statecraft is also found in a few women whom nature has raised above the others. There have been intelligent and able women in almost all periods who were capable of carrying on the weightiest negotiations, and a few have appeared in certain countries clear-headed enough to bear the burden of public affairs.

Aristo then told his friend all that his memory furnished him on the subject of wise princesses who have governed empires. He did not forget Pulcheria, the sister of Theodosius, [35] Blanche, the mother of Saint Louis, [36] Isabella, the wife of Ferdinand, [37] Catherine Paleologus, Duchess of Mantua and Marchesa de Montferrat, so that Eugene was obliged to confess finally that there were beaux esprits of all kinds and sorts among women.

The reflections they both made afterward on the admirable conduct of these princesses took them so far afield into history and politics that they were scarcely able to bring their conversation to an end.

✖ 1671

Dominique Bouhours THE JE NE SAIS QUOI FROM

"THE CONVERSATIONS OF ARISTO AND EUGENE"

When Aristo and Eugene had reached the place of their walk, they first gave expression to the joy they felt at passing such pleasant hours in each other's company. Eugene said: Though we may be solitary, yet I am not envious of the most agreeable society in the world.

Aristo thereupon said to his friend all those things which a warm friendship can suggest at such meetings; then, allowing his mind to rove wherever his heart might lead it, he said: It must be admitted, my dear Eugene, that there are few friendships like our own, for we can be always together and never tire of each other. Private conversations in which love plays no part are almost always tiresome when they are too frequent or when they are rather long. No matter what the esteem or the affection one may have for any gentleman, one gradually wearies of seeing only him and of speaking only to him; one even feels, in some inexplicable way, that this brings about a diminution in the feelings which his merits have caused, whether because one gradually becomes used to what at first appeared extraordinary in his person or whether through familiarity one discovers in him hidden defects which make his good qualities less estimable. Hence, for us daily to find new pleasures in our conversations, as we do, our friendship must necessarily be much stronger than ordinary ones, because, although it is virtuous, it arouses in us what love arouses in others.

In other words, added Eugene, we must be meant for each other, and there must be a rare sympathy between our minds.

What you say is very true, answered Aristo, and for myself I feel it deeply. The boredom which seizes upon me as soon as we are separated, the joy which our longest conversations give me, the slight attention I pay to learning new things and my lack of care in cultivating my old habits are apparently the effects of the great liking and those hidden inclinations

228

which make us feel for one person an indefinable something which we do not feel for another.

From the way you speak, replied Eugene, you appear to know pretty well the nature of that indefinable something whose effects you feel.

It is something much easier to feel than to know, rejoined Aristo. It would not be indefinable if it were understood; its nature is to be incomprehensible and inexplicable.

But can we not say, Eugene responded, that it is an influence from the stars and an invisible effect of the planet which was in the ascendant when we were born?

Naturally we can say that, answered Aristo, or even that it is the tendency and instinct of the heart, that it is the most exquisite feeling of the soul for whatever makes an impression upon it, a marvelous liking and what might be called a kinship of the heart, to use the words of a Spanish wit: *un parentesco de los corazones.*

But to say that and a thousand other things is to say nothing. These feelings, these tendencies, these instincts, these likings, these kinships, are fine words which scholars have invented to delude their ignorance and to deceive others after they have been taken in themselves. One of our poets has described it better than all the philosophers; he settles the matter in a word:

> There are strong bonds of hidden, tender liking,
> Through whose sweet pow'r each lover finds his own;
> Each to each is join'd at glances' striking
> By something hidden, never to be known.

Even if that were true of the mysterious something one feels for people deep in one's heart, said Eugene, it might not be true of whatever it is that makes people pleasing, a quality which shows in their faces and which is obvious at first sight.

I assure you, said Aristo, that this latter something is as hidden and indescribable as the other. Because it is visible it is not better known or easier to define. For it is not really beauty, or a prepossessing appearance, or charming manners, or the gaiety of good humor, or brilliance of wit, because every day we meet people who have all these qualities without the faculty of being pleasing, and we see others who are very pleasant without having any agreeable qualities except the mysterious something.

Hence, the most reasonable and the most certain thing that can be said is that the greatest merit achieves nothing without it, and that it is sufficient in itself to create a very great effect. There is no advantage in being handsome, witty, gay, or what you will, if that mysterious something is lacking; all your fine qualities are as it were dead: there is nothing striking or touching about them. They are hooks without bait, pointless arrows and dull witticisms. Yet whatever defects may be found in body or soul, with this single advantage one is always pleasing, nor can one do anything wrong: the mysterious something makes everything right.

It follows from that, said Eugene, that it is a grace which brightens beauty and other natural perfections, which corrects ugliness and other natural defects, that it is a charm and an air which informs every action and every word, which has its part in the way one walks and laughs, in the tone of the voice, and even in the slightest gesture of the socially acceptable person.

But what is that grace, that charm, that air? asked Aristo. When one examines all those terms closely one ends by not making head nor tail of them, and one is forced back upon the mysterious something. One of our clever gentlemen has said of a very likable young man:

> But most of all he had a grace
> A "something" by which to surpass
> The sweetest charms of love's young face,
> A smile whose pow'r all words doth pass,
> An air distinctive and unique
> Whose secret others vainly seek.

This grace, this charm, this air are like the light which embellishes all of nature and which is seen by everybody though we do not know what it is, and so we cannot say anything more about it, to my way of thinking, except that it can neither be explained nor understood. Indeed, it is so delicate and imperceptible that it escapes the most penetrating and subtle intelligence; the human mind, which recognizes the most highly spiritual quality of the angels and the most divine quality in God, so to speak, does not recognize what is charming in a phenomenon which is both perceptible to the senses and capable of touching the heart.

If that is true, said Eugene, we must give the lie to philosophers who have always maintained that knowledge precedes love; that the will can love nothing which is unknown to the rational faculty.

They were right in their argument, said Aristo. Love is impossible without knowledge, and one always knows the loved person; that is, we may know that she is lovable, but not always know why we love her.

But if you please, interrupted Eugene, is that knowledge sufficient by which we know the person and recognize that she is lovable? Is it possible to love her and at the same time not to know what it is that makes her the object of love?

Yes, answered Aristo, and the mystery of the "certain something" consists of exactly that. Nature, like art, is careful to hide the cause of unusual impulses: we see the machine, and with pleasure, but we do not see the spring which makes it work. A woman may be pleasing to us, or inspire love at first sight without our knowing why she has this effect. You will say that in these circumstances nature sets traps for our heart so as to catch it unawares, or rather that since she knows it to be as proud and as sensitive as it is in fact, she spares it and treats it gently by hiding the dart which is to wound it.

I am inclined to think, said Eugene, that if the soul does not perceive the quality by which it is touched in such encounters the reason is that the quality acts so fast as to be imperceptible to the soul. For, as you may have noticed, anything which moves very fast is invisible. Thus arrows, bullets, cannon balls, bolts of lightning all pass before our eyes without being seen. These things are visible in themselves but the speed with which they move hides them from our sight.

That reminds me, said Aristo, of the simple-mindedness of that savage who, having been shot and not being able to understand what had wounded him, said that it was either the flame he had seen or the noise he had heard.

If stone, fire, lead, and wood, Eugene continued, become invisible through the speed with which they fly through the air, should we be amazed that the quality which at first sight makes an impression on the soul can pass unnoticed? For of all the things which move fast the fastest is the dart which wounds the heart, and the shortest of all moments, as I may say, is that in which the "mysterious something" makes its effect.

However that may be, said Aristo, it is certain that this mysterious something belongs to that class of things which are known only by the effects they produce. Our eyes witness the wonderful movements which a magnet induces in iron filings; but who can say what the power of that marvelous stone really is? The wind which shakes mountains and rocky cliffs, which destroys towns and troubles all the elements is something unseen and which has not yet been well defined. Neither have the influences which fall from the heavens and which form minerals in the depths

231

of the earth. Let us say the same of that charm and of that peculiar fascination we are discussing: it attracts the hardest hearts, it sometimes excites violent passions in the soul, it sometimes causes very noble sentiments; but it is never known except in that way. Its importance and its advantage lie in its being hidden; it is like the source of that Egyptian river, the more famous for not having yet been discovered, or like the unknown goddess of the ancients who was adored only because she was not known.

Might one dare say, Eugene added, that it is like God Himself and that there is nothing better known nor more unknown in the world?

One can at least say this with certainty, Aristo continued, that it is one of the greatest marvels and one of the greatest mysteries of nature.

Is that not the reason, said Eugene laughing, that the most mysterious nations give it a place in everything they say? The Italians, who make a mystery of everything, use their expression *non sò che* right and left. Nothing is more usual in their poets.

Un certo non sò che
Sentesi al petto.

> An indescribable sensation is felt in the heart.

A poco a poco nacque nel mio petto
Non sò da qual radice
Com herba suol che per se stessa germini,
Un incognito affetto,
Un estranea dolcezza,
Che lascia nel fine
Un non sò che d'amaro.

> Gradually there is born in my heart from unknown roots, like grass which grows of itself, an unknown love, a strange sweetness which at the end leaves behind a mysterious bitterness.

In queste voci languide risuona
Un non sò che de flebile e soave,
Ch'al cor gli serpe, ed ogni sdegno ammorza.

> In these languorous words sounds something plaintive and sweet which enters secretly into his heart and calms all his rage.

232

Non v'e silenzio, e non v'e grido espresso,
Ma odi un non sò che roco e indistinto.

> It is not silence, nor is it a cry uttered by a human being, but there is audible something both raucous and indistinct.

Un non sò che d'inusitato e molle,
Par che nel duro petto al Re trapasse.

> Something mysterious, both rare and gentle, seems to pierce the king's hard heart.

Un non sò che d'insolito e confuso
Tra speranza e timor tutto m'ingombra.

> Something unwonted, a mixture of hope and fear, has me in its grip.

I should never finish if I tried to mention all the examples of *non sò che* which I remember. The Spaniards also have their *no sé que* which they use at all times and in all contexts, besides their *donaire* (grace) their *brio* (vigor) and their *despejo* (facility) which Gracián calls *alma de tota prenda, realce de los mismos realces, perfección de la misma perfección* (the object of all desire, splendor of all splendors, the perfection of perfection itself), and which is, according to the same author, above our thoughts and our words, *lisonjea la inteligencia, y estraña la explicación* (it deceives the intelligence and bemuses attempts at explanation).

If you took the trouble to read our books with as much care as you have read the Italians and Spaniards, said Aristo, you would find that the *je ne sais quoi* is very popular among us, and that in this we are as mysterious as our neighbors.

But to come back to what we were saying, the *je ne sais quoi* is like those beauties covered with a veil, which are the more highly prized for being less exposed to view, and to which the imagination always adds something. Hence, if by chance we were to see clearly the nature of this mysterious something which astonishes and overwhelms the heart at first glance, we should perhaps be less charmed and touched than we are; but it has not yet been unveiled and perhaps never will be since, as I have already said, once unveiled it would cease to be what it is.

Moreover, since it cannot be explained, it cannot be described either, and this is perhaps the reason why showing a person's portrait is not enough to cause her to be loved by the beholder, any more than does singing her praises, whatever romances and fables may say. The most favorable description and the most flattering portrait can produce esteem for a person and a desire to see her, but neither the one nor the other ever causes a real affection because neither the brush nor the tongue can express that mysterious something which is all-powerful.

But aside from that mysterious quality which compensates, as we have said, for natural defects and which sometimes replaces beauty, physical charm, good humor, and even intelligence, there is another which has a completely contrary effect, for it destroys, it spoils, it poisons, as you might say, the merit of those people in whom it is found.

Every day we see people who, by all the rules, ought to be very pleasant and who nevertheless are very unpleasant, like those two gentlemen well known at Court of whom it was said that they had between them more good qualities than would be needed to make four decent people, and yet they were themselves not acceptable.

We wonder sometimes why a man makes a bad impression, we ask ourselves what the reason may be, we find a thousand which indicate that he ought to make a good impression and not one which explains why he does not, except a certain disturbing quality which leads us to say in spite of ourselves: He is handsome, attractive, intelligent, but there is something about him which I dislike. Some people think that is said out of fastidiousness or caprice and is a mere pretext, yet it is a good and solid reason, although a hidden one and unknown to philosophy, and which nature alone proposes to us.

What is most astonishing to me, said Eugene, is that the same man you dislike may perhaps suit me perfectly.

There is no reason to be surprised at that, said Aristo. As there are certain mysterious qualities which are universal so that everybody is equally touched by them, so there are individual ones which affect only certain people, for these qualities are like those ghosts which are seen only in certain places and by certain people. All men have something about them which makes them attractive or unattractive at first sight, depending upon the different people who see them, and upon this are founded what we call sympathy and antipathy.

If that is true, said Eugene, we are wrong in condemning the taste or preference of another, however peculiar the taste may be and however odd the preference. We should complain of nature and not of ourselves,

234

for we only follow her and cannot withstand her promptings in these matters.

It is true, answered Aristo, that these mysterious qualities which produce the effect of beauty or ugliness, so to speak, cause in us mysterious feelings of inclination or aversion which are beyond reason and which the will cannot control. They are impulses which forestall reflection and freedom. We can stop them in their course but we cannot prevent their arising. These feelings of liking or disliking take shape in an instant and when we are least aware of them. We love or hate at once without awareness in the mind, and, if I dare say so, without knowledge in the heart.

But do you know, he went on, that these mysterious qualities are to be found almost everywhere? The expression of the face which distinguishes one person from a hundred thousand others is such a quality, being very noticeable and yet very difficult to describe, for who has ever clearly distinguished the feaures and the lineaments in which that difference precisely resides?

An intelligent face is another mysterious phenomenon. For, if one undertakes to determine why it is that an intelligent man is usually recognizable on sight, one must conclude that it is not the breadth of his forehead, nor the brilliance or fieriness of his eyes, nor the chiseled regularity of his features, nor the form and complexion of his face, but something which results from all these things, or rather that it has nothing to do with these things at all.

There is also something mysterious in sicknesses, not only in extraordinary ones in which the masters of the healing art recognize something divine, as they themselves say, but also in the commonest ones like the fever. Those regular attacks, those chills and burning fits, those intermissions in a disease which lasts for years on end, are these not all unknown quantities? And must not the same thing be said of the ebbing and flooding of the tides, the power of the magnet and the occult qualities, as they are called by philosophers?

People of breeding usually have in their faces something noble and grand which makes them respected and which makes them recognizable in a crowd.

I agree, said Eugene, and that characteristic grandeur which God has imprinted particularly on the brow of kings distinguishes our own from all the nobles of his court. There is in his whole person an air, a mysteriously majestic quality which marks him so well that people who have

235

never seen him need not ask which is he when they see him in a tiltyard or a ballet.

And so, Aristo went on, all nature is filled

With something hidden, never to be known.

At least, Eugene added, the *je ne sais quoi* is restricted to natural phenomena for, as far as works of art are concerned, all their beauties are evident and their capacity to please is perfectly understandable.

I cannot agree, answered Aristo. The *je ne sais quoi* belongs to art as well as to nature. For, without mentioning the different manners of painters, what charms us in those excellent paintings, in those statues so nearly alive that they lack only the gift of speech, or who do not even lack that if we are to believe our eyes:

Manca il parlar, di vivo altro non chiedi;
Ne manca questo ancor, s'a gli occhi credi . . .

what charms us, I say, in such paintings and statues is an inexplicable quality. Therefore the great masters, who have discovered that only that is pleasing in nature whose attraction cannot be explained, have always tried to give charm to their works by hiding their art with great care and skill.

E quel ch'el bello, e'l caro accresce a l'opre,
L'arte che tutto fa, nulla si scopre.

And what makes a work more beautiful and
gives it greater importance is that art which
does all but is nowhere to be seen.

Delicate compositions in prose and verse have something refined and genteel about them which is the source of almost all their importance and which consists in that sophisticated air, that tincture of *urbanity* which Cicero is at a loss to define. There are great beauties in Balzac's books; they are regular beauties and very pleasing; but it must be admitted that the works of Voiture, which have those secret charms, those fine and hidden graces of which we are speaking, are much more pleasing still.

Let us go further, my dear Eugene, and let us say in addition that when we examine carefully those things in this world which we most admire we see that what makes us admire them is the mysterious something which surprises us, which dazzles us, which charms us. We shall even come to see that this mysterious quality is, if it is rightly understood, the focal point of most of our passions. Besides love and hatred, which give the impetus to all the impulses of the heart, desire and hope, which fill up the whole of man's life, have practically no other foundation. For we are always desiring and hoping, because beyond the goal we have set for ourselves there is always something else to which we unceasingly aspire and which we never attain; that is why we are never satisfied with the enjoyment even of those things we have most ardently desired.

But to speak in a Christian fashion of the *je ne sais quoi,* is there not a mysterious something in us which makes us feel, despite all the weaknesses and disorders of corrupt nature, that our souls are immortal, that the grandeurs of the earth cannot satisfy us, that there is something beyond ourselves which is the goal of our desires and the centre of that felicity which we everywhere seek and never find? Do not really faithful souls recognize, as one of the Fathers of the Church says, that we were made Christians not for the goods of this life but for something of an entirely different order, which God promises to us in this life but which man cannot yet imagine?

Then, Eugene interrupted, this mysterious quality partakes of the essence of grace as well as of nature and art.

Yes, answered Aristo. Grace itself, that divine grace which has caused so much uproar in the schools and which produces such wonderful effects upon souls, that grace both strong and gentle which triumphs over hardness of heart without limiting the freedom of the will, which subjects nature by adjusting itself to her, which makes itself master of the will while leaving the will its own master, that grace, I say, what is it but a mysterious quality of a supernatural order which can be neither explained nor understood?

The Fathers of the Church have tried to define it, and they have called it "a deep and secret calling," "an impression of the spirit of God," "a divine unction," "an all-powerful gentleness," "a victorious pleasure," "a holy lust," "a covetousness for the true good;" that is to say that it is a *je ne sais quoi* which indeed makes itself felt but which cannot be explained and of which it would be better not to speak.

It is true, Aristo went on, that the *je ne sais quoi* is almost the only subject about which no books have been written and which the learned have never taken the trouble to elucidate. Lectures, dissertations and treatises have been composed on very odd subjects, but no author, as far as I know, has worked on this one.

I remember, said Eugene, reading in the *History of the French Academy*

237

that one of the most illustrious academicians gave a speech in the Academy on the subject of the *je ne sais quoi*. However, since this speech has not been published, the world was no more illumined by it than it was before, and perhaps even if this academic discourse were to see the light we should not be much more informed than we are, the subject being one of those which have an impenetrable core and which cannot be explained other than by admiration and silence.

I am very glad, said Aristo laughing, that at last you have come to the proper conclusion and that you are satisfied to admire what at first you wanted to understand. Take my advice, he added, and let us stop here without saying anything further about a thing which continues to exist only because no one can say what it is. Besides it is time to bring our walk to an end; the sky is darkening all around us, it is starting to rain, and if we do not go in soon we shall be liable to feel the fury of the coming storm.

Dominique Bouhours THE ART OF CRITICISM, OR THE

METHOD OF MAKING A RIGHT JUDGMENT UPON SUBJECTS

OF WIT AND LEARNING

Dialogue I

Eudoxus and Philanthus, who manage these following dialogues, are two scholars whom their learning has not spoiled, and whose breeding is equal to their learning. Though they had pursued the same studies and knew for the most part the same things, yet their characters are widely different. Eudoxus has a true relish, and nothing pleases him in ingenious discourses which is not reasonable and natural. He loves the ancients much, especially the authors of Augustus's age, which in his opinion was the age of good sense. Cicero, Virgil, Livy, and Horace are his heroes.

As for Philanthus, what is florid and glittering charms him. The Greeks and the Romans, in his opinion, are not comparable to the Spaniards and the Italians. Among others, he admires Lope de Vega and Tasso, and his head is so full of the *Gerusalemme liberata* that he prefers it without any ceremony to the *Iliad* or the *Aeneid*. This excepted, he has wit, is an honest gentleman, and Eudoxus's friend. Their friendship, however, is no hindrance, but they often quarrel about these things. They reproach one another at every turn with their tastes, and they differ concerning every book that is published; but what differences soever they may have, yet they love each other nevertheless, and they agree so well together that they cannot live one without the other.

Eudoxus has a very pretty country house near Paris, where he goes in fine weather to take the fresh air and to enjoy the pleasures of retirement whenever his business will permit him to quit the town.

Philanthus went, as he used to do, to see him last autumn. He found him walking alone in a little grove, and reading the *Doubts Concerning the*

French Language, Proposed to the Gentlemen of the Academy By a Country Gentleman.[1]

Philanthus, who understands the tongue more by custom than rule, fell foul upon Eudoxus presently for reading it.

What business have you with that country gentleman, says he; a man as you are needs only follow his own genius to speak and to write well. I do assure you, replies Eudoxus, that a genius alone will not go far, and that one is in danger of committing a thousand faults against custom if he does not reflect upon custom itself. This country gentleman's scruples are reasonable, and the more I read them the more necessary they seem.

For my part, says Philanthus, I should rather desire his reflections upon authors' thoughts; for it seems to me to be a more necessary thing to think well than to speak well, or rather, one can neither speak nor write correctly unless his thoughts be just.[2] He promised these reflections when he told us at the end of his book that he had several other scruples about the thoughts of authors, besides those concerning the language. But he has not performed his promise, and I see plainly that this Breton is not too much a man of his word.

Since the gentlemen of the Academy gave him no solution of his first scruples, replied Eudoxus, he believed perhaps that it was to no purpose for him to propose new ones. But take notice that this place where the Low Breton seems to promise those reflections you speak of has caused me to make several which I had not made before, and that when I examined things more nearly it seemed to me that those thoughts which sometimes appear the brightest in [compositions] of wit are not always the most solid.

I am almost dead with fear, says Philanthus, interrupting him briskly, lest with reading this book of *Doubts* so much you should have learned to doubt of everything, and that this country gentleman who is scrupulously nice has communicated something of his spirit to you. It is not the provincial that I am guided by, replied Eudoxus, it is good sense which he himself takes for his rule in those things which do not perfectly depend upon custom; for one needs only consult his own reason not to approve some thoughts which almost all the world admires, as for instance that famous one of Lucan, *Victrix causa deis placuit, sed victa Catoni,*[3] which the translator of his *Pharsalia* has thus rendered: *Les dieux servent César, mais Caton suit Pompée* (The gods serve Caesar, but Cato follows Pompey).

I could be content, says Philanthus, smiling, that this should not please you; it would, said he, going on in a serious tone, be so much the worse for you.

I protest to you, replied Eudoxus, this never pleased me, and though the adorers of Lucan should owe me a spite for it, yet I would not change my opinion. But what, returned Philanthus, can be greater or finer than to set the gods on one side and Cato on the other?

The misfortune of this thought is, answered Eudoxus, that it hath only a fair outside, and when one fathoms it he will find it unreasonable at the bottom. For in short, it represents the gods at the first view fixed to the unjust side, and so Caesar's was, who sacrificed his country to his ambition, and who [presumed] to oppress the public liberty which Pompey endeavored to defend; now good sense never allows that the gods should approve of the injustice of an usurper who breaks the laws of God and man to make himself master of the world, and one that thought rightly should have forgot the gods on such an occasion, much less have brought them into play.

Besides, Cato being a good man, according to the poet's own description of him, there was no reason to oppose him to the gods, and to set him in an interest different from theirs. This is to destroy his character, to take away his virtue; for if we believe Sallust, it was a part of the Roman goodness to be zealous in the service of the immortal gods, and the Romans did not begin to neglect them till their morals began to be corrupted.[4] It is yet less reasonable to advance Cato above the gods, and by that means to raise the credit of Pompey's party, for this is what *sed victa Catoni* signifies: *But Cato followed Pompey. But* here is a mark of distinction and preference.

The truth is, this Roman was in the judgment of the Romans themselves a living image of virtue, and in everything more like the gods than men;[5] he was, if you will, a divine man. He was a man, and the poet, how much soever a pagan, how much soever a poet, could not give a man an advantage above the gods without doing injury to the religion in which he lived, so that Lucan's thought is at once both false and impious.

I do not reason so much, says Philanthus, and all your reasonings will never hinder me from esteeming Lucan's as an admirable thought. You may judge as you please, replied Eudoxus, but I cannot admire that which is not true.

But, says Philanthus, cannot this thought be thus explained? It pleased

241

the gods that the unrighteous party should prevail over the righteous, though Cato wished otherwise. Does this shock reason? Is this not the sense of the verse? Good men every day make vows for those that are like themselves, for the success of a good cause; their vows are not always heard, and Providence sometimes turns things otherwise.

The gods declared for Caesar in the event, though Pompey's was the juster side, which Cato upheld. The *but* in the verse signifies perhaps no more than this *though*, which gives no offense to the gods, whose designs are unsearchable.

Were the poet's thoughts no more than this, replies Eudoxus, it were no great matter, and there would be no cause to cry out against it. I am sure at least that his defenders do not understand it so, and that the sense which displeases me is the very sense which they admire.

To be convinced of this, you need only remember what one of Lucan's admirers says in his reflections upon our translators. According to him, Brébeuf [6] flags sometimes, and when Lucan happily comes up to the true beauty of a thought, his translator falls very much below it; the example which this reflecter brings is that before us: *Victrix causa deis placuit, sed victa Catoni.* (The gods serve Caesar, but Cato follows Pompey.)

He maintains that the French expression does not answer the nobleness of the Latin one, and that this is misrepresenting the author's sense, because Lucan, whose mind was filled with Cato's virtues, intended to advance him above the gods when he set Cato's opinion of the merits of the cause against theirs, whereas Brébeuf turns this noble image of Cato advanced above the gods into one of Cato subject to Pompey.

I do not pretend to justify the translation, says Eudoxus, and I agree with him that it is not exact. I say only that the reflecter's censure proves what I said, that those who are fond of the Latin *Pharsalia* fancy something extraordinary in this verse, *Victrix causa deis placuit, sed victa Catoni.*

Do not refine too much, Philanthus; till just now you were of the same opinion yourself, and this new sense which you have put upon it is only an excuse to save Lucan's honor.

Be it as it will, I could have all ingenious thoughts in books of poetry or prose to be like those of a great orator whom Tully speaks of, which were as sound as they were true, as surprising as out of the way; in short, they were as natural as they were far from all that luster which has nothing in it that is not frivolous and childish. [7] For in one word, to tell you my opinion in some sort of order, truth is the first quality, and as it were the foundation of thoughts; the fairest are the faultiest, or rather those which pass for the fairest are not really so, if they want this foundation.

But tell me then, replied Philanthus, what is the exact notion of a true thought, and wherein this truth consists, without which whatever one thinks, according to you, is so imperfect and monstrous.

Thoughts, answers Eudoxus, are the images of things, as words are the images of thoughts; and generally speaking, to think is to form in oneself the picture of any object, spiritual or sensible. Now images and pictures are true no further than they resemble; so a thought is true when it represents things faithfully, and it is false when it makes them appear otherwise than they are in themselves.

I do not understand your doctrine, replies Philanthus, and I can scarce persuade myself that a witty thought should always be founded upon truth; on the contrary, I am of the opinion of a famous critic, that falsehood gives it often all its grace, and is as it were the soul of it.[8] Nay, do we not see that what strikes most in epigrams, and in other things where the wit gives all the beauty, generally turns most upon fictions, upon ambiguities, upon hyperboles, which are but so many lies?

Do not confound things, if you please, replied Eudoxus, and allow me to explain myself that I may be understood. All that appears to be false is not so, and there is a great deal of difference between fiction and falsehood; the one imitates and perfects nature in some sort, the other spoils and quite destroys it.

In truth, the fabulous world, which is the world of poets, has nothing real in it; it is altogether a work of imagination, and Parnassus, Apollo, the Muses, with the horse Pegasus, are only agreeable chimeras. But this system being once supposed, whatever is feigned within its extent passes not for falsehood amongst the learned, especially when a fiction is probable, and has some truth hidden under it.

According to the fable, for instance, flowers grow under the feet of gods and heroes, to hint, perhaps, that great men ought to spread abundance and joy everywhere. This is plausible, and has probability; so that in reading those verses of Racan upon Marie de Médicis where he bids his flock "go into the fields and take their pleasure there, making use of the happy season which the heavens had given in recompense of all these miseries, and not spare the flowers, because there would grow up enough again under Marie's feet":[9]

243

Paissez, chères brebis, jouissez de la joie
Que le Ciel vous envoie;
A la fin la clémence a pitié de nos pleurs.
Allez dans la campagne, allez dans la prairie;
N'épargnez point les fleurs;
Il en revient assez sous les pas de Marie.

I say in reading these verses, we find nothing *choquant* in the poet's thought; and if we allow a falsehood, yet it is an established one, which has an air of truth. So when we read in Homer that the goddesses of prayer are deformed and lame, we are not offended at it; this makes us imagine that prayer has something in itself that is mean, and that when one prays he goes not so quick as when he commands, which is as much as to say that commands are short and prayers are long. One might add that the one are fierce and haughty, the other humble and creeping.

Neither are we shocked with the fiction of the Graces being little and very low. Men hereby intended to show that prettinesses consist in little things, sometimes in a posture or a smile, sometimes in a negligent air and in something less. I say the same of all fictions that have wit in them, such as the Latin fable of the sun and the frogs which was published in the beginning of the Dutch war, and which was so well received in the world.

That is to say, answered Philanthus, interrupting him, that you would not condemn another vision of the same poet; that the stars jealous of the sun made a league against him, but that when he appeared he dispersed the conspirators and made all his enemies vanish. No, without doubt, replied Eudoxus, it is a very happy thought, and being conceived upon Parnassus according to the rules of fiction it has all the truth it can have. The fabulous system [saves] all the falsehood which these sort of thoughts have in themselves, and it is allowed, nay, it is even glorious for a poet to lie in so ingenious a manner. But then, setting the fiction aside, truth ought to be found in poetry as well as in prose. Hereby I do not pretend to take away the marvelous from poetry, which distinguishes it from the noblest and the sublimest prose; I mean only that poets ought never to destroy the essences of things when they would raise and adorn them.

In the humor you are, says Philanthus, you will not approve of what Ariosto says of one of his heroes, "that in the heat of the engagement not perceiving that he was killed, he still fought on vigorously, as dead as he was."

Dominique Bouhours

Il pover'uomo che non sen'era accorto
Andava combattendo, ed era morto.

Neither do I approve, replied Eudoxus, of what Tasso says of Argante, "He dying threatened, and he fainted not."

Minacciava morendo, è non languia.

I give up Ariosto, says Philanthus; but I beg quarter for Tasso, and desire you to consider that a strong and fierce Saracen who had been wounded in the fight and who died of his wounds might, when he was a-dying, threaten him that gave him the fatal blow well enough. I agree with you that he might threaten him, replied Eudoxus, and even that his dying postures, that his last words, might have something in them that was fierce, proud and terrible:

Superbi, formidabili, feroci
Gli ultimi moti fur', l'ultime voci.

This may be, and this agrees with Argante's character: at his death he might have the same sense of things which he had when he was alive; he might call together all his spirits and what strength he had left to express [what he feels]. Sometimes men make frightful outcries before their last groans, but not to faint when they are dying, *e non languia*, is what is by no means probable. Montaigne's cannibal acts much more naturally than Tasso's Saracen.[10] For in short, if the cannibal, prisoner to his enemies, braves them even in irons, speaks reproachfully to them, spits in their faces; if in the midst of torments and at the point of death, when he has not strength to speak, he makes mouths at them to mock them, and to assure them that he is not yet overcome — there is nothing in all this which is not perfectly conformable to the genius of a fierce and resolute barbarian.

But what can be more agreeable to heroic virtue, says Philanthus, than to die without any weakness? Heroes, replies Eudoxus, have resolution in dying, have constancy when they die, but the firmness of their minds preserves not their bodies from weakness; there it is that they have no privilege. And yet the *non languia* which belongs to the body exempts Argante from this common law, and in advancing the hero destroys the man.

I am afraid, answered Philanthus, that your nicety goes too far, and that you push the criticism beyond its due bounds. I believe Tasso intended to describe Argante in a rage against Tancred, and threatening him even when he was a-dying, and so did not barely say that he died, but

245

that his fury and his anger [in] some measure took away his faintness and made him appear vigorous.

It is pity, replies Eudoxus, that Tasso is not better explained. For my part, I tie myself to what an author speaks; I do not know how to make him speak what he never says.

After all, says Philanthus, some very grave authors are not of your opinion in the matter of that truth which you would establish and require in all ingenious thoughts. Not to speak of Macrobius and Seneca who call those things pleasant sophisms, which we term strokes of wit, and the Italians *vivezze d'ingegno*, and the Spaniards *agudezas*; Aristotle reduces almost the whole art of thinking ingeniously to the metaphor, which is a kind of fraud, and the Count Tesauro says, according to that philosopher's principles, that the subtlest and the finest thoughts are only figurative enthymemes, which equally please and impose upon the understanding.[11]

All this ought to be understood in a good sense, replies Eudoxus. What is figurative is not false, and metaphors have their truth as well as fictions. Let us call to mind what Aristotle teaches in his rhetoric, and consider his doctrine a little.[12]

When Homer says of Achilles he went like a lion, it is a comparison; but when he says of the same Achilles "This lion darted forth," it is a metaphor. In the comparison the hero is like a lion; in the metaphor the hero is a lion. The metaphor, you see, is brisker and shorter than the comparison; this represents but one object, whereas that shows us two. The metaphor confounds, as I may say, the lion with Achilles or Achilles with the lion, but there is no more falsehood in the one than in the other. These metaphorical ideas deceive no man; how little understanding soever a man has, he knows what they signify, and he must be very dull who takes these things literally. In a word, can we question that Homer called Achilles a lion for any other reason than to describe his strength, his fierceness, and his courage? And when Voiture says of the great Gustavus, "Behold the northern lion," who discovers not through this foreign image a king terrible for his valor and power throughout all the north?[13]

We may say then that metaphors are like transparent veils, through which we see what they cover, or like the habits of a masque under which the persons who are disguised are known.

How glad am I, for the sake of poets and orators, says Philanthus, that fiction and metaphor wound not that truth which you require in [works] of wit. But I am very much afraid that ambiguity and truth can never agree according to your principles. And yet it would be a pity that so many thoughts which are pretty only for their ambiguity should not be good, for instance Voiture's upon Cardinal Mazarin, whom his coachman overthrew one day in the water, "where he desires him to forgive his coachman who had driven so unfortunately, since it was his Eminence's reputation which made him rash; for he thought in overturning he could not do amiss, because it was the common report that whatever he did, in peace, in war, upon the road, or in business, he still recovered himself upon his feet."

> Prélat passant tous les prélats passés,
> Car les présents serait un peu trop dire,
> Pour Dieu rendez les péchés effacés
> De ce cocher qui vous sut mal conduire.
> S'il fut peu caut à son chemin élire,
> Votre renom le rendit téméraire.
> Il ne crut pas versant pouvoir mal faire,
> Car chacun dit que quoi que vous fassiez,
> En guerre, en paix, en voyage, en affaire,
> Vous vous trouvez toujours dessus vos pieds.

All ambiguities are not like this, answers Eudoxus, and this petition for the coachman who overthrew the cardinal pleases me better than another which I remember, wherein he desires his Eminence to pardon the afflicted coachmen, who by misfortune or carelessness tumbled him into the water. The too hardy coachman know not (says he) the history of Phaeton and his calamity. He had read no *Metamorphoses*, and he thought he need not fear making any false steps when he carried Caesar and his fortune.

> Plaise, Seigneur, plaise à votre Eminence
> Faire la paix de l'affligé cocher,
> Qui par malheur, ou bien par imprudence,
> Dessous les flots vous a fait trébucher.
> On ne lui doit ce crime reprocher.
> Le trop hardi meneur ne savait pas
> De Phaéton l'histoire et piteux cas:
> Il ne lisait *Métamorphose* aucune,
> Et ne croyait qu'on dût craindre aucun pas
> En conduisant César et sa fortune.

For if you mind, this coachman who had not read the *Metamorphoses* knew a considerable passage in Roman history. And yet I cannot see how a man who had never heard of Phaeton should be so well informed of Caesar's adventures. But that's not the thing we are now about, and I

247

come back again to the thought of the petition you repeated. Though it be false in one sense, yet, however, it is true in another, according to the character of thoughts expressed in ambiguous terms, which have always a double sense: one proper, which is false; the other figurative, which is true. Here the proper and false sense is that the Cardinal always so recovers himself upon his feet as never to fall on the ground; the figurative and true sense is that he always so recovers himself upon his feet so that nothing overturns his designs or his fortune.

In short, what is true is always true though it be joined to that which is false. A good pistole loses none of its value when set by a false one; you have but one due to you. There are two offered to you, a good one and a bad one; make your choice; we shall see whether you understand money, and you will have the pleasure yourself to make trial of the exactness of your skill. It is much the same in this playing with words, which in reality is only a sport of the mind. Truth there is joined to falsehood, and what is very remarkable, the false carries one to the true; for from the proper sense, which is the false sense, of a quibble, one goes on to the figurative, which is the true one; this is visible in the example which you brought. When I read what Voiture says of Cardinal Mazarin, I imagine two things, as I have already told you: one false, that his feet never fail, but that he always keeps himself upon his legs; the other true, that his mind and his fortune are always in the same posture. The first brings us immediately to the second, by letting us pleasantly into the change. These ambiguities are allowable and diverting in epigrams, madrigals, masques, and other composures where the mind diverts itself.

But not to dissemble with you, there is one sort of quibbles extremely flat which men of a true relish cannot endure, because the false rules all so that the true has no share. Saint-Amant's [14] epigram upon the burning of the Palais is of this kind.

Certes l'on vit un triste jeu
Quand à Paris Dame Justice
Se mit le Palais tout en feu
Pour avoir mangé trop d'épice.

> Surely there was sorry sport when at Paris Dame Justice set the Palais in a flame for having eaten too much spice.[15]

This quatrain dazzled formerly, and there are some people still who think it extremely witty. Why, can there be anything happier or prettier?

248

says Philanthus, interrupting him. There can be nothing more empty or more frivolous, replies Eudoxus. These are only words in the air which have no manner of sense; it is all over false. For in one word, what is called *spice* in the Palais has no relation to burning, and the palate in a flame after eating too much pepper never leads a man to the firing of a building where justice is administered and sold, if you please.

What think you, says Philanthus, of that quibble which makes all the smartness of another of Saint-Amant's epigrams?

Ci gît un fou nommé Pasquet,
Qui mourut d'un coup de mousquet,
Lorsqu'il voulut lever la crête.
Quant à moi, je crois que le sort
Lui mit du plomb dedans la tête
Pour le rendre sage en sa mort.[16]

> Here lies a fool called Pasquet who died by the shot of a musket as he lifted up his head. For my part I believe that fate put all this lead into his pate to make him wise e'er he was dead.

This may be allowed in burlesque or comical writings with catches or ballads, replies Eudoxus. These are false jewels which are worn at masques and balls; it is false money which does no injury to trade when it is paid for what it is worth, but he that would have it pass for sterling would make himself very ridiculous in the company of men of sense.

Generally speaking, there is no wit in quibbling or very little; nothing costs less, or is more easily found. Ambiguity, which makes up its character, is less an ornament of discourse than a fault; and it is that which makes it insipid, especially when he who uses it thinks he speaks finely and values himself upon it. On the other side, it is not always easy to be understood: the mysterious appearance which gives it the double meaning is the occasion that a man cannot often come at the true sense without some pains, and when he is come at it he is sorry for his labor; he thinks himself cheated, and I cannot tell but that what he feels at such a time is a sort of vexation for having searched so long to find nothing.

All these reasons sink the credit of pure quibbles very low with men of good sense. I say pure quibbles: for all figures which contain a double sense have every one in its kind their beauties and graces which make them valuable, though they have something in them of the quibble. One single example will make you understand what I mean. Martial tells Domitian, "The people of your empire speak several languages, yet they have but one language when they say that you are the true father of your country." [17] Here are two senses, as you see, and two senses which make an antithesis: speak several languages and have but one language. They are both true as they are severally taken, and one destroys not the other. On the contrary they agree very well, and from the union of these two opposite senses there arises something, I can't tell what, which is ingenious, founded upon the ambiguous word *vox* in Latin and *language* in English. Several smart things in epigrams and a great many jests and witty repartees affect us only because of the double sense which is found in them, and these are properly those thoughts which Macrobius and Seneca call agreeable sophisms.

As far as I see, says Philanthus, truth has a larger extent than I imagined, since it may agree with equivocal expressions in matters of wit; there is nothing now to be done but to reconcile it to hyperboles, and I would very willingly know your opinion about them.

The bare original of the word, replies Eudoxus, decides the thing in general. Whatever is excessive is vicious, even in virtue, which ceases to be virtue when it comes to extremities, and keeps no longer within bounds. So likewise, thoughts which turn upon an hyperbole are all false in themselves, and deserve to have no place in reasonable discourses unless the hyperbole be of a particular kind, or that such qualifications are admitted which moderate its excess; for some hyperboles are less bold than others, and go not beyond their bounds,[18] though they are above common belief. There are others naturalized, as I may say, by custom, which are so established that they have nothing *choquant*. Homer calls Nireus beauty itself,[19] and Martial says that Zoilus is not vicious, but vice itself.[20] We say daily when we are speaking of a very wise and virtuous person, "He is wisdom, he is virtue itself." We say also after the Greeks and Romans, "She is whiter than snow. He goes faster than the wind." These hyperboles, according to Quintilian, lie without deceiving; or, as Seneca says,[21] they bring the mind to truth by a lie, by causing it to comprehend what they signify when they express anything in such a manner as seems to make it incredible.

Those therefore which are prepared and brought on by little and little never shock the minds of the readers or the audience. They even gain belief, I know not how, as Hermogenes says, and the falsest things they propose become at least probable. We have a noted example in Homer. He does not say at once that Polyphemus tore off the top of a mountain; that would scarce have appeared credible. He disposes the reader by his description of that Cyclops, whom he sets forth as a person of an enormous stature, and then gives him strength equal to his height when he makes him carry the body of a great tree for a club and stop the mouth of his cave with a large rock. Besides, he makes him eat more meat at a meal than would serve several men; and at last he adds that Neptune was his father. After all these preparations, when the poet comes to say that Polyphemus tore off the top of a mountain the action does not seem so strange. Nothing seems impossible to a man who is the son of the god of the sea, and who is not made like ordinary men.

There are other ways of qualifying an hyperbole, and which give it even an air of probability. Virgil says that to have seen Antony's and Augustus's fleets at the Battle of Actium, one would have thought they had been the Cyclades floating in the sea.[22] And Florus,[23] speaking of the expedition with which the Romans built a great number of ships in the first Punic War, says that the ships did not seem to have been made by workmen, but the trees seemed to be turned into ships by the gods. They do not say that the vessels were floating islands, or that the trees were turned into ships; they say only that one would think it was so, and that they seemed to be so. This precaution serves for a passport to an hyperbole, as I may say, and makes it allowable even in prose. "For whatever is excused before it is spoke is always favorably hearkened to, be it as uncredible as it will." . . .[24]

၏   ၏   ၏

An irony seems also very proper to make an hyperbole pass, continues Eudoxus. When men are in jest or banter, they have a right to say anything. If Balzac had said smilingly that his muscadines bore enough to make half England drunk, that the superfluity at his house was as much as ought to be drunk in a whole country, that there were more perfumes in his chamber than in all Arabia Felix, and that sometimes there was so great a torrent of orange flower and jasmine water that he and his famliy could save themselves only by swimming — I say, if Balzac had said this in jest, Philarchus perhaps would have had nothing to have reproached him with upon this head; but he unhappily says this in very good earnest, and is the first man in the world who ever spoke of the extremities of things where there is not the least appearance of truth, in a grave tone. . . .[25]

But I am weary of speaking all alone, and you may perhaps be willing that I should take a little breath. I have heard you without interrupting, replies Philanthus, because I took a pleasure in hearkening to you, and I was not willing to lose anything of a doctrine whereof I had very confused notions. I am glad, however, that you will allow some little favor to an hyperbole, which is so dear to the Italians and Spaniards, my good friends. I understand reason, as you may see, replies Eudoxus, and I am not so severe as you may think; but do not deceive yourself, and remember upon what conditions these figures are allowed. Especially never forget what one of the greatest wits of our age has said upon this argument, that "nothing is fine but what is true. Truth alone is to be valued; it ought to reign everywhere, yea, even in fable."

I question then, replies Philanthus, whether it reigns in an epitaph of Francis I, composed by way of dialogue by Saint-Gelais.[26] I read it lately, and I have not forgot it. "Who is buried under this marble? *Answer*: The great Francis, that incomparable king. Why had this prince so narrow a tomb? *Answer*: Here is only his heart. Then here is not all that great conqueror? *Answer*: Here is all, for he was all heart."

Your scruple is well grounded, answered Eudoxus. A very serious piece requires something more solid and substantial. At this rate, says Philanthus, Maréchal de Ranzau's epitaph is not much better than that of Francis I. I remember the last verse, which contains the whole thought. You know that this *maréchal* left an eye and a leg in the war, and that perhaps there was never a general of an army more maimed than he was. Upon this the poet grounds his thought. After he had said that there was but one half of the great Ranzau under the tombstone, and that the other was left behind in the field, he concludes thus: *Et Mars ne lui laissa rien d'entier que le coeur.* (And Mars left him nothing entire but his heart.)

But the heart, says Eudoxus, interrupting him with a smile; were not his lungs and his liver left entire, not to speak of any more? You think then that this thought is false? replies Philanthus. Yes, returns Eudoxus, and I like much better what Voiture says to Mademoiselle Paulet. "If I durst write mournful letters, I would say things which would break your heart; but to tell you the truth, I had much rather it should keep whole, and I should be afraid that if it were once in two it might be divided in my absence. You see how I can make use of those pretty things which I hear said."

For in short, says Eudoxus, Voiture is pleasant and in jest. He laughs at somebody who had said some such thing. And I am amazed that he that writes about exactness should fall foul upon our author himself. For this without doubt, the censor did not take notice of these words: "You see how I can make use of those pretty things which I have [heard] said. . . .

ᐧᐅᐧ ᐧᐅᐧ ᐧᐅᐧ

I will not always contradict you, says Philanthus, and now we talk of justness, I would rather desire to know what your idea of a just thought is.

Truth, answers Eudoxus, which is indivisible at other times, is not so here.[27] Thoughts are more or less true as they are more or less agreeable to their object. An entire agreement makes what we call justness in a thought; that is to say, as clothes are fit when they fit well about one's body and when they are perfectly proportionable to the person who wears them, so thoughts are just likewise when they perfectly agree to the things which they represent. So that to speak properly, a thought is just when it is true on all sides and in every light in which it is viewed. We have a fine example of this in a Latin epigram upon Dido which was so happily translated into our language.[28]

> Pauvre Didon, où t'a réduite
> De tes maris le triste sort?
> L'un en mourant cause ta fuite;
> L'autre en fuyant cause ta mort.

> Unhappy Dido, you're well wed to none. One
> dies, you fly. You die when t' other's gone.

This, you see, supposes what the history tells, that Dido saved herself and all her wealth in Africa when Sichaeus was killed, and also what the poem feigns, that she killed herself after Aeneas had left her.

It is true, says Philanthus, that these proportions cannot be better observed than they are in Ausonius's epigram, where everything hits admirably. You must not imagine, however, replies Eudoxus, that returns so just as these are essential to justness. It does not always require so much symmetry nor so much pleasantness; it is enough if the thought be true in its whole extent, as I have said already, and that nothing contradicts itself on which side soever you take it. But it belongs not to all the world to think justly; one must have a ready wit, a sound judgment, and something of Homer's genius, who in Aristotle's opinion, had always thoughts and words proportioned to the subject he treated of.

Balzac, who is not so correct as Voiture in his thoughts, though he is

253

more so in his elocution and style, yet sometimes has a great deal of justness. Witness what he says of Montaigne, that "he is a wandering guide, but such a one as leads men into more agreeable countries than he promised."

In short, in what kind soever one writes, justness in thinking is necessary, though it be more so at some times than at others. Elegy, for example, and tragedy require a more exact truth than epigrams and madrigals. There are comical and pleasant subjects in prose where this exactness has less place; there are other graver and more serious subjects where it is absolutely necessary, especially those which treat of morality. And yet there are several books of that kind which have numbers of false thoughts; I have observed some in reading which I have also writ down, and which I will show you when we are in my study.

The sun being set and the time no longer proper for walking, Eudoxus and Philanthus went home. Eudoxus's study is on the top of the house, and has an admirable prospect. It is hung with maps, and on every side beautified with books — a small library composed of the best authors in Greek, Latin, Italian, Spanish, and French. Eudoxus is not contented with reading of his books, but makes extracts which he reads over again from time to time, so that he has those things much at command, and he knows almost by heart all the fine passages of his collection.

When they were in the study, Eudoxus took up some sheets, and read what follows:

"All kinds of writings please us only because of the secret corruption of our heart. If in a discourse that is well written we love the sublime of the thoughts, the free and noble air of some authors, it is because of our vanity, and because we love to be great and independent."

You have set this down, says Philanthus, for a false thought? Yes, replies Eudoxus; for what can be falser than to attribute that to the corruption of the heart which is the effect of an exquisite discretion and the mark of a true taste? Discourses that are well writ please men of sense, because it is a regular thing for them to be pleased with what is finely said, and the mind is contented for the most part with anything that is perfect in its own way. Vanity has no more part in the pleasure which the reading of Virgil and Tully gives than it has in that which is taken in seeing excellent pictures or in hearing excellent music. The humblest man in the world is touched with these beauties as much as anybody else, provided that he understands them and is able to relish them. When I read the Holy Scrip-

254

tures, whose simplicity has so much sublime, think you that it is the love of my own loftiness or the corruption of my heart which makes me relish what I read? Is it not rather that simple and majestical character of the Word of God which makes the impression on me? And may not much the same thing be said of the language of the great masters in poetry and eloquence? What a fancy is it to imagine that we love the nobleness and the easiness of their style from a spirit of haughtiness and independency! . . .

～ ～ ～

But these examples are enough, continues Eudoxus, to show you the deficiency of those thoughts in morality which are not true. For I say nothing of maxims which have the least falsehood in them, and for that reason are not worthy of the name of maxims, whose only design is to regulate men's manners and to guide their reason. Historical reflections are not much better when they are false. Truth being, as you know, the soul of history, it ought to be spread over all that an historian says, but especially in his reflections it ought to shine the brightest, and there is nothing more improper than to reason falsely upon real matters of fact.

Plutarch, who was a wise man, took notice of this when he condemned the famous thought of an historian about the burning of the temple at Ephesus, that "it was no wonder that this magnificent temple consecrated to Diana should be burnt that very night that Alexander came into the world, because the goddess was so busy in assisting at Olympia's labor that she could not quench the fire." [29]

But Tully commended this for a pleasant thought, says Philanthus interrupting him, that Tully who in your opinion always thinks and judges well. I own it freely, replies Eudoxus, that I cannot fully comprehend him here. He considered Timaeus's thought without question, only as a fiction of a poet, and not as the reflection of an historian.[30] That cannot be said, answers Philanthus, for Tully commends Timaeus for thinking so pleasantly in his history. For my part I am persuaded that the Roman orator, whose head naturally lay for drollery, and who loved a jest to such a degree as sometimes to say those that were dull enough himself, as Quintilian observes, was touched with the pleasantness of Timaeus's thought without examining any further; whereas Plutarch, who was a serious man and a critic, considered only the falsehood of it. . . .

If the reflections of historians, says Philanthus, ought to be true, those of preachers methinks should not be false. That would be to corrupt the Word of God, replies Eudoxus, to intermix it with the shadow of a lie. And yet we have seen preachers, replies Philanthus, charm the world with discourses sprinkled all over with conceits and false thoughts. The relish of the age is well altered as to that matter, says Eudoxus; a preacher would be laughed at nowadays who, to prove that young men sometimes die before those that are older, should say that John outran Peter and came before him to the sepulchre. Neither would men be endured to tell us from the pulpit that women with their patins add something to their stature against the express words of our Saviour, and make truth itself to lie.

Neither do I believe that those thoughts would be now allowed which I have seen admired formerly: as this, that the heart of man being triangular and the world round, it was plain that all worldly greatness could not fill the heart of man; or this, that the same word stood for life and death in the Hebrew, and that there was only a point between them, whence the preacher concluded that there was but a point between life and death. But the preacher talked extravagantly, and his principle was not more solid than his conclusion, for it is not true that the same word stands for life and death in the Hebrew language. . . .

∽ ∽ ∽

But what will you say of those persons who are brought into epistles dedicatory? Hear me out, if you please. The author of a book which treats of Caesar's conquests or Hippolytus's adventures makes no scruple of telling a prince to whom he dedicates the book: "Here's the conqueror of Gaul who comes to pay his homage to you. Hippolytus comes out of the thickest of the woods with a design to make his court to you." There is nothing falser than this, replies Eudoxus, and it is ridiculous to confound the book which one dedicates with the hero who is the subject of the book, unless by a kind of fiction the author makes his hero or his heroine speak instead of speaking himself, as has been ingeniously done by one of our poets in publishing a play.

And yet Voiture, who is one of your oracles, replies Philanthus, confounds the hero and the romance and takes one for the other in two of his letters. He opened the book and read the beginning of a letter superscribed *To my Lord Duke de Bellegarde when he sent him* Amadis. "My Lord, at a time when history is so confused, I thought I might send you fables,

256

and that in a place where your only care is to give a loose to your thoughts, you might allow some of those hours which are bestowed upon your country gentlemen to entertain *Amadis* with. I hope in this your present retirement he may sometimes agreeably divert you whilst he relates his own adventures, which will be without doubt the finest in the world as long as you will not suffer it to be acquainted with yours."

You see he speaks only of the book *Amadis* in the title, and in the letter our author speaks of the hero called Amadis de Gaule; he does the same in a letter superscribed to Madame de Saintot, when he sent her Ariosto's *Orlando Furioso* translated into French.

"This questionless is the finest adventure which Orlando ever met with, and when he defended Charles the Great's crown by himself and wrested scepters out of the hands of kings he never did anything so glorious for himself as now when he has the honor to kiss yours."

If I durst condemn Voiture, replies Eudoxus, I would say that in these two places he forgets himself a little, and recedes from the character of a man of true and fine sense; but I had rather say that he plays with his subject, and that letters of gallantry require not so severe truth as epistles dedicatory, which are grave and serious things of themselves. I understand you, says Philanthus, and I perceive that I begin to distinguish truth from falsehood by myself. . . .

സ   സ   സ

To conclude all that we have said, reason is of itself an enemy of falsehood, and those that would think justly ought to imitate the great painters, who give truth to all their pieces, or rather to follow nature, by which painters guide themselves. Hence comes it also that well-chosen comparisons, which are drawn from nature, are always the foundation of very reasonable thoughts, as these for instance: Grateful persons are like fertile grounds, which give much more than they receive. Princes' actions are like great rivers, whereof few men see the original and all the world sees the course.

Seneca, who does not always think justly when he follows his own genius, is true and correct in his thoughts when he copies after nature, and all his comparisons are the finest in the world.

I said the comparisons ought to be well chosen, for it is easy to mistake, and the ablest men are sometimes mistaken. Cardinal Pallavicini [31] when he was but a Jesuit dedicated one of his books which I have by

257

me, entitled *Considerations Concerning the Art of Style and Dialogue,* to Monsignor Rinuccini, Archbishop of Fermo, and in his dedication commending this prelate for several treatises which he had written concerning the episcopal function he says that "To find so dry, so austere, so empty a subject, treated of with so great variety of curious notions, with so much sweetness of style, with so great an abundance of ornaments and figures, was to me an object of as great amazement as delightful gardens built by the black art upon desert rocks would have been."

It is not a happy comparison; for besides that there is not much relation between a bishop and a magician, to say that this dry and hard subject treated of with so much wit, so much politeness, and so much eloquence has something more surprising than the delicious gardens which appear all at once upon frightful and barren rocks by the help of magic, is not this to say (without thinking of it) that this prelate's works are not solid, and that there is more show than substance in what he writes? In truth, enchanted palaces and gardens dazzle and charm men's eyes, but all this is only illusion, and there is nothing less real than what pleases most.

The late Duke of Rochefoucauld, who thought so justly and had so sound a judgment, says Philanthus, said one day, after he had read a book full of subtlety and very sparkling, that it seemed to him as if he had seen those palaces built in the air by charms, which vanish away in smoke at the time when they dazzle the most.

The Duke of Rochefoucauld's thought, replies Eudoxus, is as true as Cardinal Pallavicini's was false. But as to comparisons, says he further, one ought chiefly to avoid falsifying of nature, if I may so speak, by attributing to her what does not belong to her, as those orators or rather corrupters of eloquence whom Quintilian laughs at,[32] who thought it was a fine thing to say that great rivers are navigable at the fountainhead, and good trees bear fruit at their first springing up.

That which amazes me, replies Philanthus, is that Cardinal Pallavicini should not think justly in a book which treats of justness, and where the author accuses good writers of falsehood; among others Tasso, who, before he describes the last battle of the infidels against the Christians, says that the clouds disappeared just as the engagement began, and that heaven resolved to see without a veil those great acts of valor which were then to be showed on each side.

258

Dominique Bouhours

E senza velo
Volse mirar l'opre grandi il Cielo.

"For we know very well," says Pallavicini, "that the material heaven has no eyes to see with, nor soul to desire, and that the inhabitants of heaven, if he means them, see through the thickest clouds whatever mortals act upon the earth."

He criticizes also upon a poet of his own time (I cannot tell who it is) who, being willing to commend an ancient statuary for the statue of a goddess, said of him that he was himself a god, since it belonged to God alone to give life to marble.

Tu pur Dio sei;
Che Dio sol è, chi puo dar vita à i marmi.

The fallacy in this censor's judgment lies in taking that in a proper sense which for the most part is only taken in a metaphorical one: I mean the privilege which is allowed to excellent statuaries to give life to marbles. This privilege, literally speaking, is a mark of the power of a god, such as that of Jupiter was, who quickened the stones, according to the fable, which Deucalion and Pyrrha threw; which is not true, and cannot be said of statuaries unless in a metaphorical sense, because of the resemblance which their workmanship has to living creatures.

I am surprised, I say, that so exact and so judicious a critic should fall himself into that fault which he reproves. For my part, replies Eudoxus, I wonder not at it. Wise men have their bad intervals, as well as fools their good ones; and even in matters of morality and style those who know the rules very well do not always follow them, and sometimes philosophers use [sophisms]. You and I, with all our reflections upon the falsehood of thoughts, are capable of mistaking, and we mistake perhaps at the very time when we would correct others. Let us at least love the truth even in our mistakes, which, I say, all men love, and when we read anything that is true, it is neither the book nor the author which makes us find it out to be so; it is something we carry about us that's very much advanced above body and sensible light, and which is an impression, a spark of the eternal light of truth. So a very sensible man of our age assures us that when a natural discourse paints a passion we find within ourselves the truth of what we heard, which was there before without being taken notice of, and we find ourselves carried to love him who made us perceive it, for he showed us not his own happiness but ours.

All this is fine and curious, says Philanthus. But is it enough to think well that our thoughts have nothing false in them? No, replies Eudoxus; thoughts may be so very true that they may be sometimes trivial, and therefore it was that Tully, commending Crassus's thoughts after he had said they were as perfect as they were true, adds that they were equally new and out of the common road; [33] that is to say that besides the truth which always contents the mind there must be something else which strikes and surprises it. I do not say that all ingenious thoughts ought to be as new as Crassus's were. It would be hard to say nothing but what is new; it is enough that the thoughts made use of in discourses of wit are not common, or, if the invention be not wholly new, yet that the way of turning them at least should be so; or, if they have not the graces of being new even in the turn, yet they should have something in themselves which may create pleasure and admiration.

Ah! this is what I love, says Philanthus, and I die with longing to know all your thoughts upon this subject.

This will serve for another time, replies Eudoxus; it is already very late, and I see that the victuals is ready.

Here they ended their conversation, went to supper, and talked only of indifferent things till they parted.

Dialogue II

Philanthus's head was filled all night long with that truth and falsehood which had been the subject of their dialogue. The principles and examples upon which Eudoxus had built it came into his mind again when he awaked, but his friend's last words made him extremely impatient to renew the discourse.

He rose betimes contrary to his custom, and went immediately to seek Eudoxus whom the love of study had made a very early man, after the example of those philosophers who believed that the most precious hours of the day for scholars were those in the morning; without doubt, because the head is then freest and the images of things are clearest after sleep, or because the mind is more recollected before it is distracted with business. Philanthus found Eudoxus in his closet and let him see presently how much he desired to begin again the discourse concerning thoughts. I am at work about it now, says Eudoxus, and I have been above this hour, reviewing all my best extracts out of the ancients and moderns. To come back again then to the place where we left off yesterday, I told you that for ingenious thoughts it was not enough for them to be true; something

260

extraordinary must be added over and above to strike the mind. We have said already, and it cannot be said too often: truth is to a thought what foundations are to a building; it supports it and makes it strong. But a building which is only strong will not have wherewith to please those that understand architecture. They look for nobleness, beauty, and even fineness in well-built houses, besides strength, and this also is what I would have in those thoughts we are now speaking of. Truth which in so many other cases pleases without any ornament, requires it here, and this ornament is sometimes nothing but a new turn which is given to things. Instances will make you understand what I mean. *Death spares no man.* Here's a very true thought, and but too true, the more's the pity, adds Eudoxus; yet it is a very ordinary and a very plain one. To raise it and to make it in some sort new, one needs only turn it as Horace and Malherbe have done.

The first, as you know very well, turns it thus: "Pale Death knocks equally at kings' palaces and poor men's cottages." [34] The second takes another turn. "The poor man in his cottage covered over with straw is subject to her laws, and the guard which watches at the gates of the Louvre defends not our kings." [35]

I understand you, says Philanthus; but which of these two thoughts, or rather of these two turns pleases you most? Both in their kinds have something which pleases, replies Eudoxus. The turn of the Latin poet is more figurative and smart; that of the French poet is more natural and finer; there is something noble in them both.

For my part, replies Philanthus, I chiefly love thoughts which have [loftiness] in them, and which represent only great things to the mind. Your taste is not very bad in that, says Eudoxus; the sublime, the grandeur in a thought is that properly which carries all before it and which ravishes, provided the thought agrees to the subject. For this is a general rule, that one ought to think according to the matter he treats of, and nothing is more foolish than to have sublime thoughts on a subject which requires only mean ones, and it would almost be better to have none but mean thoughts upon an argument which might require sublime ones; so that Timaeus whom Longinus speaks of, that commended Alexander for conquering all Asia in fewer years than Isocrates composed his panegyric upon the Athenians,[36] troubles me less than Balzac, who says thus to la Motte Aigron: "Let me die if the least part of the work which you showed me be not worth more than all that ever the Hollanders did, provided you except the victories of the Prince of Orange.[37]

The truth is, Longinus condemns this comparison of the king of Macedon with a sophist, and of the conquest of Asia with a simple discourse, as low and childish. But yet there is more proportion between an illustrious conqueror and a famous orator, between an effect of heroic virtue and a masterpiece of eloquence, than there is between a small part of a little work and all that a powerful and a happy people have done. For not to speak of the Prince of Orange's victories, since our author desires they should be excepted, how far has not the Dutch Commonwealth carried her power by sea and land, notwithstanding all the forces and all the politics of Spain?

Here as I am not for Balzac, says Philanthus, so neither am I for Longinus, and I think he criticizes too far when he reproaches Timaeus with childishness for his commendation of Alexander. If anyone should say of Louis the Great that he conquered the Franche-Comté the first time in fewer days than one could write his panegyric, would he, think you, speak foolishly? And if at his return from so short and so glorious a campaign it should be said that those who were to compliment his Majesty had need of more time to prepare their harangues than had been spent in that conquest, do you believe that would be a bad thought?

I do not think it would, answers Eudoxus; but I think that Timaeus's thought is faulty, because the harangues you speak of relate to the king and his conquest, whereas Isocrates's panegyric no ways concerned Alexander or his victories. But let's not ramble too far; let us go back to that nobleness which you love so much.

Hermogenes[38] sets down several degrees of noble and majestical thoughts as he calls them. The first is of those which have a relation to the gods, and which express something divine; so that one may say according to this rhetorician's doctrine that there is a great deal of dignity in what a Greek Father said, that Christianity is an imitation of the divine life, and a Latin Father, that he takes his revenge upon God who loves his enemies. . . .

∽ ∽ ∽

The nobleness of thoughts, continues Eudoxus, arises also, according to Hermogenes, from the nature of things which are indeed human; but which pass for great and illustrious among men, as power, generosity, wit, courage, victories, and triumphs. Here are some examples which I took notice of and set down.

"There is nothing greater in your fortune than an ability to preserve great numbers of men, nor nothing better in your nature than a desire to do it." [39] It was to Caesar that this was said by the Roman orator; see also how your beloved historian, who in your opinion has something brisker than Livy, speaks of this same orator: "He owed all his advancement to himself: a man of mighty genius, who prevented our being overcome by the wit of those whose arms we had conquered." [40] But the elder Seneca says a greater thing of him when he says that Tully's was the only genius which the people of Rome had that was equal to their Empire. . . .[41]

〜 〜 〜

Methinks, replied Philanthus, that well-chosen comparisons taken from the great subjects of nature always produce very noble thoughts. Yes, replied Eudoxus, and Longinus, who gives rules of the sublime not only in words but in thoughts, thinks very nobly himself when he compares Demosthenes to a tempest and thunder that ravages and carries all away, Cicero to an everlasting fire, and who according to the proportion it goes on gets new strength.[42] The comparisons of art, pursued he, excel sometimes those we borrow from nature, and one of our panegyrists says excellently upon the surprising actions of St. Louis in a memorable battle, and which appeared above the rules of common bravery, that [such examples are to be compared to noble pictures full of shades and obscurities, which at first sight look rough to those who have no skill in it, and seem to offend the eyes and the rule, but are a happy boldness and a masterpiece of art to understanding and skillful people.]

History also furnishes us with very fine comparisons; upon one of the medals that were laid in the foundations of the Jesuits' Church of St. Louis, which Louis the Just built, these words were engraved: *Vicit ut David, aedificat ut Salomon.* What can imagination afford greater?" "He conquered like David, he built like Solomon. . . .

〜 〜 〜

All those sorts of thoughts have a deal of nobleness, because the foundation they are grounded upon has nothing but what's noble. On the contrary, mean comparisons cause the thoughts to be so too. Bacon, which you have read, and who was one of the finest geniuses of his time, says that money is like a dunghill, which is of no use but when it is spread abroad.[43] There is truth and wit in that thought, but there is nothing noble in it. The idea of a dunghill is somewhat mean and loathsome. You are mighty nice, I find, said Philanthus; I fear you'll have a disgust too for the epigram which the honest man Patrix [44] composed a few days before his death. For there a dunghill is spoken of, and even the dunghill is the turn of the poem.

> Je songeais cette nuit que de mal consumé
> Côte à côte d'un pauvre on m'avait inhumé
> Et que n'en pouvant pas souffrir le voisinage,
> En mort de qualité je lui tins ce langage:
> Retire-toi, coquin, va pourrir loin d'ici;
> Il ne t'appartient pas de m'approcher ainsi.
> Coquin, ce me dit-il, d'une arrogance extrême,
> Va chercher tes coquins ailleurs, coquin toi-même!
> Ici tous sont égaux, je ne te dois plus rien;
> Je suis sur mon fumier, comme toi sur le tien.

I dreamed this night that consumed by pain they had interred me abreast with a poor wretch, and disliking the loathsome neighborhood, like a dead man of quality I gave him this language: stand off, rascal, go and rot far from hence; it does not become you to approach me thus. Rascal, said he to me, with an extreme arrogance, go look for your rascals elsewhere, rascal yourself. Here all are equal; I owe you nothing more. I lie upon my own dunghill as you do upon yours.

That dunghill, resumed Eudoxus, is not altogether like that of Bacon; the metaphorical sense smooths the roughness of the proper; for all the seriousness of the epigram, it has a pleasant air and somewhat comical which admits the proverb and the *quodlibet*.

I am upon my own dunghill, as you are upon yours.

For [low] thoughts which are ingenious may take place in the comic and the burlesque, as they must be entirely banished from the grave and the austere, such as serious poems, harangues, panegyrics and funeral orations.

But pray you, said Philanthus, except the poem of *Magdalene in the Wilderness of Sainte Baume*, which we have read together with so much pleasure, and though it be above the rules, and of a particular kind, it has its own merit. Sure it is an original piece, replied Eudoxus, and I'll approve of it for your sake, "that the eyes of the repenting sinner are melted candles; that [from] windmills they become water mills; that the fair tresses of hair with which she wiped our Saviour's feet are a golden dishcloth; that she herself is a holy [courtesan] and is no more a dirty black kettle; that the tears of a God are nothing but a water of life; that Jesus Christ is a great operator who had the ingenuity to take away the cataracts from Magdalene's eyes, and the Hercules who cleansed the stables of her heart." All this is admirable, and suits perfectly well the dignity of the subject.

But let's leave the Provençal poet [Patrix], and speak more seriously. I hate above all meanness in a Christian discourse, continued Eudoxus, and I cannot remember without indignation what a preacher said one day to an audience of nuns, that they ought always to have their toothpicks in their hands because the regular communities resemble the teeth, which to keep fine and clean must be well ranged, very white and very neat. I was at that sermon, replied Philanthus, and I assure you that the good father applauded himself for this thought. It is one almost of the same stamp, resumed Eudoxus, as that of the Italian preacher, who on Easter Sunday preached at Milan before the Cardinal Charles Borromeo, archbishop of that city, and said to the people that they had a very holy prelate, and very like an Easter egg which is red and blessed, but a little hard: *Havete un prelato santissimo; e come l'uova de pasca, rosso e benedetto; ma è vero ch'è un poco duretto.*

After all, it is ingenious, said Philanthus. Say rather, answered Euxodus, [that it is silly]. The ministers of the Word of God should speak in another tone, not to disgrace their ministry. But concerning the Divine Word, remember, I beseech you, that the Holy Scripture is a foundation of noble thoughts, great and sublime, such as these: "I am He that is." "The Lord shall reign in all eternity and beyond." "That there be light, and there was light." The last, so plain in appearance, [in regard to the terms only], gives a magnificent idea of the power of God; and Longinus, for all he was a pagan, proposes it for a model of sublimity [of] thought.[45] For an elevated thought may agree very well with plain words; it happens even that the plainness of the expression makes us often more sensible of the greatness of things, and that is [so] true according to the sentiment of Longinus that sometimes we admire the thought of a generous and magnanimous man though he says nothing. We admire him, I say, through his silence, which shows the nobleness of his soul, and we have an example of it in the *Odyssey*. Here Ulysses makes his submissions to Ajax, to which Ajax does not so much as answer: and that very silence has something greater than all [that] he could have said.[46]

The strength of expression contributes sometimes to the height of the thought, and Scripture itself furnishes us with very rich examples. For saying that Alexander was master of the world, that the sea opened herself to the people of God, that heaven and earth cannot sustain the glance of the Divine Majesty, the Holy Ghost speaks thus: "The earth was silent at his presence;" "The sea saw the Lord, and fled;" "Earth and heaven fled before the presence of him that sate upon the throne."[47] Those terms of *silence* and *flight* have somewhat very energetical which paints the thing both lively and nobly.

As for me, said Philanthus, I have seen no pictures like those which David made of a turn of fortune: "I myself have seen the ungodly in great power and flourishing like a green bay tree." "I went by and lo he was gone: I sought him but his place could nowhere be found."[48] Observe how far David goes. All [that] poets have said of the decay of Troy, of Rome, and of Carthage, is that nothing was left but the places where those famous cities were situated. But David tells us that the very place where the impious was in the highest pitch of fortune is no more.

The prophets, answered Eudoxus, are full of strong thoughts, of magnificent ideas, which go far beyond those of Hermogenes. But what do you understand, interrupted Philanthus, by a strong thought? I understand, replied Eudoxus, a thought full of great sense, explained in few words and in a lively manner, which has a sudden and powerful effect.[49] Such are in Tacitus, to go back to the profane authors, the thoughts of Otho when determined to die in the bad condition of his affairs, and after a battle which was to decide entirely the fate of the empire between him and Vitellius. "My life is not worthy the hazard of a virtue like yours," said he to those that spurred him on to try his fortune once more; "the more you give me hopes, if I had a mind to live, the more I shall find delight in dying. Fortune and I have [tried one another] sufficiently. I don't want consolation nor vengeance; others might have kept the empire longer, but none could quit it more generously." He concludes his harangue, as strongly as he began and followed it, thus: "It is faint-heartedness to speak too much of one's own death. [Regard as the chief proof of my resolve the fact that I complain of no man. It is for him to blame gods or men who has the wish to live.]" [50]

What Germanicus said to his friend when he was dying has its force also: "Even the unknown shall lament the death of Germanicus. You gentlemen shall revenge him, if so be you love more my person than my fortune. . . ."[51]

      ∽   *∽*   *∽*

As for what remains, the comparisons taken from florid and delicious subjects make agreeable thoughts, as those that are formed of great subjects make noble ones.

"It seems to me," says Costar,[52] "that it is a great advantage to be happy without any trouble, and that [happiness] is a calm stream, which following its natural course [flows] without any obstacle between two flowery banks. I find to the contrary that those who are virtuous by reason, who sometimes make finer things than others, are like those *jets d'eau* where art commits violence on nature, and who after having spurted into the air very often [are stopped] by the least obstacle.

It is to [think] a pleasant thought to say with Balzac of a little river: "This pretty water loves this country so well that it divides itself into a thousand branches and makes an infinite number of isles and turns to amuse itself the more." [53]

I don't wonder, said Philanthus, that the eclogues of Theocritus and Virgil, and the gardens and the pastorals of one of our friends who equals them both,[54] are so agreeable that they never tire; for they have flowers in them everywhere, woods, streams, and in short all that is delicious in a country life, besides the form of the ornaments which those great masters give to their matter to enliven and embellish it.

There it is, answered Eudoxus, that poetry, which according to Hermogenes aims almost entirely at pleasure, amuses and diverts us. But if we may believe the same Hermogenes, the fiction, or something poetical, renders the thoughts very agreeable in prose. . . .[55]

      ∽   *∽*   *∽*

I judge by that, said Philanthus, that sometimes poetry imitates prose. But it seems to me that the rhetorical figures borrowed from poetry very much enliven the thought in prose. The elder Pliny, who, according to Voiture, far exceeds the younger, speaking of those Roman dictators who,

267

after having commanded armies and obtained victories, ploughed the ground and led the plough themselves, says that the earth rejoiced to be cultivated by such victorious laborers, and by a plough-share loaded with laurels.[56]

He says in another place [57] that the houses in which the statues of noble heroes were placed in order were yet sensible in themselves of their triumphs after they had changed their master, and the walls would reproach a coward which inhabited them for every day entering into a place consecrated by the monuments of the virtue and of the glory of others.

It is true, replied Eudoxus, that that joy of the earth, that sensibility of the houses, those reproaches of the walls have something lively and very fine which gives pleasure to the sense. But an animated metaphor that shows a deal of action pleases no less. Pliny, whom you have mentioned just now, says, to make one comprehend the use of arrows, that to contrive death should come sooner, we have made her fly, in giving wings to iron.[58] Is not that a brisk and lively thought, and as agreeable as that of Horace, upon the sorrows which fly about the gilded ceilings, which the guards can't keep out? Let's observe by the by, said Philanthus, that the thought of Malherbe upon death is taken from thence.[59]

Et la garde qui veille aux barrières du Louvre
N'en défend pas nos rois.

> And the guard which watches at the gates of the
> Louvre defends not our kings [from it].

As for what remains, resumed Eudoxus, the metaphor is, of its nature, a spring of agreeableness, and perhaps nothing flatters the sense more than the representation of an object under a strange image. According to the remark of Aristotle, we love to see one thing in another, and what does not affect of itself or with a naked face surprises in a borrowed habit and masked. So of a common and plain proposition, such as the following, "The girls in France don't succeed to the crown," we make an ingenious and agreeable thought in saying according to the Gospel, "The lilies don't spin," or according to the fable, "A spinning-wheel does not agree with the Gallic Hercules." . . .

꙳   ꙳   ꙳

It must be owned, said Philanthus, that antitheses well managed are infinitely pleasant in pieces of wit. They have almost the same effect, answered Eudoxus, as the lights and shades in a picture, which good painters have the art to dispose in their proper places, or as in music the high and low notes, which a master knows how to order.

In the meantime don't believe, continued he, that a thought cannot be agreeable but where the [passages] are bright and witty; simplicity alone sometimes makes all their beauty. This simplicity consists in I don't know what air that is plain and ingenuous but sprightly and reasonable, like that of a [rustic] with sense, or a witty child; and most of the epigrams of the [Greek] *Anthology* have this character: they do not sting the taste, yet they have something that tickles it, and one may say that without having Martial's salt they are not insipid. . . .

৩৮ ৩৮ ৩৮

The authors of these epigrams, added Eudoxus, are a little of the genius of some painters which excelled in a certain graceful plainness, and amongst others of Corregio, whose pictures of children have particular graces and something so childish that art is like nature itself.[60] Amongst the Latins, Ovid and Catullus are originals in that kind; you need but open the books of *Metamorphoses*, *Fasti*, and *Tristia* to find some example of ingenuity, and the number of them there hindered me from writing any of them. What Catullus said of an excellent perfume was agreeable because plain. "When you smell it, you'll desire the gods to make you all nose." . . .

৩৮ ৩৮ ৩৮

. . . I must tell you of a third way of thinking, which with [its agreeableness] has a delicacy, or rather whose grace, beauty, and value rises from its being nice. Tell me, I pray, replied Eudoxus, what is precisely delicacy? Nothing else is talked of, and I talk of it every minute without well understanding what I say and having a clear notion of it. I only know that there are good wits, as well as good painters, [who] are not delicate. The works of Rubens, [in relation to] the masters of that art, savor more of a Dutch genius than of the beauty of the ancients, and though there is vivacity and nobleness in all his pieces, they are more coarse than delicate; whereas the pictures of Raphael have a great deal of grandeur, of inimitable graces, and all the delicacy possible.

Delicacy strictly taken, replied Eudoxus, is easier to be defined than in the figured way. If you would ask me what delicacy is in matters of perfume, in meat, or in music, I could tell you, perhaps, by saying that a

269

delicate perfume is a subtle scent which never offends the brain; and that delicate meat is that which will not charge the stomach; and delicate music is a concert of vocal and instrumental music which tickles the ears and excites [only gentle] motions of the heart. But when you ask me what a delicate thought is, I don't know in what terms to explain myself; it is a difficult thing to bring them under one view, for when we think we have them they flee from us; all that we can do is to look nearly and divers ways till we come by degrees to know them. Let us endeavor to form [for] ourselves [some idea of ingenious delicacy, and above all let us not be content with saying that] a delicate thought is the finest production, [and, as it were,] the flower of wit; for that is to say nothing, [and in] a subject so difficult, we [cannot disentangle ourselves] with a synonym or a metaphor.

We must, in my mind, reason on the delicacy of [works of wit in the same way as we reason on the delicacy in works of nature]; the most delicate are those [61] where nature takes pleasure to work in little, and where the matter, almost imperceptible, makes us doubt whether she has a mind to show or hide her address:[62] such is an insect perfectly well formed, so much the more worthy of admiration as it less affects the sight, according to the author of the *Natural History*.

Let's say by way of analogy that a thought wherein there is delicacy [ought] to be included in few words, and [that] the sense which it contains [be] neither so visible nor so plain; it seems now to me that it is hid to the end that we may look for it, and that we should guess at it, and keeps us in suspense to give us the pleasure of discovering it all at once when we have knowledge enough;[63] for as we should have good eyes, and assist the same with art, as spectacles, microscopes, etc., to search into the works of nature, [so only intelligent and enlightened persons can penetrate the whole sense of a delicate thought.] This little mystery is, [as it were, the soul of delicacy of thoughts, so that thoughts] which have nothing mysterious, neither in the depth or turnings, and show themselves clearly at the first sight, [are not properly delicate], however sprightly they may be in other respects. We may conclude that delicacy adds something to the agreeable and sublime, and that the thoughts which are noble and pretty have some sort of resemblance [to] the heroines or romantic shepherdesses, whose faces are not covered with masks nor veils, but all their beauty is quickly discovered by those who see them. . . .

Dominique Bouhours

The first thought that comes into my mind of that nature is in Pliny's panegyric.[64] The panegyrist said to his prince, who had long time refused the title of Father of his Country, and would not admit it till he thought he merited it, "You are the only person that has merited to be styled the Father of your Country before you had the title."

The Cardinal Bentivoglio, interrupts Philanthus, has almost the same notion upon the dignity of a grandee of Spain, in speaking of the Marquess of Spinola: "His illustrious birth and great merit made him grandee of Spain before he had the title." . . .

ဢ ဢ ဢ

As far as I see, replied Eudoxus, you understand very well what a delicate thought means, and in what it differs from a sublime one, or purely agreeable. But do you believe that surprising and elevating thoughts, which affect most by [their] delicacy or sublim[ity], or by [their] plain agreeableness, are in some kind vicious if they be not natural, as that of Crassus, which we have took for our model, which has none of the appearance of [affectation]? [65] I always fear, said Philanthus, lest that by pretending to be natural one should become dull and insipid, or lest the thought should lose something which renders it lively and sharp. That's not my intention, replied Eudoxus, and as in the language I do not like an exactness which makes the discourse dry and weak, what I call natural would not suit with my inclination if it made a thought flat and languid; but that may be avoided. There is a difference between being flat and [being] nauseous; sauce may be good without a great deal of pepper and salt, and [a] strengthening broth pleases those of a refined taste more than a bisque.

What do you mean, then, said Philanthus, by what you call natural thoughts? I mean, replied Eudoxus, something which is not farfetched, which follows from the nature of the subject.[66] I mean a kind of a simple beauty, plain without art, such as the ancients describe true eloquence; one would say that a natural thought should come into anybody's mind, and that it was in our head before we read it; it seems easy to be found and costs nothing wherever we meet it; they come less in some manner out of the mind of him that thinks than of the thing that was spoke of.[67]

For what remains, by the word *natural* I understand not this [ingenu-ous] character which is [one of the sources] of the agreeable in thoughts; all [ingenuous] thoughts are natural, [but not all natural thoughts are in-

271

genuous,] to take the word [ingenuous], in its proper signification.[68] The great and the sublime are not [ingenuous], nor can they be, for the [ingenuous] carries in it somewhat low or less elevated. Did you not tell me, interrupts Philanthus, that simplicity and grandeur were not incompatible? Yes, replied Eudoxus, and I say so still; but there is a certain difference between a noble simplicity and pure [ingenuousness]: one only excludes ostentation, and the other greatness itself.

But to explain myself more sensibly, a natural thought in some measure resembles a spring which is found in a garden without the help of art, or like a fine complexion without paint. In the time of Augustus they have thoughts of this kind, especially Cicero, Virgil, and Ovid.

The thought of Cicero upon the colossi of Ceres and Triptolemus, which Verres could not carry away because of their weight, whatever temptation he had, comes from the subject, and presents [itself] of itself. "Their beauty puts them in danger of being taken: their magnitude saves them." [69] But that upon the death of Crassus is one of the most natural that can be seen. He takes notice that Crassus dies before the troubles of the Republic, and that that great man saw neither the war begun in Italy, nor the exile of his son-in-law, nor the affliction of his daughters, nor, in short, the fatal condition of Rome quite disfigured by a continual course of sorrows; after that it appears to one that "the gods did not take away his life, but made a present of death." [70]

The thought, [as] you see, is drawn from the bottom of the subject; there is nothing in it strange or foreign; there is nothing flat or insipid. . . .[71]

◌ ◌ ◌

Affectation, pursued Eudoxus, is the fault directly opposed to that natural style we speak of. It is according to Quintilian,[72] said Philanthus, the worst of all vices in eloquence, because the others are avoided, and the former is looked for; but it is complete in the elocution. Without offence to Quintilian, replied Eudoxus, [that fault so specious and so beautiful] in appearance has no less part in thought than in language. And it is the sentiment of a [clever] Italian, who dares give the lie to Quintilian upon the last article of the passage you spoke of; *questo ultimo*, says he, *è falso, perochè l'affettazione consiste anche ne concetti*;[73] he speaks it after an ancient rhetor, who produces for example of affectation in the thought, the centaur on horseback upon himself; but some other examples shall explain it better.

272

Virgil says that the giant Enceladus, burned with the lightning of Jupiter, spews flames through the overtures of the mountain which the gods threw upon him; and Guarini says that the same giant pours fire out of anger and indignation against heaven without discovering him that was stricken with thunderbolts, or him that strikes.

> La dove sotto a la gran mole Etnea
> Non so sè fulminato u fulminante
>   Vibra il fiero gigante
> Contra l'enemico ciel fiamme disdegno.[74]

The one is natural and the other affected.

According to the ancient Pliny, human blood, to revenge itself to its mortal enemy, the sword, which helps to spill it, makes it rusty.[75] According to Pliny the Younger, one Lucinianus, who from senator turned professor of rhetoric to get a livelihood, revenged himself of fortune by the harangues he made against her.[76] There is affectation in the thought of the former, for that revenge we attribute to the blood does not arise from nature, and the rust that spoils the sword proceeds as well from the blood of a beast as that of man. The thought of the latter is natural, and the vengeance the degraded senator takes has its foundation in nature, which throws unfortunate men into a passion against anything which they think to be the cause of their disgrace. . . .

❧   ❧   ❧

For the rest, affectation which regards the thoughts commonly proceeds from the excess to which we carry them;[77] that's to say, from too much sublime or too much agreeable or delicacy pursuant to the three kinds we have established: the one of noble, great, and sublime thoughts, the other of pretty and agreeable thoughts, and the third of gentle and delicate thoughts. For if we take no care to manage our understanding according to the rules of good sense and include ourselves within the bounds of nature, we spoil all. The bombast style takes the place of the great and sublime; agreeableness is nothing but affectation, and delicacy is pure refining.

I fear, said Philanthus, that with all your distinctions you refine a little yourself, and wish you would give me some examples of this bombast, of this affectation and refining, to see whether you don't carry the matter too far. I shall easily satisfy you in that, replied Eudoxus, for in reading authors I have observed several thoughts which are vicious in those three kinds, and which sometimes err by too much wit.

They were thus far when one came in and told Eudoxus that some company was coming; they were three fine wits from his neighborhood, great talkers and laughers of the number of those honest troublesome fellows that disturb all agreeable societies, and the more impertinent because they don't believe themselves to be so. [As] one has not in the country the conveniencies that are to be had in town of shunning such sort of people or getting rid of them soon, Eudoxus was forced to receive them. They dined; after dinner they [played; then they walked] till evening; the visit was pretty long, and the night sent away the three troublesome companions.

As soon as they were gone, Philanthus, who could not believe that ever anyone could have too much wit, [and who] was impatient to know how a thought could be vicious that way, begged his friend to explain it a little, but Eudoxus was so fatigued by the company he had just quitted that he had no strength to speak one word. He begged Philanthus's pardon and put the conversation off till next day.

✤ 1674

Rene Rapin REFLECTIONS ON ARISTOTLE'S TREATISE OF POESY IN GENERAL

I

The true value of poetry is ordinarily so little known that scarce ever is made a true judgment of it. It is the talent of wits only that are above the common rank to esteem of it according to its merit, and one cannot consider how Alexander, Scipio, Julius Caesar, Augustus, and all the great men of antiquity have been affected therewith without conceiving a noble idea of it. In effect, poesy, of all arts, is the most perfect: for the perfection of other arts is limited, but this of poesy has no bounds; to be excellent therein one must know all things. But this value will best appear by giving a particular of the qualities necessary for a poet.

II

He must have a genius extraordinary; great natural gifts; a wit just, fruitful, piercing, solid, universal; an understanding clean and distinct; an imagination neat and pleasant; an elevation of soul that depends not on art nor study, and which is purely a gift of heaven, and must be sustained by a lively sense and vivacity; a great judgment to consider wisely of things, and a vivacity to express them with that grace and abundance which gives them beauty. But as judgment without wit is cold and heavy, so wit without judgment is blind and extravagant. Hence it is that Lucan often in his *Pharsalia* grows flat for want of wit. And Ovid in his *Metamorphoses* sometimes loses himself through his defect of judgment. Ariosto has too much flame; Dante has none at all. Boccaccio's wit is just but not copious; the Cavalier Marino is luxuriant, but wants that justness. For in fine, to accomplish a poet is required a temperament of wit and of fancy, of strength and of sweetness, of penetration and of delicacy, and above all things he must have a sovereign eloquence and a profound ca-

275

pacity. These are the qualities that must concur together to form the genius of a poet and sustain his character.

III

But the first injustice that poets suffer is that commonly what is merely the effect of fancy is mistaken for wit. Thus an ignorant person shall start up and be thought a poet in the world for a lucky hit in a song or catch, where is only the empty flash of an imagination heated perhaps by a debauch, and nothing of that celestial fire which only is the portion of an extraordinary genius. "One must be careful," saith Horace, "of profaning that name by bestowing it without distinction on all those who undertake to versify. For," saith he, "there must be a greatness of soul, and something divine in the spirit. There must be lofty expressions, and noble thoughts, and an air of majesty to deserve that name." [1] A sonnet, ode, elegy, epigram, and those little kind of verses that often make so much noise in the world are ordinarily no more than the mere productions of imagination; a superficial wit with a little conversation of the world is capable of these things. True poetry requires other qualifications; a genius for war or for business comes nothing near it. A little phlegm, with a competency of experience, may fit a man for an important negotiation, and an opportunity well managed, joined with a little hazard, may make the success of a battle, and all the good fortune of a campaign; but to excite these emotions of the soul and transports of admiration that are expected from poetry, all the wit that the soul of man is capable of is scarce sufficient.

VI

One may be an orator without the natural gift of eloquence, because art may supply that defect; but no man can be a poet without a genius, the want of which no art or industry is capable to repair. This genius is that celestial fire intended by the fable, which enlarges and heightens the soul and makes it express things with a lofty air. Happy is he to whom nature has made this present; by this he is raised above himself, whereas others are always low and creeping, and never speak but what is mean and common. He that hath a genius appears a poet on the smallest subjects by the turn he gives them and the noble manner in which he expresses himself. This character the French gave their Monsieur Racan;[2] but in truth where shall we find all these qualities I have mentioned? Where is that sparkling

276

René Rapin

wit and that solid judgment? that flame and that phlegm? that rapture and that moderation which constitute that genius we inquire after? It is the little wits always who think they versify the best; the greatest poets are the most modest. . . .

VII

It is not easily decided what the nature and what precisely is the end of this art; the interpreters of Aristotle differ in their opinions. Some will have the end to be delight, and that it is on this account it labors to move the passions, all whose motions are delightful, because nothing is more sweet to the soul than agitation; it pleases itself in changing the objects to satisfy the immensity of its desires. It is true, delight is the end poetry aims at, but not the principal end, as others pretend. In effect, poetry, being an art, ought to be profitable by the quality of its own nature and by the essential subordination that all arts should have to polity, whose end in general is the public good. This is the judgment of Aristotle and of Horace, his chief interpreter.

VIII

After all, since the design of poetry is to delight, it omits nothing that may contribute thereto; it is to this intent that it makes use of numbers and harmony, which are naturally delightful, and animates its discourse with more lively draughts and more strong expressions than are allowed in prose, and does affranchize itself from that constraint and reservedness that is ordinary with orators, and permits a great liberty to imagination, and makes frequent images of what is most agreeable in nature; and never speaks but with figures, to give a greater luster to the discourse; and is noble in its ideas, sublime in the expressions, bold in the words, passionate in the motions, and takes pleasure in relating extraordinary adventures to give the most common and natural things a fabulous gloss, to render them more admirable and heighten truth by fiction. It is finally for this that it employs whatever art has that is pleasant, because its end is to delight. [Empedocles and Lucretius, who used not this art in their poems (as Homer and Virgil did), are not true poets.] Homer is delightful even in the description of Laertes' swineherd's lodge in his *Odyssey*, and Virgil in the dung and thistles in his *Georgics* as he expresses himself, for everything becomes beautiful and flowery in the hands of a poet who hath a genius.

277

IX

However, the principal end of poesy is to profit, not only by refreshing the mind to render it more capable of the ordinary functions and by assuaging the troubles of the soul with its harmony and all the elegancies of expression, but furthermore, by purging the manners with wholesome instructions which it professes to administer to human kind; for virtue being naturally austere by the constraint it imposes on the heart in repressing the desires, morality, which undertakes to regulate the motions of the heart by its precepts, ought to make itself delightful that it may be listened to, which can by no means be so happily effected as by poetry. It is by this that morality, in curing the maladies of men, makes use of the same artifice that physicians have recourse to in the sickness of children: they mingle honey with the medicine to take off the bitterness. The principal design therefore of this art is to render pleasant that which is wholesome, in which it is more wise than other arts, which endeavor to profit without any care to please. Eloquence itself by its most passionate discourse is not always capable to persuade men to virtue with that success as poetry, because men are more sensible and sooner impressed upon by what is pleasant than by reason. For this cause, all poetry that tends to the corruption of manners is irregular and vicious, and poets are to be looked on as a public contagion whose morals are not pure; and it is these dissolute and debauched poets that Plato banished his commonwealth. And true it is that the petty wits only are ordinarily subject to say what is impious or obscene. Homer and Virgil were never guilty in this kind; they were sweet and virtuous as philosophers. The Muses of true poets are as chaste as Vestals.

X

For no other end is poetry delightful than that it may be profitable. Pleasure is only the means by which the profit is conveyed, and all poetry, when it is perfect, ought of necessity to be a public lesson of good manners for the instruction of the world. Heroic poesy proposes the example of great virtues and great vices to excite men to abhor these and to be in love with the other. It gives us an esteem for Achilles in Homer, and contempt for Thersites; it begets in us a veneration for the piety of Aeneas in Virgil and horror for the profaneness of Mezentius. Tragedy rectifies the use of passions by moderating our fear and our pity, which are obstacles of virtue; it lets men see that vice never escapes unpunished when it

278

René Rapin

represents Aegisthus in the *Electra* of Sophocles, punished after the ten years' enjoyment of his crime. It teaches us that the favors of fortune and the grandeurs of the world are not always true goods when it shows on the theatre a queen so unhappy as Hecuba, deploring with that pathetic air her misfortunes, in Euripides. Comedy, which is an image of common conversation, corrects the public vices by letting us see how ridiculous they are in particulars. Aristophanes does not mock at the foolish vanity of Praxagora (in his *Parliament of Women*) but to cure the vanity of the other Athenian women; and it was only to teach the Roman soldiers in what consisted true valor that Plautus exposed in public the extravagance of false bravery in his braggadoccio captain in that comedy of *The Glorious Soldier*.

XI

But because poetry is only profitable so far as it is delightful, it is of greatest importance in this art to please; the only certain way to please is by rules. These therefore are to be established that a poet may not be left to confound all things, imitating those extravagances which Horace so much blames — that is to say, by joining things naturally incompatible, "mixing tigers with lambs, birds with serpents, to make one body of different species, and thereby authorize fancies more indigested than the dreams of sick men;" [3] for unless a man adhere to principles, he is obnoxious to all extravagances and absurdities imaginable; unless he go by rule, he slips at every step towards wit, and falls into errors as often as he sets out. Into what enormities hath Petrarch run in his *Africa*, Ariosto in his *Orlando Furioso*, Cavalier Marino in his *Adone*, and all the other Italians who were ignorant of Aristotle's rules and followed no other guides but their own genius and capricious fancy. Truth is, the wits of Italy were so prepossessed in favor of the romantic poetry of Pulci, Boiardo, and Ariosto that they regarded no other rules than what the heat of their genius inspired. The first Italian poet who let the world see that the art was not altogether unknown to him was Giorgio Trissino,[4] in his poem of Italy delivered from the Goths under the pontificates of Leo X and Clement VIII. . . .

XII

Aristotle drew the platform of these rules from the poems of Homer and other poets of his time by the reflections he had a long time made on their works. I pretend not by a long discourse to justify the necessity, the

279

justness, and the truth of these rules, nor to make an history of Aristotle's treatise of poesy, or examine whether it is complete, which many others have done; all these things I suppose. Only I affirm that these rules well considered, one shall find them made only to reduce nature into method, to trace it step by step, and not suffer the least mark of it to escape us. It is only by these rules that the verisimility in fictions is maintained which is the soul of poesy. For unless there be the unity of place, of time, and of the action in the great poems, there can be no verisimility. In fine, it is by these rules that all becomes just, proportionate, and natural, for they are founded upon good sense and sound reason rather than on authority and example. Horace's book *Of Poetry*, which is but an interpretation of that of Aristotle, discovers sufficiently the necessity of being subject to rules by the ridiculous absurdities one is apt to fall into who follows only his fancy; for though poesy be the effect of fancy, yet if this fancy be not regulated it is a mere caprice, not capable of producing anything reasonable.

XIII

But if the genius must indispensably be subjected to the servitude of rules, it will not easily be decided whether art or nature contributes more to poetry; it is one of those questions unresolved which might be proper for a declamation, and the decision is of small importance. It suffices that we know both the one and the other are of that moment that none can attain to any sovereign perfection in poetry if he be defective in either. So that both (saith Horace) must mutually assist each other and conspire to make a poet accomplished. But though nature be of little value without the help of art, yet we may approve of Quintilian's opinion, who believed that art did less contribute to that perfection than nature.[5] And by the comparison that Longinus makes betwixt Apollonius and Homer, Eratosthenes and Archilocus, Bacchilides and Pindar, Ion and Sophocles, the former of all which never transgressed against the rules of art whereas these others did, it appears that the advantage of wit is always preferred before that of art.[6]

XVI

Nothing can more contribute to this perfection than a judgment proportioned to the wit, for the greater that the wit is and the more strength and vigor that the imagination has to form these ideas that enrich poesy, the more wisdom and discretion is requisite to moderate that heat and govern its natural fury. For reason ought to be much stronger than the fancy to discern how far the transports may be carried. It is a great talent to forbear speaking all one thinks and to leave something for others to employ their thoughts. It is not ordinarily known how far matters should be carried; a man of an accomplished genius stops regularly where he ought to stop, and retrenches boldly what ought to be omitted. It is a great fault not to leave a thing when it is well, for which Apelles so much blamed Protogenes.[7] This moderation is the character of a great wit; the vulgar understand it not, and (whatever is alleged to the contrary) never any save Homer and Virgil had the discretion to leave a thing when it was well.

XVIII

The art of poetry in general comprehends the matters of which a poet treats and the manner in which he handles them; the invention, the contrivance, the design, the proportion and symmetry of parts, the general disposition of matters, and whatever regards the invention belong to the matters of which this art ought to treat. The fable, the manners, the sentiments, the words, the figures, the numbers, the harmony, the versification regard the manner in which the matters are to be handled. So that the art is, as it were, the instrument of the genius, because it contains essentially all the different parts which are employed in the management. So that those who are furnished with a naked wit only, and who, to be great poets, rely principally on their fancy, as Cavalier Marino among the Italians, Théophile among the French; and those likewise who place the essence of poetry in big and pompous words, as Statius among the Latins and Du Bartas among the French, are much mistaken in their account when they aspire to the glory of poetry by such feeble means.

XIX

Among the particulars of this art, the subject and design ought to have the first place because it is, as it were, the first production of the wit, and the design in a poem is what they call the *ordonnance* in a picture. The great painters only are capable of a great design in their draughts, such as Raphael, a Giulio Romano, a Poussin, and only great poets are capable of a great subject in their poetry. An indifferent wit may form a vast design in his imagination, but it must be an extraordinary genius that can work this design, and fashion it according to justness and proportion. For it is necessary that the same spirit reign throughout, that all contribute to the

281

same end, and that all the parts bear a secret relation to each other; all depend on this relation and alliance, and this general design is nothing else but the form which a poet gives to his work. This also is the most difficult part, being the effect of an accomplished judgment; and because judgment is not the ordinary talent of the French, it is generally in the contrivance of their design that their poets are defective, and nothing is more rare among them than a design that is great, just, and well conceived. They pretend to be more happy in the talents of wit and fancy, as likewise the Italians. The most perfect design of all modern poems is that of Tasso; nothing more complete has appeared in Italy, though great faults are in the conduct of it. And the most judicious, the most admirable, the most perfect design of all antiquity is that of Virgil in his *Aeneid*; all there is great and noble, all proportionable to the subject, which is the establishment of the empire of Rome, to the hero, who is Aeneas, to the glory of Augustus and the Romans, for whom it was composed. Nothing is weak or defective in the execution; all there is happy, all is just, all is perfect. But the sovereign perfection of a design, in the opinion of Horace, is to be simple, and that all turn on the same center. Which is so true that even in little things, that is to say, in an eclogue, elegy, song, or epigram, and in the meanest compositions, there ought to be a just cast, and that all of it turn on the same point. Ovid did much violence to himself to unite his *Metamorphoses* and close them in one design, in which he was not altogether so happy as afterwards in his elegies, where wellnigh always one may find a certain turn which binds the design and makes thereof a work that is just by the dependence and relation of its parts. In this the ancient poets were always more exact than the modern, for most of the modern express their thoughts higgle-piggle, without any order or connection. If there be design, it is never with that scrupulous unity which is the principal virtue that should be predominant to make it just and complete. I know there are a kind of works which, by the quality of their character, ought to be writ with a free air, without other design than that of writing things naturally and without constraint; such are the hymns of Orpheus, Homer, Callimachus; and such are certain odes of Pindar, Anacreon, and Horace, that have no other rule but enthusiasm; and such likewise are the most part of the elegies of Tibullus and Propertius. But it must be granted that these are not the best and most beautiful, and who reflects on the elegies of Ovid shall always there perceive a secret turn which makes the design; and this is ordinarily the principal beauty in these little works

René Rapin

of verse, as may be seen in most epigrams of the *Anthology*, in those of Catullus, in the correct odes of Horace, and in the phaleusiacs of Bonnefons,[8] who within this last age has writ in Latin verse with all the softness and delicacy possible. Thus every sort of poesy ought to have its proportionable design — a great design in great poems, and in little, a little design. But of this the ordinary wits know nothing; their works, which generally are mere productions of imagination, have scarcely any design, unless it be by chance. It must be the work of an accomplished genius to close his thoughts in a design, whence results an agreement and proportion of parts that makes the harmony perfect.

XXI

Aristotle divides the fable, which serves for argument to a poem, into simple and compound. The simple is that which hath no change of fortune, as is the *Prometheus* of Aeschylus and the *Hercules* of Seneca. The compound fable is that which hath a turn from bad fortune to good, or from good to bad, as the *Oedipus* of Sophocles. And the contrivance of each fable must have two parts, the intrigue and the discovery. The intrigue embroils matters, casting troubles and confusion among the affairs. The discovery remits all into a calm again. Whatever goes before the change of fortune is called the intrigue; all that makes the change or follows it is the discovery. The intrigue in the *Andromache* of Euripides is that this princess, after she had lost Hector, her husband, and seen her father Priam murdered, the chief city of his kingdom burnt, became a slave to Neoptolemus. Hermione, the wife of this prince, pricked with jealousy against Andromache, was minded to kill her. Menelaus, father of Hermione causes her with her son Astyanax to be dragged to execution; this is the intrigue. Now she is rescued from death by Tethys and Peleus, who prefer the son to be king of the Molosians, and the mother to be queen by a marriage with Helenus; this is the discovery. And every fable must have these two parts to be the subject of a just poem. Thus Aeneas, chased from his country, spoiled of all that he possessed, beaten by tempests, wandering from coast to coast, destitute of all succors, persecuted by Juno and the other deities of her cabal, after all these disgraces became the founder of the greatest monarchy in the world. This is the fable of the Aeneid with its intrigue and its discovery. And it is to be observed that only by this change of fortune the fable pleases and has its effect, in which

283

the simple fable is defective, in Aristotle's opinion, because it wants variety.

XXIII

The admirable is all that which is against the ordinary course of nature. The probable is whatever suits with common opinion. The changing of Niobe into a stone is an event that holds of the admirable; yet this becomes probable when a deity, to whose power this change was possible, is engaged. Aeneas, in the twelfth book of the *Aeneid*, lifts by himself a stone that ten men could scarce remove; this prodigy is made probable by the assistance of the gods that took his part against Turnus. But most part of those that make verse, by too great a passion they have to create admiration, take not sufficient care to temper it with probability. Against this rock most ordinarily fall the poets, who are too easily carried to say incredible things that they may be admirable. . . .

XXIV

Besides that probability serves to give credit to whatever poesy has the most fabulous, it serves also to give to whatever the poet saith a greater luster and air of perfection than truth itself can do, though probability is but the copy. For truth represents things only as they are, but probability renders them as they ought to be. Truth is wellnigh always defective by the mixture of particular conditions that compose it. Nothing is brought into the world that is not remote from the perfection of its idea from the very birth. Originals and models are to be searched for in probability and in the universal principles of things, where nothing that is material and singular enters to corrupt them. For this reason the portraits of history are less perfect than the portraits of poesy, and Sophocles, who in his tragedies represents men as they ought to be, is, in the opinion of Aristotle, to be preferred before Euripides, who represents men as really they are; and Horace makes less account of the lessons of Crantor and Chrysippus for the manners than of those of Homer.[9]

XXV

After the design or fable, Aristotle places the manners for the second part; he calls the manners the cause of the action, for it is from these that a man begins to act. Achilles retires from the Grecian army in Homer because he is discontent. Aeneas in Virgil carries his gods into Italy because

284

he is pious. Medea kills her children in Seneca because she is revengeful; so the manners are, as it were, the first springs of all human actions. The painter draws faces by their features, but the poet represents the minds of men by their manners, and the most general rule for painting the manners is to exhibit every person in his proper character: a slave, with base thoughts and servile inclinations; a prince, with a liberal heart and air of majesty; a soldier, fierce, insolent, surly, inconstant; an old man, covetous, wary, jealous. It is in describing the manners that Terence triumphed over all the poets of his time, in Varro's opinion, for his persons are never found out of their characters. He observes their manners in all the niceties and rigors of decorum, which Homer himself has not always done, as some pretend. Longinus cannot endure the wounds, the adulteries, the hatred, and all the other weaknesses to which he makes the gods obnoxious, contrary to their character. Philostratus finds much to object against his portraits, but Justin Martyr excuses him, alleging that he took these notions from Orpheus, and that he had followed the opinion that publicly prevailed in those days. However it be, it may be granted that Homer has not treated the gods with all the respect due to their condition. Aristotle condemns Euripides for introducing Melanippa to speak too much like a philosopher of the sect of Anaxagoras, whose opinions were then new in his time.[10] Theon the Sophist cannot endure the unseasonable discourses of Hecuba on her misfortunes, in the same author. Sophocles makes Oedipus too weak and low-spirited in his exile after he had bestowed on him that character of constancy and resolution before his disgrace. Seneca, for his part, knows nothing of the manners. He is a fine speaker who is eternally uttering pretty sayings, but is in no wise natural in what he speaks, and whatever persons he makes to speak, they always have the mien of actors. The Angelica of Ariosto is too immodest. The Armida of Tasso is too free and impudent. These two poets rob women of their character, which is modesty. Rinaldo is soft and effeminate in the one, Orlando is too tender and passionate in the other. These weaknesses in no wise agree with heroes; they are degraded from the nobleness of their condition to make them guilty of folly. The sovereign rule for treating of manners is to copy them after nature, and above all to study well the heart of man to know how to distinguish all its motions. It is this which none are acquainted with. The heart of man is an abyss, where none can sound the bottom; it is a mystery which the most quick-sighted cannot pierce into, and in which the most cunning are mistaken. At the worst the poet is obliged to speak of manners according to the common opinion. Ajax must be represented grim, as Sophocles; Polyxena and Iphigenia generous, as Euripides has represented them. Finally, the manners must be proportionable to the age, to the sex, to the quality, to the employment, and to the fortune of the persons; and it is particularly in the second book of Aristotle's *Rhetoric* and in Horace's book *Of Poetry* that this secret may be learned. Whatever agrees not with his principles is false. Nothing tolerable can be performed in poetry without this knowledge, and with it all becomes admirable. And Horace, in that place of his book *Of Poetry* [153 sqq.] where he makes distinction of ages to draw their portraits, affirms that it is only by the "representation of manners" that any can have success on the stage, for there all is frivolous if the manners be not observed.

XXVI

The third part of the art consists in the thoughts or sentiments, which are properly the expressions of the manners as words are the expressions of the thoughts. Their office, saith Aristotle, is to approve or dislike, to stir or to calm the passions, to magnify or diminish things. . . . Thoughts must not only be comformable to the persons to whom they are given, but likewise to the subject treated of; that is to say, on great subjects are required great thoughts, as those of Evadne in the *Suppliants* of Euripides. There this queen, after the death of her husband Capaneus, may be seen to express all the extremity of her grief by force of a sorrow the most generous that ever was; her affliction oppresses her without extorting from her one word that betrays anything of weakness. The Greek poets are full of these great thoughts, and it is much by this greatness of their sentiments that they are particularly signalized in their works. Demetrius and Longinus perpetually propose them for models to those who study the sublime style, and it is in these great originals that our modern poets ought to consult nature, to learn how to raise their wits and be lofty. We may flatter ourselves with our wit and the genius of our (the French) nation, but our soul is not enough exalted to frame great ideas; we are busied with petty subjects, and by that means it is that we prove so cold in the great, and that in our works scarce appears any shadow of that sublime poesy of which the ancient poets have left such excellent models, and above all Homer and Virgil. For great poetry must be animated and sustained by

286

great thoughts and great sentiments; but these we ordinarily want, either because our wit is too much limited, or because we take not care to exercise on important matters. Thus we are low on high subjects. For example, how feeble are we when we speak of the conquests of a king! Our poets make their expressions swell to supply the want of noble sentiments, but it is not only the greatness of the subjects and the thoughts that give this air of majesty to poetry; there is likewise required lofty words and noble expressions.

XXVII

The last part is the expression and whatever regards the language; it must have five qualities to have all the perfection poetry demands: it must be apt, clear, natural, splendid, and numerous. The language must in the first place be apt, and have nothing impure or barbarous. For though one may speak what is great, noble, and admirable, all is despicable and odious if the purity be wanting; the greatest thoughts in the world have not any grace if the construction be defective. This purity of writing is of late so strongly established among the French that he must be very hardy that will make verse in an age so delicate, unless he understand the tongue perfectly. Secondly, the language must be clear that it may be intelligible, for one of the greatest faults in discourse is obscurity. In this Camoëns, whom the Portuguese call their Virgil, is extremely blamable, for his verses are so obscure that they may pass for mysteries, and the thoughts of Dante are so profound that much art is required to dive into them. Poetry demands a more clear air and what is less incomprehensible. The third quality is that it be natural, without affectation, according to rules of decorum and good sense. Studied phrases, a too florid style, fine words, terms strained and remote, and all extraordinary expressions are insupportable to the true poesy; only simplicity pleases, provided it be sustained with greatness and majesty. But this simplicity is not known except by great souls; the little wits understand nothing of it. It is the masterpiece of poesy, and the character of Homer and Virgil. The ignorant hunt after wit and fine thoughts because they are ignorant. The language must be lofty and splendid, which is the fourth quality. For the common and ordinary terms are not proper for a poet; he must use words that partake nothing of the base and vulgar; they must be noble and magnificent, the expressions strong, the colors lively, the draughts bold. His discourse must be such as may equal the greatness of the ideas of a workman who is the creator of his work. The fifth quality is that it be numerous, to uphold that greatness and air of majesty which reigns throughout in poesy, and to express all the force and dignity of the great things it speaks. Terms that go off roundly from the mouth and that fill the ears are sufficient to render all admirable, as poesy requires. But this is not enough that the expressions be stately and great; there must likewise be heat and vehemence, and above all, there must shine throughout the discourse a certain grace and delicacy which makes the principal ornament and most universal beauty.

XXIX

The loftiness of expression is so important that for the attaining it it is not enough to propose Homer and Virgil; it must be searched in Pindar, in Sophocles, in Euripides, and it must be had in grave and serious subjects that of themselves are capable to furnish with great thoughts, as the great thoughts are capable to furnish with noble expressions. "But the way to heighten discourse," saith Aristotle, "is to make good use of metaphors, and to understand perfectly their nature, that they may not be abused." [11] And he adds in the same place that this discernment is the mark of an excellent wit. And because, as saith Quintilian,[12] this loftiness which is aimed at by the boldness of a metaphor is dangerous, insomuch that it comes nigh to rashness, Aristotle must be consulted on this matter to employ them with discretion, as Virgil has done, who, treating of bees in the fourth book of his *Georgics*, that he might heighten the meanness of his subject, speaks not of them but in metaphorical terms — of a court, of legions, of armies, of combats, pitched fields, kings, captains, soldiers — and by this admirable art forms a noble image of the lowest subject, for after all, they are still but flies. Finally, the poet must above all things know what eloquence has of art and method for the use of figures, for it is only by the figures that he gives force to the passions, luster to the discourses, weight to the reasons, and makes delightful all he speaks. It is only by the most lively figures of eloquence that all the emotions of the soul become fervent and passionate. Nature must be the only guide that can be proposed in the use of these figures and metaphors, and must therefore be well understood that it may be traced and followed without mistake; for no portraits can be drawn that have resemblance without it, and all the images that poetry employs in expressing itself are false unless they be natural.

288

XXX

But this sublime style is the rock to the mean wits; they fly out in too vast and boisterous terms from what is natural when they endeavor to be high and lofty. For this haughty and pompous kind of speech becomes vain and cold if not supported with great thoughts, and the great words that are indiscreetly affected to heighten the discourse for the most part only make a noise. . . . For the most essential virtue of speech, next to the clearness and perspicuity, is that it be chaste and modest, as Demetrius Phalerius observes.[13] There must be, saith he, a proportion betwixt the words and the things; and nothing is more ridiculous than to handle a frivolous subject in a sublime style, for whatsoever is disproportionate is altogether false or at the least is trifling and childish. [It is for this that Socrates reproaches the Sophist Gorgias Leontinus], whom he pleasantly plays upon for affecting to speak petty things with a great and solemn mien.[14] Most French poets fall into this vice for want of genius; their verses, where logic is much neglected, most commonly are either pedantry or nonsense. . . .

XXXI

Of late some have fallen into another extremity by a too scrupulous care of purity of language: they have begun to take from poesy all its nerves and all its majesty by a too timorous reservedness and false modesty, which some thought to make the character of the French tongue by robbing it of all those wise and judicious boldnesses that poesy demands. They would retrench without reason the use of metaphors and of all those figures that give life and luster to the expressions, and study to confine all the excellency of this admirable art within the bounds of a pure and correct discourse without exposing it to the danger of any high and bold flight. The gust of the age, which loved purity, the women, who naturally are modest, the court, which then had scarce any commerce with the great men of antiquity, through their ordinary antipathy to learning and the general ignorance in the persons of quality, gave reputation to this way of writing. But nothing more authorized it than the verses of Voiture and Sarasin, the *Metamorphosis of the Eyes of Phillis into Stars, The Temple of Death*, the eclogues of Lane, and some other works of that character that came abroad at that time with a success which distinguished them from the vulgar.[15] In this way they were polite and writ good sense, and it agreed with the gust of the age and was followed. And who succeeded therein would make a new kind of refinement in poetry, as if the art consisted only in the purity and exactness of language. This indeed pleased well, and was much to the advantage of women that had a mind to be tampering and writing in verse; they found it their concern to give vogue to this kind of writing, of which they were as capable as the most part of men, for all the secret was no more but to make some little easy verses, in which they were content if they could close some kind of delicateness of sweet and passionate thoughts, which they made the essence of poetry. The ill fortune is, Horace was not of their mind. "It is not enough," saith he, "to write with purity to make a poet; he must have other qualities." . . .[16]

XXXVI

. . . But that I may not repeat what hath been said in the twenty-fifth Reflection, I proceed to the passions, which give no less grace to poetry than the manners, when the poet has found the art to make them move by their natural springs. Without the passions all is cold and flat in the discourse, saith Quintilian,[17] for they are, as it were, the soul and life of it; but the secret is to express them according to the several estates and different degrees from their birth. And in this distinction consists all the delicacy wherewith the passions are to be handled to give them that character which renders them admirable by the secret motions they impress on the soul. Hecuba in Euripides falls into a swound on the stage, the better to express all the weight of her sorrow that could not be represented by words. But Achilles appears with too much calmness and tranquillity at the sacrifice of Iphigenia, designed for him in marriage by Agamemnon; his grief has expressions too little suiting to the natural impetuosity of his heart. Clytemnestra much better preserves her character; she discovers all the passion of a mother in the loss of a daughter so lovely as was this unfortunate princess, whom they were about to sacrifice to appease the gods. And Agamemnon generously lays aside the tenderness of a father to take, as he ought, the sentiments of a king; he neglected his own interest to provide for the public. Seneca, so little natural as he is, omits not to have of these strokes that distinguish the passion, as that of Phaedra in the second act of his *Hippolytus*; for she affects a negligence of her person, and considered it as not very proper to please a hunter, who hated ornament and neatness. It is finally this exact distinction of the different degrees of passion that is of most effect in poetry. For this gives the

290

René Rapin

draught of nature, and is the most infallible spring for moving the soul, but it is good to observe that the most ardent and lively passions become cold and dead if they be not well managed or be not in their place. The poet must judge when there must be a calm and when there must be trouble, for nothing is more ridiculous than passion out of season. But it is not enough to move a passion by a notable incident; there must be art to conduct it so far as it should go. For by a passion that is imperfect and abortive the soul of the spectator may be shaken, but this is not enough; it must be ravished.

XXXVII

Besides the graces that poetry finds in displaying the manners and the passions, there is a certain I know not what in the numbers, which is understood by few, and notwithstanding gives great delight in poetry. Homer hath excelled generally all the poets by this art, whether the nature of his language was favorable to him by the variety in the numbers and by the noble sound of the words, or that the delicacy of his ear made him perceive this grace, whereof the other poets of his time were not sensible; for his verse sound the most harmoniously that can be imagined. Athenaeus pretends that nothing is more proper to be sung than the verses of Homer, so natural is the harmony of them.[18] It is true I never read this poet or hear him read, but I feel what is found in a battle when the trumpets are heard. . . .

XXXIX

Besides all the rules taken from Aristotle, there remains one mentioned by Horace, to which all the other rules must be subject as to the most essential, which is the decorum, without which the other rules of poetry are false, it being the most solid foundation of that probability so essential to this art.[19] Because it is only by the decorum that this probability gains its effect; all becomes probable where the decorum is strictly preserved in all circumstances. One ordinarily transgresses this rule, either by confounding the serious with the pleasant, as Pulci has done in his poem of *Morgante*; or by giving manners disproportionate to the condition of the persons, as Guarini has done to his shepherds, which are too polite, in like manner as those of Ronsard are too gross; or because no regard is had to make the wonderful adventures probable, whereof Ariosto is guilty in his *Orlando*; or that a due preparation is not made for the great events by a natural conduct, in which Bernardo Tasso transgressed in his poem of *Amadis* and in

291

his *Floridante*; or by want of care to sustain the characters of persons, as Théophile in his tragedy of *Pyramus and Thisbe*; or by following rather a capricious genius than nature, as Lope de Vega, who gives his wit too much swing, and is ever foisting in his own fancies on all occasions; or by want of modesty, as Dante, who invokes his own wit for his deity; and as Boccaccio, who is perpetually speaking of himself; or by saying everything indifferently without shame, as Cavalier Marino in his *Adone*. Finally, whatever is against the rules of time, of manners, of thoughts, of expression, is contrary to the decorum, which is the most universal of all the rules.

Rene Rapin REFLECTIONS ON ARISTOTLE'S BOOK OF

POESY IN PARTICULAR

II

The epic poem is that which is the greatest and most noble in poesy; it is the greatest work that human wit is capable of. All the nobleness and all the elevation of the most perfect genius can hardly suffice to form one such as is requisite for an heroic poet; the difficulty of finding together fancy and judgment, heat of imagination and sobriety of reason, precipitation of spirit and solidity of mind, causes the rareness of this character and of this happy temperament which makes a poet accomplished; it requires great images and yet a greater wit to form them. Finally, there must be a judgment so solid, a discernment so exquisite, such perfect knowledge of the language in which he writes, such obstinate study, profound meditation, vast capacity, that scarce whole ages can produce one genius fit for an epic poem. And it is an enterprise so bold that it cannot fall into a wise man's thoughts but affright him. Yet how many poets have we seen of late days who, without capacity and without study, have dared to undertake these sort of poems, having no other foundation for all but the only heat of their imagination and some briskness of spirit.

VII

The unity of the action, however simple and scrupulous it ought to be, is no enemy to those delights which naturally arise from variety when the variety is attended with that order and that proportion which makes uniformity, as one palace may contain the various ornaments of architecture and a great diversity of parts, provided it be built in the same order and after the same design. This variety hath a large field in heroic poesy; the enterprises of war, the treaties of peace, embassies, negotiations, voyages, councils, debates, building of palaces and towns, manners, passions, unexpected discoveries, unforeseen and surprising revolutions, and the different images of all that happens in the life of great men, may there be employed, so be that all go to the same end; without this order, the most beautiful figures become monstrous, and like those extravagances that Horace taxes as ridiculous in the beginning of his book *Of Poetry*.

X

The principal character of an heroic poem consists in the narration; it is in this that it is opposed to the dramatic, which consists altogether in the action. But as nothing is more difficult than to relate things as one ought, the poet must employ all his art to succeed herein. The qualities a narration must have to be perfect are these: it must be short and succinct, that nothing may be idle, flat, or tedious; it must be lively, quick, and delightful, that it may have nothing but what is attractive; finally, it must be simple and natural, but it is a great art to know how to relate things simply and yet the simplicity not appear. The most ordinary graces of a narration must come from the figures, the transitions, and from all those delicate turns that carry the reader from one thing to another without his regarding it; and in this chiefly consists all the artifice of the narration. It must never pour out all the matter, that some place may always be left for the natural reflections of the reader; it must likewise avoid the particulars and the length of affected description. Homer, great speaker as he is, amuses not himself, says Lucian, to discourse of the torments of the unhappy in Hell when Ulysses descended thither, though this was a fair occasion for him.[20] But the poet, when he is judicious, makes no descriptions but to clear the matters, and never to show his wit. Finally, the narration must be delightsome, not only by the variety of things it relates, but likewise by the variety of the numbers. It is this variety that makes the Greek versification more harmonious and more proper for narration than the Latin, and though Tasso has been successful enough in the narrations of his poem, and likewise Ariosto, who to me seems more natural than he, yet the pauses and interruptions to which the Italian poesy is subjected by the stanzas do weaken, methinks, and enervate that force and vigor which makes one part of the character of heroic verse. That monotony of the Alexandrine verse, which can suffer no difference nor any variety of numbers, seems to me likewise a great weakness in the French poetry. And though the vigor of the verse might be sustained either by the great subjects or by an extraordinary genius and wit above the common rate, yet this sort of verse will grow tedious and irksome in a long poem. For the rest, one shall scarce ever meet with narrations that are continued with the same force and the same spirit except in Homer and Virgil. It is true the narration of the death of Polyxena in the *Hecuba* of Euripides is the most lively and most moving in the world, and that of Tecmessa in the *Ajax* of Sophocles is the most tender and most passionate that can be imagined. It is by these great models that a poet must learn to be pathetical in what he relates without amusing himself to make subtle and witty narrations by ridiculous affectations. In the other Greek and Latin poets are found only some imperfect essays of narrations. He among the moderns who has the best genius to sustain all the nobleness of a narration in heroic verse is Hierom Vida, Bishop of Alba, in his poem on the death of Jesus Christ,[21] and if sometimes he fell not into low expressions and harshnesses like those of Lucretius, his style had been incomparable. Scaliger objects against the long narrations which Homer makes his heroes speak in the heat and fury of a battle; in effect this is neither natural nor probable. Neither can I approve the descriptions of Alcina's palace in Ariosto, nor of Armida's in Tasso, no more than the particulars of the pleasant things which both of them mix in their narrations; hereby they degenerate from their character, and show a kind of puerility that is in no wise conformable to the gravity of an heroic poem, where all ought to be majestic.

XIII

Finally, the sovereign perfection of an epic poem, in the opinion of Aristotle, consists in the just proportion of all the parts. The marvelous of tragedy consists in the pathetical style; but the marvelous of an heroic poem is that perfect connection, that just agreement and the admirable relation that the parts of this great work have each to other, as the perfection of a great palace consists in the uniformity of design and in the proportion of parts. It is this symmetry that Horace so much commends in the beginning of his book *Of Poetry*, where he taxes the ridiculousness of the extravagant disproportions in the picture he speaks of, and which he compares to the prodigious adventures of dolphins in the forests and wild boars in the sea, and all the other images he so much blames because disproportionable to the subject. And this proportion that Aristotle demands is not only in the quantity of the parts, but likewise in the quality. In which point Tasso is very faulty, who mixes in his poem the light character with the serious, and all the force and majesty of heroic with the softness and delicacy of the eclogue and lyric poesy. For the shepherd's adventures with Herminia in the seventh canto, and the letters of her lover's name which she carved on the bark of bays and beeches, the moan she made to the trees and rocks, the purling streams, the embroidered meadows, the singing of birds, in which the poet himself took so much pleasure, the enchanted wood in the thirteenth canto, the songs of Armida in the fourteenth to inspire Rinaldo with love, the caresses this sorceress made him, the description of her palace where nothing is breathed but softness and effeminacy, and those other affected descriptions have nothing of that grave and majestic character which is proper for heroic verse. It is thus that Sannazarius in his poem *De Partu Virginis* has injudiciously mingled the fables of paganism with the mysteries of Christian religion, as also Camoens,[22] who speaks without discretion of Venus and Bacchus and the other profane deities in a Christian poem. It is not sufficient that all be grand and magnificent in an epic poem; all must be just, uniform, proportionable in the different parts that compose it.

XVII

Tragedy, of all parts of poesy, is that which Aristotle has most discussed, and where he appears most exact. He alleges that tragedy is a public lecture, without comparison more instructive than philosophy, because it teaches the mind by the sense, and rectifies the passions by the passions themselves in calming by their emotion the troubles they excite in the heart. The philosopher had observed two important faults in man to be regulated, pride and hardness of heart, and he found for both vices a cure in tragedy. For it makes man modest by representing the great masters of the earth humbled, and it makes him tender and merciful by showing him on the theatre the strange accidents of life and the unforeseen disgraces to which the most important persons are subject. But because man is naturally timorous and compassionate, he may fall into another extreme, to be either too fearful or too full of pity; the too much fear may shake the constancy of mind, and the too great compassion may enfeeble the equity. It is the business of tragedy to regulate these two weaknesses; it prepares and arms him against disgraces by showing them so frequent in the most considerable persons, and he shall cease to fear ordinary accidents when he sees such extraordinary happen to the highest part of mankind. But as the end of tragedy is to teach men not to fear too weakly the common misfortunes, and manage their fear, it makes account also to teach them to spare their compassion for objects that deserve it. For there is an injustice in being moved at the afflictions of those who deserve to be miserable. One may see without pity Clytemnestra slain by her son Orestes in Aeschylus, because she had cut the throat of Agamemnon, her husband, and one cannot see Hippolytus die by the plot of his stepmother Phaedra in Euripides without compassion, because he died not but for being chaste and virtuous. This to me seems, in short, the design of tragedy according to the system of Aristotle, which to me appears admirable but which has not been explained as it ought by his interpreters; they have not, it may seem, sufficiently understood the mystery to unfold it well.

XVIII

But it is not enough that tragedy be furnished with all the most moving and terrible adventures that history can afford, to stir in the heart those motions it pretends, to the end it may cure the mind of those vain fears that may annoy it, and those childish compassions that may soften it. It is also necessary, says the philosopher, that every poet employ these great objects of terror and pity as the two most powerful springs in art to produce that pleasure which tragedy may yield. And this pleasure which is properly of the mind consists in the agitation of the soul moved by the passions. Tragedy cannot be delightful to the spectator unless he become sensible to all that is represented; he must enter into all the different thoughts of the actors, interest himself in their adventures, fear, hope, afflict himself, and rejoice with them. The theatre is dull and languid when it ceases to produce these motions in the soul of those that stand by. But as of all passions fear and pity are those that make the strongest impressions on the heart of man by the natural disposition he has of being afraid and of being mollified, Aristotle has chosen these amongst the rest, to move more powerfully the soul by the tender sentiments they cause when the heart admits and is pierced by them. In effect, when the soul is shaken by motions so natural and so humane, all the impressions it feels become delightful; its trouble pleases, and the emotion it finds is a kind of charm to it which does cast it into a sweet and profound meditation and which insensibly does engage it in all the interests that are managed on the theatre. It is then that the heart yields itself over to all the objects that are proposed, that all images strike it, that it espouses the sentiments of all those that speak, and becomes susceptible of all the passions that are presented because it is moved. And in this agitation consists all the pleasure that one is capable to receive from tragedy, for the spirit of man does please itself with the different situations caused by the different objects and the various passions that are represented.

XX

Modern tragedy turns on other principles; the genius of our (the French) nation is not strong enough to sustain an action on the theatre by moving only terror and pity. These are machines that will not play as they ought but by great thoughts and noble expressions, of which we are not indeed altogether so capable as the Greeks. Perhaps our nation, which is naturally gallant, has been obliged by the necessity of our character to frame for ourselves a new system of tragedy to suit with our humor. The Greeks, who were popular estates and who hated monarchy, took delight in their spectacles to see kings humbled and high fortunes cast down because the exaltation grieved them. The English, our neighbors, love blood in their sports by the quality of their temperament. These are *insulaires*, separated from the rest of men; we are more humane. Gallantry moreover agrees with our manners, and our poets believed that they could not succeed well on the theatre but by sweet and tender sentiments; in which, perhaps, they had some reason, for, in effect, the passions represented become deformed and insipid unless they are founded on sentiments conformable to those of the spectator. It is this that obliges our poets to stand up so strongly for the privilege of gallantry on the theatre, and to bend all their subjects to love and tenderness, the rather to please the women, who have made themselves judges of these divertissements and usurped the right to pass sentence. And some besides have suffered themselves to be prepossessed and led by the Spaniards, who make all their cavaliers amorous. It is by them that tragedy began to degenerate, [that we have slowly become accustomed to seeing] heroes on the theatre smitten with another love than that of glory, and that by degrees all the great men of antiquity have lost their characters in our hands. It is likewise perhaps by this gallantry that our age would devise a color to excuse the feebleness of our wit, not being able to sustain always the same action by the greatness of words and thoughts. However it be; for I am not hardy enough to declare myself against the public; it is to degrade tragedy from that majesty which is proper to it to mingle in it love, which is of a character always light, and little suitable to that gravity of which tragedy makes profession. Hence it proceeds that these tragedies mixed with gallantries never make such admirable impres-

298

sions on the spirit as did those of Sophocles and Euripides, for all the bowels were moved by the great objects of terror and pity which they proposed. It is likewise for this that the reputation of our modern tragedies so soon decays, and yield but small delight at two years' end; whereas the Greek please yet to those that have a good taste, after two thousand years, because what is not grave and serious on the theatre, though it give delight at present, after a short time grows distasteful and unpleasant, and because what is not proper for great thoughts and great figures in tragedy cannot support itself. The ancients who perceived this did not interweave their gallantry and love save in comedy. For love is of a character that always degenerates from that heroic air of which tragedy must never divest itself. And nothing to me shows so mean and senseless as for one to amuse himself with whining about frivolous kindnesses when he may be admirable by great and noble thoughts and sublime expressions. But I dare not presume so far on my own capacity and credit to oppose myself of my own head against a usage so established. I must be content modestly to propose my doubts, and that may serve to exercise the wits in an age that only wants matter. But to end this reflection with a touch of Christianism, I am persuaded that the innocence of the theatre might be better preserved according to the idea of the ancient tragedy, because the new is become too effeminate by the softness of latter ages; and the Prince de Conti,[23] who signalized his zeal against the modern tragedy by his treatise on that subject, would, without doubt, have allowed the ancient, because that has nothing that may seem dangerous.

XXV

Comedy is an image of common life; its end is to show on the stage the faults of particulars in order to amend the faults of the public, and to correct the people through a fear of being rendered ridiculous. So that which is most proper to excite laughter is that which is most essential to comedy. One may be ridiculous in words or ridiculous in things. There is an honest laughter, and a buffoon laughter. It is merely a gift of nature to make everything ridiculous. For all the actions of human life have their fair and their wrong side, their serious and their ridiculous. But Aristotle, who gives precepts to make men weep, leaves none to make them laugh. This proceeds purely from the genius; art and method have little to do with it; it is the work of nature alone. The Spaniards have a genius to discern the ridiculous of things much better than the French, and the Italians, who are naturally comedians, express it better; their tongue is more proper for it by a drolling tone peculiar to them. The French may be capable of it when their language has attained its perfection. Finally, that pleasant turn, that gaiety which can sustain the delicacy of his character without falling into coldness nor into buffoonery, that fine raillery which is the flower of wit, is the talent which comedy demands. But it must always be observed that the true ridiculous of art, for the entertainment on the theatre, ought to be no other but the copy of the ridiculous that is found in nature. Comedy is as it should be when the spectator believes himself [to be in the midst of a group of neighbors or among members of a family instead of in a theatre, and when] he there sees nothing but what he sees in the world. . . .

XXVII

The eclogue is the most considerable of the little poems; it is an image of the life of shepherds. Therefore the matter is low, and nothing great is in the genius of it; its business is to describe the loves, the sports, the piques, the jealousies, the disputes, the quarrels, the intrigues, the passions, the adventures, and all the little affairs of shepherds. So that its character must be simple, the wit easy, the expression common; it must have nothing that is exquisite, neither in the thoughts, nor in the words, nor in any fashions of speech; in which the Italians, who have writ in this kind of verse, have been mistaken, for they always aim at being witty, and to say things too finely. The true character of the eclogue is simplicity and modesty. Its figures are sweet, the passions tender, the motions easy, and though sometimes it may be passionate and have little transports and little despairs, yet it never rises so high as to be fierce or violent; its narrations are short, descriptions little, the thoughts ingenious, the manners innocent, the language pure, the verse flowing, the expressions plain, and all the discourse natural, for this is not a great talker that loves to make a noise. . . .

XXX

The ode ought to have as much nobleness, elevation, and transport as the eclogue has of simplicity and modesty. It is not only the wit that heightens it, but likewise the matter. For its use is to sing the praises of the gods and to celebrate the illustrious actions of great men, so it requires to sustain all the majesty of its character an exalted nature, a great wit, a daring fancy, an expression noble and sparkling, yet pure and correct. All the

300

briskness and life which art has by its figures is not sufficient to heighten the ode so far as its character requires. But the reading alone of Pindar is more capable to inspire this genius than all my reflections. . . .

XXXII

It remains to speak of the madrigal, the rondelay, the sonnet, the ballad, and all the other little verse that are the invention of these latter ages; but as a little fancy may suffice to be successful in these kind of works without any genius, I shall not amuse myself in making reflections on the method that is to be observed in composing them. Not but that he who has a genius would have a much different success, either by a more happy turn he gives to what he writes, or by a more lively air, or by more natural beauties, or finally, by more delicate fashions of speech; and generally, the genius makes the greatest distinction in whatsoever work a man undertakes. The character of the smaller verse and of all the little works of poesy requires that they be natural, together with a delicacy; for, seeing the little subjects afford no beauty of themselves, the wit of the poet must supply that want out of its own stock. . . .

XXXIV

Finally, to conclude with a touch of morality. Since the reputation of being modest is more worth than that of making verses, were I to make any, I would never forsake honesty nor modesty. For if nothing renders men more ridiculous than the kind opinion they conceive of themselves and of their performances, the poets are yet more ridiculous than other men when their vanity rises from the difficulty of succeeding well in their mystery. But if I made verse better than another, I would not force any man to find them good; I would not have a greater opinion of myself though all the world applauded them, nor should the success blind me. Amongst the praises that were bestowed on me, I could not persuade myself to suffer those where appeared ought of favor, and I would impose silence on them who, in commending me, spoke further than my conscience, to save myself from that ridiculousness which some vain spirits fall into who would have praises and admirations eternally for everything they do. I would employ all my reason and all my wit to gain more docility and more submission to the advice my friends should give me; I would borrow their lights to supply the weakness of mine; and I would listen to all the world, that I might not be ignorant of any of my faults. In the praises

301

that I gave to those I found worthy, I would be so conscientious that for no interest whatsoever would I speak against my opinion, and there should never enter into anything that went from my hands any of those mercenary glances which so greatly debase the character of a poet. Lastly, I would rid myself of all the ridiculous vanities to which those who make verse are ordinarily obnoxious, and by this prudent conduct I would endeavor to destroy those fripperies which by custom are said of a profession that might continue honorable, were it only exercised by men of honorable principles.

❧ 1675

Rene Le Bossu TREATISE OF THE EPICK POEM

Book I, Chapter 2

The fables of poets were originally employed in representing the Divine Nature according to the notion then conceived of it. This sublime subject occasioned the first poets to be called divines, and poetry the language of the gods. They divided the divine attributes into so many persons because the infirmity of a human mind cannot sufficiently conceive or explain so much power and action in a simplicity so great and indivisible as that of God. And, perhaps, they were also jealous of the advantages they reaped from such excellent and exalted learning, and of which they thought the vulgar part of mankind was not worthy.

They could not describe the operations of this almighty Cause without speaking at the same time of its effects; so that to divinity they added physiology, and treated of both without quitting the umbrages of their allegorical expressions.

But man being the chief and most noble of all that God produced, and nothing being so proper or more useful to poets than this subject, they added it to the former, and treated of the doctrine of morality after the same manner as they did that of divinity and philosophy; and from morality thus treated is formed that kind of poem and fable which we call epic.

The poets did the same in morality that the divines had done in divinity. But that infinite variety of the actions and operations of the Divine Nature (to which our understanding bears so small a proportion) did, as it were, force them upon dividing the single idea of the only one God into several persons, under the different names of Jupiter, Juno, Neptune, and the rest.

And on the other hand, the nature of moral philosophy being such as never to treat of things in particular but in general, the epic poets were obliged to unite in one single idea, in one and the same person and in an

303

action which appeared singular, all that looked like it in different persons and in various actions which might be thus contained as so many species under their genus.

The presence of the Deity and the care such an august cause is to be supposed to take about any action obliges the poet to represent this action as great, important, and managed by kings and princes. It obliges him likewise to think and speak in an elevated way above the vulgar, and in a style that may in some sort keep up the character of the divine persons he introduces. To this end serve the poetical and figurative expression and the majesty of the heroic verse.

But all this, being divine and surprising, may quite ruin all probability; therefore the poet should take a peculiar care as to that point, since his chief aim is to instruct, and without probability any action is less likely to persuade.

Lastly, since precepts ought to be concise to be the more easily conceived and less oppress the memory, and since nothing can be more effectual to this end than proposing one single idea and collecting all things so well together as to be present to our minds all at once, therefore the poets have reduced all to one single action, under one and the same design, and in a body whose members and parts should be homogeneous.

Book I, Chapter 3

What we have observed of the nature of the epic poem gives us a just idea of it, and we may define it thus:

The epic poem is a discourse invented by art to form the manners by such instructions as are disguised under the allegories of some one important action, which is related in verse after a probable, diverting, and surprising manner.

Book I, Chapter 8

In every design which a man deliberately undertakes, the end he proposes is the first thing in his mind, and that by which he governs the whole work and all its parts; thus, since the end of the epic poem is to regulate the manners, it is with this first view the poet ought to begin.

But there is a great difference between the philosophical and the poetical doctrine of manners. The schoolmen content themselves with treating of virtues and vices in general; the instructions they give are proper for all states of people and for all ages. But the poet has a nearer regard to his

René Le Bossu

own country and the necessities of his own nation. With this design he makes choice of some piece of morality, the most proper and just he can imagine; and in order to press this home, he makes less use of the force of reasoning than of the power of insinuation, accommodating himself to the particular customs and inclinations of those who are to be the subject, or the readers, of his work.

Let us now see how Homer has acquitted himself in all these respects.

He saw the Grecians, for whom he designed his poem, were divided into as many states as they had capital cities. Each was a body politic apart, and had its form of government independent from all the rest. And yet these distinct states were very often obliged to unite together in one body against their common enemies. These were two very different sorts of government, such as could not be comprehended in one maxim or morality and in one single poem.

The poet, therefore, has made two distinct fables of them. The one is for Greece in general, united into one body but composed of parts independent on each other, and the other for each particular state considered as they were in time of peace, without the former circumstances and the necessity of being united.

As for the first sort of government, in the union or rather in the confederacy of many independent states experience has always made it appear that nothing so much causes success as a due subordination and a right understanding among the chief commanders. And on the other hand, the inevitable ruin of such confederacies proceeds from the heats, jealousies, and ambition of the different leaders and the discontents of submitting to a single general. All sort of states, and in particular the Grecians, had dearly experienced this truth. So that the most useful and necessary instructions that could be given them was to lay before their eyes the loss which both the people and the princes must of necessity suffer by the ambition, discord, and obstinacy of the latter.

Homer then has taken for the foundation of his fable this great truth, that a misunderstanding between princes is the ruin of their own states. "I sing," says he, "the anger of Achilles, so pernicious to the Grecians, and the cause of many heroes' deaths, occasioned by the discord and separation of Agamemnon and that prince."

But that this truth may be completely and fully known, there is need of a second to support it. It is necessary in such a design not only to represent the confederate states at first disagreeing among themselves and

305

from thence unfortunate, but to show the same states afterwards reconciled and united and of consequence victorious.

Let us now see how he has joined all these in one general action.

Several princes independent of one another were united against a common enemy. The person whom they had elected their general offers an affront to the most valiant of all the confederates. This offended prince is so far provoked as to relinquish the union and obstinately refuse to fight for the common cause. This misunderstanding gives the enemy such an advantage that the allies are very near quitting their design with dishonor. He himself who made the separation is not exempt from sharing the misfortune which he brought upon his party. For having permitted his intimate friend to succor them in a great necessity, this friend is killed by the enemy's general. Thus the contending princes, being both made wiser at their own cost, are reconciled and unite again; then this valiant prince not only obtains the victory in the public cause, but revenges his private wrongs by killing with his own hands the author of the death of his friend.

This is the first platform of the poem, and the fiction which reduces into one important and universal action all the particulars upon which it turns.

In the next place it must be rendered probable by the circumstances of times, places, and persons. Some persons must be found out, already known by history or otherwise, whom we may with probability make the actors and personages of this fable. Homer has made choice of the siege of Troy, and feigned that this action happened there. To a phantom of his brain, whom he would paint valiant and choleric, he has given the name of Achilles; that of Agamemnon, to his general; that of Hector, to the enemy's commander; and so, to the rest.

Besides, he was obliged to accommodate himself to the manners, customs, and genius of the Greeks his auditors, the better to make them attend to the instruction of his poem, and to gain their approbation by praising them so that they might the better forgive him the representation of their own faults in some of his chief personages. He admirably discharges all these duties by making these brave princes and those victorious people all Grecians and the fathers of those he had a mind to commend.

But not being content, in a work of such a length, to propose only the principal point of the moral, and to fill up the rest with useless ornaments and foreign incidents, he extends this moral by all its necessary consequences. As for instance in the subject before us it is not enough to know that a good understanding ought always to be maintained among confederates, it is likewise of equal importance that, if there happens any division, care must be taken to keep it secret from the enemy, that their ignorance of this advantage may prevent their making use of it. And in the second place, when their concord is but counterfeit and only in appearance, one should never press the enemy too closely, for this would discover the weakness which we ought to conceal from them.

The episode of Patroclus most admirably furnishes us with these two instructions. For when he appeared in the arms of Achilles, the Trojans, who took him for that prince now reconciled and united to the confederates, immediately gave ground, and quitted the advantages they had before over the Greeks. But Patroclus, who should have been contented with this success, presses upon Hector too boldly, and, by obliging him to fight, soon discovers that it was not the true Achilles who was clad in his armor, but a hero of much inferior prowess. So that Hector kills him and regains those advantages which the Trojans had lost on the opinion that Achilles was reconciled.

Book I, Chapter 10

The *Odyssey* was not designed, like the *Iliad*, for the instruction of all the states of Greece joined in one body, but for each state in particular. As a state is composed of two parts, the head which commands and the members which obey, there are instructions requisite for both, to teach the one to govern and the others to submit to government.

There are two virtues necessary to one in authority: prudence to order, and care to see his orders put in execution. The prudence of a politician is not acquired but by a long experience in all sorts of business, and by an acquaintance with all the different forms of governments and states. The care of the administration suffers not him that has the government to rely upon others, but requires his own presence, and kings who are absent from their states are in danger of losing them, and give occasion to great disorders and confusion.

These two points may be easily united in one and the same man. A king forsakes his kingdom to visit the courts of several princes, where he learns the manners and customs of different nations. From hence there naturally arises a vast number of incidents, of dangers, and of adventures, very useful for a political institution. On the other side, this absence gives way to the disorders which happen in his own kingdom, and which end not till his return, whose presence only can re-establish all things. Thus the absence of a king has the same effects in this fable as the division of the princes had in the former.

The subjects have scarce any need but of one general maxim, which is to suffer themselves to be governed and to obey faithfully, whatever reason they may imagine against the orders they receive. It is easy to join this instruction with the other by bestowing on this wise and industrious prince such subjects as in his absence would rather follow their own judgment than his commands, and by demonstrating the misfortunes which this disobedience draws upon them, the evil consequences which almost infallibly attend these particular notions, which are entirely different from the general idea of him who ought to govern.

But as it was necessary that the princes in the *Iliad* should be choleric and quarrelsome, so it is necessary in the fable of the *Odyssey* that the chief person should be sage and prudent. This raises a difficulty in the fiction, because this person ought to be absent for the two reasons aforementioned, which are essential to the fable and which constitute the principal aim of it; but he cannot absent himself without offending against another maxim of equal importance, viz., that a king should upon no account leave his country.

It is true there are sometimes such necessities as sufficiently excuse the prudence of a politician in this point. But such a necessity is a thing important enough of itself to supply matter for another poem, and this multiplication of the action would be vicious. To prevent which, in the first place, this necessity and the departure of the hero must be disjoined from the poem; and in the second place, the hero having been obliged to absent himself for a reason antecedent to the action and placed distinct from the fable, he ought not so far to embrace this opportunity of instructing himself as to absent himself voluntarily from his own government. For at this rate, his absence would be merely voluntary, and one might with reason lay to his charge all the disorders which might arise.

Thus in the constitution of the fable he ought not to take for his action and for the foundation of his poem the departure of a prince from his own country nor his voluntary stay in any other place, but his return, and this return retarded against his will. This is the first idea Homer gives us of it. His hero appears at first in a desolate island, sitting upon the side of the sea, which, with tears in his eyes, he looks upon as the obstacle which had so long opposed his return and detained him from revisiting his own dear country.

And lastly, since this forced delay might more naturally and usually happen to such as make voyages by sea, Homer has judiciously made choice of a prince whose kingdom was in an island.

Let us see then how he has feigned all this action, making his hero a person in years, because years are requisite to instruct a man in prudence and policy.

A prince had been obliged to forsake his native country and to head an army of his subjects in a foreign expedition. Having gloriously performed this enterprise, he was marching home again, and conducting his subjects to his own state. But spite of all the attempts with which his eagerness to return had inspired him, he was stopped by the way by tempests for several years, and cast upon several countries differing from each other in manners and government. In these dangers his companions, not always following his orders, perished through their own fault. The grandees of his country strangely abuse his absence, and raise no small disorders at home. They consume his estate, conspire to destroy his son, would constrain his queen to accept of one of them for her husband, and indulge themselves in all violence, so much the more because they were persuaded he would never return. But at last he returns, and discovering himself only to his son and some others who had continued firm to him, he is an eyewitness of the insolence of his enemies, punishes them according to their deserts, and restores to his island that tranquillity and repose to which they had been strangers during his absence.

As the truth which serves for foundation to this fiction is that the absence of a person from his own home or his neglect of his own affairs is the cause of great disorders, so the principal point of the action, and the most essential one, is the absence of the hero. This fills almost all the poem. For not only this real absence lasted several years, but even when the hero returned he does not discover himself; and this prudent disguise, from whence he reaped so much advantage, has the same effect upon the authors of the disorders, and all others who knew him not, as his real absence had before, so that he is absent as to them till the very moment of their punishment.

After the poet had thus composed his fable and joined the fiction to the truth, he then makes choice of Ulysses, the king of the isle of Ithaca, to maintain the character of his chief personage, and bestowed the rest upon Telemachus, Penelope, Antinous, and others, whom he calls by what names he pleases.

I shall not here insist upon the many excellent advices which are so many parts and natural consequences of the fundamental truth, and which the poet very dexterously lays down in those fictions which are the episodes and members of the entire action. Such for instance are these advices: not to intrude oneself into the mysteries of government[1] which the prince keeps secret; (this is represented to us by the winds shut up in a bullhide, which the miserable companions of Ulysses would needs be so foolish as to pry into); not to suffer oneself to be led away by the seeming charms of an idle and inactive life, to which the Sirens' song invited; not to suffer oneself to be sensualized by pleasures, like those who were changed into brutes by Circe; and a great many other points of morality necessary for all sorts of people.

This poem is more useful to the people than the *Iliad*, where the subjects suffer rather by the ill conduct of their princes than through their own miscarriages. But in the *Odyssey* it is not the fault of Ulysses that is the ruin of his subjects. This wise prince leaves untried no method to make them partakers of the benefit of his return. Thus the poet in the *Iliad* says he sings the anger of Achilles, which had caused the death of so many Grecians, and, on the contrary, in the *Odyssey* he tells his readers that the subjects perished through their own fault.

Book I, Chapter 16

Aristotle bestows great encomiums on Homer for the simplicity of his design because he has included in one single part all that happened at the siege of Troy. And to this he opposes the ignorance of some poets who imagined that the unity of the fable or action was sufficiently preserved by the unity of the hero, and who composed their Theseids, Heraclids, and the like, wherein they only heaped up in one poem everything that happened to one personage.

Book I, Chapter 17

He finds fault with those poets who were for reducing the unity of the fable into the unity of the hero, because one man may have performed several adventures which it is impossible to reduce under any one [general and] simple head. This reducing of all things to unity and simplicity is what Horace likewise makes his first rule.

Denique sit quod vis simplex dumtaxat, et unum [1]

310

According to these rules, it will be allowable to make use of several fables, or (to speak more correctly) of several incidents, which may be divided into several fables provided they are so ordered that the unity of the fable be not spoiled. This liberty is still greater in the epic poem, because it is of a larger extent and ought to be entire and complete.

I will explain myself more distinctly by the practice of Homer.

No doubt but one might make four distinct fables out of these four following instructions.

I. Division between those of the same party exposes them entirely to their enemies.

II. Conceal your weakness, and you will be dreaded as much as if you had none of those imperfections of which they are ignorant.

III. When your strength is only feigned and founded only in the opinion of others, never venture so far as if your strength was real.

IV. The more you agree together, the less hurt can your enemies do you.

It is plain, I say, that each of these particular maxims might serve for the groundwork of a fiction, and one might make four distinct fables out of them. May one not, then, put all these into one single epopea? Not unless one single fable can be made out of all. The poet indeed may have so much skill as to unite all into one body as members and parts, each of which taken asunder would be imperfect; and if he joins them so, as that this conjunction shall be no hindrance at all to the unity and regular simplicity of the fable. This is what Homer has done with such success in the composition of the *Iliad*.

1. The division between Achilles and his allies tended to the ruin of their designs. 2. Patroclus comes to their relief in the armor of this hero, and Hector retreats. 3. But this young man, pushing the advantage which his disguise gave him too far, ventures to engage with Hector himself; but not being master of Achilles's strength (whom he only represented in outward appearance) he is killed, and by this means leaves the Grecian affairs in the same disorder from which, in that disguise, he came to free them. 4. Achilles, provoked at the death of his friend, is reconciled, and revenges his loss by the death of Hector. These various incidents being thus united do not make different actions and fables, but are only the uncomplete and unfinished parts of one and the same action and fable, which alone, when taken thus complexly, can be said to be complete and entire;

and all these maxims of the moral are easily reduced into these two parts, which, in my opinion, cannot be separated without enervating the force of both. The two parts are these, that a right understanding is the preservation, and discord the destruction, of states.

Though then the poet has made use of two parts in his poems, each of which might have served for a fable, as we have observed, yet this multiplication cannot be called a vicious and irregular polymythia, contrary to the necessary unity and simplicity of the fable; but it gives the fable another qualification altogether necessary and regular, namely, its perfection and finishing stroke.

Book II, Chapter 1

The action of a poem is the subject which the poet undertakes, proposes, and builds upon. So that the moral and the instructions, which are the end of the epic poem, are not the matter of it. Those the poets leave in their allegorical and figurative obscurity. They only give notice at the exordium that they sing some action: the revenge of Achilles, the return of Ulysses, etc.

Since then the action is the matter of a fable, it is evident that whatever incidents are essential to the fable or constitute a part of it are necessary also to the action and are parts of the epic matter, none of which ought to be omitted. Such, for instance, are the contention of Agamemnon and Achilles, the slaughter Hector makes in the Grecian army, the reunion of the Greek princes, and lastly, the resettlement and victory which was the consequence of that reunion.

Book II, Chapter 7

There are four qualifications in the epic action: the first is its unity, the second its integrity, the third its importance, the fourth its duration.

The unity of the epic action, as well as the unity of the fable, does not consist either in the unity of the hero or in the unity of time; three things, I suppose, are necessary to it. The first is to make use of no episode but what arises from the very platform and foundation of the action, and is as it were a natural member of the body. The second is exactly to unite these episodes and these members with one another. And the third is never to finish any episode so as it may seem to be an entire action, but to let each episode still appear in its own particular nature as the member of a body and as a part of itself not complete.

312

Book II, Chapter 9

Aristotle not only says that the epic action should be one, but adds that it should be entire, perfect, and complete, and for this purpose ought to have a beginning, a middle, and an end. These three parts of a whole are too generally and universally denoted by the words *beginning, middle* and *end*; we may interpret them more precisely and say that the causes and designs of an action are the beginning, that the effects of these causes and the difficulties that are met with in the execution of these designs are the middle, and that the unraveling and resolution of these difficulties are the end.

Book II, Chapter 11

Homer's design in the *Iliad* is to relate the anger and revenge of Achilles. The beginning of this action is the change of Achilles from a calm to a passionate temper. The middle is the effects of his passion, and all the illustrious deaths it is the cause of. The end of the same action is the return of Achilles to his calmness of temper again. All was quiet in the Grecian camp, when Agamemnon, their general, provokes Apollo against them, whom he was willing to appease afterwards at the cost and prejudice of Achilles, who had no part in his fault. This then is an exact beginning; it supposes nothing before, and requires after it the effects of this anger. Achilles revenges himself, and that is an exact middle: it supposes before it the anger of Achilles; this revenge is the effect of it. Then this middle requires after it the effects of this revenge, which is the satisfaction of Achilles; for the revenge had not been complete unless Achilles had been satisfied. By this means the poet makes his hero, after he was glutted by the mischief he had done to Agamemnon, by the death of Hector, and the honor he did his friend by insulting over his murderer; he makes him, I say, to be moved by the tears and misfortunes of King Priam. We see him as calm at the end of the poem, during the funeral of Hector, as he was at the beginning of the poem, whilst the plague raged among the Grecians. This end is just, since the calmness of temper Achilles re-enjoyed is only an effect of the revenge which ought to have preceded; and after this nobody expects any more of his anger. Thus has Homer been very exact in the beginning, middle and end of the action he made choice of for the subject of his *Iliad*.

His design in the *Odyssey* was to describe the return of Ulysses from the siege of Troy and his arrival at Ithaca. He opens this poem with the

313

complaints of Minerva against Neptune, who opposed the return of this hero, and against Calypso, who detained him in an island from Ithaca. Is this a beginning? No; doubtless the reader would know why Neptune is displeased with Ulysses, and how this prince came to be with Calypso. He would know how he came from Troy thither. The poet answers his demands out of the mouth of Ulysses himself, who relates these things and begins the action by the recital of his travels from the city of Troy. It signifies little whether the beginning of the action be the beginning of the poem. The beginning of this action is that which happens to Ulysses when, upon his leaving Troy, he bends his course for Ithaca. The middle comprehends all the misfortunes he endured and all the disorders of his own government. The end is the reinstating of this hero in the peaceable possession of his kingdom, where he was acknowledged by his son, his wife, his father, and several others. The poet was sensible he should have ended ill had he gone no farther than the death of these princes who were the rivals and enemies of Ulysses, because the reader might have looked for some revenge which the subjects of these princes might have taken on him who had killed their sovereign; but this danger over, and the people vanquished and quieted, there was nothing more to be expected. The poem and the action have all their parts and no more.

Book II, Chapter 12

But the order of the *Odyssey* differs from that of the *Iliad* in that the poem does not begin with the beginning of the action.

The causes of the action are also what the poet is obliged to give an account of. There are three sorts of causes: the humors, the interests, and the designs of men; and these different causes of an action are likewise often the causes of one another, every man taking up those interests in which his humor engages him and forming those designs to which his humor and interest incline him. Of all these the poet ought to inform his readers, and render them conspicuous in his principal personages.

Homer has ingeniously begun his *Odyssey* with the transactions at Ithaca during the absence of Ulysses. If he had begun with the travels of his hero, he would scarce have spoken of anyone else, and a man might have read a great deal of the poem without conceiving the least idea of Telemachus, Penelope, or her suitors, who had so great a share in the action; but in the beginning he has pitched upon, besides these personages whom he discovers, he represents Ulysses in his full length, and from the very first opening one sees the interest which the gods take in the action.

The skill and care of the same poet may be seen likewise in inducing his personages in the first book of his *Iliad*, where he discovers the humors, the interests, and the designs of Agamemnon, Achilles, Hector, Ulysses, and several others, and even of the deities. And in his second he makes a review of the Grecian and Trojan armies, which is full evidence that all we have here said is very necessary.

Book II, Chapter 13

As these causes are the beginning of the action, the opposite designs against that of the hero are the middle of it, and form that difficulty or intrigue which makes up the greatest part of the poem; the solution or unraveling commences when the reader begins to see that difficulty removed and the doubts cleared up. Homer has divided each of his poems into two parts, and has put a particular intrigue and the solution of it into each part.

The first part of the *Iliad* is the anger of Achilles, who is for revenging himself upon Agamemnon by the means of Hector and the Trojans. The intrigue comprehends the three days' fight which happened in the absence of Achilles, and it consists on one side in the resistance of Agamemnon and the Grecians and on the other in the revengeful and inexorable humor of Achilles, which would not suffer him to be reconciled. The loss of the Grecians and the despair of Agamemnon prepare for a solution by the satisfaction which the incensed hero received from it. The death of Patroclus, joined to the offers of Agamemnon, which of itself had proved ineffectual, remove this difficulty, and make the unraveling of the first part.

This death is likewise the beginning of the second part, since it puts Achilles upon the design of revenging himself on Hector. But the design of Hector is opposite to that of Achilles; this Trojan is valiant, and resolved to stand on his own defense. This valor and resolution of Hector are on his part the cause of the intrigue. All the endeavors Achilles used to meet with Hector and be the death of him, and the contrary endeavors of the Trojan to keep out of his reach and defend himself, are the intrigue, which comprehends the battle of the last day. The unraveling begins at the death of Hector; and besides that, it contains the insulting of Achilles over his body, the honors he paid to Patroclus, and the entreaties of King Priam. The regrets of this king and the other Trojans in the sorrowful obsequies they paid to Hector's body end the unraveling; they justify the satisfaction of Achilles, and demonstrate his tranquillity.

The first part of the *Odyssey* is the return of Ulysses into Ithaca. Neptune opposes it by raising tempests, and this makes the intrigue. The unraveling is the arrival of Ulysses upon his own island, where Neptune could offer him no farther injury. The second part is the reinstating this hero in his own government. The princes that are his rivals oppose him, and this is a fresh intrigue; the solution of it begins at their deaths, and is completed as soon as the Ithacans were appeased.

These two parts in the *Odyssey* have not one common intrigue. The anger of Achilles forms both the intrigues in the *Iliad*, and it is so far the matter of this epopea that the very beginning and end of this poem depend on the beginning and end of this anger. But let the desire Achilles had to revenge himself and the desire Ulysses had to return to his own country be never so near allied, yet we cannot place them under one and the same notion; for that desire of Ulysses is not a passion that begins and ends in the poem with the action: it is a natural habit; nor does the poet propose it for his subject as he does the anger of Achilles. . . .

Book II, Chapter 14

We have already observed what is meant by the intrigue and the unraveling thereof; let us now say something of the manner of forming both. These two should arise naturally out of the very essence and subject of the poem, and are to be deduced from thence. Their conduct is so exact and natural that it seems as if their action had presented them with whatever they inserted without putting themselves to the trouble of a farther inquiry.

What is more usual and natural to warriors than anger, heat, passion, and impatience of bearing the least affront or disrespect? This is what forms the intrigue of the *Iliad*, and everything we read there is nothing else but the effect of this humor and these passions.

What more natural and usual obstacle to those who take voyages than the sea, the winds, and the storms? Homer makes this the intrigue of the first part of the *Odyssey*, and for the second he makes use of almost the infallible effect of the long absence of a master whose return is quite despaired of, viz., the insolence of his servants and neighbors, the danger of his son and wife, and the sequestration of his estate. Besides, an absence of almost twenty years, and the insupportable fatigues joined to the age of which Ulysses then was, might induce him to believe that he should not be owned by those who thought him dead and whose interest it was to have him really so. Therefore if he had presently declared who he was and had called himself Ulysses, they would easily have destroyed him as an impostor before he had an opportunity to make himself known.

There could be nothing more natural nor more necessary than this ingenious disguise, to which the advantages his enemies had taken of his absence had reduced him, and to which his long misfortunes had inured him. This allowed him an opportunity, without hazarding anything, of taking the best measures he could against those persons who could not so much as mistrust any harm from him. This way was afforded him by the very nature of his action to execute his designs and overcome the obstacles it cast before him. And it is this contest between the prudence and the dissimulation of a single man on one hand and the ungovernable insolence of so many rivals on the other which constitutes the intrigue of the second part of the *Odyssey*.

Book II, Chapter 15

If the plot or intrigue must be natural and such as springs from the very subject, as has been already urged, then the winding up of the plot by a more sure claim must have this qualification and be a probable consequence of all that went before. As this is what the readers regard more than the rest, so should the poet be more exact in it. This is the end of the poem and the last impression that is to be stamped upon them.

We shall find this in the *Odyssey*. Ulysses by a tempest is cast upon the island of the Phaeacians, to whom he discovers himself and desires they would favor his return to his own country, which was not very far distant. One cannot see any reason why the king of this island should refuse such a reasonable request to a hero whom he seemed to have in great esteem. The Phaeacians, indeed, had heard him tell the story of his adventures, and in this fabulous recital consisted all the advantage they could derive from his presence; for the art of war which they admired in him, his undauntedness under dangers, his indefatigable patience and other virtues, were such as these islanders were not used to. All their talent lay in singing and dancing and whatsoever was charming in a quiet life. And here we see how dexterously Homer prepares the incidents he makes use of. These people could do no less for the account with which Ulysses had so much

317

entertained them than afford him a ship and a safe convoy, which was of little expense or trouble to them.

When he arrived, his long absence and the travels which had disfigured him made him altogether unknown, and the danger he would have incurred had he discovered himself too soon forced him to a disguise. Lastly, this disguise gave him an opportunity of surprising those young suitors, who for several years together had been accustomed to nothing but to sleep well and fare daintily.

It was from these examples that Aristotle drew this rule, that whatever concludes the poem should so spring from the very constitution of the fable as if it were a necessary or at least a probable consequence.

Book II, Chapter 18

The time of the epic action is not fixed like that of the dramatic poem; it is much longer, for an uninterrupted duration is much more necessary in an action which one sees and is present at than in one which we only read or hear repeated. Besides, tragedy is fuller of passion, and consequently of such a violence as cannot admit of so long a duration.

The *Iliad* containing an action of anger and violence, the poet allows it but a short time, about forty days. The design of the *Odyssey* required another conduct: the character of the hero is prudence and long-suffering; therefore the time of its duration is much longer, above eight years.

Book III, Chapter 9

The passions of tragedy are different from those of the epic poem. In the former, terror and pity have the chief place; the passion that seems most peculiar to epic poetry is admiration.

Besides this admiration, which in general distinguishes the epic poem from the dramatic, each epic poem has likewise some peculiar passion which distinguishes it in particular from other epic poems, and constitutes a kind of singular and individual difference between these poems of the same species. These singular passions correspond to the character of the hero. Anger and terror reign throughout the *Iliad* because Achilles is angry and the most terrible of all men. The *Aeneid* has all soft and tender passions, because that is the character of Aeneas. The prudence, wisdom, and constancy of Ulysses do not allow him either of these extremes; therefore the poet does not permit one of them to be predominant in the *Odyssey*. He confines himself to admiration only, which he carries to an higher pitch than in the *Iliad*, and it is upon this account that he introduces a great many more machines in the *Odyssey* into the body of the action than are to be seen in the actions of the other two poems.

Book IV, Chapter 4

The manners of the epic poem ought to be poetically good, but it is not necessary they be always morally so. They are poetically good when one may discover the virtue or vice, the good or ill inclinations of every one who speaks or acts; they are poetically bad when persons are made to speak or act out of character, or inconsistently or unequally. The manners of Aeneas and of Mezentius are equally good, considered poetically, because they equally demonstrate the piety of the one and the impiety of the other.

Book IV, Chapter 5

It is requisite to make the same distinction between a hero in morality and a hero in poetry as between moral and poetical goodness. Achilles had as much right to the latter as Aeneas. Aristotle says that the hero of a poem should be neither good nor bad, neither advanced above the rest of mankind by his virtues or sunk beneath them by his vices, that he may be the properer and fuller example to others, both what to imitate and what to decline.

Book IV, Chapter 7

The other qualifications of the manners are that they be suitable to the causes which either raise or discover them in the persons; that they have an exact resemblance to what history or fable have delivered of those persons to whom they are ascribed; and that there be an equality in them so that no man is made to act or speak out of his character.

Book IV, Chapter 12

But this equality is not sufficient for the unity of the character; it is further necessary that the same spirit appear in all sorts of encounters. Thus Aeneas, acting with great piety and mildness in the first part of the *Aeneid*, which requires no other character, and afterwards appearing illustrious in heroic valor in the wars of the second part (but there without any appearance either of a hard or a soft disposition), would doubtless be far from offending against the equality of the manners; but yet there would be no simplicity or unity in the character. So that besides the qualities that claim their particular place upon different occasions there must be one appearing throughout which commands over all the rest, and without this we may affirm it is no character.

One may indeed make a hero as valiant as Achilles, as pious as Aeneas, and as prudent as Ulysses. But it is a mere chimera to imagine a hero that has the valor of Achilles, the piety of Aeneas, and the prudence of Ulysses at one and the same time. This vision might happen to an author who would suit the character of a hero to whatever each part of the action might naturally require without regarding the essence of the fable or the unity of the character in the same person upon all sorts of occasions. This hero would be the mildest, best-natured prince in the world, and also the most choleric, hard-hearted, and implacable creature imaginable; he would be extremely tender like Aeneas, extremely violent like Achilles, and yet have the indifference of Ulysses, that is incapable of the two extremes. Would it not be in vain for the poet to call this person by the same name throughout?

Let us reflect on the effects it would produce in several poems whose authors were of opinion that the chief character of a hero is that of an accomplished man. They would be all alike; all valiant in battle, prudent in council, pious in the acts of religion, courteous, civil, magnificent, and, lastly, endued with all the prodigious virtues any poet could invent. All this would be independent from the action and the subject of the poem, and upon seeing each hero separated from the rest of the work we should not easily guess to what action and to what poem the hero belonged. So that we should see that none of those would have a character, since the character is that which makes a person discernible and which distinguishes him from all others.

Book IV, Chapter 11 [2]

This commanding quality in Achilles is his anger; in Ulysses, the art of dissimulation; in Aeneas, meekness. Each of these may be styled, by way of eminence, the character in these heroes.

But these characters cannot be alone. It is absolutely necessary that some other should give them a luster and embellish them as far as they are capable, either by hiding the defects that are in each by some noble and shining qualities, as the poet has done the anger of Achilles by shading it with extraordinary valor, or by making them entirely of the nature of a true and solid virtue, as is to be observed in the two others. The dis-

René Le Bossu

simulation of Ulysses is a part of his prudence, and the meekness of Aeneas is wholly employed in submitting his will to the gods. For the making up this union, our poets have joined together such qualities as are by nature the most compatible: valor with anger, meekness with piety, and prudence with dissimulation. This last union was necessary for the goodness of Ulysses, for without that his dissimulation might have degenerated into wickedness and double-dealing.

Book V, Chapter 1

We now come to the machines of the epic poem. The chief passion which it aims to excite being admiration, nothing is so conducive to that as the marvelous, and the importance and dignity of the action is by nothing so greatly elevated as by the care and interposition of heaven.

These machines are of three sorts. Some are theological, and were invented to explain the nature of the gods. Others are physical, and represent things of nature. The last are moral, and are the images of virtues and vices.

Book V, Chapter 2

Homer and the ancients have given to their deities the manners, passions, and vices of men. The poems are wholly allegorical, and in this view it is easier to defend Homer than to blame him. We cannot accuse him for making mention of many gods, for his bestowing passions upon them, or even introducing them fighting against men. The Scripture uses the like figures and expressions.

If it be allowable to speak thus of the gods in theology, much more in the fictions of natural philosophy, where, if a poet describes the deities, he must give them such manners, speeches, and actions as are conformable to the nature of the things they represent under those divinities. The case is the same in the [morals of the deities]: Minerva is wise, because she represents prudence; Venus is both good or bad, because the passion of love is capable of these contrary qualities.

Book V, Chapter 3

Since among the gods of a poem some are good, some bad, and some indifferently either, and since of our passions we make so many allegorical deities, one may attribute to the gods all that is done in the poem, whether good or evil. But these deities do not act constantly in one and the same manner.

321

Sometimes they act invisibly and by mere inspiration, which has nothing in it extraordinary or miraculous, being no more than what we say every day, that some god has assisted us, or some demon has instigated us.

At other times they appear visibly, and manifest themselves to men in a manner altogether miraculous and preternatural.

The third way has something of both the others; it is in truth a miracle, but is not commonly so accounted: this includes dreams, oracles, etc.

All these ways must be probable; for so necessary as the marvelous is to the epic action, as nothing is so conducive to admiration, yet we can, on the other hand, admire nothing that we think impossible. Though the probability of these machines be of a very large extent since it is founded upon divine power, it is not without limitations. There are numerous instances of allowable and probable machines in the epic poem, where the gods are no less actors than the men. But the less credible sort, such as metamorphoses, etc., are far more rare.

This suggests a reflection on the method of rendering those machines probable which in their own nature are hardly so. Those which require only divine probability should be so disengaged from the action that one might subtract them from it without destroying the action. But those which are essential and necessary should be grounded upon human probability, and not on the sole power of God. Thus the episodes of Circe, the Sirens, Polyphemus, etc., are necessary to the action of the *Odyssey* and yet not humanly probable; yet Homer has artificially reduced them to human probability by the simplicity and ignorance of the Phaeacians, before whom he causes those recitals to be made.

Book V, Chapter 4

The next question is where and on what occasions machines may be used. It is certain Homer and Virgil make use of them everywhere, and scarce suffer any action to be performed without them. Petronius makes this a precept: *Per ambages, deorumque ministeria*, etc.[3] The gods are mentioned in the very proposition of their works, the invocation is addressed to them, and the whole narration is full of them. The gods are the causes of the action; they form the intrigue and bring about the solution. The precept of Aristotle and Horace, that the unraveling of the plot should not proceed from a miracle or the appearance of a god, has place only in dramatic poetry, not in the epic. For it is plain that both in the solution of the *Iliad* and *Odyssey* the gods are concerned. In the former, the deities meet to appease the anger of Achilles; Iris and Mercury are sent to that purpose, and Minerva eminently assists Achilles in the decisive combat with Hector. In the *Odyssey* the same goddess fights close by Ulysses against the suitors, and concludes that peace betwixt him and the Ithacensians which completes the poem.

Book V, Chapter 5

We may therefore determine that a machine is not an invention to extricate the poet out of any difficulty which embarrasses him, but that the presence of a divinity and some action surprising and extraordinary are inserted into almost all the parts of the work in order to render it more majestic and more admirable. But this mixture ought to be so made that the machines might be retrenched without taking anything from the action, at the same time that it gives the readers a lesson of piety and virtue, and teaches them that the most brave and the most wise can do nothing and attain nothing great and glorious without the assistance of heaven. Thus the machinery crowns the whole work and renders it at once marvelous, probable, and moral.

Jean de La Bruyère OF POLITE LEARNING FROM

"CHARACTERS"

We are come too late, after above seven thousand years that there have been men, and men have thought, to say anything which has not been said already. The finest and most beautiful thoughts concerning manners are carried away before us, and we can do nothing now but glean after the ancients and the most ingenious of the moderns.

We must only endeavor to think and speak justly ourselves, without aiming to bring others over to our taste and sentiments. We shall find that too great an enterprise.

To make a book is like making a pendulum: a man must have experience as well as wit to succeed in it. A certain magistrate arriving by his merit to the first dignities of the gown thought himself qualified for everything; he printed a treatise of morality and published himself a coxcomb.

It is not so easy to raise a reputation by a complete work as to make an indifferent one valued by a reputation already acquired.

A satire or a libel when it is handed privately from one to another with strict charge of secrecy, if it is but mean in itself, passes for wonderful; the printing it would ruin its reputation.

Take away from most of our moral essays the advertisement to the reader, the epistle dedicatory, the preface, the table, and the commendatory verses, there will seldom be enough left to deserve the name of a book.

Several things are insupportable if they are but indifferent, as poetry, music, painting, and public speeches.

It is the worst punishment in the world to hear a dull declamation delivered with pomp and solemnity, and bad verses rehearsed with the emphasis of a wretched poet.

Some poets in their dramatic pieces are fond of big words and sounding verses, which seem strong, elevated, and sublime. The people stare, gape, and hear them greedily; they are transported at what they fancy is rare, and where they understand least are sure to admire most; they scarce allow themselves time to breathe, and are loath to be interrupted by claps or applauses. When I was young I imagined these places were clear and intelligible to the actors, the pit, boxes, and galleries; that the authors understood them, and that I was in the wrong to know nothing of the matter after much attention. But I am now undeceived.

There never was seen any piece excellent in its kind that was the joint labor of several men; Homer writ his *Iliad*, Virgil his *Aeneid*, Livy his *Decades*, and Cicero his *Orations*.

As there is in nature, so there is in art a point of perfection. He who is sensible of it and is touched with it has a good taste; he who is not sensible of it, but is wavering, has a vicious taste. Since, then, there is a good and a bad taste, we may with reason dispute the difference.

Everyone has more fire than judgment, or rather there are few men of wit who are good critics.

The lives of heroes have enriched history, and history has adorned the actions of heroes; and thus it is difficult to tell who are most indebted, the historians to those who furnished them with such noble materials or the great men to their historians.

It is a sorry commendation that is made up of a heap of epithets; it is actions and the manner of relating them which speak a man's praise.

The chief art of an author consists in making good definitions, good pictures. Moses, Homer, Plato, Virgil, and Horace excel other writers mostly in their expressions and images. Truth is the best guide to make a man write forcibly, naturally, and delicately.

We should do by style as we have done by architecture, banish entirely the Gothic order, which the barbarians introduced in their palaces and temples, and recall the Doric, Ionic, and Corinthian. Let what we see in the ruins of ancient Rome and old Greece shine in our porticoes and peristyles, and become modern, since we cannot arrive to perfection, or, if possible, surpass the ancients in building or writing but by imitating them.

How many ages were lost in ignorance before men could come back to the taste of the ancients in the arts and sciences, or recover at last the simple and the natural.

We nourish ourselves by the ancients and ingenious moderns; we draw from them as much as we can, and, at their expense, in the end become authors. Then we quickly think we can walk alone and without help; we oppose our benefactors and treat them like those children who, grown pert and strong with the milk they have sucked, turn themselves against their nurses.

It is the practice of a modern wit to prove the ancients inferior to us by two ways, reason and example. He takes the reason from his particular opinion and the example from his writings.

He confesses the ancients, as unequal and incorrect as they are, have a great many good lines; he cites them, and they appear so fine that they ruin his criticisms.

Some learned men declare in favor of the ancients against the moderns. But we are afraid they judge in their own cause, and so many of their works are made after the model of antiquity that we except against their authority.

An author should be fond of reading his works to those who know how to correct and esteem them.

He that will not be corrected nor advised in his writings is a pedant.

An author ought to receive with equal modesty the praises and the criticisms which are passed on his productions.

Amongst all the different expressions which can render any one of our thoughts, there is but one good. We are not always so fortunate as to hit upon it in writing or speaking; however, it is true that it exists, that all the rest are weak and will not satisfy a man of sense who would make himself understood.

A good author who writes with care, when he meets with the expression he has searched after for some time without knowing it, finds it at last the most simple and the most natural, and fancies it ought to have presented itself to him at first without search or inquiry.

Those who write by humor are frequently subject to revise their works and give them new touches. And as their humors are never fixed, but vary on every slight occasion, they quickly spoil their writings by new expressions and terms which they like better than the former.

The same true sense which makes an author write a great many good things tells him that there are not enough to deserve reading.

A man of little sense is ravished with himself, and thinks his writings divine; a man of good sense is harder to be pleased, and would only be reasonable.

One, says Aristus, engaged me to read my book to Zoilus. I read it; he was satisfied, and before he had leisure to dislike it, he commended it coldly in my presence. Since that, he takes no notice on it, nor says a word in its favor. However, I excuse him; I desire no more of an author, and even pity him the hearing so many fine things which were not his own making.

Such as by their circumstances are free from the jealousies of an author have other cares and passions to distract them and make them cold towards another man's conceptions. It is difficult to find a person whose fortune and good humor put him in a condition to taste all the pleasure a complete piece can give him.

The pleasure of criticizing takes away the pleasure of being sensibly charmed with very fine productions.

Many men who perceive the beauties of a manuscript when they hear it read will not declare themselves in its favor till they see what success it has in the world when it is printed, and what character the ingenious give it. They will not hazard their votes before its fortune is made, and they are carried away with the crowd or engaged by the multitude. Then they are very forward to publish how early they were in their approbation, and how glad they are to find the world is of their opinion.

These men lose a fair opportunity to convince us that they are persons of capacity and insight, that they make a true judgment, and distinguish an excellent thing from one that is good. A fine piece falls into their hands, the author's first work, before he has got a name, or they are yet prepossessed in his behalf; he has not endeavored to make his court to the great men by flattering their writings; neither is it required that they should proclaim to please some man of quality or topping wit who has declared himself in its favor, "This is a masterpiece. Human wit never went so far. We will judge of nobody's opinion but in proportion to what thoughts he has of this book." Extravagant and offensive expressions, which smell of the pension or the abbey, [1] and are injurious to what is really commendable. Why did they not profess it by themselves? When they might have been alone in their praises, why did they not then commend it? It is true, at last they cry aloud, "It is an admirable book," when the whole kingdom has approved it; when foreigners as well as their own countrymen are fond of it; when it is printed all over Europe, translated into all languages; in short, when it is too late, and the author is not obliged to them for their applauses.

Some of them read a book, collect certain lines which they do not understand, and rob them of their value by what they put in of their own. Yet these lines, so broken and disguised that they are indeed their proper style and thoughts, they expose to censure, maintain them to be bad, and as they cite them the world readily agrees with them. But the passage they pretend to quote is never the worse for their injustice.

"Well," says one, "what's your opinion of Hermedorus's book?" "That it is bad," replies Anthimus. "That it is bad? What d'ye mean, sir?" "That it is bad," continues he; "at least it deserves not the character people give it." "Have you read it?" "No," says Anthimus, "but Fulvia and Melania have condemned it without reading, and I am a friend to Fulvia and Melania."

Arsenes from the altitudes of his understanding contemplates mankind, and at the distance from whence he beholds them seems affrighted at their littleness. He is commended, exalted, and mounted to the skies by certain persons who have reciprocally covenanted to admire one another. Contented with his own merit, he fancies he has as much wit as he wants, and more than he ever will have. Thus employed by his high thoughts, and full of sublime ideas, he scarcely finds time to pronounce the sacred oracles. He is elevated by his character above human judgments, and leaves it for common souls to value a common and uniform life, being answerable for his inconstancy to none but his particular friends who have resolved to idolize him. For this reason, they only know how to judge or think; they only know how to write, and it is only in them a duty. As for other pieces, however received in the world or universally liked by men of honor and worth, he is so far from approving them that he never condescends to read them, and is incapable of being corrected by this picture, which will not be so happy as to reach him.

Theocrines is very well acquainted with what is trivial and unprofitable. He is less profound than methodical. He is the abstract of disdain, and seems continually laughing in himself at such as he thinks despise him. By chance I once read him something of mine. He heard it out with impatience; he cried presently, "Is it done?" and then talked of his own. "But what said he of yours," say you? "I have told you already, sir, he talked of his own."

The most accomplished piece which the age has produced would fail under the hands of the critics and censurers if the author would hearken to their objections and allow them to throw out what is not to their satisfaction.

Experience tells us, if there are ten persons who would blot a thought or an expression out of a book, there are a like number who would oppose it. These will allege, "For what would you suppress that thought? It is new, fine, and handsomely expressed." Those, on the contrary, affirm it should be omitted; at least they would have given it another turn. "In your work," says one, "there is a term exceedingly witty; it points out your meaning very naturally." "Methinks," says another, "that word is too bold, and yet does not signify so much as you would have it." It is the same word and the same line these critics differ so much about, and yet they are all judges, or pass for such amongst their acquaintance. What then shall an author do but follow the advice of those who approve it?

A serious author is not obliged to trouble his head with all the extravagant banters and bad jests which are thrown on him, or to be concerned at the impertinent constructions which a sort of men may make on some passages of his writings; neither ought he to give himself the trouble to suppress them. He is convinced that if a man is never so exact in his manner of writing, the dull raillery and wretched buffoonry of certain worthless people are unavoidable, since they make use of the best things only to turn them into ridicule.[2]

There is a prodigious difference between a fine piece and one that is regular and perfect. I question if there is anything to be found in the last kind, it being less difficult for a rare genius to hit upon the great and sublime than to avoid all errors. The *Cid* at its first appearance was universally admired. It lived in spite of policy or power, which attempted in vain to destroy it. The wits, who were otherwise divided in their sentiments, united in favor of this tragedy. The persons of quality and the common people agreed to keep it in their memory; they were beforehand with the actors in rehearsing it at the theatre. The *Cid,* in short, is one of the finest poems which can be made, and one of the best critiques which ever was written on any subject is that on the *Cid.*[3]

Capys sets up for a judge of style, and fancies he writes like Bouhours [and] Rabutin; he opposes himself to the voice of the people, and says all alone Damis is not a good author. However, Damis gives way to the multitude, and affirms ingenuously with the public that Capys is a dull writer.[4]

It is the business of a newsmonger to inform us when a book is to be published, for whom it is printed, for Cramoisy or for whom else, in what character, how bound and what paper, how many of them are gone off, and at what sign the bookseller lives. This is his duty; it is foolish in him to pretend to be a critic.

The highest reach of a newsmonger is an empty reasoning on policy and vain conjectures on the public management.

Boevius [5] lies down at night in great tranquillity at some false news which dies before morning, and he is obliged to abandon it as soon as he awakes.

The philosopher wastes his life in observing men and exposing foppery and vice; he gives his thoughts no other turn than what serves to set a truth he has found out in a proper light, that it may make the impression he designs. He has little of the vanity of an author, and yet some readers think they do very well by him if they say with a magisterial air they have read his book and there is some sense in it. But he returns them their praises, having other ends than bare applause in his sweating so much and breaking his rest. He has higher aims, and acts by a more elevated policy; he requires from mankind a greater and more extraordinary success than commendation or even rewards. He expects amendment and reformation.

A fool reads a book and understands nothing in it; a little wit reads it and is presently master of all without exception; a man of sense sometimes does not comprehend it entirely: he distinguishes what is clear from what is obscure, whilst the beaux esprits will have those passages dark which are not, and cannot understand what is really intelligible.

An author endeavors in vain to make himself admired by his productions. A fool may sometimes admire him, but then he is a fool. And a man of sense has in him the seeds of all truth and opinions; nothing is new to him. He admires little, it being his province chiefly to approve.

I question if it is possible to find in letters of wit a better manner, more agreeableness, and a finer style than we see in Balzac's and Voiture's.[6] It is true they are void of those sentiments which have since taken among us, and were invented by the ladies. That sex excels ours in this kind of writing. Those expressions and graces flow from them which are in us the effect of tedious labor and troublesome inquiry. They are happy in their terms, and place them so justly that everyone presently lights upon their meaning. As familiar as they are, yet they have the charm of novelty, and seem only designed for the use they put them to. They only can express a whole sentence in a single word, and render a delicate thought in a turn altogether as delicate. We find in all their letters an inimitable connection continued through the whole very naturally and always bounded by good sense. If the ladies were more correct, I might affirm that they have produced some letters the best written of anything in our language.

Terence wanted nothing but warmth; with what purity, exactness, politeness, elegance, and characters are his plays adorned! Molière wanted nothing but to avoid jargon and to write purely. What fire, what naivety, what a source of good pleasantry, what imitation of manners, what images, what a flail of ridicule are in his comedies! What a man could we make of these two comedians!

I have read Malherbe and Théophile.[7] They both understood nature, with this difference: the first in a plain, uniform style discovered at once something noble, fine, simple, and natural like a good painter or a true historian; the other, without choice or exactness, with a free and uneven pen, sometimes loaden with descriptions, grows heavy in particulars and gives you an anatomy, and sometimes he feigns, exaggerates, and goes so much beyond the natural truth that he makes a romance.

Ronsard[8] and Balzac have each in their kind good and bad things, enough to form after them very great men in verse or prose.

Marot[9] by his turn and style seems to have written since Ronsard. There is little difference between the first and us but the alteration of a few words.

Ronsard and his contemporaries were more prejudicial than serviceable to style. They kept it back in the way to perfection and exposed it to the danger of being always defective. It is surprising that Marot's works, which are so easy and natural, had not taught Ronsard, otherwise full of rapture and enthusiasm, to make a greater poet than Marot or himself, and that on the contrary Belleau, Jodelle, and Saint-Gelais were so soon followed by a Racan and a Malherbe;[10] or that our language ere it was scarce corrupted should be so quickly recovered.

Marot and Rabelais are inexcusable for scattering so much ribaldry in their writings; they had both genius and wit enough to have omitted it without striving to please such as would rather meet matter of laughter than admiration in an author. Rabelais is incomprehensible. His book is an inexplicable enigma, a mere chimera; it has a woman's face, with the feet and tail of a serpent or some beast more deformed. It is a monstrous collection of political and ingenious morality, with a mixture of beastliness. Where it is bad it is abominable and fit for the diversion of the rabble, and where it is good it is exquisite, and may entertain the most delicate.

Two writers in their works have condemned Montaigne. I confess he

331

sometimes exposes himself to censure, but neither of these gentlemen will allow him to have anything valuable. One of them thinks too little to taste an author who thinks a great deal, and the other thinks too subtly to be pleased with what is natural.

A grave, serious, and scrupulous style will live a long while. Amyot and Coëffeteau are read, and who else of their contemporaries? [11] Balzac for his phrase and expression is less old than Voiture. But if the wit, genius, and manner of the last is not modern nor so conformable to our present writers, it is because they can more easily neglect than imitate him, and that the few who followed could never overtake him.

The *Mercure galant* [12] is a trifle, next to nothing, and there are [a good many works like it]; however, the author has had the good luck to live well by his invention, and there have been fops always ready to take off an impression of his foolish book. Whence we may perceive it is the ignorance of the people's judgment which makes men sometimes fearful to venture abroad a great many dull pieces.

An opera is the sketch of some magnificent show, of which it serves to give one an idea.

I wonder how an opera, with all its charge and music, should yet so suddenly tire me.

There are some places in an opera which make us desire more, and others that dispose us to wish it all over, according as we are pleased or offended with the scenes, the action, and the things represented.

An opera is not nowadays a poem, it is verses; nor a show, since machines have disappeared by the dexterous management of Amphion and his race. It is a concert of voices assisted by instruments. We are cheated by those who tell us machines are the amusements of children and proper only for puppet plays. It increases and embellishes the fiction, and keeps the spectators in that sweet illusion which is the highest pleasure of the theatre, especially where it has a mixture of the marvelous. There is no need of wings or cars or metamorphoses; but it is, however, the design of an opera and its representation to hold the mind, the eye, and the ear in an equal enchantment.[13]

The critics, or such as would be thought so, will ever have the decisive voice at all public sights. They canton and divide themselves into parties, pushed on of both sides by a particular interest opposite to that of the public or equity, admiring only such a poem or such a piece of music, and condemning all the rest. They are sometimes so warm in their prejudices that they are at a loss how to defend them, and injure the reputation of their cabal by their visible injustices and partiality. These men discourage the poets and musicians by a thousand contradictions, retarding the progress of the arts and sciences, depriving several masters of the fruit they would draw from emulation, and the world of many excellent performances.

What's the reason that we laugh so freely and are ashamed to weep at the theatre? Is nature less subject to be softened by pity than to burst forth at what is comical? Is it the alteration of our looks that prevents us? It is as great in an extraordinary laughter as in the most bitter weeping and we turn away our faces to laugh as well as to weep in the presence of people of quality, or such as we respect. Is it our backwardness to be thought tender or to show any emotion at a false subject where we fancy we are made cullies? Without naming some grave men or persons of sound judgments who think there is as much weakness shown in laughing excessively as in weeping, what is it that we look for at a tragedy? Is it to laugh? Does not truth reign there as lively by its images as in a comedy? And does not the soul imagine things true in either kind before it suffers itself to be moved? Or is it so easy to be pleased that verisimility is not necessary towards it? If not, we must suppose it is the natural effect of a good tragedy to make us weep freely in sight of the whole audience without any other trouble than drying our eyes and wiping our faces. It being no more ridiculous to be seen weeping than to be heard to laugh by the whole theatre, on the contrary we then conclude there was something acted very pleasantly and to the life, and the restraint a man puts on himself to hide his tears by an affected grimace plainly demonstrates that he ought not to resist the main design of a tragedy, but give way to his passions, and discover them as openly and with as much confidence as at a comedy. Besides, when we have been so patient as to sit out a whole play we should be less ashamed to weep at the theatre than to sit there three hours for nothing.

It is not sufficient that the manners of the theatre ought not to be bad; they should be decent and instructive. Some things are so low, so mean, so dull and insignificant in themselves, that the poet is not permitted to write nor the audience to be diverted by them. The peasant or the drunkard may furnish out some scenes for a farce-maker; they must never enter into true comedy, for since such characters cannot answer the main end, they should not be the main action of the play. Perhaps you will say they are natural. So is a whistling lackey, or a sick man on his closet-stool. By the same rule you may bring them on the stage, or the drunkard snoring and vomiting;

is there anything more natural? It is the property of a beau to rise late, to pass the best part of the day at his toilet, to adjust himself at his glass, to be perfumed and powdered, to put on his patches, to receive and answer his *billets*. When this part is brought on the stage, if it is continued two or three acts it may be the more natural and conformable to the original, but it is the more dull and insipid.

Plays and romances, in my opinion, may be made as useful as they are prejudicial to such as read them. There are so many great examples of constancy, virtue, tenderness, and disinterest, so many fine and perfect characters, that when a young person turns his prospect thence on everything about him and finds nothing but unworthy objects, very much below what he [has just been] admiring, I wonder how he can be guilty of the least [interest in] them.

Corneille cannot be equalled where he is excellent; he is then an original and unimitable, but he is unequal. His first plays are dry and languishing, and gave us no reason to hope he would afterwards rise to such a height, and his last plays make us wonder he could fall from it. In some of his best pieces there are unpardonable faults against the manners, the action is embarrassed with the declamatory style, there are such negligences in the verse and expression that we can hardly comprehend how so great a man could be guilty of them. The most eminent thing in him is his sublime wit, though he is very happy sometimes in his verses, and generally in the conduct of his plays, where he often ventures against the rules of the ancients. He is admirable in unraveling his plots, and in this does not always subject himself to the judgment of the Greeks or their great simplicity. On the contrary, he loads the scene with events, and most commonly comes off with success. He is above all to be admired for his great variety and the little agreement we find in his designs amongst the great number of poems he composed. In Racine's plays there are more likenesses; they lead more to the same thing. But he is even and everywhere supported, as well in the design and conduct of his pieces, which are just, regular, full of good sense, and natural, as for the versification, which is rich in rhymes, elegant, numerous, harmonious, and correct. He is an exact imitator of the ancients, whom he follows religiously in the simplicity of action. He wants not the sublime and the marvelous, and where it is proper he is ever master of the moving and the pathetic as well as his predecessor Corneille. Where can we find greater tenderness than is diffused through the *Cid*, *Polyeucte*, and *Horace*? What greatness of soul is there in Mithradate, Porus, and Burrhus! [14] They were both well acquainted with horror and pity, the favorite passions of the ancients, which the poets are fond of exciting on the theatre, as Oreste in the *Andromaque* of Racine, the Phèdre of the same author, and the *Oedipe* and the *Horace* of Corneille sufficiently prove. If I may be allowed to make a comparison or to show the talent of both the one and the other as it is to be discovered in their writings, I should probably say that Corneille reigns over us by his characters and ideas; Racine's are more conformable to our own. The one paints men as they ought to be; the other describes them as they are. There is in the first more of what we admire and ought to imitate, and in the second more of what we know in others and approve in ourselves. Corneille elevates, surprises, triumphs, and instructs. Racine pleases, affects, moves, and penetrates. The former works on us by what is fine, noble, and commanding. The latter insinuates himself into us by the delicacy of his passions. One is full of maxims, rules, and precepts, the other of opinions and judgments; we are engaged more at Corneille's pieces, at Racine's more softened and concerned. Corneille is more moral, Racine more natural. The one seems to imitate Sophocles, the other Euripides.

Some persons have a faculty of speaking alone and a long time, joined with extravagant gestures, a loud voice, and strong lungs: this the people call eloquence. Pedants never admit [eloquence] but in public orations, and cannot distinguish [it from] a heap of figures, the use of [big] words, and the roundness of periods.

Logic is the art to make truth prevalent, and eloquence a gift of the soul that renders one master of the sense and hearts of other men, by which we persuade and inspire them with what we please.

Eloquence may be found in all discourses and all kinds of writings; it is rarely where we seek it, and sometimes where it is least expected.

Eloquence is to the sublime what the whole is to its part.

What is the sublime? We talk much about it, but nobody pretends to define it. Is it in itself a figure? Is it composed of one or more figures? Does the sublime enter into all sorts of writing, or are great subjects only capable of it? [Can anything shine in eclogues but] a fine wit and a natural simplicity, [or] in familiar letters and conversation [anything but] a great delicacy; or rather [are not the natural and the delicate] the sublime of those works where they make the perfection? What is this sublime, and in what does it consist?

Synonyms are several dictions or phrases that signify the same thing.

An antithesis is the opposition of two truths which give light to each other. A metaphor or comparison borrows from a strange thing the natural and sensible image of a true one. An hyperbole expresses things above truth to reclaim the mind that it may the better understand it. The sublime paints nothing but the truth, only in a noble subject it paints it all entire in its causes and effects. It is the expression or image most worthy the dignity of the truth it treats of. Little wits cannot find the simple expression, and use synonyms. Young men are dazzled with the luster of antitheses, and generally make use of them. True wits, who would be exact in their images, are for metaphors and comparisons. Quick wits, full of fire and vast imagination, carry themselves above rules or justice, and are never satisfied without an hyperbole. As for the sublime, [even among the great geniuses only the most elevated are capable of it].

Everyone who would write purely should put himself in the place of his readers, examine his own work as a thing that is new to him, which he never read before, where he is not at all concerned; and the author must submit to the critic. He should not suppose another man will understand them himself but forasmuch as they are in themselves really intelligible.

An author should not only endeavor to make himself understood; he must strive to inform us of such things as deserve it. He ought, it is true, to have pure language and a chaste expression, but they ought also to express lively, noble, and solid thoughts, full of good sense and sound reason. He prostitutes chastity and clearness of style who wastes it on some frivolous, puerile, dull, and common subject, having neither spirit, fire, nor novelty, where the reader may perhaps easily find out the meaning of the author, but he is much more certain to be tired with his productions.

If we aim to be profound in certain writings, if we affect a polite turn and sometimes too much delicacy, it is merely for the good opinion we have of our readers.

We have this disadvantage in reading books written by men of party and cabal: we seldom meet with the truth in them. Actions are there disguised; the reasons of both sides are not alleged with all their force nor with an entire exactness. He who has the greatest patience must read an abundance of hard, injurious reflections on the gravest men, with whom the writer has some personal quarrel about a point of doctrine or matter of controversy. These books are particular in this, that they deserve not the prodigious sale they find at their first appearance, nor the profound oblivion that attends them afterwards. When the fury and division of these authors cease, they are forgotten, like an almanac out of date.

It is the glory and merit of some men to write well, and of others not to write at all. For this last twenty years we have been regular in our writings. We have faithfully observed constructions and enriched our language with new words, thrown off the yoke of Latinism, and reduced our style to a pure French phrase. We have almost found again the numbers which Malherbe and Balzac hit upon first and so many authors after them suffered to be lost. We have, in short, brought into our discourses all the order and clearness they are capable of, and this will insensibly lead us at last to add wit.

There are some artists and skillful men whose genius is as vast as the art or science they profess. They restore with interest, by their contrivance and invention, what they borrow from its principals. They frequently break through the rules of art to ennoble it, and thwart the common roads if they don't conduct them to what is great and extraordinary. They go alone; they leave their company a long way behind, whilst they are by themselves mounting high and penetrating far into the secrets of their profession, emboldened by their success and encouraged by the advantages they draw from their irregularity, whilst men of ordinary, soft, and moderate parts, as they can never reach them, so they never admire them; they can't comprehend, and much less imitate them. They live peaceably within the compass of their own sphere, aiming at a certain point, which makes the bounds of their insight and capacity. They go no farther because they feel nothing beyond it. They are at best but the first of a second class, and excellent in mediocrity.

I may venture to call certain wits inferior or subaltern; they seem as if they were born only to collect, register, and raise magazines out of the productions of other geniuses. They are plagiaries, translators, or compilers. They never think, but tell you what other men have thought; and as the good choice of thoughts proceeds from invention, having none of their own, they are seldom just in their collections, but choose rather to make them large than excellent. They know nothing of what they learn, and learn what the rest of the world are unwilling to know: a vain and useless science, neither agreeable nor profitable in commerce or conversation. Like false money, it has no currency, for we are at once surprised with these coxcombs' reading and tired with their company and writings. However, the great ones and the vulgar mistake them for men of learning; but wise men know very well what they are, and rank them with the pedants.

Criticism is commonly a trade, not a science; it requires more health than wit, more labor than capacity, and habit than genius. If a person pretends to it who has less discernment than reading, he will be at a loss where to exercise himself, and corrupt his own judgment as well as his readers'.

I advise an author born only to copy, who in extreme modesty works after another man, to choose for his patterns such writings as are full of wit, imagination, and even good learning; if he does not understand his originals, he may at least come at them and read them. He ought, on the contrary, to avoid as he would destruction any desire to imitate those who write by humor, who speak from their hearts, which inspired them with figures and terms, and draw, if I may say it, from their very entrails what they express on their paper. These are dangerous models, and will infallibly make him write meanly, dully, and ridiculously. Besides, I should laugh at a man who would seriously endeavor to speak in my tone of voice or be like me in the face.

A man born a Christian and a Frenchman is confined in satire. Some subjects are forbidden him by the greatness of their quality; others are too low, but he is obliged frequently to fall on them to ease him of his resentment, and by this means he raises them in the beauties of his style and genius.

Everyone should avoid imitating [. . .] a vain, puerile style; a man may be sometimes bold in his expressions, use transpositions and anything which paints his subject to the life, pitying those who are not sensible of the pleasure there is in this liberty to such as understand it.

He who regards nothing more in his works than the taste of the age has a greater value for his person than his writings. He should always aim at perfection, and, though his contemporaries refuse him justice, posterity will give it him.

We must never put a jest in the wrong place; it offends instead of pleasing, and vitiates our own judgments as well as other men's. The ridicule is only proper when it comes in with a good grace, and in a manner which both pleases and instructs.

"Horace and Boileau have said such a thing before you." I take your word for it, but I said it as my own; and may not I think a just thought after them, as others may do the same after me?

338

Bernard Le Bovier de Fontenelle OF PASTORALS

Of all kinds of poetry the pastoral is probably the most ancient, as the keeping of flocks was one of the first employments which men took up. It is very likely that these primitive shepherds, amidst the tranquility and leisure which they enjoyed, bethought themselves of singing their pleasures and their loves; and then their flocks, the woods, the springs, and all those objects that were most familiar to them, naturally came into the subject of their songs. They lived in great plenty after their way, without any control by superior power, being in a manner the kings of their own flocks, and I do not doubt but that a certain joy and openness of heart that generally attends plenty and liberty induced them to sing and to make verses. Society in time was brought to perfection, or [perhaps] declined and was perverted, and men took up employments that seemed to them of greater consequence. More weighty affairs filled their minds; towns and cities were built everywhere, and mighty states at last were founded and established. Then those who lived in the country became slaves to those who dwelt in cities, and the pastoral life, being grown the lot of the most wretched sort of people, no longer inspired any delightful thought.

To please others in ingenious compositions, men ought to be in a condition to free themselves from pressing want, and their minds ought to be refined through a long use of civil society. Now a pastoral life has always wanted one of these two circumstances: the primitive shepherds, of whom we have spoken, lived indeed in plenty enough, but in their times the world had not yet had leisure to grow polite. The following ages might have produced something more refined, but the shepherds of those days were too poor and dejected, so that the country way of living and the poetry of shepherds must needs have been always very homely and artless.

And indeed nothing is more certain than that no real shepherds can be altogether like those of Theocritus. Can anyone think that it is natural for shepherds to say like his:

Gods! When she view'd, how strong was the surprise!
Her soul took fire, and sparkled through her eyes!
How did her passions, how her fury move!
How soon she plung'd into th'abyss of love!

Let the following passages be examined:

O that, to crown what e'er my wish can crave,
I were that bee which flies into your cave!
There softly through your garland would I creep,
And steal a kiss when you are fast asleep!

I know what love is now, a cruel god,
A tigress bore and nursed him in a wood,
A cruel god, he shoots through ev'ry vein —

The fair Calistris, as my goats I drove,
With apples pelts me, and still murmurs love.

The pastures flourish, and the flocks improve,
All smiles, so soon as here resorts my love;
But oh! when e'er the dear one leaves the place,
At once there fade the shepherds and the grass.

Ye gods, I wish not heaps of gold refin'd,
Nor rapid swiftness to outstrip the wind;
But let me sit and sing by yonder rock,
Clasp thee, my dear, and view my feeding flock.

I am of opinion that there will be found in these expressions more beauty and more delicacy of imagination than real shepherds have.

But I don't know how Theocritus, having sometimes raised his shepherds in so pleasing a manner above their native genius, could let them so very often fall to it again. I wonder he did not perceive it was fit that a certain gross clownishness, which is always very unbecoming, should be omitted. When Daphnis in the First Idyllium is ready to die for love, and a great number of deities are come to visit him, in the midst of that honorable company he is reproved for being like the goatherds, who envy the pleasure of their copulating goats and are jealous of them; and it is most certain that the terms used by Theocritus to represent this are much of the kind of the idea which they give.

Ah Daphnis, loose and wanton in thy love!
A herdsman thought, thou dost a goatherd prove:
A goatherd, when he sees the kids at rut,
Sits down and grieves that he's not born a goat.

Bernard Le Bovier de Fontenelle

Thus, when you see the virgins dance, you grieve
Because refus'd, and now disdain to live.

In another idyllium the goatherd Comatas and the herdsman Laco contend about some theft which they had committed against each other; Comatas stole Laco's pipe, and Laco had stolen the skin which Comatas used to wear to cover himself withal, so that he had left him bare. They rail at each other, and vent their passion in reviling and abusive words, which might become a couple of Grecians, but certainly are not over civil; and then, after a gentle item which one of them gives the other of smelling rank, they both sing for a wager, the one having challenged the other to that musical fight, though it should rather have been to a rubbers at fisticuffs, considering what went before; and what seems the more odd is that whereas they begun with gross taunts and ill language, now they are going to sing against each other, they affect an uncommon niceness concerning the choice of a place where they are to sing, each proposing one, of which he makes a florid description. For my part, I have a much-a-do to believe that all this is very well set together. Their songs are as oddly diversified; for among the things that relate to their amours and that are pretty, Comatas puts Laco in mind of a beating which he bestowed upon him, and Laco answers him that he does not remember it, but that he has not forgot how Comatas was bound and soundly lashed by his master Eumaras. I do not fancy that those who say that Venus, the Graces, and Cupid composed Theocritus's idyllia will pretend that they had a hand in these passages.

There are some other places in Theocritus that are not altogether so low which yet are not very entertaining, because they barely treat of country matters. His Fourth Idyllium is wholly of this kind. The subject of it is only a certain Aegon, who, being gone to the Olympic Games, has left his herds to one Corydon. Battus tells the trustee that the herds are in a pitiful condition since Aegon left them. Corydon answers that he does his best, that he drives them to the best pastures he knows, and feeds them at a rack of hay. Battus says that Aegon's pipe is spoiled and mouldy in his absence; Corydon replies that it is not so, that Aegon when he went gave it him, and that he is a notable piper. Then Battus desires Corydon to pull a thorn out of his foot, and the other having advised him never to walk over mountains without his shoes, the idyllium presently concludes, a thing which those who are not conversant with antiquity would scarce have believed possible.

341

When in a pastoral strife one says, "Ho! My goats go on the brow of yonder hill"; and the other answers, "Go, my sheep, feed on to the eastward"; or, "I hate the brush-tailed fox, which comes at night and devours our grapes"; and the other, "I hate the beetles that eat the figs"; or, when one says, "I have made myself a bed with cow's skins near a cool stream,"

> And there I value summer's burning heats
> No more than children do their father's threats,
> Their mother's kind complaints, etc.

And the other answers, "I live in a large shady cave, where"

> Soft chitterlings afford me pleasing food
> And when the winter comes I'm stor'd with wood;
> So that I value cold no more, not I,
> Than toothless men do nuts when pap is by.

May not these discourses be thought too clownish, and fitter to be spoken by real country fellows than by such shepherds as are introduced in eclogues?

Virgil, who, having had the example of Theocritus before his eyes, has had an opportunity to outdo him, hath made his shepherds more polite and agreeable. Anyone who compares his Third Eclogue with that of Laco and Comatas in Theocritus will easily find how well he could rectify and surpass what he did imitate; not but that he still somewhat too much resembles Theocritus when he loses some time in making his pastors say,

> [Graze not too near the banks, my jolly sheep:
> The ground is false; the running streams are deep:
> See, they have caught the father of the flock,
> Who dries his fleece upon the neighboring rock.] [1]

And

> Kids from the river drive, and fling your hook;
> Anon I'll wash them in the shallow brook.

And

> Boys, drive to shades when milk is drained by heat;
> In vain the milkmaid strokes an empty teat.

All this is the less pleasing, considering that it comes after some tender things which are very pretty and genteel, and which have made the reader the more unfit to relish such things as altogether relate to the country.

Calpurnius, a writer of eclogues who lived almost three hundred years after Virgil,[2] and whose works however are not wholly destitute of beauty, seems to have been sorry that Virgil did express but with the words *novi-*

mus et qui te [3] those injurious terms with which Laco and Comatas treat one another in Theocritus, though after all it had yet been better had Virgil wholly suppressed that short hint. Calpurnius has judged this passage worthy a larger extent, and therefore wrote an eclogue which is made up of nothing but those invectives with which two shepherds ready to sing for a prize, ply each other with a great deal of fury, till the shepherd who was to be their judge is so affrighted that he runs away and leaves them. A very fine conclusion!

But no author ever made his shepherds so clownish as J. Baptista Mantuanus,[4] a Latin poet, who lived in the foregoing age and who has been compared to Virgil, though he has indeed nothing common with him besides his being of Mantua. The shepherd Faustus, describing his mistress, says that she had a good big bloated red face, and that, though she was almost blind of an eye, he thought her more beautiful than Diana. It were impossible to guess what precaution another shepherd takes before he begins a discourse of considerable length. And who knows but that our modern Mantuan valued himself mightily upon having copied nature most faithfully in those passages?

I therefore am of opinion that pastoral poetry cannot be very charming if it is as low and clownish as shepherds naturally are, or if it precisely runs upon nothing but rural matters. For to hear one speak of sheep and goats and of the care that ought to be taken of those animals has nothing which in itself can please us; what is pleasing is the idea of quietness, which is inseparable from a pastoral life. Let a shepherd say, "My sheep are in good case, I conduct them to the best pastures, they feed on nothing but the best grass," and let him say this in the best verse in the world, I am sure that your imagination will not be very much delighted with it. But let him say, "How free from anxious cares is my life! In what a quiet state I pass my days! All my desires rise no higher than that I may see my flocks in a thriving condition, and the pastures wholesome and pleasing; I envy no man's happiness, etc." You perceive that this begins to become more agreeable. The reason of it is that the idea runs no longer immediately upon country affairs, but upon the little share of care which shepherds undergo, and upon the quietness and leisure which they enjoy, and, what is the chiefest point, upon the cheapness of their happiness.

For all men would be happy, and that too at any easy rate. A quiet pleasure is the common object of all their passions, and we are all controlled by a certain laziness. Even those who are most stirring are not precisely such for business' sake, or because they love to be in action, but because they cannot easily satisfy themselves.

Ambition, as it is too much an enemy to this natural laziness, is neither a general passion nor very delicious. A considerable part of mankind is not ambitious; many have begun to be such but by the means of some undertakings and ties that have determined them before they seriously reflected on what they did, and that have made them unfit ever to return to calmer inclinations; and even those who have most ambition do often complain of the cares which it exacts and the pains that attend it. The reason of this is that the native laziness of which we were speaking is not wholly suppressed, though it has been sacrificed to that presumptuous tyrant of the mind; it proved the weakest, and could not overbalance its rival, yet it still subsists and continually opposes the motions of ambition. Now no man can be happy while he is divided by two warring inclinations.

However, I do not say that men can relish a state of absolute laziness and idleness; no, they must have some motion, some agitation; but it must be such a motion and agitation as may be reconciled, if possible, to the kind of laziness that possesses them; and this is most happily to be found in love, provided it be taken in a certain manner. It must neither be a hot, jealous, touchy, furious, desperate love, but tender, pure, simple, delicate, faithful, and, that it may preserve itself in this state, attended with hopes. Then the heart is taken up but not disturbed; we have cares but no uneasinesses; we are moved but not torn; and this soft motion is just such as the love of rest and our native laziness can bear it.

Besides, it is most certain that love is the most general and the most agreeable of all the passions. So in the state of life which we have now described there is a concurrence of the two strongest passions, laziness and love, which thus are both satisfied at once; and that we may be as happy as it is possible we should by the passions, it is necessary that all those by which we are moved agree together in us.

This is properly what we conceive of a pastoral life. For it admits of no ambition, nor of anything that moves the heart with too much violence; therefore our laziness has cause to be contented. But this way of living, by reason of its idleness and tranquillity, creates love more easily than any other, or at least indulges it more. But after all, what love! A love more innocent because the mind is not so dangerously refined, more assiduous because those who feel it are not diverted by any other passions, more full of discretion because they hardly have any acquaintance with vanity, more faithful because, with a vivacity of imagination less used, they have also less uneasiness, less distaste, and less fickleness; that is to say, in short, a love purged of whatever the excesses of human fancy have sophisticated it with.[5]

This considered, it is not to be admired why the pictures which are drawn of a pastoral life have always something so very smiling in them, and indulge our fancies more than the pompous description of a splendid court, and of all the magnificence that can shine there. A court gives us no idea but of toilsome and constrained pleasures. For, as we have observed, the idea is all in all.[6] Could the scene of this quiet life, with no other business but love, be placed anywhere but in the country, so that no goats nor sheep should be brought in, I fancy it would be never the worse, for the goats and sheep add nothing to its felicity; but as the scene must lie either in the country or in towns, it seems more reasonable to choose the first.

As the pastoral life is the most idle of all others, it is also the most fit to be the groundwork of those ingenious representations of which we are speaking. So that no ploughmen, reapers, vine-dressers, or huntsmen can by any means be so properly introduced in eclogues as shepherds; which confirms what I said, that what makes this kind of poetry please is not its giving an image of a country life, but rather the idea which it gives of the tranquillity and innocence of that life.

Yet there is an idyllium of Battus and Milo, two reapers in Theocritus, which has beauties. Milo asks Battus why he does not reap as fast as he used to do. He answers that he is in love, and then sings something that is very pretty about the woman that he loves. But Milo laughs at him, and tells him he is a fool for being so idle as to be in love; that this is not an employment fit for one who works for food; and that, to divert himself and excite one another to work, he should sing some songs which he denotes to him, and which altogether relate to the harvest. I must needs own that I do not so well like this conclusion. For I would not be drawn from a pleasing and soft idea to another that is low and without charms.

Sannazarius has introduced none but fishermen in his eclogues,[7] and I always perceive when I read those piscatory poems that the idea I have of fishermen's hard and toilsome way of living shocks me. I don't know what moved him to bring in fishermen instead of shepherds, who were in possession of the eclogue time out of mind; but had the fishermen been in possession of it, it had been necessary to put the shepherds in their place. For singing and above all an idle life becomes none but shepherds. Besides, methinks it is prettier and more genteel to send flowers or fruit to one's mistress than send her oysters, as Sannazarius's Lyco doth to his.

It is true that Theocritus hath an idyllium of two fishermen, but it doth not seem to me so beautiful as to have deserved to tempt any man to write one of that kind. The subject of it is this: two old fishermen had but sparingly supped together in a wretched little thatched house by the seaside. One of them wakes his bedfellow to tell him he had just dreamt that he was catching a golden fish, and the other answers him that he might starve [even] though he had really caught such a one. Was this worth writing an eclogue!

However, though none but shepherds were introduced in eclogues, it is impossible but that the life of shepherds, which after all is yet very clownish, must lessen and debase their wit, and hinder their being as ingenious, nice, and full of gallantry as they are commonly represented in pastorals. The famous Lord d'Urfé's *L'Astrée* seems a less fabulous romance than *Amadis de Gaule*;[8] yet I fancy that in the main it is as incredible as to the politeness and graces of his shepherds as *Amadis* can be as to all its enchantments, all its fairies, and the extravagance of its adventures. How comes it then that pastorals please in spite of the falsity of the characters, which ought always to shock us? Could we be pleased with seeing some courtiers represented as having a clownishness which should resemble that of real shepherds as much as the gallantry which shepherds have in pastorals resembles that of courtiers? No, doubtless; but indeed that character of the shepherds is not false after all, if we look upon it one way. For we do not mind the meanness of the concerns that are their real employment, but the little trouble those concerns bring. This meanness would wholly exclude ornaments and gallantry, but on the other hand the quiet state promotes them; and it is only on that tranquillity that whatever pleases in a pastoral life is grounded.

Our imagination is not to be pleased without truth, but it is not very hard to please it, for often it is satisfied with a kind of half truth. Let it see only the half of a thing, but let that half be shown in a lively manner, then it will hardly bethink itself that you hide from it the other half; and you may thus deceive it as long as you please, since all the while it imagines that this single moiety, with the thoughts of which it is taken up, is the whole thing. The illusion and at the same time the pleasingness of pastorals therefore consists in exposing to the eye only the tranquility of a shepherd's life, and in dissembling or concealing its meanness, as also in showing only its innocence and hiding its miseries; so that I do not comprehend why Theocritus dwelt so much upon its miseries and clownishness.

If those who are resolved to find no faults in the ancients tell us that Theocritus had a mind to draw nature just such as it is, I hope that according to those principles we shall have some idyllia of porters or watermen discoursing together of their particular concerns, which will be every whit as good as some idyllia of shepherds speaking of nothing but their goats or their cows.

The business is not purely to describe; we must describe such objects as are delightful. When the quiet that reigns in the country, and the simplicity and tenderness which [are] discovered there in making love, are represented to me, my imagination, moved and affected with these pleasing ideas, is fond of a shepherd's life; but though the vile and low employments of shepherds were described to me with all the exactness possible, I should never be taken with them, and my imagination would not in the least be touched. The chief advantage of poetry consists in representing to us in a lively manner the things that concern us, and in striking strongly a heart which is pleased with being moved.

Here's enough and perhaps too much against these shepherds of Theocritus, and those who, like them, have too much of the shepherd in them. What we have left of Moschus and Bion in the pastoral kind makes me extremely lament what we have lost of theirs. They have no manner of rusticity, but rather a great deal of delicacy and grace, and some ideas wholly new and pleasing. They are accused of being too florid, and I do not deny but that they may be said to be such in some few places; yet I don't know why the critics are more inclined to excuse Theocritus's clownishness than Moschus and Bion's elegancy; methinks they should have done the contrary. Is it not that Virgil has prejudiced everyone for Theocritus, having done to no other the honor of imitating and copying him? Or is it not rather than the learned have a taste [accustomed to disdaining] what is delicate and genteel? Whatever it is, I find that all their favor is for Theocritus, and that they have resolved to dub him prince of the bucolic poets.

The moderns have not often been guilty of making their shepherds thus clownish. The author of *L'Astrée*, in that romance which otherwise is full of admirable things, has rather run into the other extreme. Some of his shepherds are absolutely drawn such as they ought to have been, but some others, if I am not mistaken, might better have been placed in *Le Grand Cyrus* or in *Cléopâtre*. These shepherds often seem to me courtiers dis-

guised in a pastoral dress, and ill mimics of what they would imitate; sometimes they appear to me most cavilling sophisters. For though none but
Sylvandre has studied in the school of the Massilians, there are some
others who happen to be as full of subtlety as himself, though I don't comprehend how they could even but understand him, not having like him took
their degrees in the Massilian schools.

It does not belong to shepherds to speak of all sorts of matters, and when
a poet has a mind to raise his style, he may make use of other persons.
When Virgil desired to give a pompous description of the imaginary return
of the Golden Age, which he promises to the world at the birth of Pollio's
son, he should not have excited the pastoral muses to leave their natural
strain and raise their voices to a pitch which they can never reach; his business was to have left them, and have addressed himself to some others. Yet
I do not know after all if it had not been better to have kept to the pastoral
muses, for he might have given a pleasing description of the good which
the return of peace was ready to cause in the country; and this, methinks,
had been as acceptable at least as all those incomprehensible wonders
which he borrows of the Cumaean Sibyl, this new race of men which is to
descend from heaven, these grapes which are to grow on briars, and these
lambs whose native fleece is to be of a scarlet or crimson hue to save mankind the trouble of dyeing the wool. He might have flattered Pollio more
agreeably with things that might have seemed more consistent with it, at
least to the party concerned; for praise is seldom thought such by those on
whom it is lavished.

Shall I dare to say that Calpurnius, an author much inferior to Virgil,
seems to have handled a subject of the same nature much more to the purpose? Take notice that I only speak of the design or fable, and not at all of
the style. He brings in two shepherds, who to be screened from the sun's
sultry heat shelter themselves in a cave, where they find some verses written
with the god Faunus's own hand, which contain a prophecy about the happiness which the Roman Empire is to enjoy under the Emperor Carus. According to the duty of a pastoral poet, he dwells sufficiently on the
prosperity and plenty that relates to the country, and then proceeds to
higher matters, because, as he makes a god speak, he has a right to do so;
but he brings in nothing like the Sibyl's prophecies.

It is pity that Virgil did not write the verses of this piece; neither had
there been need to have had them all written by him.

Virgil makes Phoebus say to him at the beginning of his Sixth Eclogue that a shepherd ought not to sing kings nor wars, but to stick to his flocks, and such subjects as only require a plain style. Without doubt Phoebus's counsel was very good, but I cannot imagine how Virgil could forget it so much as to fall a-singing, immediately after, the original of the world and the framing of the universe according to Epicurus's system, which was a great deal worse than to sing kings and wars. I must needs own that I cannot in the least tell what to make of this piece; I do not understand what is the design, nor what coherence there is between the several parts of it. For after these philosophical notions we have the fables of Hylas and Pasiphae and of Phaeton's sisters, which have no manner of relation to them; and in the middle of these fables, which are all borrowed from very remote times, we have Cornelius Gallus, Virgil's contemporary, and the honors which he receives on Parnassus; after which we presently come to the fables of Scylla and Philomela. It is honest Silenus that gives all this fine medley, and, as Virgil tells us that according to his laudable custom he had taken a hearty carouse the day before, I am afraid the fumes were hardly yet got out of his head.

Here let me once more take the freedom to own that I like better the design of an eclogue of this kind by Nemesianus, [9] an author who was Calpurnius's contemporary, and who is not altogether to be despised. Some shepherds, finding Pan asleep, try to play on his pipe; but as a mortal can make a god's pipe yield only a very unpleasing sound, Pan is awaked by it, and tells them that if they are for songs he'll gratify them presently. With this he sings to them something of the history of Bacchus, and dwells on the first vintage that ever was made, of which he gives a description which seems to me very agreeable. This design is more regular than that of Virgil's Silenus, and the verses also are pretty good.

The moderns have been often guilty of handling high subjects in their eclogues. The French poet Ronsard has given us in his the praises of princes and of France, and almost all that looks like bucolic in them is his calling Henry II Henriot [or Harry], Charles IX Carlin [or Charlie], and Queen Catharine de Medicis Catin [or Kate]. It is true that he owns that he did not follow the rules, but it had been better to have done it, and thus have avoided the ridicule which the disproportion that is between the subject and the form of the work produces. Hence it happens that in his first eclogue it falls to the lot of the shepherdess Margot to sing the elegy of Turnebus, Budaeus, and Vatable, [10] the greatest men of their age for Greek and Hebrew, but with whom certainly Peg ought not have been acquainted.

349

Because shepherds look well in some kinds of poetry, many writers prostitute them to every subject. They are often made to sing the praises of kings in the sublimest style the poet can write, and provided he has but talked of oaten pipes, meads, and plains, fern or grass, streams or valleys, he thinks he has written an eclogue. When shepherds praise a hero they should praise him shepherd-like, and I do not doubt but that this would be very ingenious and taking; but it would require some art, and the shortest cut, it seems, is to make the shepherds speak the common dialect of praise, which is very big and lofty indeed, but very common, and consequently easy enough of conscience.

Allegorical eclogues also are not very easy. J. B. Mantuanus, who was a Carmelite friar, has one in which two shepherds dispute, the one representing a Carmelite friar who is of that party of the order which they call *the strict observance*, and the other of that which they call the *mitigated*. The famous Bembus is their judge, and it is worth observing that he prudently makes them lay down their crooks lest they fall together by the ears.

Now though in the main our Mantuan has pretty well kept the allegory, it is too ridiculous to find the controversy between these two sorts of Carmelitans handled ecloguewise.

Yet I had rather see a shepherd represent one of these than have him act the Epicurean and say impious things; it is what happens sometimes to some of Mantuanus's shepherds, though they are very clownish, and he himself was of a religious order. Amyntas, one of them, in an angry fit which makes him rail against the laws and virtue merely because he is in love, says that men are great fools to feed themselves up with a fancy of being taken up to heaven after their death, and he adds that the most that is like to happen then is that they may chance to transmigrate into some birds and so flutter up and down through the air. In vain to make this excusable, our friar says that Amyntas had lived a long time in town; and as much in vain Badius his commentator — for as much a modern as Mantuanus is, he has one, and as bigoted and hot for his author as those of the ancients — in vain, I say, he takes from thence an opportunity to make this rare reflection, that love causes us to doubt of matters of faith. It is certain that these errors, which ought to be detested by all those who have heard of them, ought not to be known, much less mentioned by shepherds.

To make amends, sometimes our Mantuan makes his shepherds mighty godly. In one of his eclogues you have a catalogue of all the Virgin Mary's holidays; in another an apparition of the Virgin, who promises a shepherd

350

that when he shall have passed his life on Mount Carmel she'll take him to a more pleasant place, and will make him dwell in heaven with the dryads and hamadryads, a sort of new-fashioned saints whom we did not yet know in heaven.

Such gross and inexcusable indecencies may be easily avoided in the character of shepherds, but there are some that are not so observable, of which some writers cannot so easily be freed: it is the making their shepherds speak too wittily. Sometimes even those of the Marquess de Racan [11] are guilty of this, though they generally use to be very reserved in that point. As for the Italian authors, they are also so full of false and pointed thoughts that we must resolve, right or wrong, to give them leave to indulge themselves in that darling style of theirs, as natural to them as their mother tongue. They never take the pains to make their shepherds speak in a pastoral style, but make use of as bold and exaggerated figures, and are as full of conceits in that sort of poetry, as they are in others.

Father Bouhours, in his excellent treatise *Of the Manner of Thinking Justly in Ingenious Composures*, finds fault with Tasso's Sylvia, who, seeing the reflection of her face in a fountain and adorning herself with flowers, tells them she does not wear them to mend her beauty, but to lessen them and disgrace them by being placed near her brighter charms. Our judicious critic thinks this thought too full of affectation, and not natural enough for a shepherdess, and none can refuse their assent to this criticism, which is the result of a very delicate taste. But when this is done, let none give themselves the trouble of reading Guarini's, Bonarelli's, and Marini's pastoral poetry with a design to find anything in them truly pastoral, for Sylvia's thought is one of the most unaffected and simple things in the world, if compared to most of those of which these authors are full.[12]

And indeed Tasso's *Amynta* is the best thing that Italy has produced in the pastoral kind, and has certainly very great beauties; even the passage of Sylvia, except what we have observed in it, is one of the most ingenious and best-described things I ever read, and we ought to own ourselves extremely obliged to an Italian author for not having been more prodigal of pointed thoughts.[13]

Monsieur de Segrais, whose works are the most excellent pattern we have of pastoral poetry, owns himself that he did not always keep exactly to the style which it requires.[14] He says that he has sometimes been obliged to humor the genius of this age, which delights in figures and glittering things. But this must be said on his behalf, that he only condescended to

351

follow this method after he had sufficiently proved that he could when he pleased perfectly hit the true beauties of pastoral. After all, none can well tell which is the taste or genius of this age; it is not determined either what is good or bad, but seems wavering sometimes on this and sometimes on that side. So I believe that, since there is still a hazard to be run whatever side we take, it were better to follow the rules and true ideas of things.

Between the usual clownishness of Theocritus's shepherds and the too much wit of most of our modern shepherds, a certain medium should be kept, but it is so far from being easily followed in the performance that it is even difficult to denote it. The shepherds ought to have wit, and it ought to be fine and genteel too, for they could not please without it; but they ought to have that wit only in a certain degree, otherwise they are no more shepherds. I'll endeavor to determine this degree, and adventure to give my notion of it.

The men who have the most wit and those who have but an indifferent share of it do not differ so much in the sense which they have of things as they do in their manner of expressing it. The passions, amidst all the disturbance which they cause, are attended by a kind of light which they impart almost equally to all those whom they possess. There is a certain penetration, certain ideas, which, without any regard to the difference of the minds, are always found in men in whatever concerns and affects them. But these passions, at the same time that they in a manner inform the mind of all men alike, do not enable them to speak equally well. Those whose mind is more refined, more capacious, and more improved by study or conversation do, while they express their sentiments, add something that hath the air of a reflection, and that is not inspired by the passion alone; whereas the others speak their minds more simply, and add in a manner nothing that is foreign. Any ordinary man will easily say, "I so passionately desired that my mistress might be faithful that I believed her such"; but it only belongs to a refined wit, as the Duke de la Rochefoucauld, to say, "My understanding was fooled by my will," or, "My reason was cullied by my desire [l'esprit a été en moi la dupe du coeur]." The sense is the same, the penetration equal, but the expression is so different that one would almost think it is no more the same thing.

We take no less pleasure in finding a sentiment expressed simply than in a more thoughtlike and elaborate manner, provided it be always equally fine. Nay, the simple way of expressing it ought to please more, because it occasions a kind of gentle surprise and a final admiration. We are amazed to find something that is fine and delicate in common and unaffected terms; and on that account the more the thing is fine without ceasing to be natural, and the expression common without being low, the deeper we ought to be struck.

Admiration and surprise are so powerful that they can even raise the value of things beyond their intrinsic worth. All Paris has lavished exclamations of admiration on the Siamese ambassadors for their ingenious sayings.[15] Now had some Spanish or English ambassadors spoken the same things, nobody would have minded it. This happened because we wrongfully supposed that some men who came from the remotest part of the world, of a tawny complexion, dressed otherwise than we are, and till then esteemed barbarians by those of Europe, were not to be endowed with common sense; and we were very much surprised to find they had it, so that the least thing they said filled us with admiration, an admiration which after all was injurious enough to those gentlemen.

The same happens of our shepherds, for we are the more pleasingly struck with finding them thinking finely in their simple style because we the least expected it.

Another thing that suits with the pastoral style is to run only on actions, and never almost on reflections. Those who have a middling share of wit, or a wit but little improved by a converse with polite books or persons, use to discourse only of those particular things of which they have had a sense, while others, raising themselves higher, reduce all things into general ideas. The minds of the latter have worked and reflected upon their sentiments and experiments; it happens that what they have seen hath led them to what they have not seen; whereas those of an inferior order, not pursuing their ideas beyond what they have a sense of, it may happen that what resembles it most may still be new to them. Hence proceeds the insatiable desire of the multitude to see the same objects, and their admiring always almost the same things.

A consequence of this disposition of mind is the adding to the things that are related any circumstances, whether useful or not. This happens because the mind has been extremely struck with the particular action, and with all that attended it. Contrary to this a great genius, despising all these petty circumstances, fixes on what is most essential in things, which commonly may be related without the circumstances.

It is truer than it seems that in such composures wherein passion is to be described it is better to imitate the way of speaking used by men of in-

353

different capacity than the style of more refined wits. I must own that thus there is little related besides actions, and we do not rise to reflections, but nothing is more graceful than actions so displayed as to bring their reflection along with them. Such is this admirable touch in Virgil: "Galatea throws an apple at me, then runs to hide herself behind the willows, and first would be perceived." The shepherd does not tell you what is Galatea's design, though he is fully sensible of it; but the action has made a deep, pleasing impression on his mind, and according as he represents it, it is impossible but you must guess its meaning. Now the mind is delighted with sensible ideas because it easily admits of them, and it loves to penetrate, provided it be without effort; whether it be that it loves to act but to a certain degree, or that a little penetration indulges its vanity. So the mind hath the double pleasure, first of getting an easy idea, then of penetrating, whenever such cases as that of Galatea are laid before it. The action and in a manner the soul of the action all at once strike the eyes of the mind; it can see nothing more in the matter, nor more quickly; neither can it ever be put to less expense.

In Virgil's Second Eclogue, Corydon, to commend his pipe, tells us that Damaetas gave it him when he died, and said to him, "Thou art the second master it hath had," and Amyntas was jealous because it was not bequeathed him. All these circumstances are altogether pastoral. It might not perhaps be disagreeable to bring in a shepherd who is puzzled in the midst of his story, and who finds some difficulty in recovering himself; but this would require some art in the management.

There are no persons whom it becomes better to lengthen a little their narrations with circumstances than lovers. They ought not indeed to be absolutely needless or too far-fetched, for this would be tedious, though it may be natural enough; but those that have but a half relation to the action which is talked of, and that show more passion than they are considerable, can never fail to please. So when, in one of Monsieur de Segrais's eclogues, a shepherdess says,

> The songs which Lysis and Menalcas sing
> Please ev'ry swain, and make the valleys ring;
> But I like better those which near this tree
> My jealous shepherd lately made for me.

The circumstance of the [tree] is pretty only as it had been needless for any other but a lover. According to our idea of shepherds, tales and narrations become them very well; but for them to make speeches such as those in *L'Astrée*, full of general reflections and chains of arguments, is a thing which I do not think their character allows.

It is not amiss to make them give descriptions, provided they be not very long. That of the cup which the goatherd promises to Thyrsis in Theocritus's first idyllium somewhat exceeds the bounds. Yet, according to that example, Ronsard and Belleau, his contemporary, have made some that are yet longer. When their shepherds are about describing a basket, a goat, or a blackbird, which they make the prize of a pastoral combat, they never have done. Not that their descriptions are sometimes without great beauties, and are writ without admirable art; far from this, they have too much of it for shepherds.

Vida, a Latin poet of the last age and of great reputation, in his eclogue of Nicé, whom I take to be Vittoria Colonna, the Marquess of Pescario's widow, brings in the shepherd Damon giving a description of a rush basket which he is to make for her. He says that he will represent in it Davalos, that is the marquess, dying, and grieved that he does not die in battle; some kings, captains, and nymphs in tears about him, Nicé praying the gods in vain, Nicé fainting away at the news of Davalos's death, and with difficulty recovering her senses by the means of the water which her women throw on her face; and he adds that he would have expressed many complaints and moans if they could be expressed on rush. Here are a great many things to be showed on a basket! Neither do I relate them all; but I cannot tell how all this can be expressed on rush, nor how Damon, who owns he cannot express on it the complaints of Nicé is not at a loss to display on it the marquess's grief for dying in his bed. I shrewdly suspect that Achilles's shield is the original from which this basket has been imitated.

I find that Virgil has used similitudes very often in his pastoral discourses. These similitudes are very properly brought in to supply the place of those trivial comparisons, and principally of those clownish proverbial sayings, which real shepherds use almost continually. But as there is nothing more easily to be imitated than this way of using similitudes, it is what Virgil hath been most copied in. We find in all your writers of eclogues, nothing more common than shepherdesses who exceed all others as much "as lofty pines o'ertop the lowly reed, or highest oaks the humblest shrubs exceed"; we see nothing but the cruelty of ungrateful shepherdesses who are to a shepherd "what frosts or storms are to the tenderest flowers, like hail to rip'ning corn, etc." I think all this old and worn threadbare at this time of day, and to say the truth on it, it is no great pity. Similitudes naturally are not very proper for passion, and shepherds should only use them when they find it difficult to express themselves otherwise; then they would have a very great beauty; but I know but very few of that kind.

Thus we have pretty near discovered the pitch of wit which shepherds ought to have, and the style they should use. It is methinks with eclogues as with those dresses which are worn at masques or balls; they are of much finer stuff than those which real shepherds usually wear; nay, they are even adorned with ribbands and points, and are only made after the country cut. In the same manner the thoughts which are the subject matter of eclogues ought to be finer and more delicate than those of real shepherds, but they must have the most simple and most rural dress possible.

Not but that we ought to use both simplicity and a country-like plainness even in the thoughts, but we ought to take notice that this simplicity and country-like plainness only exclude your excessive delicacy in the thoughts, like that of the refined wits in courts and cities, and not the light which nature and the passions bestow of themselves; otherwise the poet would degenerate and run into childish talk that would beget laughter rather than admiration. Something of this kind is pleasant enough in one of Rémi Belleau's eclogues, where a young shepherd, having stolen a kiss from a pretty shepherdess, says to her,

> I've kissed some new-fawned kids, like other swains,
> I've kissed the sucking calf, which in our plains
> Young Colin gave me; but this kiss, I swear,
> Is sweeter much than all those kisses were.

Yet such a childishness seems more pardonable in this young shepherd than in the Cyclops Polyphemus. In Theocritus's idyllium that bears his name, and which is fine, he is thinking how to be revenged on his mother, a sea nymph, because she never took care to make Galatea, another sea nymph, have a kindness for his giantship; so he says to his mistress that he'll tell his mother, to make her mad, that he has a pain in his head and in his thighs.

It is hard to imagine that, ugly as he was, his mother could dote on him so much as to be very much concerned to hear the poor little urchin have those petty ills, or that the clownish giant could invent so gentle a revenge; his character is better kept when he promises his mistress to make her a present of a litter of cubs or young bears, which he breeds for her in his cave. And now that I speak of bears, I would gladly know why Daphnis when he is going to die bids adieu to the bears, the lions, and the wolves, as well as to the fair fountain Arethuse, and to the silver streams of Sicily. Methinks a man does not often use to regret the loss of such company.

I have but one remark more to make, which hath no manner of connection with those that go before. It is concerning those eclogues which have a burthen much like those in ballads, that is, a verse or two repeated several times. I need not say that we ought to place those repeated verses in such parts of the eclogue as may require, or at least bear such a verse to interlard them; but it may not be amiss to observe that all the art that Theocritus hath used in an idyllium of this kind was only to take this burthen and scatter it up and down through his idyllium, right or wrong, without the least regard to the sense of the places where he inserted it, nay, without even so much as respecting some of the phrases which he made no difficulty to split in two.

I have here spoken with a great deal of freedom of Theocritus and Virgil, notwithstanding they are ancients, and I do not doubt but that I shall be esteemed one of the profane by those pedants who profess a kind of religion which consists in worshipping the ancients. It is true, however, that I have often commended Virgil and Theocritus, but yet I have not always praised them; much less have I said, like the superstitious, that even their faults (if they had any) were beautiful; neither have I strained all the natural light of reason to justify them. I have partly approved and partly censured them, as if they have been some living authors whom I saw every day, and there lies the sacrilege! [16]

Bernard Le Bovier de Fontenelle A DIGRESSION

ON THE ANCIENTS AND THE MODERNS

Once the whole question of the pre-eminence of the ancients and moderns is properly understood, it boils down to knowing whether the trees which used to be seen in the countryside were taller than those of today.[17] If they were, Homer, Plato, Demosthenes cannot be equaled in these latter centuries; but if our trees are as tall as those of former times, then we can equal Homer, Plato, and Demosthenes.

Let us explain this paradox. If the ancients were more intelligent than we, the reason must be that brains in those days were better arranged, made of firmer or more delicate fibers, and filled with more animal spirits;[18] but why should the brains of those days have been better arranged? Trees too, then, would have been taller and more beautiful; for if Nature was then younger and more vigorous, trees as well as human brains must have felt the effect of that vigor and youth.

The admirers of the ancients ought to be very careful when they tell us that the ancients are the sources of good taste and reason as well as of knowledge destined to illuminate all other men; that one is intelligent only in proportion as one admires them; and that Nature wore herself out in producing those great originals; for in fact these admirers make the ancients of another species from ourselves, and science is not in agreement with all these fine phrases. Nature has at hand a certain clay which is always the same and which she unendingly turns and twists into a thousand different shapes, thus forming men, animals, and plants; and certainly she did not shape Plato, Demosthenes, or Homer from finer or better-prepared clay than she used for our philosophers, orators, and poets of today. As to our minds, which are not of a material nature, I am concerned here only with their connection with the brain (which is material) and which by its varying arrangements produces the differences between one man and another.

358

But if trees are equally tall in all centuries they are not so in all countries. Similar differences occur also among minds. The various ideas are like plants or flowers which do not flourish equally in all climates.[19] Perhaps French soil is not suitable for Egyptian lines of thought as it is not for their palm trees; and not to go so far afield, perhaps orange trees, which do not grow so well here as in Italy, are an indication that in Italy there is a certain kind of mind which does not have its exact equal in France. In any case it is sure that through the connection and reciprocal interdependence which exist among the parts of the material world, the differences of climate, whose effect is observable in plants, must produce some effect on human brains as well.[20]

However, this effect is smaller and less obvious because art and culture work more successfully on brains than on the land, which is of a harder and less manipulable substance. Thus the thoughts of one country can be more easily carried to another than its plants, and we would not have as much difficulty in capturing the Italian genius in our literary works as we would have in raising orange trees.

It is ordinarily said that there is more diversity among minds than among faces. I am not so sure. Faces, merely because they look at each other, do not come to look like each other; but minds develop resemblances as a result of reciprocal contacts. Thus minds, which naturally would differ as much as faces, come to differ less.

The ease with which minds use each other for models produces the result that nations do not persevere in whatever habits of thought they derive from their climate. The reading of Greek books produces in us proportionately the same effect as if we were to marry Greek women. It is certain that after many alliances of this kind the blood of Greece and that of France would be changed and the facial expression peculiar to each of the two nations would be somewhat altered.

What is more, since it is not possible to judge which climates are the most favorable for the mind, and since they all apparently have complementary advantages and disadvantages, and since those climates which of themselves would give a higher degree of liveliness would also produce less precision (and so on for the other pairs of good and bad qualities), it follows that the differences between climates must be counted for nothing provided minds are otherwise equally cultivated. At the very most one might think that the torrid zone and the two frigid zones are not well adapted to learning.[21] Up to the present day education has not gone farther than Egypt and Mauritania in one direction and Sweden in the other; perhaps it is not by chance that learning has been restricted to the area between the Atlas Mountains and the Baltic Sea; but we do not know whether these are the limits which nature has set for it or whether we may hope some day to see great Negro or Lapp authors.

However that may be, the main question concerning the ancients and the moderns now seems to me resolved. Centuries do not put any natural differences among men. The climate of Greece or Italy and that of France are too much alike to be the cause of a perceptible difference between the Greeks and the Romans and ourselves. Even if some such difference existed it would be very easy to eliminate, and after all would be no more to their advantage than to ours. So we are now all perfectly equal, ancients and moderns, Greeks, Romans, and Frenchmen.

I cannot guarantee that this reasoning will seem convincing to everybody. If I had used the great tricks of eloquence, if I had balanced facts of history favorable to the moderns with facts of history favorable to the ancients, and passages praising the ones with passages praising the others, if I had called "obstinate pedants" those who call us "ignorant and superficial thinkers"; and if according to the code established among men of letters I had given back exactly insult for insult to the partisans of the ancients, perhaps my proofs would have been more to the common taste; but it seemed to me that if the business were gone about that way it would never end, and after many fine declamations on either side we should be amazed to see that we had not advanced one step. I thought it would be quicker to consult science on this question, for science has the secret of shortening many of the disputes which rhetoric makes endless.

On this subject, for instance, after we have recognized the equality existing between the ancients and ourselves, there remains no further difficulty. It is obvious that all the differences, whatever they may be, must be caused by exterior circumstances, such as the historical moment, the government, and the state of things in general.

"The ancients discovered everything"; on this point their partisans triumph. "Therefore they were much more intelligent than we"; not at all, but they were ahead of us. I should be just as willing to see them praised for having drunk first the waters of our rivers and for us to be blamed because we drink only what they left. If we had been in their place we would have done the discovering; if they were in ours, they would add to what has already been discovered. There is no great mystery about that.

360

I am not speaking here of the discoveries brought about by chance and for which credit may perhaps be given to the stupidest man in the world; I am concerned only with those discoveries which required thought and some mental effort. It is sure that the crudest of these were reserved for the greatest geniuses, and that all Archimedes could have done in the earliest ages would have been to invent the plough. Archimedes living in another century burns the Roman fleet with mirrors — if indeed that is not just a tale.

A man concerned to utter specious and brilliant remarks would maintain to the glory of the moderns that the mind need not make a great effort for first discoveries, and that Nature seems herself to lead us to them; but more effort is needed to add to them and a still greater effort in proportion to the amount already added because the subject is more nearly exhausted and what remains in it to be discovered is less apparent to the naked eye. Perhaps the admirers of the ancients would not neglect a line of reasoning as good as that if it favored their side, but I admit in all good faith that it is not very solid.

It is true that to add to earlier discoveries often requires a greater effort of mind than the original discoveries did, but one is in a much more advantageous position to make the effort. The mind has already been enlightened by the very discoveries one has before one's eyes; we have conceptions borrowed from others which can be added to those we form ourselves; and if we surpass the first discoverer, he himself has helped us to do so; thus he still has a share in the glory of our work, and if he withdrew what belongs to him we should have nothing more left than he.

So far do I carry the equity with which I consider this point that I give the ancients credit for numberless false ideas they had, for faults of logic they committed, and for foolish statements they made. In the nature of things it is not given to us to arrive quickly at a reasonable opinion on anything; we must first wander about for a long time and pass through many kinds of mistakes and many kinds of irrelevancies. It seems now that it would always have been easy to conceive the idea that the whole working of nature is explained by the shapes and movements of various bodies; however, before arriving at that point we had first to try the ideas of Plato, the numbers of Pythagoras, and the qualities of Aristotle; only when these had been recognized as false were we driven to accept the correct theory. I say we were driven to it, for in fact no other remained, and it seems that we avoided the truth as long as we could. We are grateful to the ancients for having worn out most of the false ideas conceivable; it was absolutely necessary to pay to ignorance and error the tribute the ancients paid, and we ought not to be harsh towards those who discharged this debt for us. The same thing is true of various subjects about which we would say foolish things if they had not already been said and, so to speak, preempted; however there still are occasionally moderns who return to them, perhaps because these things have not yet been said as many times as necessary. Thus, enlightened by the ideas of the ancients and by their very mistakes, we might be expected to surpass them. If we only equaled them we should be far inferior to them by nature; we should barely be men compared with them.

However, if the moderns are to be able to improve continually on the ancients, the fields in which they are working must be of a kind which allows progress. Eloquence and poetry require only a certain number of rather narrow ideas as compared with other arts, and they depend for their effect primarily upon the liveliness of the imagination. Now mankind could easily amass in a few centuries a small number of ideas, and liveliness of imagination has no need of a long sequence of experiences nor of many rules before it reaches the furthest perfection of which it is capable. But science, medicine, mathematics, are composed of numberless ideas and depend upon precision of thought which improves with extreme slowness; sometimes indeed these studies must be helped by experiences which chance alone brings forth and which it does not produce at the desired place. It is obvious that all this is endless and that the last physicists or mathematicians will naturally have to be the ablest.

And in fact, the most important aspect of philosophy, and that which is applicable not only to philosophy but to everything, I mean the way we think, has been very much improved in this century. I doubt that many will be able to understand the remark I am about to make; nevertheless I shall make it for the sake of those who understand the problem of philosophical thought; and I may boast that it is evidence of courage to expose oneself for the sake of truth to the criticisms of all the others, whose number is assuredly not negligible. No matter what the subject is, the ancients rarely reason with absolute correctness. Often mere expediency, petty similarities, frivolous witticisms, or vague and confused discourse pass among them for proofs; therefore, it cost them very little effort to prove anything. However, what an ancient could prove in all frivolity would cause a good deal of trouble nowadays to a modern, for are we not much

362

more rigorous in the matter of reasoning? Reasoning must be intelligible, it must be exact, it must be conclusive. Scholars are cunning enough to pick out the slightest ambiguity in ideas or in words; they are harsh enough to condemn the cleverest thing in the world if it does not bear on the point. Before Descartes reasoning was done more comfortably; past centuries are very fortunate not to have had that man. It is he, as I believe, who introduced this new method of reasoning which is much more estimable than his philosophy itself, for of that a considerable part has been shown to be false or uncertain according to the very rules he taught us. In sum, there now reigns not only in our good scientific and philosophical works but also in those on religion, ethics, and criticism a precision and an exactness which have scarcely been known until now.

I am even convinced that these will be carried yet further. A few arguments in the style of the ancients still slip into our best books, but we shall be the ancients some day, and will it not be just for our posterity in its turn to rectify our mistakes and to go beyond us, especially in the technique of reasoning which is a science in itself and the most difficult as well as the least cultivated of all?

As far as eloquence and poetry are concerned, since these are the subject of the principal dispute between the ancients and the moderns although they are not very important in themselves, I think the ancients may have attained perfection in them because, as I have said, such perfection can be achieved in a few centuries, and I do not know exactly how many are necessary. I say that the Greeks and the Romans may have been excellent poets and orators, but were they? Clarification of this point would require an endless discussion which, however just and exact it might be, would never satisfy the partisans of the ancients. How can one debate with them? They have resolved to excuse all the faults of the ancients. What am I saying, to "excuse" them? They are determined to admire those faults above all else. This is the particular characteristic of textual commentators, the most superstitious of all the groups which are swayed by the cult of antiquity. What charming ladies would not be happy to inspire in their lovers a passion as intense and as tender as that which a Greek or Roman author inspires in his respectful commentator?

Nevertheless I shall say something more precise about the eloquence and the poetry of the ancients, not that I am unaware of the danger which lurks in such a declaration, but because it seems to me that the slight authority I have and the little attention people will pay to my opinions set me at liberty to say whatever I want. I think eloquence was further developed among the ancients than poetry, and that Demosthenes and Cicero are more perfect in their art than Homer and Virgil in theirs. I see an entirely natural reason for this. Eloquence was the key to success in the Greek and Roman republics, and it was as advantageous to be born with the talent for speaking well as it would be today to be born with an income of a million a year. Poetry, on the other hand, was good for nothing, as it has always been under all kinds of governments; that failing is of the essence of poetry. I think too that in both poetry and eloquence the Greeks are inferior to the Romans. I shall make an exception for one kind of poetry wherein the Romans have nothing to compare with the Greeks; I am, of course, speaking of tragedy. To my individual taste Cicero is better than Demosthenes, Virgil than Theocritus and Homer, Horace than Pindar, Livy and Tacitus than all the Greek historians.

In the light of the theory we established at the beginning, this order is a natural one. The Romans were modern compared to the Greeks, but since eloquence and poetry are rather limited there must have been a time when they were carried to their ultimate perfection; I hold that for eloquence and for history that time was the century of Augustus. I cannot imagine anything surpassing Cicero and Livy. Not that they do not have their faults, but I do not believe it is possible to have fewer faults with so many great qualities, and, as everyone knows, this is the only way in which men may be described as perfect in anything.

Virgil's is the most beautiful versification in the world; perhaps, however, it would not have been harmed if he had had the leisure to touch it up a little. There are great passages in the *Aeneid* of a finished beauty which I do not think will ever be surpassed. Insofar as the structure of the poem as a whole is concerned, or the manner of handling events or of producing agreeable surprises, or the nobility of the characters or the variety of the incidents, I shall not be surprised if Virgil is far surpassed; our novels, which are prose poems, have already shown the possibility of outdoing him.

My intention is not to go into critical detail; I merely wish to point out that since the ancients were able to achieve ultimate perfection in certain things and not in others, we ought, in gauging their success, to show no respect for their great names nor have any indulgence for their faults; we ought, instead, to treat them as though they were moderns. We must be capable of saying, or of hearing others say without blinking the fact, that

364

there are irrelevancies in Homer or in Pindar; we must make bold to believe that mortal eyes can see faults in these great geniuses; we must be able to accept a comparison between Cicero or Demosthenes and a man with a French name, perhaps even a commoner's name: this will require a great, a prodigious effort of the reason!

In this connection I cannot keep from laughing at the ridiculousness of men. Prejudice for prejudice, it would be more reasonable to favor the moderns than the ancients. Naturally the moderns have outdone the ancients: prepossession in their favor is thus well founded. What are, on the other hand, the foundations of prejudice in favor of the ancients? Their names, which sound better in our ears because they are Greek or Latin; the reputation they had of being the greatest men of their century; the number of their admirers, which is very great because it has had time to grow through a long period of years. Taking all that into consideration, it would still be better to be prejudiced in favor of the moderns, but mankind, not content to abandon reason for prejudices, often chooses among these the ones which are the most unreasonable.

Once we have decided that the ancients have reached the point of perfection in something, let us be satisfied to say they cannot be surpassed, but let us not say they cannot be equaled, as their admirers are very prone to do. Why should we not equal them? As men we always have the right to aspire to do so. Is it not odd that we need to prick up our courage on this point and that we, whose vanity is often based on nothing solid, should sometimes show a humility no less insecure? It is thus certain that no manifestation of the ridiculous will be spared us.

No doubt Nature still remembers well how she shaped the head of Cicero and Livy. In every century she produces men fit to be great men, but the historical moment does not always let them use their talents. Inundations of barbarians, governments either wholly opposed or generally unfavorable to the sciences and the arts, prejudices and imaginings which can take endlessly different forms, as in China the respect for dead bodies which prevents all dissections, universal wars — phenomena such as these often put ignorance and bad taste into the saddle, and for a long time. Add to these all the various turns which personal fortune can take, and you will see how vainly Nature sows Ciceros and Virgils in this world, and how rare it must be that some of them, so to speak, yield their fruit. It is said that Heaven, in bringing forth great kings, brings forth also great poets to sing their praises and fine historians to set down their lives. At least this much of that is true: in all periods the historians and the poets are ready, and princes need only want to set them to work.

The barbarous centuries which followed that of Augustus and preceded this one provide the partisans of the ancients with that one among their arguments which seems most sound. How does it happen, they say, that in those centuries ignorance was so thick and so deep? Because the Greeks and Romans were not known in those times and were no longer read; but from the moment that men again perceived those excellent models reason and good taste were reborn. That is true, and yet it proves nothing. If a man having a good start in learning and in literature happened to fall ill of a disease which led him to forget them, would it be right to say that he had become unable to learn them? No, for he could pick them up again at will, beginning with their most elementary aspects. If a medicine suddenly gave him back his memory he would be spared a great deal of trouble, for he would find himself in possession of all he had known before; and to go on he would have only to start again where he had left off. The reading of ancient authors [they say] dissipated the ignorance and barbarism of earlier centuries. I am sure it did. It brought back to us, all of a sudden, ideas of the good and the beautiful which we should otherwise have been a long time in conceiving, but which we would have arrived at in the end without the help of the Greeks and Romans if we had thought diligently enough. And where should we have found them? Where the ancients did. Even the ancients, before they found them, groped about for a long time.

The comparison we have just made between the men of all periods and an individual man may be extended to the whole question of the ancients and the moderns. A cultivated intelligence is composed, so to speak, of all the intelligences of preceding centuries; one intelligence only has been cultivated during all that time. Thus Mankind, which has lived from the beginning of the world to the present day, has had a childhood, during which he concerned himself only with the most pressing needs of life; and a youth, during which he succeeded rather well in the things of the imagination such as poetry and eloquence, and when he even began to think, but with less soundness than enthusiasm. He is now in the prime of life and reasons more forcefully and more incisively than ever; but he would be much farther advanced if the passion of war had not occupied him for a long time and filled him with scorn for that learning to which he has at last returned.

It is a shame not to be able to carry to the end a comparison which is going so well; but I am forced to admit that mankind will never have an old age; in each century men will be able to do the things proper to youth as they will more and more those which are suited to the prime of life; that is to say, to leave the allegory, that mankind will never degenerate, and the sound views of all subsequent thinkers will forever be added to the existing stock.

That endlessly growing stock of ideas to be followed up, of rules to be carried out, also continually increases the difficulty of all branches of the sciences and the arts; but on the other hand, gains are made which compensate for these difficulties. I can best explain by examples. In Homer's time it was a great wonder that a man was able to subject his speech to rhythm, to long and short syllables, and at the same time to make of it something reasonable. Poets were given endless license, and the public was only too glad to have verses at all. Homer might speak five different languages in one line; he might use the Doric dialect when the Ionian was not suitable; if neither suited, he could use the Attic, the Eolic, or the common tongue, that is to say, speak Picard, Gascon, Norman, Breton, and plain French at the same time. He could lengthen a word if it was too short or shorten it if it was too long; nobody found anything to criticize in such procedures. This odd mixture of languages, this outlandish gathering of disfigured words, was the speech of the gods; at least it certainly was not that of men. Bit by bit the ridiculousness of such poetic license was recognized. One by one permissible variants were excluded, and at the present time poets, despoiled of their former privileges, are reduced to speaking in a natural manner. It would seem that the task has grown harder and the difficulty of making verses greater. No, for our minds are enriched with many poetic ideas supplied by our study of the ancients; we are guided by the many rules and reflections which have been made concerning the poetic art, and since Homer lacked all those aids he was justly compensated by the broad poetic license he was allowed. To tell the truth, however, I think his condition better than ours; compensation in these matters is never exact.

Mathematics and physics are sciences whose yoke grows daily heavier on all who practice them; in the end we would be compelled to give up except that methods are improving at the same time; the same intelligence which brings disciplines nearer to perfection by adding new aspects to them also perfects and abridges the manner of learning them and provides new means with which to grasp the wider range which science has. A scientist in our day knows ten times as much as a scientist of the time of Augustus, but he has had ten times as many opportunities of becoming a scientist.

I should like to paint Nature with scales in her hand, like Justice, to indicate how she weighs and measures out almost equally whatever she distributes among men, happiness, talent, the advantages and disadvantages of different social stations, the facilities and difficulties associated with the things of the mind.

By virtue of these compensations we can hope to be excessively admired in the centuries to come just as we are little valued today in our own. Efforts will be made to find in our works beauties we did not claim to put there. An indefensible mistake, recognized as such by the author himself today, will find defenders of an invincible courage; and Heaven only knows with what scorn they will treat, in comparison with us, the thinkers of those times, who may well be Red Indians. So the same prejudice abases us at one time only to exalt us at another; so we are first its victim and then its god; it all makes a rather amusing game which one can follow with indifferent eyes.

I can even carry prediction still further. Once the Romans were moderns and complained of the stubbornness with which the Greeks were admired, they being then the ancients. The difference of time between them disappears in our eyes because of the great distance at which we find ourselves from them; they are both ancients for us, and we have no scruples in ordinarily preferring the Romans to the Greeks, because as between ancients and ancients there is no harm in preferring one to the other; but as between ancients and moderns it would be a great scandal for the moderns to win. We need only be patient, and after a long succession of centuries we shall become the contemporaries of the Greeks and Romans; it is easy to foresee that then nobody will hesitate to prefer us openly to them in many things. The best works of Sophocles, of Euripides, of Aristophanes will not stand up before *Cinna, Horace, Ariane, Le Misanthrope,* and many other tragedies and comedies of the great period; for we must honestly admit that the great period has been ended for several years. I do not think that *Théagène et Chariclée,* or *Clitophon et Leucippe* will ever be compared to *Cyrus,* to *L'Astrée,* to *Zaïde,* or to *La Princesse de Clèves.*[22] There are even new literary types such as amatory letters, tales, operas, in each of which we have an excellent author[23] and with which antiquity provides nothing for comparison; apparently posterity will not surpass us in these. Let the new types be represented only by popular ballads, a kind of writing which is very ephemeral and to which we do not pay great attention; it must be admitted that we have an enormous number of them, all filled with fire and wit. I maintain that if they had been known to Anacreon, he would have sung them rather than most of his own. We see by the example of many works of poetry that versification can be just as noble today as it ever was, and at the same time more precise and exact. I intend to omit details and I shall not dwell any longer on our riches; but I am convinced we are like great lords who do not always take the trouble to keep an accurate account of all their possessions, and who are unaware of some of them.

If the great men of this century had charitable feelings towards posterity, they would warn it not to admire them too much, but always to aspire to equal them at least. Nothing so limits progress, nothing narrows the mind so much as excessive admiration of the ancients. When the authority of Aristotle was unquestioned, when truth was sought only in his enigmatic writings and never in Nature, not only did philosophy not advance at all, but it fell into an abyss of nonsense and unintelligible ideas whence it was rescued only with great difficulty. Aristotle has never made one true philosopher, but he has stifled many who might have become philosophers if they had been allowed. And the worst is that once a fancy of that kind is established among men it lasts for a long time; whole centuries are needed for recovery from it, even after its preposterousness has been recognized. If some day we should become equally stubborn about Descartes and put him in Aristotle's place very much the same bad effect would result.

However, I must keep nothing back, and so I shall say that I am not at all sure posterity will count as one of our merits the two or three thousand years which one day will separate it from us as we do the time that separates the Greeks and Romans from ourselves. In all probability reason will have made progress and the generality of men will be freed from the crude prejudice in favor of the old. Perhaps that prejudice will not last much longer; perhaps at this moment we admire the ancients vainly and are never to be similarly admired ourselves. That would be somewhat unfortunate.

If after all I have just said I am not excused for having dared to attack the ancients in the *Discourse on the Eclogue*, it must be that such an attack is an unpardonable crime. I shall therefore say no more about it. I shall add only that if I have shocked past centuries by my criticism of the eclogues of the ancients, I very much fear that I shall not please this century by my own. Aside from the defects they contain, they always present a tender, delicate, diligent love which is faithful to the point of superstition; and from all that I hear, this century is ill chosen for the painting of such perfect love.

NOTES AND INDEX

Notes

The following are some of the chief works, in English and French, on literary criticism in seventeenth-century France.

Adams, Henry H., and Baxter Hathaway, *Dramatic Essays of the Neoclassic Age*, New York, 1950.

Borgerhoff, E. B. O. E., *The Freedom of French Classicism*, Princeton, 1950.

Clark, A. F. B., *Boileau and the French Classical Critics in England (1660–1830)*, Paris, 1925.

Clark, Barrett H., *European Theories of the Drama*, New York, 1947.

Kern, Edith G., *The Influence of Heinsius and Vossius upon French Dramatic Theory*, Baltimore, 1949.

Lancaster, H. C., *A History of French Dramatic Literature in the Seventeenth Century*, Baltimore, 1929–1942.

Morrissette, Bruce A., "French Criticism: Seventeenth Century," in Joseph T. Shipley, *Dictionary of World Literature*, New York, 1953, pp. 174–180.

Saintsbury, George, *A History of Criticism* (New York, 1905), II, 239–322.

Spingarn, Joel E., *A History of Literary Criticism in the Renaissance*, 2nd ed., New York, 1908.

Bourgoin, Auguste, *Les Maîtres de la critique au XVIIᵉ siècle*, Paris, 1889.

Bray, René, *La Formation de la doctrine classique en France*, Paris, 1927.

Brunetière, Ferdinand, *L'Evolution des genres dans l'histoire de la littérature*, Paris, 1890.

Gasté, Armand, *La Querelle du Cid*, Paris, 1898.

Gillot, Hubert, *La Querelle des anciens et des modernes en France*, Paris, 1914.

Lemaître, Jules, *Corneille et la poétique d'Aristote*, Paris, 1888.

Mornet, D., *Histoire de la littérature française classique (1660–1700)*, Paris, 1940.

Peyre, Henri, *Le Classicisme français*, New York, 1942.

Rigault, Hippolyte, *Histoire de la querelle des anciens et des modernes*, Paris, 1856.

Chapelain (pages 3–54)

Jean Chapelain (1595–1674) is perhaps most commonly known as the author of *La Pucelle*, an unreadable epic poem about Joan of Arc, of which Boileau said:

> *La Pucelle est encore une oeuvre bien galante,*
> *Et je ne sais pourquoi je bâille en la lisant.*

But Chapelain deserves to be remembered for his contributions to French criticism, chiefly in his letters (ed. Tamizey de Larroque, 2 vols., Paris, 1880–1883), in *Les Sentiments de l'Académie sur le Cid* (1638), and in the two essays here translated.

Though the essay on Marino's *Adone* (1623) is an early and perhaps not typical work, it is interesting on two counts: (1) it shows both Chapelain's derivation from

373

Italian critical method in its rationalistic analysis of the question of genre, and his disposition to consider the possibility of new forms not provided for in classical criticism; (2) it seems to have been influential in the criticism of Davenant (see Preface to *Gondibert*) and Dryden. W. P. Ker, in his Introduction to the *Essays of John Dryden* (I, xxviii), said: "The ancestors of Dryden's prose are to be traced in Chapelain's Preface to the *Adone* of Marino, in Mesnardière's *Poétique*, in the Dialogues and Essays of Sarasin, in the Prefaces of Scudéry, in the *Discours* and *Examens* of Corneille."

Thomas Rymer, in the Preface to his translation of Rapin's *Reflections on Aristotle's Treatise of Poesie* (1674), was influential in making the name of Giovan Battista Marino (1569–1625) a symbol in English criticism for stylistic excess. His reputation in France is summarized in the *Petit Larousse*: "[Marino's] style précieux et contourné (marinisme) eut la plus fâcheuse influence sur le développement du goût français." His poem *Adone*, published in Paris in 1623, similarly became an easy point of reference. For example, in the Dedication of the *Aeneis* (1697), Dryden said: "Whereas poems which are produced by the vigor of imagination only have a gloss upon them at the first which time wears off, the works of judgment are like the diamond. . . . Such is the difference betwixt Virgil's *Aeneis* and Marini's *Adone*."

The essay on the reading of old romances was written about 1646; it was first published in *Continuations des mémoires de littérature et histoire* (Paris, 1728), VI, i, 281–342, and was later edited by Feuillet (Paris, 1870). In "A Seventeenth-Century French Source for Hurd's *Letters on Chivalry and Romance*" (*PMLA*, LII (1937), 820–828) Victor Hamm shows that Chapelain anticipated Hurd's opinion about the likenesses between the romances and the classical epics.

The present translations were made from the edition of Alfred C. Hunter, Jean Chapelain, *Opuscules Critiques* (Paris, 1936).

[1] Giovanni Francesco Straparola (d. 1557?), author among other works of *Piacevole Notte* (Venice, 1550–1557).

[2] One of the Seven against Thebes. He defied Jupiter and was struck by lightning while scaling the walls.

[3] There is no extant Greek tragedy by this name, but at Rome Varius and Seneca treated the subject under the title *Thyestes*.

[4] A novel in Greek by Heliodorus (fl. A.D. 225).

[5] Musaeus was a Greek poet (fl. end of the 4th or beginning of the 5th century A.D.); author of *History of Hero and Leander*. He was later than and belonged to the school of Nonnus of Panopolis, who lived in the 5th century A.D. and is the author of a *Dionisyaca* in forty-eight books.

[6] Latin poet (A.D. 365?–408), author of *De raptu Proserpinae*, of which three books survive.

[7] See Catullus, *Carm.* lxiv. The poem has 408 lines of which 205 (ll. 50–255) are devoted to the episode of Ariadna.

[8] Literally *from the egg*, i.e., from the ultimate source of the action (Cf. Horace, *Ars poet.* 147).

[9] On the various interpretations of Aristotle's word περιπέτεια see S. H. Butcher, *Aristotle's Theory of Poetry and Fine Art* (fourth edition, 1951), note on pp. 329–331.

[10] "departure from logical order."

[11] Diomedes: one of the principal heroes in the *Iliad*. Mezentius: legendary king of Caere in Etruria. He appears in the *Aeneid*.

[12] Armida appears in Tasso's *Gerusalemme liberata*.

[13] Gilles Ménage (1613–1692), a lawyer who entered the service of the Cardinal de Retz and took orders (1648). Later he left the Cardinal and lived independently. Molière pilloried him as Vadius in *Les Femmes savantes*. His works include the *Dictionnaire étymologique* (Paris, 1650), referred to in the dialogue, and *Observa-*

tions sur la langue française. A man of the *salons*, he refused an invitation from Queen Christina of Sweden in a Latin eclogue, which was the cause of a quarrel between Ménage and Gilles Boileau. Ménage's detestation of Boileau later forced him to break off his friendship with Chapelain.

Jean-François Sarasin (1614–1654), author of much light verse, of a work in Latin, *Bellum Parasiticum* (1644), of an *Histoire du siège de Dunkerque* (1649), and of an *Apologie de la morale d'Epicure* often attributed to Saint-Evremond. He was a courtier and professional wit whose natural habitat was the *salon*. See also headnote to his *Remarks on Scudéry's L'Amour Tyrannique,* below.

[14] *Lancelot*, an interminable prose romance, written about 1225, whose success assured the popularity of tales of that sort.

[15] Perhaps an allusion to Sarasin's *Histoire du siège de Dunkerque.*

[16] Valentin Conrart (1603–1675). At his house were held the meetings which led to the establishment of the Académie française, whose first secretary he was. Conrart published no such work as the one here mentioned.

[17] Jean de Joinville (1224?–1317) accompanied Saint Louis (Louis IX) to Egypt and chronicled the life of that king (1309); Geoffroi de Villehardouin (1150–1218) is the chronicler of an adventure in which he participated: *La Conquête de Constantinople*, the first printed edition of which appeared at Venice in 1573.

[18] Julius Caesar Scaliger (1484–1558) in his commentary on Aristotle's *Poetics, Poetices libri septem* (1561), was one of the first to praise Virgil above Homer.

[19] Olaüs Magnus (1490–1558), Swedish author of the famous *Historia de gentibus septentrionalibus* (Rome, 1555); Saxo Grammaticus (1150–1206?), Danish historian and poet, author of *Gesta danorum* (Paris, 1514); Polydore Virgil (1470?–1555), English historian also known as P. V. Castellensis, author of the *Historia anglica* (1534); George Buchanan (1506–1582), author of numerous tragedies in Latin and of *Rerum scoticarum historia* (1582); the *Life* of Saint Louis is by Joinville (see above, note 17); Bertrand du Guesclin, Constable of France (1320?–1380), eclipsed the fame of all the military leaders of his time; Jean le Meingre Bouciquaut II, Marshal of France (1366?–1421), was taken prisoner in the battle of Agincourt and died in England; Pierre Terrail, seigneur de Bayard (1473?–1524), called the *chevalier sans peur et sans reproche*, was considered the perfect incarnation of French chivalry; Jean Froissart (1333?–1400), best-known chronicler of events in the fourteenth century, whose writings are the mirror of the aristocratic society of his time; Enguerrand de Monstrelet (1390?–1453), whose *Chronique* details events in the period 1400–1444.

[20] André Duchesne (1584–1640), author among other works of *Les Antiquités et recherches de la grandeur et de la majesté des rois de France* (1609) and of a *Series auctorum omnium qui de Francorum historia et de rebus Francicis, cum ecclesiasticis tum secularibus, ab exordio regni ad nostra usque tempora* (1633).

[21] Marc de Vulson de Colombière (d. 1658) created the science of heraldry. In 1648 appeared his *Vrai théâtre d'honneur et de la chevalerie, ou Mémoires historiques de la noblesse, contenant les combats, les triomphes, les tournois, les joutes, les carrousels, les courses de bague, les cartels, les duels, les dégradations de noblesse.*

[22] Ménage was the author of a *Mamurrae, parasito-sophistae metamorphosis* and of a *Vita Gargilii Mamurrae parasito-pedagogi*, satires aimed at the pedantry of Pierre de Montmaur (1654–1648), professor of Greek in the Collège de France. Sarasin's sentence, with its exuberant Latinity, also parodies the pedantic style. "Apedestic" means ignorant.

[23] William II, Bishop of Tyre (d. 1190), a historian of the crusades, is the author of *Historia rerum in partibus transmarinis gestarum,* two books of which have the value of personal memoirs.

[24] *Silvestres homines sacer interpresque deorum caedibus et victu foedo deterruit*

Orpheus. Horace *Ars poet.* 391: "While men still roamed the woods, Orpheus, the holy prophet of the gods, made them shrink from bloodshed and brutal living." — Trans. H. R. Fairclough in Loeb Classical Library.

[25] *Ars poet.* 122: "He denies that laws were framed against him; he arrogates everything to himself by force of arms." — Fairclough.

[26] Gothia is the Crimea; Scandia is Scandinavia; Sarmatia designates central and southern Russia; Scythia is the name for regions north and northeast of the Black Sea.

[27] Eurystheus, King of Tiryns, who imposed the famous labors upon Hercules. See *Iliad* xix. 76 ff.

[28] *Morata* rather than *urbana*: that is to say suited to their primitive way of life rather than refined and genteel.

[29] Numa Pompilius is the second legendary king of Rome (715–672 B.C.). His name is here synonymous with primitive conditions as opposed to the refinement of the Republic and the Empire.

[30] *Toxaris* is one of Lucian's dialogues. It describes remarkable instances of friendship among the Scythians and the Greeks.

[31] Logres is variously identified in the Arthurian romances as Gascony, Saxon England, and as a town in England.

[32] Tannegui Lefèvre (1615–1672) produced numerous editions of classical authors. No work by him on the Arthurian legends is known.

Sarasin (pages 55–79)

Jean-François Sarasin (1614–1654) published his *Discours sur la tragédie* in 1639 to support Scudéry in the quarrel over Corneille's *Cid*. Scudéry probably hoped to show by his play *L'Amour tyrannique*, the plot of which Sarasin summarizes in his essay, that he could write as good a play as *Le Cid* and still not violate any of the classical rules. One of the interesting things about Sarasin's treatment is his use of Heinsius's *De constitutione tragoediae* (1610), which was beginning to influence the common interpretation of Aristotle's *Poetics*. See Albert Mennung (i.e., Georg Heinrich Albert), *Jean-François Sarasin's Leben und Werke*, etc., (Halle, 1902–1904), I, 76. The present translation was made from the text of Sarasin's *Oeuvres*, edited by Paul Festugière (Paris, 1926), II, 3–36. See also Chapelain, *On the Reading of Old Romances*, note 13.

[1] Horace *Epist.* II. i. 175: "That done, he cares not whether his play fall or stand square on its feet." — Trans. H. R. Fairclough, Loeb Classical Library.

[2] Jean Mairet (1604–1686). His *La Silvanire ou la morte-vive*, a pastoral tragicomedy, was presented in 1625. *Sophonisbe*, a tragedy, was presented in 1629.

[3] Daniel Heinsius (1580–1655), to whose commentary on Aristotle, *De constitutione tragoediae* (Leyden, 1611), Sarasin is much indebted.

[4] Seneca *Hercules Oetaeus* 797: "Then with dreadful cries he filled the air."— Trans. Frank Justus Miller, Loeb Classical Library.

[5] Ibid. 739: "And whatever that poison touched begins to shrink." — Miller.

[6] *Aeneid* II. 26: "So all the Teucrian land frees herself from her long sorrow." — Fairclough.

[7] Ibid. 554: "Such was the close of Priam's fortunes." — Fairclough.

[8] Aristotle *Poetics* xxvi. 5: "Moreover the art attains its end within narrower limits; for the concentrated effect is more pleasurable than one which is spread over a long time and so diluted." — Trans. S. H. Butcher.

[9] *Ars poet.* 147: "Nor does he begin . . . the war of Troy from the twin eggs" (i.e., from the birth of Helen). — Fairclough.

[10] Joachim du Bellay (1522–1560), author of the famous *Défense et illustration de la langue française* (1549).

Notes

[11] Alexandre Hardy (1560–1632). The full title of the play mentioned is *Elmire ou l'heureuse bigamie.*

[12] "Complex." *Poetics* x.

[13] Seneca *Agamemnon* 918: "I am Strophius—I have just left Phocis my kingdom, and am now returning, honored and distinguished through having gained a prize in the chariot race at the Olympic Games." — Trans. Watson Bradshaw.

[14] Ibid, 919: "And the cause for my coming on hither was simply to congratulate an old friend." — Bradshaw.

[15] Ibid. 942: "And Greece! be now my witness that you, my swift coursers, fly with your headlong speed from these treacherous regions." — Bradshaw.

[16] *Poetics* xi.

[17] *Ars poet.* 450: "He will prove an Aristarchus. He will not say, 'Why should I give offense to a friend about trifles?' " — Fairclough. The name of Aristarchus had become proverbial as that of a keen critic.

[18] *Poetics* xvi: "But, of all recognitions, the best is that which arises from the incidents themselves." — Butcher.

[19] *Ars poet.* 186: "Medea is not to butcher her boys before the people, nor impious Atreus cook human flesh upon the stage, nor Procne be turned into a bird, Cadmus into a snake." — Fairclough.

[20] Suetonius *Nero* xii.

[21] *Poetics* xiv.

[22] *Ars poet.* 12: "But not so far that savage should mate with tame or serpents couple with birds, lambs with tigers." — Fairclough.

[23] Apparently a reference to the last part of *Poetics* xiv, where Aristotle says that of the events that move pity and fear the best is one in which the agents are related to one another, and in which one in ignorance is about to kill the other but discovers the truth in time. This seems inconsistent with his earlier (xiii) statement that in the best tragedies the fortune of the hero goes from good to bad.

[24] Horace *Epist.* II. i. 174.

[25] Hippolyte-Jules Pilet de la Mesnardière (1610–1663) published the first volume of his *Poétique* in 1639. The remainder of the work was never published.

[26] Virgil *Eclog.* vii. 5: "Ready in a match to sing, as well as to make reply." — Fairclough.

Scudéry (pages 80–95)

When Madeleine de Scudéry (1607–1701), author of many long romances, published *Ibrahim, ou l'illustre Bassa* (1641), her brother Georges (1601–1667) wrote a preface for it, in which he discussed such topics as the importance of verisimilitude, the abuse of the marvelous, problems of characterization, tragic flaws appropriate to romantic heroes, and poetic justice. Interesting as that preface is, it does not deal with several of the most important questions discussed by those who theorized about the art of the romance, particularly the question of what stories were appropriate sources for plots. This topic and others Scudéry discussed in the Preface to his own epic, *Alaric* (1654). The earlier Preface was probably better known in England because a translation of *Ibrahim* by George Cogan was published in London in 1652. It has been reprinted by the Augustan Reprint Society (No. 42), Los Angeles, 1953.

[1] The proper title of Boiardo's poem is *Orlando Innamorato.*

[2] By Giovanni Graziani.

[3] See H. B. Charlton, *Castelvetro's Theory of Poetry*, Manchester, 1913, 58–59.

[4] Procopius, *History of the Wars*, Book III; Orosius, *Seven Books of History Against the Pagans*, VII, 39; Ritius (Michele Ricci) *Rerum secularum scriptores ex recentioribus praecipui in unum corpus nunc primum congesti* . . . (Francofurti ad Moenum apud Wechelum, MDLXXIX), V, 3.

377

[5] Marc-Antoine Gérard, sieur de Saint-Amant (1594–1661), *Moïse sauvé* (1653).

[6] Cf. Tasso, *Discorsi dell'arte poetica* (Discorso secondo): ". . . perocchè essendo il fine della poesia il dilettare . . ." *Opera in verso et in prosa*, 4 vols., (Napoli, 1840, III, 11.) This is an oversimplification of Tasso's position. See the *Trattato del Poema eroico*, ibid. 30–31.

[7] *Jerusalem Delivered*, I, 3:

> The world, thou know'st, on tiptoe ever flies
> Where warbling most Parnassus' fountain winds,
> And that Truth, robed in song's benign disguise,
> Has won the coyest, sooth'd the sternest minds:
> So the fond mother her sick infant blinds,
> Sprinkling the edges of the cup she gives
> With sweets; delighted with the balm it finds
> Round the smooth brim, the medicine it receives,
> Drinks the delusive draught, and, thus deluded, lives.
>
> — Trans. J. H. Wiffen

[8] ". . . to delight and to refresh the spirits of the crude multitude and of the common people."

[9] Théophile de Viau, "Elégie à une dame," 101–102.

[10] For a summary of Castelvetro's argument see Charlton, *op. cit.*, pp. 72–78.

[11] Quintilian *Instit. orat.* i. 4: "Nor again if he [the teacher of literature] be ignorant of astronomy can he understand the poets; for they, to mention no further points, frequently give their indications of time by reference to the rising and setting of the stars. Ignorance of philosophy is an equal drawback, since there are numerous passages in almost every poem based on the most intricate questions of natural philosophy, while among the Greeks we have Empedocles and among our own poets Varro and Lucretius, all of whom have expounded their philosophies in verse." — Trans. H. F. Butler, Loeb Classical Library.

[12] Cicero *De Orat.* i. 217: a "distinguished poem."

[13] *Ars poet.* 46–48: "Moreover, with a nice taste and care in weaving words together, you will express yourself most happily, if a skillful setting makes a familiar word new." — Fairclough.

[14] Ibid. 343–344: "He has won every vote who has blended profit with pleasure, at once delighting and instructing the reader."

[15] Queen Christina of Sweden.

[16] *Poetics* ix.

[17] *Poetics* xv. 6: "As in the structure of the plot, so too in the portraiture of character, the poet should always aim either at the necessary or the probable." — Butcher.

[18] This is a translation of a sentence from Tasso's *Discorsi dell'arte poetica* (Discorso terzo, 16): "Avendosi a trattare dell'elocuzione, si tratterà per conseguenza dello stile, perchè non essendo quella altro che accoppiamento di parole, e non essendo altro le parole che immagini imitatrici de' concetti, che seguono la natura loro, si viene per forza a trattare dello stile, non essendo quello altro che quel composto che risulta dai concetti e dalle voci."

[19] *Aeneid* vi. 129: "This is the task, this the labor."

[20] Heliodorus (fl. A.D. 225) is the author of a prose narrative called the *Aethiopica*. "Athenagoras" is probably a reference to Chariton (fl. A.D. 260), author of *Chaereas and Callirrhoë*, "who tells us he served as a copyist to one Athenagoras." F. A. Wright, *A History of Later Greek Literature*, London, 1932, p. 307. But cf. note 32, p. 384.

[21] "It blazes and does not burn, illumines and does not harm, burns and does not consume, glows and does not wound, purifies and does not inflame, and warms besides, yet does not pain."

Notes

[22] *Iliad* iii. 179: "King Agamemnon/Goodly, insooth, as a king and as powerful too, as a spearman." — Trans. W. B. Smith and Walter Miller.

[23] For Camilla see *Aeneid* vii. 803 and xi. 432 ff. Penthesilea does not appear in Homer but belongs rather to post-Homeric legend.

[24] Ovid; for Nisus see *Ibis* 362 and *Ars Am.* i. 331; Euryale appears in *Fasti* iv. 57.

[25] Johannes Magnus (1488–1544) is the author of *Gothorum Sueonumque historia* (1554) and his brother Olaüs Magnus (1490–1558) of *Historia de gentibus septentrionalibus . . .* (1555).

[26] Jean Chapelain (1595–1674). The first twelve cantos of his epic poem on Joan of Arc, *La Pucelle* (The Maid), were published in 1656. See headnote to selections from his writings, above.

[27] Isaiah 45: 1–3: "Thus saith the Lord to his anointed, to Cyrus, whose right hand I have holden, to subdue nations before him; and I will loose the loins of kings, to open before him the two-leaved gates; and the gates shall not be shut; I will go before thee and make the crooked places straight; I will break in pieces the gates of brass, and cut in sunder the bars of iron: and I will give thee the treasures of darkness, and hidden riches of secret places. . . ."

Hédelin (pages 96–116)

François Hédelin, abbé d'Aubignac (1604–1676) was perhaps the most mechanical and dogmatic of all the neoclassical critics of the drama. His criticism of Corneille, in which he was encouraged by Richelieu, was only part of his campaign to establish correctness. In 1647 he published a prose tragedy called *Zénobie*, of which Saint-Evremond said: "I remember that the Abbé d'Aubignac wrote one according to the laws he had imperiously prescribed for the stage. This piece had no success, notwithstanding which he boasted in all companies that he was the only French writer who had exactly followed the precepts of Aristotle; whereupon the Prince of Condé said wittily: 'I am obliged to Monsieur d'Aubignac for having so exactly followed Aristotle's rules, but I will never forgive the rules of Aristotle for having put Monsieur d'Aubignac upon writing so bad a tragedy.' "

La Pratique du théâtre (1657) is a long treatise (385 pages in a modern edition), consisting of four books. The three unities are discussed in Book Two. It is hard to say definitely how strong was d'Aubignac's influence. Much of the evidence is collected in A. F. B. Clark, *Boileau and the French Classical Critics in England* (Paris, 1925), pp. 239–241. Certainly Dennis, Dryden, Addison, and Joseph Warton knew his work. The anonymous English translation does not always stay very close to the original, and a few obscure passages in the text have been retranslated. Most of the following notes are from the excellent modern edition of *La Pratique* by Pierre Martino (Paris, 1927).

[1] Josias de Soulas (1608–1672), a famous actor who under the stage name of Floridor played in Corneille's tragedy *Horace* (1639).

[2] *La Dorinde* (1631), by le Sieur Auvray.

[3] *Trucul.*, the opening lines.

[4] Samuel Petit (1594–1643), author of several scholarly works, notably *Miscellaneorum libri novem* (1630) and *Observationum libri tres* (1641).

[5] Aelius Donatus, fourth-century commentator on Terence.

[6] Scudéry's *L'Amour tyrannique*, I, i.

[7] Alessandro Piccolomini (1508–1578) and Bernardo Segni (d. 1558), Italian commentators on the *Poetics*.

[8] Martino's note: *Discorsi di Nic. Rossi vicentino, intorno alla tragedia*. Vicenza, 1590.

[9] *La Mariamne* (1637), by Tristan.

THE CONTINENTAL MODEL

Corneille (pages 117–131)

The dramatic criticism of Pierre Corneille (1606–1684) consists of three discourses on drama and a series of short criticisms, called *Examens*, of his own plays. They were published in 1660 in a three-volume edition of his works. Each play was followed by its *examen*, and each volume of the edition was prefaced by one of the *Discours*. None of these was translated into English until the twentieth century, nor is there much reference to them in English criticism. But, if for no other reason than that they greatly influenced Dryden in the *Essay of Dramatic Poesy*, we can say that they had a significant influence on eighteenth-century England.

The three discourses should be read together. The first, translated (and slightly abridged) in Barrett H. Clark (*op. cit.*, pp. 139–147), deals with the moral "uses" of tragedy and with its "parts." The morality of a play can be expressed by (1) speeches put in the mouths of characters, (2) simple descriptions of virtues and vices, (3) poetic justice, (4) the total effect of the tragedy — the purgation of pity and fear. After a brief notice of the "quantitative parts" — prologue, episode, exodus, and chorus — Corneille devotes the last half of the discourse to an interpretation of Aristotle's "parts" — subject, manner, sentiment, and diction, neglecting music and stage setting. The second discourse, translated in Adams and Hathaway (*op. cit.*, pp. 1–34), is on the subject of Aristotelian purgation and the means of effecting it. The third is different from the first two in its more technical concern for dramaturgical problems. It shows as well as the other two what is meant by "the vacillating compromises of [Corneille's] long duel with Aristotle," a phrase of Jules Lemaître, in *Corneille et la poétique d'Aristote* (Paris, 1888).

¹ Corneille's note: *Poetics* x. 3.
² Corneille's note: *Ibid.*
³ Corneille's note: *Ibid.* xviii. 1.
⁴ Seneca *Medea* 975: "But thee, poor senseless corse, within mine arms I'll bear." — Trans. Frank Justus Miller. Corneille *Médée*, IV, 5.
⁵ Corneille's note: *Ars poet.* 189: *Neve minor, neu sit quinto productior actu/ fabula.* ["A play should consist of five acts — no more, no less."]
⁶ Corneille's note: See *Poetics* xxvi.
⁷ Corneille's note: *Rodogune*, V, 3.
⁸ Corneille's note: *Poetics* v. 4.
⁹ Corneille's note: *Suppliants* 598–634. Besides, Aethra says nothing and merely listens to the chorus, which is divided into two parts.
¹⁰ Corneille's note: See Aeschylus *Agamemnon* 650 ff.
¹¹ In the *Examen de Mélite*, which precedes the present *Discourse* in the editions published by Corneille.

Saint-Evremond (pages 132–185)

Charles de Marguetel de Saint-Denis, seigneur de Saint-Evremond (1610–1703) lived the last forty years of his life in England, where he wrote almost all of the essays for which he is now remembered, and where most of his work was first published. Some of the essays were privately circulated in manuscript; some were pirated and printed without Saint-Evremond's knowledge. The first authorized edition of his complete works was published posthumously by his friends Dr. P. Silvestre and Pierre Des Maizeaux, *Les Véritables oeuvres de M. de Saint-Evremond, publiées sur les manuscrits de l'auteur*, 3 vols., London, 1705. Later editions appeared in 1706 (Amsterdam), 1708, 1709, etc. But the English translations of various essays had been published in London as early as 1684. In 1692 Dryden wrote an introductory essay on Saint-Evremond for a volume of *Miscellaneous Essays by Monsieur St. Evremond*, which contained anonymous translations previously published. To this volume a second was added in 1694, containing translations by "Dr. Drake, Mr.

Notes

Brown, Mr. Savage, Mr. Manning," and others. In 1700 a two-volume *Works* appeared, claiming to be a "translation . . . done from a copy of the last French Edition and corrected in many Places by the Pen of the Author." This was, however, only a reprint of the 1692–1694 edition with minor changes. When in 1714 Des Maizeaux published his scholarly edition of the works in translation, based on his 1705 edition of *Les Véritables oeuvres* he followed the earlier translations, but these he carefully corrected and revised. Our text follows Des Maizeaux's second edition (1728); we have made a very few changes for the sake of clarity.

The dates accompanying the titles are those of composition, not publication.

Saint-Evremond's influence on Dryden, Temple, and Dennis can be discovered in their essays and in modern editions of those essays. The evidence has been summarized by Clark (*op. cit.*, pp. 288–293). See also W. Melville Daniels, *Saint-Evremond en Angleterre* (Versailles, 1907).

[1] Racine's play was first performed in 1665.

[2] Velleius Paterculus *Hist. Rom.* 11. 41: "He greatly resembled Alexander the Great, but only when Alexander was free from the influence of wine and master of his passions." — Frederick W. Shipley.

[3] Quintus Curtius *De rebus gestis Alexandri Magni.*

[4] Corneille, *La Mort de Pompée.*

[5] Corneille, *Cinna*, I, i.

[6] Corneille, *La Mort de Pompée.*

[7] Corneille, *Oedipe.*

[8] Corneille, *Sophonisbe.*

[9] Elegance, charm, grace, urbanity, loveliness, delight, agreeableness.

[10] *De bell. civ.* i. 128: "If the victor had the gods on his side, the vanquished had Cato." — J. D. Duff.

[11] *De rerum nat.* i. 101: "So potent was religion in persuading to evil deeds." Trans. W. H. D. Rouse, Loeb Classical Library.

[12] *Ars poet.* 343: "He has won every vote who has blended profit and pleasure." — Fairclough.

[13] Cicero *Part orat.* xvii: "For a tear dries quickly, especially one prompted by another's misfortune."

[14] *Don Quixote*, I, i: "Because he was of a temperament which adjusted itself to any event; neither was he so cynical nor such a whining lover as his brother."

[15] The title of the play is *Bérénice.*

[16] Corneille, *Tite et Bérénice.*

[17] *Ars poet.* 121: Impiger, iracundus, inexorabilis, acer / iura neget sibi nata, nihil non arroget armis.

[18] *Ars poet.* 169: Multa senem circumveniunt incommoda, vel quod / quaerit et inventis miser abstinet ac timet uti, / vel quod res omnis timide gelideque ministrat, / dilator, spe longus, iners avidusque futuri, difficilis, / querulus, laudator temporis acti / se puero, castigator censorque minorum.

[19] Corneille, *Sophonisbe*, II, ii:

> Quand sous un front ridé, qu'on a droit de haïr,
> Il croit se faire aimer à force d'obéir.

[20] Tasso, *Aminta*, III, ii; Corneille, *Suréna*, V, v.

[21] Tristan l'Hermite, *Mariamne*; Mairet, *Sophonisbe*; Du Ryer, *Alcionée*; Rotrou, *Venceslas*; Thomas Corneille, *Stilicon*; Racine, *Andromaque* and *Britannicus.*

[22] A mistranslation of *Le Festin de pierre*, apparently a version of the Don Juan legend. There were two Italian plays on the legend in the seventeenth century, both called *Il Convitato di pietra*, one by Onofrio Giliberto (Naples, 1652), now lost, and one by Andrea Cicognini, which served as the basis for the scenario used by the Commedia dell' Arte.

THE CONTINENTAL MODEL

²³ Guidobaldi Bonarelli (1563–1608), *Filli di Sciro* (1607).

²⁴ *Satyricon* 90 ff.; Théophile de Viau (1590–1626), French poet and playwright.

²⁵ Luigi Rossi was the composer of *Orfeo*, the first opera performed at Paris (1647). Francesco Cavalli (d. 1676) was master of the chapel at St. Mark's Cathedral in Venice, and the composer of thirty-eight operas, including *Xerxes*, which was performed in Paris at the celebration of Louis XIV's marriage. Marco Antonio Cesti (d. 1688) presented eight operas in Venice between 1649 and 1669 which were subsequently performed throughout Italy. He also composed cantatas.

²⁶ Jean-Baptiste Lulli (1633?–1687), Florentine musician, later naturalized French citizen. Court composer and superintendent of music to Louis XIV, he is called the founder of national French opera. His operas, with Quinault as librettist, include *Alceste* (1674), *Thesée* (1675), and *Armide* (1686); he also composed *pastorali*, ballets, masques, and church music.

²⁷ Des Maizeaux's note: "An entertainment of music and dancing between the acts, which has no connection with the play."

²⁸ Robert Cambert (1628–1677) was *surintendant de la musique* for Anne of Austria, mother of Louis XIV. He was the first French musician to compose an opera — a *pastorale*, presented in 1647.

²⁹ "The Spaniard wails, the Italian laments, the German bellows, the Belgian shrieks, and only the Frenchman sings."

³⁰ Philippe Quinault (1635–1688), dramatic poet, author of *Les Rivales* (1653), *La Mort de Cyrus* (1656), *Le Mariage de Cambyse* (1656), and of the libretti of fourteen operas in association with Lulli. He was frequently ridiculed by Boileau.

³¹ Des Maizeaux gives the following account of the occasion for the essay: "I shall now acquaint you how he came to write his *Dissertation on the Word* Vast. Madame Mazarin having, amongst other praises, said of Cardinal Richelieu that he had a vast mind or genius, M. de Saint-Evremond maintained that that expression was not just; that a *vast genius* was taken either in a good or bad sense, according to what accompanied it; that a vast, wonderful, and penetrating genius denoted an admirable capacity; and that, on the contrary, a vast and immoderate genius was a genius that lost itself in rambling thoughts, in fine but airy ideas, in designs too great, and not at all proportioned to the means that may render them successful. After a long dispute, they agreed to refer the matter to the gentlemen of the French Academy. The Abbot de Saint-Réal, then at Paris, having been desired to consult them, they gave their judgment in favor of Madame Mazarin. M. de Saint-Evremond had retracted and confessed his error before their decision was known, but when he saw it, he wrote [this] dissertation. . . ."

³² *Satyricon* 118: "Homer proves this, and the lyric poets, and Roman Virgil, and the studied felicity of Horace." — Michael Heseltine.

³³ Antoine Nervèze (b. 1570) and Jean-Louis Guez de Balzac (1594–1654) were poets; Nicolas Coëffeteau (1574–1623) and Anthyme-Denis Cohon (1594–1643) were popular preachers.

³⁴ Claude Favre de Vaugelas (1585–1650), grammarian and academician, author of *Remarques sur la langue française* (Paris, 1647); Nicolas Perrot d'Ablancourt (1606–1664), translator of Cicero, Caesar, Tacitus, Thucydides, and others; Olivier Patru (1604–1681), lawyer and academician, one of the literary and grammatical arbiters of his day, as well as a successful orator.

³⁵ *Aeneid* iii. 647: "I see the huge Cyclopes from a rock." iii. 655: "The shepherd Polyphemus moving his mighty bulk." — Fairclough.

³⁶ See *De oratore* i. 115; *De re publica* vi. 20; *De divinatione* i. 49.

³⁷ In the last half of the essay, Saint-Evremond makes similar analyses of the characters and careers of Pyrrhus, Catiline, Caesar, Charles the Fifth, and Cardinal Richelieu.

³⁸ *De rerum nat.* v. 107: "Which may pilot fortune steer from us." — Rouse.

³⁹ *Ars poet.* 61.

Notes

[40] Des Maizeaux's note: "Diogenes Laertius has transmitted to us that saying of Epicurus. M. de Saint-Evremond quotes it according to the translation of my Lord Bacon, *Serm. Fidel.* XVI, but this is more literal: *Impius est, non is qui multitudinis deos tollit, sed qui multitudinis opiniones diis adhibet.* Diog. Laert. x. 123." — "There is no profanity in refusing to believe in the gods of the vulgar; the profanity is in believing of the gods what the vulgar believe of them." — Trans. Spedding and Ellis.

[41] *De bell. civ.* ix. 1035 ff. and ix. 550.

Huet (pages 186–205)

Pierre Daniel Huet (1630–1721), Bishop of Avranches, was one of the most devoted scholars of his day. A few of his works bear such titles as: *Origenes commentaria in sacram Scripturam* (1668), *Demonstratio evangelica* (1679), *Censura philosophiae Cartiseanae* (1689), *De la situation du Paradis terrestre* (1691), and *Histoire du commerce et de la navigation des anciens* (1716). The following essay, *De l'Origine des romans*, appeared first as an introduction to the 1670 edition of Mme. de La Fayette's novel *Zayde*, which was published under the name of Jean-Regnauld de Segrais (1624–1701), to whom the letter is addressed. An English translation of the essay was published anonymously in London in 1672. A translation by Stephen Lewis, *The History of Romances*, was published in 1715. The present text is that of a third translation, which was prefixed to Volume I of *A Select Collection of Novels*, edited by S. Croxall, in 1720.

It cannot be proved that Huet's essay had much influence on English scholarship. Thomas Warton refers to it once in his *History of English Poetry*, and to William Warburton's criticism of it in a Supplement to the Translator's Preface of Charles Jarvis's *Don Quixote* (1742). Clara Reeve devoted several pages (90–96) to ridiculing it in her *Progress of Romance* (1785). Nevertheless, the number of times it was reprinted in English suggests that it was one of the classics in what became an important subject of study in the eighteenth century. And its intrinsic interest in not inconsiderable.

[1] Lilio Gregorio Giraldi (1479–1552), author of numerous learned works. Giambattista Nicolucci Pigna (1530–1575) is the author, among other works, of *I Romanzi* (Venice, 1554) which treats of Ariosto.

[2] *Satyricon* v.

[3] On Hanno see Diodorus Siculus xiii. 80. Philostratus intended to rehabilitate his hero and to defend him against the charge of being a magician in his *Life of Apollonius of Tyana* (about A.D. 220).

[4] Annius Viterbensis (Giovanni Nanni, 1432–1502) attributed hitherto unknown works to ancient authors in his *Antiquitatum variarum volumina* XVIII (1498).

[5] Tarik (born second half of the seventh century) was the leader of the Arab forces in the invasion of Spain, although subordinate to the Emir Musa Ben Nasser (660?–718).

[6] *Geography* XV, ii. 18 and XI. vi. 2.

[7] *Instit.* V. xi. 1, ff.

[8] *On Sacrifices* xiv; *The Goddesse of Surrye.*

[9] The work of Clearchus of Soli (born about 355) is described in the *Histoire de la littérature grecque* of A. and M. Croiset (Paris, Foutemoing, 1901, Vol. V, p. 32) as "clever badinage, elegant in form, serious in intention, and passably original."

[10] The reference is to Parthenius of Nicaea, who came to Rome in A.D. 73. He is the author of *The Pangs of Love* (περὶ ἐρωτικῶν παθημάτων), a collection of legends dealing with love which usually end in catastrophes or metamorphoses.

[11] Longus composed a well-known work in four books entitled *Daphnis and Chloë.*

[12] Eustathius of Epiphanius (end of fifth century A.D.) is known only from frag-

ments. Theodorus Prodromus, Byzantine writer of the first half of the twelfth century, is the author of a verse novel, *The Loves of Rhodonte and Dosicles*.

[13] Apparently a reference to Xenophon, the author of the *Anabasis*; to Xenophon, a historian of the third century A.D. about whom nothing is known; and Xenophon of Ephesus (third century A.D.), the author of a novel entitled *The Ephesian Tales* concerning the loves and trials of Habrocomes of Ephesus and Antheia.

[14] Hesychius of Miletus, Greek biographer, lived during the sixth century. He composed a work on the same plan as the *Lives of the Philosophers* of Diogenes Laertius entitled *Concerning Those Distinguished for Their Learning*.

[15] Suidas, Greek lexicographer of the eleventh century. The work bearing his name is a dictionary, an encyclopedia, and a collection of biographies.

[16] Probably "The Old Commentary," the famous Alexandrian variorum edition of Aristophanes.

[17] Claudius Aelian, *Various History* XIV. xx.

[18] See *The Ignorant Book-Collector*, 23.

[19] Taliessin, a late sixth-century British bard to whom is attributed the collection of poems known as the *Book of Taliessin*.

[20] Balaeus (John Bale, 1495–1563) is the author of a work called *Illustrium majoris Britanniae scriptorum summarium in quasdam centurias divisum*, Basle, 1559.

[21] Hunibaldus, author of a chronicle history from the fall of Troy to the time of Clovis.

[22] The so-called *Chronicle of Turpin*, composed at some unknown date before 1122 by a monk, purports to be the work of Charlemagne's friend Turpin, Archbishop of Rheims.

[23] *Geography* IV. i. 1.

[24] Salmasius (Claude de Saumaise, 1588–1653) published many editions of Latin and Greek authors.

[25] Aristotle *Rhetoric* ii. 20.

[26] Claude Fauchet (1529–1601), author of *Antiquités gauloises* (1579) and of *Recueil de l'origine de la langue et poésie françaises* (1581). Thibaut de Champagne, King of Navarre, and the Châtelain de Couci were poets who took part in the fourth crusade (1204). "Gace's Brussez" should read "Gace Brulé," a poet of about 1180.

[27] *Symposium* 203.

[28] François de Malherbe (1555–1628), official poet to Henry IV and a favored poet under Louis XIII and Richelieu.

[29] *Eunuchus* iii. 584.

[30] The famous novel by Honoré d'Urfé (1568–1625) appeared at intervals between 1610 and 1627.

[31] *Epist.* I. ii. 3.

[32] Photius, Patriarch of Constantinople, lived during the ninth century; the reference is to remarks made in his *Bibliotheca*, a valuable work consisting of abstracts of 280 Greek works, together with criticisms. Lucius Apuleius, a Roman neo-Platonist of the second century, wrote *The Golden Ass*, a prose romance. "Athenagoras" is the pseudonym of Martin Fumée de Genille. His *Du vray et parfaict amour . . . contenant les amours honnestes de Théogènes et de Charide* (Paris, 1599) purports to be a translation; but it was in fact written by him. L. Cornelius Sisenna (c. 120–67 B.C.) was a Roman historian known for his translation of the *Milesian Fables* of Aristides. The *Satyricon* of Petronius is a work of prose fiction. Clodius Albinus, a Roman general of the second century, may have been the same Clodius Albinus who was a senator and who wrote the *Milesian Fables* in verse. Heliodorus, a fourth-century Greek sophist and Christian bishop, wrote the romance *Aethiopica*. Achilles Tatius, a fourth-century Greek of Alexandria who became a Christian and later a bishop, wrote the *Amours de Clitophon et de*

384

Notes

Leucippe. To Saint John Damascenus was ascribed (without convincing evidence) the *Histoire du saint ermite Barlaam et de Josaphat, fils d'un roi des Indes*, a "roman de spiritualité."

Bouhours (pages 206–238)

In addition to religious works and biographies of St. Ignatius Loyola and St. Francis Xavier, Dominique Bouhours (1628–1702), a Jesuit teacher of classical studies at Paris and Tours, published two influential works of literary criticism. *Les Entretiens d'Ariste et d'Eugène* (1671), consisting of six dialogues on "La Mer," "La Langue française," "Le Secret," "Le Bel esprit," "Le Je ne sais quoi," and "Les Devises," went through at least three editions, and has been edited in modern times by René Radouant (Paris, 1920). It was never translated into English, but it was almost as well known in eighteenth-century England as Bouhours's other, more ambitious work of criticism, *La Manière de bien penser dans les ouvrages d'esprit*, which was published in 1687. At least five editions of the latter work had appeared by the middle of the eighteenth century, as well as two translations into English: *The Art of Criticism . . . Translated . . . by a person of quality* (London, 1705), and *The Arts of Logick and Rhetorick*, by John Oldmixon (London, 1728), which is an English adaptation "to which are added parallel quotations out of the most eminent English authors in verse and prose." The present text is an abridgment of the first two of the four dialogues which make up the book. The third dialogue consists mainly of a collection and discussion of examples of false wit, and the fourth, of examples of "obscurities." Bouhours's critical doctrine is fully outlined in the first two dialogues. One of the disadvantages of the present abridgment is that many of the examples have been omitted, and it is the loving and leisurely concern with the hundreds of examples that gives the work its characteristic style.

Clark (*op. cit.*, pp. 262–274) has summarized the evidence of Bouhours's influence in England. The list of English critics who admired, or quoted, or referred to Bouhours is long: Rymer, Dennis, Addison, Spence, Joseph Warton, Arthur Murphy, and George Campbell. Lord Chesterfield several times in letters to his son recommended Bouhours. In his poem "An Essay Upon Unnatural Flights in Poetry" (1701), George Granville, Lord Lansdowne (1667–1735), "borrowed freely from Bouhours's *La Manière de bien penser*," and several of his "Explanatory Annotations" are paraphrases from Bouhours. (See J. E. Spingarn, *Critical Essays of the Seventeenth Century* [New York, 1908], III, 292–298, 337.) For a full study of the background of the *Je ne sais quoi*, see Samuel H. Monk, "Grace Beyond the Reach of Art," in *The Journal of the History of Ideas*, V (1944), 131–150.

In *La Manière de bien penser* we have enclosed in brackets the places where we have corrected or improved the translation of the "person of quality."

[1] ["Its splendor is proportionate to its solidity."]

[2] [Pierre Fortin de la Hoguette, French military man, composed a *Testament, ou Conseils d'un père à ses enfants* which appeared in 1655 and in which the author examines the duties of man toward God, toward himself, and toward his fellow men.]

[3] Suet. in *Caesar*.

[4] August. in Psalms 58.

[5] [Charles, Duke of Schomberg (1601–1656) had a brilliant military career under Louis XIII.]

[6] ["first in that coarseness than second in delicacy."]

[7] ["It always bears ripe fruit along with blossoms."]

[8] Ludov. Vives *de Budaeo*.

[9] [Daniel Bartoli (1608–1685) was an Italian Jesuit. His *Man of Letters* was translated into French by Father Livoy.]

[10] [Vincent Voiture (1597–1648) was a master of light poetry and a much-admired wit of the *salons*.]

[11] *The History of the French Academy.*

[12] [Giovanni Baptista Mancini was a Bolognese writer of the first half of the seventeenth century, several of whose works were translated into French by Scudéry; Virgilio, marquis de Malvezzi (1599–1644) wrote many works dealing with history and diplomacy, among them an historical novel entitled *Il Romulo* (1629) translated into French in 1645; Giovanni Francesco Loredano (1606–1651) wrote *Dianea* (1636), a collection of libertine tales, and published various collections of *concetti* which were very successful not only in Italy but abroad.]

[13] Tacitus *Annals* xiii. 45: ["She paraded modesty and practiced wantonness. In public she rarely appeared, and then with her face half-veiled, so as not quite to satiate the beholder, — or, possibly, because it so became her." — Trans. John Jackson, Loeb Classical Library.]

[14] ["She neither hid her beauties nor did she display them."]

[15] I Cor. 13:12.

[16] [Claude de Mesmes, comte d'Avaux (1595–1650), French diplomat. For Cardinal Duperron, see below, note 18.]

[17] ["Talent and intelligence are the two axes of splendor and success: one without the other leads only to half of the desired goal; intelligence is not enough, for talent too is needed."] Baltasar Gracián, *Oraculo manual y arte de prudencia.*

[18] [Bouhours cites for this anecdote the collection (*Perroniana*) made by Christophe Dupuy of the witticisms and criticisms attributed to Jacques Davy, Cardinal Duperron (1556–1618).]

[19] [In the first edition of the *Conversations* (1671) Bouhours credited the reform to Ronsard but apparently repented of this rashness. All later editions mention Malherbe.]

[20] [Paris, comte de Saint-Pol, second son of the Duc de Longueville, whose tutor Bouhours had been. The young prince died in 1672, the year following the first appearance of the *Conversations.*]

[21] [Tasso, *Jerusalem Delivered*, Canto I, stanza 58:

Hope and his years he far outstrips; scarce blown
Appear his blossoms, than the fruit's reveal'd;
So sweetly fierce, that when his face is shown
You deem him Love, but Mars when helm'd and steel'd.

— Wiffen.]

[22] [*L'Art de connaître les hommes* . . .(Paris, 1659, 1664, 1666), by Marin Cuneau de la Chambre. De la Chambre had convinced Louis XIV of his ability to judge character and even talent from physiognomy. In the work mentioned he shows himself an opponent of the whole female sex.]

[23] [Sappho.]

[24] [Athenaïs is better known as Eudoxia, wife of Theodosius II.]

[25] [Vittoria Colonna (1490–1547) was a friend of Michelangelo.]

[26] [Isotta Nogarola (1420–1466) composed a Latin dialogue in defense of Eve.]

[27] [Serafina Contarini is known as a letter-writer.]

[28] [Margareta Sarrochi was the center of an enthusiastic literary group at the beginning of the seventeenth century.]

[29] [Margaret More (1505–1544) was the eldest daughter of Sir Thomas More. Her devotion to him was exemplary.]

[30] [Elizabeth Tanfield (1585–1639) married Sir Henry Cary, first Viscount Falkland. She mastered French, Spanish, Italian, Latin, Hebrew, and Transylvanian.]

[31] [Isabel de Roseres preached in Barcelona Cathedral (sixteenth century).]

[32] [Catherine, wife of John II of Portugal, defended her country against Philip II in 1580. She was as learned as she was energetic.]

[33] [Queen Margaret of Navarre, first wife of Henry IV of France, left some very interesting *Mémoires* (1552–1615).]

Notes

[34] [Louise Marguerite de Lorraine, later Princess de Conti (1577–1631), wrote a description of life at the court of Henry IV under the title *Les Amours du grand Alcandre* (1652).]

[35] [Saint Pulcheria, Empress of the Eastern Roman Empire (399–453) served as regent for Theodosius II, her younger brother.]

[36] [Blanche of Castile (1188–1252) became regent of France after the death of Louis VIII, during which time she broke up a league of the barons and repelled an attack by the king of England.]

[37] [Isabella (1451–1504), la Católica, queen of Castile and León, married Ferdinand of Aragon. She supported Columbus in his project.]

Bouhours (pages 239–274)

[1] [*Doutes sur la langue françoise proposez à messieurs de l'Académie françoise par un gentilhomme de province*, 1674. This work is by Bouhours himself.]

[2] *Ars poet.* [309.]

[3] [Lucan *De bell. civ.* i. 128.]

[4] Sallust *Bell. Catil.*

[5] Velleius Paterculus *Hist. Rom.* ii.

[6] [Guillaume de Brébeuf (1618–1661), whose epic poem *Pharsale* was ridiculed by Boileau in *L'Art poétique*.]

[7] *De orat.* ii.

[8] Vavasseur, *De epigramm. lib.*

[9] [Honoré de Bueil, marquis de Racan, (1589–1670) composed a pastoral *Arthenice ou les Bergeries*, elegiac verse, and translations of the Psalms.]

[10] [See Montaigne, *Essays*, I, 31.]

[11] *Cavillationes*, Macrob.; *Vafrae et ludicrae conclusiones*, Senec.; *Cannochiale Aristotelico* [by Manolo Tesauro (1591–1677). The *Cannochiale* appeared at Venice in 1669.]

[12] *Rhetoric* iii. 4.

[13] [Vincent Voiture (1597–1648) during the last half of his life enjoyed a great reputation as one of the leading wits among the brilliant writers who gathered at the Hôtel de Rambouillet (Malherbe, Chapelain, Saint-Evremond, La Rochefoucauld, the Scudérys, and others). His letters and poems were widely read. The reference here is to the opening sentence of a letter to Mlle. de Rambouillet written over the name of the King of Sweden. The poems quoted in the following paragraph are called *Placets*.]

[14] [Marc-Antoine Gerard, sieur de Saint-Amant (1594–1660).]

[15] [The pun turns on *palais*, "palate" and *palais*, "palace."]

[16] [The pun turns on *plomb*, "lead" and *plomb*, "plumb," with overtones of "aplomb."]

[17] *In amphit. Caesar.*

[18] Quint. viii. 6.

[19] *Iliad* ii. [This appears to be a mistake; Homer says "Nireus the comeliest man that came beneath Ilios . . ." (ii. 673).]

[20] Lib. ii [epigram 92].

[21] *De ben.* vii. 23.

[22] *Aeneid* viii.

[23] *Hist. Rom.* [i. 17.]

[24] Senec. Rhet. *Suasor.* ii.

[25] [Jean-Louis Guez de Balzac (1594–1654) was much admired by his contemporaries for his prose style, first revealed in his collection of *Lettres* (1624), carefully turned essays, which went through many editions (and several English translations) during the century. He is said to have done for French prose what Malherbe did for French poetry, freeing it from excesses of ornament and imposing upon it a kind

of classical discipline. Bouhours's reference is to a letter written to M. de Bois Robert, in 1623.]

[26] [Mellin de Saint-Gelais (1491–1558), poet and musician, a favorite wit of Francis I.]

[27] Quint. viii. 5

[28] Auson.

[29] Plutarch in *Alexandri vita*.

[30] *De natura deorum.*

[31] [*Trattato dello stile e dialogo*, by Cardinal Sforza Pallavicini, appeared in 1662.]

[32] *Institutiones* iii. 4.

[33] *De orat.* ii.

[34] *Carm.* i. 2.

[35] [This is the sense of the penultimate stanza of Malherbe's poem "Consolation à Monsieur du Périer . . . sur la mort de sa fille."]

[36] Longin. *De sublimi. i.*

[37] [*Lettres*, see note 25, above.]

[38] [Hermogenes of Tarsus (b. ca. A.D. 150)] *De formis orat.* vi.

[39] *Cicero Orat. pro Ligar.*

[40] Vellei. Patercul. ii. 34.

[41] *Controvers.* i.

[42] [*On the Sublime* xii.]

[43] [Perhaps a reference to Bacon's *Natural History*, VI, 595 ff.]

[44] [Pierre Patrix (1583–1671), friend of Voiture, is the author of *Poésies diverses*, where the quoted madrigal will be found.]

[45] [*On the Sublime* ix.]

[46] Longin. ii.

[47] Macc. I; Psalm 113; Apocal. XX.

[48] Psalm 36.

[49] Demet. Phaler. *De elocut.*

[50] *Histor.* ii. [The English translation of the French translation from the Latin is faulty. The version here substituted is that of C. N. Moore, in the Loeb Classical Library.]

[51] Tacit. *Annal.* ii.

[52] [Pierre Costar (or Costaud, or Coustart) (1603–1660) was a friend of Voiture and Guez de Balzac and frequented the *salon* of Mme. de Rambouillet.]

[53] [Letter to M. de la Motte Aigron, September 26, 1622.]

[54] [I.e., René Rapin, who had written on both subjects: *Hortum libri IV* (1665), and *de Carmine pastorale* (1659).]

[55] Hermog. *De formis orat.* vi [and] iv.

[56] *Histor. Nat.* xviii. 3.

[57] xxxv. 2.

[58] xxxiv. 14.

[59] *Carm.* ii. 16.

[60] Longin. xix.

[61] Pliny ii. 2.

[62] Ibid. xxxvii. proem.

[63] Quintil. viii. 2.

[64] *Panegyricus*, an oration praising Trajan.

[65] Cic. *De orat.* ii.

[66] Quintil. viii. proem.

[67] Ibid. iv.

[68] [Bouhours's word *naïf* we have translated *ingenuous*. The passage is obscure in the original translation.]

Notes

[69] [Cicero] in *Verr*. iii.
[70] *De orat*. iii.
[71] Cicero *De optimo genere or*.
[72] Quintil. viii. *proem de verbis*.
[73] Benedetto Fioretti (1579–1642), *Proginnasmi poetici di Udeno Nisieli* [pseud.] *accademico apatista* . . .
[74] [*Il Pastor fido*, prologue, ll. 10–13. The paraphrase should read, "without our knowing whether he is the hurler of the thunderbolts or him that is struck."]
[75] xxxiv. 14.
[76] iv. 11.
[77] Diomed. *Grammatic*. ii.

Rapin (pages 275–302)

Among all the French critics of the seventeenth century, René Rapin (1621–1687) shared with Saint-Evremond the distinction of having all his critical works translated into English. The *Whole Critical Works* appeared in London in two volumes in 1706 (second and third editions in 1716 and 1731), but the *Réflexions sur la Poétique* had been translated and published by Thomas Rymer in 1674, the same year in which the essay first appeared in France, and had been reprinted in 1694. Rymer's important Preface is in Spingarn's *Critical Essays of the Seventeenth Century*. Rapin was thus not only "the first of the formalist critics to be translated into English" (Curt A. Zimansky, *The Critical Works of Thomas Rymer*, New Haven, 1956, p. 179), he was also one of the most widely read. Some of his other works translated and published separately were *A Comparison Between Demosthenes and Cicero* (1672); *A Comparison of Plato and Aristotle* (1673); *Reflections Upon the Eloquence of These Times* (1672 and 1673); *A Discourse of Pastorals* (1684); and *Of Gardens* (1673).

Rapin's influence in the criticism of the Augustan period was pervasive. In 1677, in *The Author's Apology for Heroic Poetry*, Dryden called Boileau and Rapin "the greatest of this age" in France, and said that "were all the other critics lost," Rapin alone was "sufficient to teach anew the rules of writing." And from then on through the first half of the eighteenth century English critics referred frequently to him. Clark (*op. cit.*, pp. 275–285) has sketched his career.

Our text, over half the whole essay, follows that of the 1694 edition.

[1] A paraphrase of *Epist*. ii. 1.
[2] Honorat de Bueil, marquis de Racan (1589–1670), follower of Malherbe and author of the pastoral drama *Les Bergeries*.
[3] *Ars poet*. 5–15.
[4] Giovan-Giorgio Trissino (1478–1550) worked twenty years on *l'Italia liberata da' Goti*.
[5] *Inst. Orat*. II. xix.
[6] *On the Sublime*, XXXIII.
[7] Apelles and Protogenes were Greek painters of the fourth century B.C.
[8] Jean Bonnefons (1554–1614), a French poet who wrote erotic verse in Latin. Phaleusiacs are lines in an ancient meter consisting of a spondee, a dactyl, and three trochees.
[9] Aristotle *Poetics* xxv; Horace *Epist*. I. ii. 3.
[10] *Poetics* xv.
[11] *Rhetoric* III. ii.
[12] *Inst. Orat*. VIII. iii.
[13] The reference is to the treatise *On Style* (first century A.D.) commonly, but probably wrongly, attributed to Demetrius Phalerius.
[14] In the dialogue *Gorgias*.
[15] Vincent Voiture (1597–1648) was a master of light verse and a much-admired wit of the *salons*. For Sarasin, see headnote to his *Discourse on Tragedy*, above.

389

Phillippe Habert (c. 1605–1637) wrote an elegy called "Le Temple de la Mort" (1637). Pierre de Lalane (d. 1661?) wrote love poems, in a highly artificial style.

[16] *Ars poet.* 99.

[17] *Inst. Orat.* vi.

[18] [Athenaeus *Deipnosophists* XIV. 620. b.]

[19] *Ars poet.* 178 sqq.

[20] [In *Of the Writing of History*.]

[21] Marco Girolamo Vida (1490–1560) author of a Latin poem, *The Art of Poetry*, and of the *Christiad*.

[22] Giacomo Sannazaro (1458–1530) Italian poet, author of the pastoral romance *Arcadia* and called by his contemporaries "the Christian Virgil." Luís de Camoëns (1524–1580), Portuguese poet, author of the *Lusiads*.

[23] Armand, prince de Conti (1629–1668) opposed the theater in a *Traité de la comédie et des spectacles* (1666) although he had previously been a friend of Molière.

Le Bossu (pages 303–323)

No work of French criticism was better known in eighteenth-century England than the *Traité du poème épique*, by René Le Bossu (1631–1680). First published in Paris in 1675, and reissued several times during the following years, it was well known in England before it was translated by "W. J." in 1695. During the next thirty years the translation was reprinted in England in various forms at least fourteen times (Clark, *op. cit.*, p. 243). Our abridgment is that which Pope published in the first edition of his translation of the *Odyssey* (1725–1726).

As early as 1727 Voltaire said, in his English essay *On Epic Poetry*, that "to believe Homer and Virgil submitted beforehand to the rules laid down by Le Bossu, who bids an epic poet invent and dispose the constitution of his fable before he thinks of the name of his heroes, is indeed not natural." And Johnson in his *Life of Milton* indirectly criticized Le Bossu's thesis by saying that Milton was the only poet to compose an epic by Bossu's method. Nevertheless, critics from Dryden and Dennis and Shaftesbury to Blair and Twining took the *Treatise* very seriously either by following it as a guide in criticism or by condemning it. Clark (*op. cit.*, pp. 243–261) has a long and interesting account of Le Bossu's fame in England. The *Treatise* is divided into six Books: I, "The Nature of the Epic Poem and of the Fable"; II, "The Matter, or the Action"; III, "The Form, or the Narration"; IV, "The Manners"; V, "The Machines"; VI, "The Sentiments and the Expression." Pope's abridgment represents about one tenth of the original.

[1] *Ars poet.* 23: "In short, be the work what you will, let it at least be simple and uniform." — Fairclough.

[2] Pope puts Chapter 11 after Chapter 12.

[3] *Satyricon* 118: "It is not a question of recording real events in verse; historians can do that far better. The free spirit of genius must plunge headlong into allusions and divine interpositions." — Heseltine.

La Bruyère (pages 324–338)

The fame of Jean de La Bruyère (1644–1696) rests on one book, *Les Caractères de Théophraste, traduits du grec, avec les caractères ou les moeurs de ce siècle*, published in Paris in 1687. With various alterations, it went through several editions before La Bruyère's death. It was translated "by several hands" and published in London in 1699; later editions appeared in 1700, 1702, 1708, 1709, 1713. The translation by Henri Van Laun (London, 1885), from whom we have borrowed a few notes, was reprinted in 1929. The text used here, except for a few corrections, is that of the anonymous translation of 1699.

The popularity of La Bruyère in England, attested by the numerous editions of his work, is about all there is to suggest that his "Des Ouvrages de l'esprit" ("Of Polite Learning") was familiar to English critics. Clark found no references to him among the English critics. But Addison, Dennis, Swift, Pope, and others all referred at least once to him. Though Murphy (*Johnson Miscellany*, I, 416) said Dr. Johnson was a "profound admirer of Boileau and La Bruyère," Johnson scolded Mrs. Piozzi for preferring La Bruyère to La Rochefoucauld. Perhaps no argument need be made for the intrinsic interest of the essay.

We have omitted from our notes most of the identifications of the characters supplied by the "key" which accompanied later editions.

[1] "Qui sentent la pension ou l'abbaye." Presumably, "which suggest the style of one who hopes to gain a pension or the office of abbot."

[2] Here the translator omitted the following paragraph:

"If certain men of quick and resolute mind are to be believed, words would even be superfluous to express feelings; signs would be sufficient to address them, or we could make ourselves be understood without speaking. However careful you may be to write closely and concisely, and whatever reputation you may have for so doing, they will think you diffuse. You must give only the merest suggestion of what you mean, and write for them alone. They understand a whole phrase by reading the first word, and an entire chapter by a single phrase. It is sufficient for them to have heard only a bit of your work, they know it all and understand the whole. A collection of riddles would be amusing reading to them; they regret that the wretched style which delights them becomes rare, and that so few authors employ it. Comparisons of a river flowing rapidly, though calmly and uniformly, or of a conflagration which, fanned by the winds, spreads afar in a forest, where it devours oaks and pine-trees, give to them not the smallest idea of eloquence. Show them some fireworks to astonish them, or a flash of lightning to dazzle them, and they will dispense with anything fine or beautiful." — Van Laun.

[3] Here the translator omitted the following paragraph:

"When, after having read a work, loftier thoughts arise in your mind and noble and heartfelt feelings animate you, do not look for any other rule to judge it by; it is fine and written in a masterly manner." — Van Laun.

[4] "Capys" is Edmé Boursault (1638–1701), whom Boileau ("Damis") attacked in his Satire IX. Roger de Rabutin, comte de Bussy (1618–1693), was "banished from the court for more than twenty years for writing the 'licentious and satirical' *Histoire amoureuse des Gaules*." — Van Laun.

[5] The original reads simply, "Le nouvelliste se couche . . ."

[6] See discussion of prose style of Voiture and Balzac in Bouhours's *The Art of Criticism*, and notes to it (13 and 25).

[7] François de Malherbe (1555–1628), official poet under Henri IV and later under Louis XIII and Richelieu, was famous for his vigorous opposition to the excesses of style of earlier poets, the followers of Ronsard, the Pléiade. Théophile de Viau (1590–1626) disagreed in theory and practice with Malherbe.

[8] La Bruyère is here disagreeing with the then current estimate of Ronsard, who was no longer considered a great poet.

[9] Clément Marot (1495–1544), a court poet in the reign of Francis I.

[10] Rémy Belleau (1528–1577), Etienne Jodelle (1532–1573), poets of the Pléiade, and Mellin de Saint-Gelais (1491–1558), a court poet. In later editions La Bruyère replaced Saint-Gelais with Guillaume du Bartas (1544–1590), the author of a long poem on the Creation. Honorat de Bueil, marquis de Racan (1589–1670), follower of Malherbe, wrote the pastoral *Les Bergeries*.

[11] Jacques Amyot (1513–1593) and Nicolas Coëffetau (1574–1623), Bishop of Marseilles, were translators of classical writing.

[12] A periodical.

[13] Here the translator omitted the following paragraph:

"Busybodies have created the theatre and its machinery, composed ballets, verses, and music; theirs is the whole spectacle, even to the room where the performance was held, from the roof to the very foundation of the four walls. Who has any doubt that the hunt on the water, the delights of "La Table," the marvels of the Labyrinth were also invented by them? I think so, at least, by the agitation they are in and by the self-satisfied air with which they applaud their success. Unless I am deceived, they have not contributed anything to a festival so splendid, so magnificent, and so long kept up, and which one person planned and paid for; so that I admire two things: the ease and quietness of him who directed everything, and the fuss and gesticulations of those who did nothing." — Van Laun. "La Table" was an ingenious meal served in the Labyrinth, which was itself in the forest of Chantilly.

[14] Mithridates, King of Pontus (132–63 B.C.) is the hero of Racine's *Mithridate*; Porus and Burrhus are characters in his *Alexandre* and *Britannicus*, respectively.

Fontenelle (pages 339–370)

The Quarrel between the Ancients and the Moderns has been said to have begun on January 27, 1687, at a special meeting of the Academy held to celebrate the convalescence of the king. There, as Charles Perrault read his poem *Le Siècle de Louis le Grand*, Boileau became so indignant that he interrupted Perrault by shouting that the poem was a shame to the Academy. What so moved Boileau was Perrault's suggestion that the age of Louis the Great was the equal of the age of Augustus:

> Que l'on peut comparer, sans crainte d'être injuste,
> Le siècle de Louis au beau siècle d'Auguste.

Shortly thereafter Boileau wrote two violent epigrams about Perrault and within a year Boileau and Perrault had lined up their teams. Most of the leading writers supported Boileau in his thesis that the works of the ancient poets had not been, and were not likely to be, equaled by the work of modern poets. La Fontaine, Racine, and La Bruyère, as well as the critics Ménage, Huet, and Dacier, defended Boileau. Perrault's chief allies were Saint-Evremond and Bernard le Bovier de Fontenelle (1657–1757), a nephew of Corneille, who published in 1688, as appendices to a collection of pastoral poems, "A Discourse on the Nature of the Pastoral" and "A Digression on the Ancients and the Moderns."

Actually, Fontenelle had, like others before 1687, concerned himself with some of the ideas involved in the Quarrel, in particular with the idea of progress, which he treated in his *Dialogues of the Dead* (1683) in a colloquy between Socrates and Montaigne. Fontenelle was not a good poet or dramatist but his essays must have been effective against the intense seriousness of men like Boileau and Dacier. The definitive treatment of the Quarrel is Hubert Gillot, *La Querelle des anciens et des modernes* (Paris, 1914).

As J. E. Congleton has made clear in his *Theories of Pastoral Poetry in England, 1684–1798* (University of Florida Press, 1952), Fontenelle's "Discourse" in its rationalistic and "impertinent" disregard for the Ancients was not, as Pope implied, similar to René Rapin's *De Carmina pastorali* (1659), which was translated into English in 1684. Rapin's work was, as its author claimed, modeled on Aristotle's *Poetics* in that the rules were derived from a study of the practice of the great classical pastoral poets — chiefly Virgil. Fontenelle's work was, therefore, completely different from Rapin's both in assumptions and in method.

Motteux's translation of the "Discourse" was published with "Monsieur Bossu's Treatise of the Epick Poem" in London in 1695. Motteux omitted two introductory paragraphs, which reveal Fontenelle's bias:

"While I was composing the preceding eclogues, several ideas on the nature of this kind of poetry came to me, and to investigate the matter a little further I undertook to review the majority of those authors who have any reputation as pastoral

Notes

poets. These ideas, and the criticism of these authors, make up the following essay. I place it after the eclogues, for that represents the order in which the essay and the poems were written. The eclogues came before the reflections; I wrote the poems first; then I thought of the theories; and, to the shame of reason, that is what usually happens. So I shall not be surprised if it is discovered that I have not followed my own rules — I did not yet know them very well when I wrote. Besides, it is much easier to make rules than to follow them, and it has been established by custom that the one never requires the other.

"I hope that the criticism I have rather liberally made of a large number of authors, will not render me suspect of having wished to insinuate that my eclogues are better than all others. I would much rather suppress this essay than excite such a belief in the minds of others. But I maintain that because I have sometimes recognized where others have gone astray, I do not consider myself less likely to be wrong even in the matters where I have seen their mistakes. Criticism exercised on the works of others does not require the writer to do better, unless it is bitter, peevish, and arrogant, like that of professed satirists. But criticism which is an examination, not a satire, which is unrestrained but without hatred and without spite, and above all which is accompanied by a sincere recognition of one's own limitations allows one the liberty of doing even worse, if one wishes, than all those one has undertaken to correct. It is this latter kind of criticism that I have chosen together with its privileges, which, I flatter myself, no one will deny me."

The "Digression" was translated by John Hughes and appeared as an addition to the fourth edition (1719) of John Glanvill's translation of Fontenelle's *Conversations with a Lady on the Plurality of Worlds.*

There is a good text of the original, edited, together with *Entretiens sur la pluralité des mondes*, by Robert Shackleton (Oxford, 1955), from which we have taken our notes on the "Digression."

[1] Dryden's translation has been here substituted for Motteux's, which makes nonsense of the passage.

[2] Titus Calpurnius Siculus (fl. A.D. 50–60) wrote seven pastorals that are extant. Fontenelle refers specially to number VII.

[3] Eclog. iii. 8.

[4] The *Bucolica* of Johannes Baptista Spagnuolus Mantuanus (1448–1516) were published in Paris in 1513; they were widely read, translated, and imitated during the following one hundred and fifty years.

[5] Fontenelle says, "have added to it in the way of what is foreign and evil."

[6] Fontenelle says, "c'est cette idée qui fait tout," meaning "that notion [of simple pleasures] produces the happiest effect."

[7] The five piscatory eclogues of Jacopo Sannazaro (1458–1530) were first published in Naples in 1526.

[8] The famous romance *Amadis de Gaule* was written in the fifteenth century; the pastoral romance *L'Astrée*, by Honoré d'Urfé (1568–1626), is set in the seventh century.

[9] Marcus Aurelius Olympius Nemesianus (fl. A.D. 290) wrote four pastorals that were long supposed to have been by Calpurnius.

[10] Adrien Turnèbe (1512–1565), Guilaume Budé (1467–1540), and François Vatable (d. 1547).

[11] Honoré de Racan (1589–1670) wrote a pastoral play called *Les Bergeries.*

[12] Giovan Battista Guarini (1537–1612) wrote *Il Pastor Fido* (1590) at about the same time Tasso wrote the other famous, similar, Italian pastoral drama, *L'Aminta.* Guidobaldi Bonarelli della Rovere (1563–1608) wrote *Filli di Sciro* (1607), a poor pastoral drama (his only work), which was several times translated into French during the century. For Marino, see headnote to notes on Chapelain, above.

[13] Here Motteux omitted a one-sentence criticism of a "ridiculous" passage from an eclogue of Marot.

[14] Jean de Segrais (1624–1701), a contemporary of Fontenelle's and secretary of Mme. de La Fayette, was famous for his eclogues.

[15] France exchanged ambassadors with Siam for the first time in 1680.

[16] Motteux omitted Fontenelle's last paragraph, which is as follows:

"I beg then permission to add here a short digression which will serve both as my apology and as a plain expression of my feelings on the question of the ancients and moderns. I hope this permission will the more easily be forthcoming since M. Perrault's poem has made the question one of current interest. Since he is preparing to treat it more fully and more deeply, I shall touch on it only lightly: I esteem the ancients highly enough to leave them the honor of being opposed by an adversary both illustrious and worthy of them."

[17] (This and the following notes are from Shackleton's edition, as explained in the headnote.) The comparison of men to trees was first made by Montaigne (in the *Apologie de Raymond Sebond*), in a discussion of the effects of external physical influences on men.

[18] Fontenelle here speaks in the terms of Cartesian physiology.

[19] The theory of climatic influence was very popular in the sixteenth and seventeenth centuries, its principal exponent being Jean Bodin in his *République* and *Methodus*. Montaigne and Charron caused the theory to become well known. In *De l'origine des fables* Fontenelle rejects the climatic explanation of fables, as inspired by the vivid imagination of the inhabitants of the torrid zone. In the *Digression*, on the other hand, he accepts climatic influence. Shortly before the *Digression* . . . there appeared a work which argued vigorously in favor of climatic influence. This was *De l'utilité des voyages*, by Baudelot de Dairval (Paris, 1686). Baudelot, in the Quarrel, was a supporter of the ancients, and it seems likely that Fontenelle in the *Digression* is turning against the ancients one of their own arguments.

[20] The effects of climate on the brain had been discussed by Juan Huarte, whose *Examen de Ingenios* (1577) had been translated into French and had been widely read.

[21] The notion that the temperate zone was the best region in the world for intellectual achievement was common. See Girolamo Cardano, *De animorum immortalitae* (*Opera omnia* (1663), II, 533–4), and Huarte, *Examen de Ingenios* (ed. R. Sanz, Madrid, 1930, p. 182).

[22] Theagenes and Charicleia are characters in the Greek prose narrative *Aethiopica*, by Heliodorus (fl. A.D. 225); Clitophon and Leucippe are characters in a romance by Achilles Tatius, an Alexandrian Christian of the fourth century. Both these romances were popular in French translations. The French romances are *Cyrus*, by Mlle. de Scudéry, *L'Astrée*, by Honoré d'Urfé, and *Zayde* and *Princesse de Clèves*, by Mme. de La Fayette.

[23] The "excellent authors" of these three types were, presumably: Quinault, of operas; La Fontaine, of tales; and Fontenelle, himself, whose *Lettres galantes de M. de chevalier d'Her**** appeared anonymously in 1683.

Index

Abelard, Pierre, 215
Académie française. *See* French Academy
Achilles Tatius, 193, 205, 368
Action, unity of: in *Adone*, 5; lacking in some romances, 5; relation of diversity to, 17; without it a poem becomes a romance, 18; Aristotle on, 64–66; Scudéry on, 87; Corneille on, 117–25; no enemy of variety, 295; Le Bossu's account of origin of, 303–4; in the epic, 310; three means to, 312. *See also* Plot
Admirable. *See* Marvelous, the
Aelian, Claudius, 194
Aeneid. See Virgil
Aeschylus, 107, 109, 125, 283, 297
Aesop, 189, 193
Affectation, Bouhours on, 272–73
Albinus, Clodius, 205
Alexandrine verse: a weakness of French poetry, 294
Allegory: defined, 14; in *Rome Defeated*, explained, 83; should pervade poem, 83; in pastoral poetry, 350
Amadis de Gaule, 197, 346
Ambiguities. *See* Tropes
Amyot, Jacques, 332
Anacreon, 222, 282, 369
Ancients and moderns: "brilliance of antiquity" and "graces of moderns" in *Adone*, 9; Sarasin on, 68; practical rules of drama embodied in work of a., neglected by m., 97; d'Aubignac defends authority of a. in dramaturgy, 108; Latin authors never cloying, 139; compared as playwrights, 141–48; divine and human badly mixed in a. drama, 142; plays of a. lacked credibility, 142; morality of m. superior to that of a. drama, 147; m. superior to a. in tragedy, 155–58; no one painted juster characters than the a., 156; a. tragedians neg-

lected representation of passions, 157; religion and manners of moderns make ancient literature less effective, 176–81; m. write poor poetry because they imitate the a., 180; fables and mysteries of a. unsatisfactory to m., 180, 181; a *bel esprit* does not plagiarize a., 211; unity of design better in a., 282; a. have already said everything, 324; a. can be surpassed only by imitating them, 325; m., children of the a., 325–26; m. make shepherds too refined rather than too natural, 347; Fontenelle on, 358–70
Annius Viterbensis, 188
Anthology (Greek), 269, 283
Apuleius, Lucius, 193, 197, 205
Aquinas, Saint Thomas, 198
Ariosto, Ludovico: *Orlando* no true epic, 65; model for romance, 80, 186; use of historical characters, 81; long episodes in, 87; love a subject in, 90; begins at middle of action, 90; imitated Homer, 91; valiant women in, 93; undisciplined imagination of, 210; criticized for hyperbole, 244; too much flame, 275; violated rules of epic, 279; guided only by genius, 279; his Angelica too immodest, 285; marvelous improbable in, 291; his narrations more natural than Tasso's, 294; descriptions too long in, 295
Aristides, 193
Aristophanes, 222, 279, 368
Aristotle: Corneille discovered beauties of stage A. ignorant of, 142; Saint-Evremond on A.'s theory of purgation, 145; his vast genius, 174; Clearchus his disciple, 191; reference to ideal statesman, 221; system of qualities rejected, 361; his authority delayed advance in philosophy, 369; *Ethics*, 72; *Poetics*, 6, 37, 55 *bis*, 56, 61–66, 72–73, 80, 86 *bis*,

287; what seems sublime may be bombastic, 324–25

Didacticism: in dramatic poetry, d'Aubignac on, 111–16; instruction in drama should be indirect, 114; in Sophocles and Euripides, compared, 112; *See also* Sentences

Diogenes, Antonius, 193

Diversity: as an aspect of plot, defined, 15; achieved by Marino in conceits, 25

Donatus, Aelius, 105

Don Belianus, 197

Double titles defended by Scudéry, 89

Du Bartas, Guillaume de Saluste, 281

Du Bellay, Joachim, 64

Duchesne, André, 40

D'Urfé, Honoré, his *Astrée*: somewhat licentious, 203–4; shepherds too refined in, 343; less fabulous than *Amadis*, 346; excessive reflection in, 355; superior to classical romances, 368

Du Ryer, Pierre, 157

Eclogue. *See* Pastoral poetry

Eclogues of Virgil, 267, 342, 348–49, 354

Empedocles, 34, 277

Energy in descriptions the essence of poetry, 27

Epic: Homer or Orpheus inventor of, 5; the non-heroic e., its usefulness detailed, 9; proper length of, 10; Scudéry on the rules for, 80–93; Rapin calls it greatest kind of poetry, 292; proportion of parts, symmetry of design, the highest perfection of, 295; Le Bossu's definition of, 304

Epic hero: may be a foreigner, 92; religion of, 94

Episodes: with descriptions, make up fable, 20; must be connected with plot, 86; length of, 87

Euripides: *Medea*, 6; *Cyclops*, 78; *Suppliants*, 101, 105, 111, 286; *Ion*, 101, 111; *Andromache*, 105, 283; compressed period of action to a few hours, 107, 109; his use of night time, 110; didacticism criticized, compared with Sophocles', 112; use of machines censured in, 122; unity of time in, 125; *Iphigenia*, 152, 286; loses much in translation, 155; *Hecuba*, 279, 290, 295; the sublime in, 288; *Hippolytus*, 297; inferior to 17th-century French dramatists, 368; mentioned, 147, 222, 284, 298–99

Eustathius, 192

Events. *See* Episodes

Fable: three kinds of defined, 18–19; consists of events and descriptions, 20. *See also* Plot

Faculties, the three of the mind, 174

False wit. *See* Wit, false

Fancy: one of three faculties of the mind, 174; confused with wit, 276

Fauchet, Claude, 198, 202

Fiction distinguished from falsehood, 243–44

Figures give force to passions, 288. *See also* Tropes

Fioretti, Benedetto, 272

Floridor (Josias de Soulas), 99

Florus, 251

French Academy: power to regulate language, 170; Bouhours addresses, 240

Froissart, Jean, 40

Garin le Loheran, 202

"Gay science," 195, 196, 198

Genius: poetic g. not agreeable with good sense, 140; g., mind, or soul divided into three faculties, 174; inadequate alone for writing well, 240; defined, 276; rewards of irregularity in men of g., 337

Genre: novelty of, 4–10; the non-heroic epic a new g., 8; *Adone* a mixture of heroic, tragic, comic, and epic, 11

Giraldi, Lilio, 186, 187, 188, 196

Good sense. *See* Judgment

Gothic: characters and events in *Lancelot*, 33; courage and ignorance of Goths, 45; should be banished, 325

Gracián, Baltasar, 212, 220, 233

Grace. *See* Delicacy

Graziani, Giovanni, 80

Grotius, Hugo, 119

Guarini, Giovanni Battista, his *Pastor fido*: too long for spectators, 106; censured for didacticism, 113; example of affectation, 273, 351; shepherds too polite in, 291; mentioned, 158

Guevarra, Luis Velez de, 90

Hardy, Alexandre, 66

Hédelin, François, abbé d'Aubignac: 96–116; Saint-Evremond on, 142

Heinsius, Daniel, 61, 119

Heliodorus, 10, 90, 193, 205, 368

Hemitheon the Sybarite, 194

Heraclitus, 214

Index

Hermogenes, 250, 262, 266, 267
Herodotus, 188, 189, 193
Hesiod, 84
Hesychius of Miletus, 193
History: compared with poetry, 13, 17–18; *Lancelot* as good history of mores as Livy, 38; false wit in, 255; writing of h. reached height in Augustan age, 364
Hoguette, Pierre Fortin de la, 208
Homer: inventor of epic, 5; descriptions in, 27; compared with *Lancelot*, 36; not guided by rules, 37; seeds of modern arts and sciences in, 38, 84; unity of action in, 64; function of episodes in, 86, 87; his poems have short titles, 89; love as subject in, 90; opens with origin of subject, 90; imitated by Virgil, 90; got ideas from Egyptians, 91; valiant women in, 93; technical learning in, 94; faulty characterization of Achilles in, 152; false character of gods in, 174–75, 184; gods essential to his poems, 176–78; his faults those of his times, 178; his poems masterpieces but not models, 181; metaphorical license in, 244, 246; his use of hyperbole, 250, 251; his thoughts and words proportioned to subject, 253; example of the sublime, 265; delightful descriptions in, 277; never uttered impiety or obscenity, 278; source of Aristotle's rules, 279; no false wit in, 281; hymns of, 282; treatment of gods, 285; simplicity of expression, 287; loftiness of expression, 288; harmony of his verses, 291; not self-indulgent, 294; long speeches in, unnatural, 295; moral of *Iliad* and of *Odyssey*, 305–9; praised for uniting four morals in one fable in *Iliad*, 311–12; complication in his poems analyzed, 316–17; structures of *Iliad* and *Odyssey* compared, 314–16; denouement in his poems analyzed, 317–18; characterization of his heroes, 320–21; analysis of machines in, 321–23; excels in making vivid images, 325; moderns can equal him, 358; inferior to Demosthenes, Cicero, Virgil, 364; irrelevancies in, 365; poetic license in, 367; mentioned, 10, 80, 91, 209, 284, 286
Horace: *Ars poet.*, 64, 69, 80, 84, 88, 122, 148, 151, 152, 180, 279, 280, 282, 286, 290, 291, 294, 295, 310, 322, 338; superior to contemporaries in taste, 140; *Epist.*, 204, 276, 284; imitated by Voi-

ture, 211; gives new turn to the obvious, 261; *Carm.*, 268; chief interpreter of Aristotle, 277; his odes praised, 282, 283; superior to Pindar, 364; mentioned, 171, 239
Hortensius, 171
Huet, Pierre-Daniel, 186–205
Humors: in English comedies, 161; mixture required for a *bel esprit*, 214
Hunibaldus Francus, 195, 196
Hyperbole: in Tasso and Ariosto, 245; more acceptable if ironic, 251

Imagination: one of three faculties of the mind, 174; distinct from understanding, judgment, wit, 275
Imitation in descriptions, 27. *See also* Plagiarism
Irony: as didactic device, 115; may be hyperbolic, 251
Isocrates, 222

Jamblicus of Chalcis, 193
Je ne sais quoi, Bouhours on, 228–38
Jodelle, Etienne, 331
John Damascenus, Saint, 193, 205
Joinville, Jean de, 35, 44
Jongleurs, origin of, 195
Jonson, Ben, 163
Judgment: genius of poets agrees not with good sense, 140; one of faculties of mind, 174; as distinct from understanding, wit, imagination, 275; should be stronger than wit, 280–81; rarer than imagination, 325
Justin, Saint (the Martyr), 285
Justness, defined as agreement between thought and object, 253

Kyrie Eleison of Montauban, 197

La Fayette, Marie Madeleine, Comtesse de, 2–5, 368
Lalane, Pierre de, 289
Lancelot: its virtues discussed, 31–54; source of all romances for four or five centuries, 32; rich source of information about language, 34; example of elegantly simple language in, 35; magic no more irregular than Homer's divinities, 37; compared with Livy, 38; lacks wit, 40; reflects characters and lives of people of the time, 42; accurately reflects state of Christianity in Europe, 43; Lancelot like Hercules, 46; praised for

399

Index

Index